Social Inequality Series

Marta Tienda and David B. Grusky, Series Editors

*Generating Social Stratification: Toward a
New Research Agenda,* edited by Alan C. Kerckhoff

*The New Role of Women: Family Formation
in Modern Societies,* edited by Hans-Peter Blossfeld

*Social Stratification: Class, Race, and Gender
in Sociological Perspective,* edited by David B. Grusky

Careers and Creativity: Social Forces in the Arts,
Harrison C. White

*Persistent Inequality:
Changing Educational Attainment in Thirteen Countries,*
edited by Yossi Shavit and Hans-Peter Blossfeld

*The Arab Minority in Israel's Economy: Patterns of
Ethnic Inequality,* Noah Lewin-Epstein and Moshe Semyonov

Equality and Achievement in Education,
James S. Coleman

*Ethnicity and the New Family Economy:
Living Arrangements and Intergenerational Financial Flows,*
edited by Frances K. Goldscheider and Calvin Goldscheider

FORTHCOMING

*Social Differentiation and Social Inequality: Essays
in Honor of John Pock,* edited by James Baron,
David B. Grusky, and Donald Treiman

Education and Social Class in Comparative Perspective,
edited by Robert Erikson and Jan O. Jonsson

Inequality and Aging, John Henretta and Angela O'Rand

*Prejudice or Productivity: Ethnicity, Languages,
and Discrimination in Labor Markets,* M.D.R. Evans

*Between Two Worlds: Southeast Asian Refugee
Youth in America,* Ruben G. Rumbaut and Kenji Ima

Children, Schools, and Inequality,
Doris R. Entwisle and Karl Len Alexander

Generating
Social Stratification:

Toward a New Research Agenda

EDITED BY

Alan C. Kerckhoff
Duke University

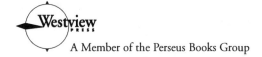

A Member of the Perseus Books Group

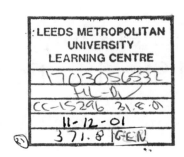
Social Inequality Series

Copyright © 2000 by Westview Press, A Member of the Perseus Books Group

Published in 2000 in the United States of America by Westview Press, 5500 Central Avenue, Boulder, Colorado 80301-2877, and in the United Kingdom by Westview Press, 12 Hid's Copse Road, Cumnor Hill, Oxford OX2 9JJ

Library of Congress Cataloging-in-Publication Data
Generating social stratification : toward a new research agenda /
  edited by Alan C. Kerckhoff
    p. cm.—(Social inequality series)
  Includes bibliographical references.
  ISBN 0-8133-8967-4 (hc) ISBN 0-8133-6796-4 (pbk).
  1. Students—United States—Social conditions. 2. Academic
achievement—United States. 3. Social mobility—United States.
I. Kerckhoff, Alan C. II. Series.
LC205.G46 1996
371.8'0973—dc20   95-45691
                                                                        CIP

10   9   8   7   6   5   4   3   2   1

Contents

Preface   xi

PART ONE
Conceptualizing Careers and Stratification Processes

    Introduction to Part One   1

1 Structuration and Individualization: The Life Course
    as a Continuous, Multilevel Process,
    Angela M. O'Rand, Duke University   3

2 Social Psychological Aspects of Achievement,
    Jeylan T. Mortimer, University of Minnesota   17

3 Building Conceptual and Empirical Bridges between
    Studies of Educational and Labor Force Careers,
    Alan C. Kerckhoff, Duke University   37

PART TWO
Educational Contexts and Processes

    Introduction to Part Two   57

4 Educational Stratification and Individual Careers,
    Adam Gamoran, University of Wisconsin, Madison   59

5 Educational Tracking during the Early Years:
    First Grade Placements and Middle School Constraints,
    Karl L. Alexander and Doris R. Entwisle
    The Johns Hopkins Univerisity   75

6   Peer Social Networks and Adolescent Career
    Development, *Charles E. Bidwell*
    and Stephen Plank, The University of Chicago;
    Chandra Muller, The University of Texas, Austin   107

7   School Choice and Community Segregation:
    Findings from Scotland, *J. Douglas Willms*
    University of New Brunswick and University of Edinburgh   133

8   Educational Processes and School Reform,
    Maureen T. Hallinan, University of Notre Dame   153

PART THREE
Education and Labor Force Linkages

    Introduction to Part Three   171

9   Educational Credentials and the Labor Market:
    An Inter-Industry Comparison,
    W.P. Bridges, University of Illinois at Chicago   173

10 Education, Earnings Gain, and Earnings Loss in
    Loosely and Tightly Structured Labor Markets:
    A Comparison between the United States and Germany,
    Thomas A. DiPrete, Duke University;
    Patricia A. McManus, Indiana University   201

11 Education and Credentialing Systems, Labor Market
    Structure and the Work of Allied Health Occupations,
    Robert Althauser, Indiana University;
    Toby Appel, Yale University   223

12 Creating Capitalists: The Social Origins of
    Entrepreneurship in Post-Communist Poland,
    Barbara Heyns, New York University   257

PART FOUR
Social System Contexts

Introduction to Part Four   291

13 The Politics of Mobility,
Michael Hout, University of California, Berkeley   293

14 Stratification and Attainment in a Large Japanese Firm,
Seymour Spilerman, Columbia University;
Hiroshi Ishida, University of Tokyo   317

15 Changing Contexts of Careers: Trends in
Labor Market Structures and Some Implications
for Labor Force Outcomes, *Arne L. Kalleberg*
University of North Carolina at Chapel Hill   343

About the Book and Editor   359

Preface

Ganzeboom, Treiman and Ultee (1991) refer to three generations of social stratification research. In the first generation, research was concerned with comparing tables that cross-classified categories of the occupational positions of fathers and sons as they varied across societies and over time. They see the second generation as having begun with Blau and Duncan's (1967) introduction of a "basic model" of status attainment. That model shifted the focus from father-son comparisons to stages in a process by which sons are distributed in a continuous status hierarchy. The third, most recent, generation of stratification research, they observe, has returned to the earlier focus on tables of parent-child locations in occupational or social class categories, although the current analyses are much more intricate due to more sophisticated theories, new analytic models, and much better data.

This volume could be viewed as a continuation of what Ganzeboom et al. call the second generation, but I prefer to see it as part of an emerging fourth generation of stratification research. It clearly has many of the features of the second generation, but the kind of research reflected in this volume moves us well beyond the second. And, as with the comparison of the first and third generations, the advance has been due to improvements at the level of theory, analytic techniques, and improved data sources.

The difference between the first and third generations, on the one hand, and the second and fourth, on the other, is the focus of the latter two on stratification processes. Rather than modeling patterns of intergenerational or career mobility, the goal is to identify and take account of the processes by which a birth cohort is distributed in the stratification system, given their positions of origin in that system. It is increasingly apparent that this is an awesome task, and we are far from reaching that goal. Yet, there have been important gains during the past two decades, many of which are reflected in the chapters of this book.

Ever since Blau and Duncan's (1967) introduction of a path model conceptualization, there has been a tendency to look at the overall stratification process as having three cumulative stages: the process by which social origins affect educational attainments; the process by which origins and educational attainments affect the level of labor force entry; the process by which origins, educational attainments, and first jobs affect workers' moves from their initial positions to later positions in the labor force. The

Blau-Duncan three-stage model served to describe the relationships among origin, educational attainment, first job, and later job, but it did not tell us very much about how those relationships come about.

Attempts were soon made to explain the relatively strong relationship between social origins and educational attainments. The "Wisconsin model of status attainment" (Sewell et al. 1969) showed how social psychological measures (ambition, influence from significant others), reflecting family and school processes, helped to explain that relationship. Much less was done to analyze the second and third stages of the attainment process, and some writers (e.g., Horan 1978) questioned the adequacy of a social psychological approach to explaining the status attainment process. They argued that there are features of the social structure that alter the free influence of personal qualities and interpersonal relations on individuals' achievements.

Such critiques served to direct attention to structured contexts and allocation processes. They also shifted the focus from the first stage to the later stages of the Blau-Duncan model because they were largely concerned with the structured nature of the labor force. They argued that the labor force is far from an open opportunity structure, and which jobs individuals enter and move between are determined by more than their personal characteristics.

Industrial sectors provide different opportunity structures (Piore 1975). "Internal labor markets," consisting of firms' job ladders and promotion regimes, favor those already in the firm (Althauser and Kalleberg 1981), and as those at the lower levels on the job ladder move up, this creates a "vacancy chain" (Sorensen 1977). Since not all jobs in a firm are on job ladders, however, some openings are "closed" to all who are not at the next lower level on a job ladder while others are "open" to outsiders (Sorensen and Tuma 1981). The central point of these analyses was that workers' locations in the highly structured labor force strongly affect their opportunities for mobility during their work careers.

Similar structural effects were identified in the educational attainment process. In particular, students' locations in the ability groups or tracks in schools were shown to have significant effects on both their aspirations (Heyns 1974) and their achievements (Alexander, Cook and McDill 1978). Here too, it was argued, the structure of opportunities within schools affected both the individuals' personal qualities and the outcomes available to them. And, in much the same way that internal labor markets limit access to favored structural locations in the labor force, access to the favored locations in the school structure is also far from fully "open" (Hallinan and Sorensen 1983).

As Baron (1994:390) has observed, however: "We have many more coherent findings now about how specific variables affect mobility or attainment than we have coherent stories about why (and under what circumstances) those results obtain." One of Baron's concerns is that "the new structuralism" has been too narrowly concerned with the structural contexts within which social mobility occurs and has ignored the social psychological processes that help explain the effects of those contexts.

As research has demonstrated the interplay among personal qualities, structured contexts, and outcomes, the conceptualization of stratification processes has become more and more complex. It has become necessary to take into account cumulative processes that occur throughout the formative years as well as during workers' careers in the labor force. There have been increasing attempts to take into account the interplay between institutional arrangements and social psychological dynamics.

As more and better data sources have become available and the facilities and methods for multivariate analyses have become more widespread, cross-societal comparisons have become feasible, and societal differences in even the basic form of the status attainment model are apparent (Treiman and Yip 1989). There are notable societal differences in the specific processes involved, as demonstrated in several of the contributions to this volume.

In part because of the increasingly complex conceptualizations and observations and the difficulty of encompassing the full range of relevant factors in any single analysis, there has also evolved a division of labor in the study of stratification processes. One sharp division is between those who focus on stratification processes that occur early in life, especially in educational institutions, and those who focus on processes within the labor force.

It was my concern about that division that led me to organize the conference at which the papers in this volume were presented. The goal of the conference was to bring together scholars who have specialized in the study of one or the other of these two parts of the stratification process in order to increase mutual interest in each other's work and to provide a basis for greater integration of the two parts both conceptually and empirically. We wanted to resensitize specialized scholars, including ourselves, to the nature of the entire stratification process and to how each of our more focused efforts contributes to an overall understanding of the full process.

We hope that this volume will contribute to a broader recognition and appreciation of the challenge of developing a more coherent understanding of stratification processes. It is the attempt to develop such a coherent understanding, firmly founded on a focus on institutional arrangements and the associated social psychological processes, that leads me to view this book as a contribution to an emerging fourth generation of social stratification research. I believe that the papers in this volume do make a contribution to such an understanding and point the way to further clarification. I anticipate a continuing effort to build on this initial contribution.

The conference was held during a three-day period in April 1994. It began with a session at the annual meeting of the Southern Sociological Society in Raleigh, N.C. on April 9th and continued in a series of sessions on the Duke University campus on April 10th and 11th. The conference was made possible and the publication of this book was significantly facilitated through generous support from The Howard E. Jensen Fund, and additional grants were received from the Provost and the Dean of Faculty of Arts and Sciences of Duke University. All of us who participated in this joint effort are very grateful for this financial support.

Several people made important contributions along the way. Judith Dillon helped immensely in organizing the conference. Elizabeth Glennie and Lorraine Bell participated in and handled many of the details of the conference. Lisa Shander took on the challenging task of collating the individual papers into a well-organized manuscript. The entire enterprise depended heavily on their assistance, and I am pleased to offer them my warm thanks. Finally, I very much appreciate the interest in the book shown by Marta Tienda and David Grusky, the editors of this series, and the patience of Dean Birkenkamp, the Westview editor, in working through the complexities of bringing the book into existence.

Alan C. Kerckhoff

References

Alexander, Karl L., Martha A. Cook, and Edward L. McDill. 1978. "Curriculum Tracking and Educational Stratification." *American Sociological Review* 43: 47-66.

Althauser, Robert P. and Arne L. Kalleberg. 1981. "Firms, Occupations and the Structure of Labor Markets: A Conceptual Analysis and Research Agenda." Pp. 119-49 in *Sociological Perspectives on Labor Markets*, edited by Ivar Berg. New York: Academic Press.

Baron, James N. 1994. "Reflections on Recent Generations of Mobility Research." Pp. 384-93 in *Social Stratification: Class, Race, and Gender in Sociological Perspective*, edited by David B. Grusky. Boulder, CO: Westview Press.

Blau, Peter M. and Otis Dudley Duncan. 1967. *The American Occupational Structure*. New York: Wiley.

Ganzeboom, Harry B. G., Donald J. Treiman and Woot C. Ultee. 1991. "Intergenerational Class Mobility in Comparative Perspective." *Research in Social Stratification and Mobility* 9:277-302.

Hallinan, Maureen T. and Aage B. Sorensen. 1983. "The Formation and Stability of Instructional Groups." *American Sociological Review* 48:838- 51.

Heyns, Barbara. 1974. "Social Selection and Stratification Within Schools." *American Journal of Sociology* 79:1434-51.

Horan, Patrick M. 1978. "Is Status Attainment Research Atheoretical?" *American Sociological Review* 43:534-41.

Piore, Michael. 1975. "Notes for a Theory of Labor Market Stratification." Pp. 125-50 in *Labor Market Segmentation*, edited by Richard C. Edwards, Michael Rich, and David M. Gordon. Lexington, KY: Heath.

Sewell, William H., Archibald O. Haller and Alejandro Portes. 1969. "The Educational and Early Occupational Attainment Process." *American Sociological Review* 34:82-92

Sorensen, Aage B. 1977. "The Structure of Inequality and the Process of Attainment." *American Sociological Review* 42:965-78.

Sorensen, Aage B. and Nancy B. Tuma. 1981. "Labor Market Structures and Job Mobility." *Research in Social Stratification and Mobility* 1:67-94.

Treiman, Donald T., and Kam-Bor Yip. 1989. "Educational and Occupational Attainment in 21 Countries." Pp. 373-94 in Melvin L. Kohn (ed.), *Cross-National Research in Sociology*. Newbury Park, CA: Sage.

PART ONE

Conceptualizing Careers and Stratification Processes

The emerging conceptualization of the processes by which societal stratification is generated includes a consideration of factors at multiple levels of analysis ranging from the dynamics of individual functioning to the nature of the society's economic and political system. The challenge we face is to integrate our knowledge of these multiple levels in ways that clarify the nature of stratification generating processes. The three papers included in Part I suggest some of the features of the broad conceptualization we need. In this way, they help to set the stage for the other papers that follow.

In the first paper in Part I, Angela O'Rand emphasizes the importance of this multilevel conceptualization. She reminds us that the life course is an on-going process whose shape is dependent on multiple sources of influence. She succinctly reviews bodies of literature dealing with the full life course, showing how institutional and individual factors help to produce the observed trajectories. She shows how what she calls the "traditional institutional approaches" differ from "relational approaches" and how they complement each other in contributing to an understanding of the role of social structure in shaping the life course.

The second paper, by Jeylan Mortimer, concentrates on the social psychology of achievement, emphasizing the significance of socialization processes both within the family and outside it. Mortimer rightly argues that it is not a question of choosing between a structural and a social psychological approach to achievement; it is essential that we see the connections between the two. She also points out that, of the two bodies of literature dealing with education and labor force processes, the literature on the labor force has been less concerned with the role of social psychological processes. She speculates about how educational and labor force experiences can alter attitudes and values and asks us to think more deeply and clearly about how structures and social psychological processes are interrelated.

In the third paper in Part I, Alan Kerckhoff directs our attention to the structured contexts of individual careers, devoting much of the discussion to an analysis of important differences in those contexts among industrial societies. The effects of both educational and labor force contexts are discussed, but perhaps the most important issue dealt with is the societal variation in the nature of the linkages between those two contexts. Kerckhoff uses the identified inter-societal differences to generate some tentative hypotheses that deal with social psychological effects on individuals as well as overall societal patterns of social stratification.

Together, these three papers provide an indication of the breadth of the research agenda to whose development this volume is dedicated. Each of them makes reference to the other papers in this collection, but they also point up additional kinds of investigation that are, or need to become, part of the overall effort. The papers in Parts II, III and IV point to the complexities of societal stratifying processes. They bring into focus the general observations O'Rand makes about the life course being a multilevel process. They provide numerous examples of the need to take both social structural and social psychological processes into account, as Mortimer suggests. And, they demonstrate the importance of the kinds of inter-organizational linkages dealt with by Kerckhoff as well as the global characteristics of the societies studied.

1

Structuration and Individualization: The Life Course as a Continuous, Multilevel Process

Angela M. O'Rand
Duke University

Sociologists have long recognized the promise of cross-level analysis for linking individual behaviors to social structures and for distinguishing the separate processes operating between levels. However, until recently methodological obstacles have hindered the successful achievement of this promise. Theoretical expositions on the transposition between levels of analysis extend back to the early fifties, including a particularly insightful and prophetic discussion by C. Wright Mills (1953) who anticipated the pivotal role of methodological as opposed to conceptual innovations for the ultimate resolution of these issues. The specification of the properties of collectivities at successive levels of analysis (e.g. Coleman, 1970) and the separation of structural from individual effects (e.g. Blau, 1960) are among the earliest and most persistent conceptual concerns that are now arriving at some methodological solution (e.g. Huber, 1991; DiPrete and Forristal, 1994).

Social transitions over the life course provide strategic subject matter for cross-level analyses. The movement of individuals within and between institutional contexts brings into focus how lives are shaped at social interfaces and, in turn, how institutions may themselves be transformed in response to the social friction exerted by demographic processes, i.e. by aggregate patterns of individual transitions (O'Rand, 1995). As such, cross-level analysis reveals what Anthony Giddens refers to as *structuration*, or how social structures are both constituted by human agency and at the same time the medium of this constitution (Giddens, 1976: 121).

Studies of life-course transitions—from the transition to adulthood, through midlife transitions associated with employment or labor force shifts and family change, to the transition to retirement—are revealing patterned variations in their trajectories and temporal organizations that emerge from the interaction between institutional contexts and individual biographies (Mayer and Tuma, 1990; Elder and O'Rand, 1994). These pathways of individual trajectories indicate what might be referred to as the essential tension between the structuration and the individualization of the life course across institutional contexts. As such, the continuous, cumulative process of the life course organized by multilevel forces is a strategically appropriate domain for cross-level analysis.

In the present essay, recent examinations of life course processes will be reviewed in light of their implications for the study of both the variability of individual trajectories and the institutional patterning of variability. Two themes in these studies will be considered. The first is individualization, or what is referred to in aging research as the thesis of heterogeneity, an idea supported principally by longitudinal demographic research on populations in advanced western societies (particularly the U. S.). Second, is the specification of social structure. Here there are alternative approaches to structuration: chief among these are what might be referred to as traditional institutional examinations and relational approaches. Both have developed rapidly in the new structuralism benefitting from methodological innovations in multilevel modeling and network analysis and from growing databases that span social contexts. Each makes a distinctive contribution to the analysis of structure.

Individualization Over the Life Course

The focus on transitions among life phases and the structural interfaces that shape these transitions is revealing the demographic and institutional mechanisms that organize lives. It is also unveiling the considerable heterogeneity of life trajectories. We have learned, for example, that the so-called *transition to adulthood* in the United States is *not* a crisp, sequence of statuses following strong age or timing norms (Hogan and Astone, 1985; Rindfuss, 1991). Rather it is a demographically dense yet temporally heterogeneous ordering of multiple transitions (including leaving school, leaving home, starting work, forming households, becoming a parent) that is driven less by age norms *per se* than by institutionalized linkages or pathways across education, work, and family domains that differentiate among subgroups of the adolescent population.

John Modell (1989) argues that the trend towards the normative "loosening" of this transition has emerged steadily over this century. His social history of the transition from youth to adulthood between 1920 and 1975— aptly titled *Into One's Own*—documents the extension of education later into the life course, changes in marital and parental timing and their determinants, changes in the transition to stable employment, and changes in the propensity for marriage and divorce and in their covariates (especially parenthood), among other trends. Overall, he observes that men's and women's life-course trajectories in family and work participation patterns are becoming increasingly similar and that the life paths between black and white populations in which earlier inequalities appear to be exacerbated over time by structural opportunities and demographic patterns are becoming more dissimilar.

The master trend, according to Modell, has been in the "liberating of one transition from the next—the weakening...of determinate sequences and intervals" by the "injection of increasing volition into the youthful life course" (Modell, 1989: 332-333). The ever-growing availability of economic and cultural resources provided to the young by family, governmental, and market structures is argued by Modell to be the principal source of this intercohort trend. But his argument accounts less rigorously for within-cohort variations and divergence among class, race and gender categories. The stratified bases of "volition" and the primary institutional contexts that define the options available to segments of succeeding cohorts of U. S. adolescents over this century are less clearly delineated by him.

Studies reported in this volume would suggest that the increased heterogeneity in the transition to adulthood in the U.S. may be in part accounted for by the jointly influential phenomena of (1) expansion of educational opportunities; (2) the stratification of the educational institution along class-related ability groupings or tracks as well as across private and public school contexts; and (3) the weak coupling of educational and employment institutions. Paradoxically, school-to-job linkages have grown increasingly ambiguous as more and more adolescents achieve secondary school educations. All in all, the impact of schooling on early life-course trajectories is a model of cross-level influences on divergent life pathways (Kerckhoff, 1993).

Midlife—a life phase once typified as demographically sparse—appears actually to be more and more punctuated by status transitions that increase the heterogeneity of life trajectories. And as we are finding for the transition to adulthood, these transitions have diverse temporal features; their timing, ordering, density, even reversibility yield multiple trajectories. Family formation and dissolution, movements into and out of jobs, and changing intergenerational dependencies pervade the adult life course. These heterogeneities, like those evident in the transition to adulthood, appear to be products of the interplay among demographic and structural processes channeling individuals. And, they are producing divergent socioeconomic trajectories anchored in early opportunities but deflected by adult transitions related to work, family, health and other contingencies of adulthood.

Even the *retirement transition* is becoming more demographically varied as its boundaries are being pushed backward and forward by reversible transitions among work, family, leisure and health statuses over a more and more extended period of life (Dannefer, 1988). Retirement is not a narrowly demarcated, absorbing, and determinate sequence of events defined by straightforward exits from work. We are identifying multiple pathways in and out of work that follow different schedules in later years. Employment in "post-career" or bridge jobs, partial and intermittent work, and disability are among several alternative routes to retirement that can be added to the traditional pension and health pathways studied for 80 many years among older male workers. These multiplying patterns emanate from the interplay of biography and social change (Henretta, 1992; O'Rand, 1995; Elder and O'Rand, 1995).

The Thesis of Heterogeneity

Demographers, epidemiologists, social historians and sociologists have observed patterns of increasing differentiation within aging cohorts from birth to death (Dannefer, 1987, 1988, 1991). These patterns are constructed by sequentially contingent status transitions or life pathways in which later transitions are constrained by earlier ones. Over time, the general pattern of differentiation produces diverse outcomes of interest, including individualization and inequality. The most striking patterns of individualization have been found in the study of health and illness in aging populations (Maddox, 1987). Health-related experiences and behaviors interact with other life transitions with cumulative and relatively highly individualized outcomes in old age. Intertwined life trajectories of health, work, family, leisure reflect highly individualized exposures to opportunities and risks related to health and functioning in later life.

Similarly, older populations exhibit greater social and economic inequalities than younger age groups due to the cumulative effects of differential opportunities and achievements over time. For example, conventional measures of income inequality across age groups (specifically gini coefficients) repeatedly reveal higher levels of dispersion among older groups (Crystal and Shea, 1990). The cumulative advantage hypothesis, initially proposed by Robert Merton (1968) to explain the high levels of inequality in productivity and recognition among scientific careers, is now more widely applied to study aging or life-course processes of social inequality linking individual behaviors with structural phenomena related to systems of advantage and disadvantage that continuously stratify cohorts over time (see Dannefer, 1987, 1991).

Social psychologists have observed across multiple studies that stability coefficients of personal characteristics such as attitudes, performance levels, and patterns of social relations increase with age (Elder and O'Rand,

1995 for review; Alwin, 1993). Here it is observed that patterns of self-definition, actualization or legitimation are sequentially reinforced or otherwise reestablished as individuals move across opportunity contexts. Short durations between transitions appear to increase stability coefficients; longer durations seem to attenuate them.

The social psychology of achievement appears to reflect a similar persistence across contexts. At a structural level, achievements in earlier structural contexts regulate the access to new contexts of achievement. Accordingly, the interfaces between institutional environments, as those between schools and jobs or between jobs, constrain individual transitions and allocate individuals selectively between contexts (Kerckhoff, 1993; see Kalleberg's contribution to this volume).

At the individual level, earlier achievements enhance self-selection processes via mechanisms related to self-esteem, identity formations, social competency and reinforced achievement motivation. Thus, structural allocation and self-selection processes enhance intraindividual stability and interindividual heterogeneity over time (Alwin, 1993). Jeylan Mortimer's essay in this volume aptly depicts these processes in the social psychology of achievement.

The growing heterogeneity of life pathways following different transition sequences and timing patterns is shedding more light on the complex interplay of changing institutional arrangements and changing lives. Even the idea of the 'triangularization' or the 'tripartitioning' of life into pre-work, work, and non-work phases correlated with age is losing its usefulness for conceptualizing the social organization of the life course (Wilensky, 1981; Kohli, 1988; Riley, 1993). Lives move along asynchronous tracks which multiply with age, especially following the transition to adulthood, and appear to produce a pattern of individualization. The synchronization of educational, family, work, leisure, health and other transitions is the central generating mechanism of the life course.

The institutional and contextual mechanisms for these changes after the transition from secondary education are anchored in the workplace, the family, and in the wider cultural and political-economic environments in which these proximate life contexts are embedded (Mayer and Schoepflin, 1989). And while we are learning that educational transitions may follow the one from secondary education in adolescence in late-20th century societies, the strong differentiating effects of this transition for later ones continues to attract our attention. This volume is devoted to identifying the structural mechanisms that operate to organize lives at the transition to adulthood.

Structuration: Two Approaches to Opportunity Structure

How does this cumulative process linking systemic and biographical components take place? Is it a simple accumulation ("adding up") of individual statuses in succeeding contexts over time? Probably not. If it were, then there would be less heterogeneity with age than we observe. Institutional structures in modern societies shape the life course via individuals' simultaneous participation in segmented and co-occurring role schedules over time. They also provide the conditions for the progressive definition, actualization and legitimation of the self (Kohli, 1986). Thus, the seemingly contradictory phenomena of the structuration and individualization of adult lives are observed.

The cumulative life-course is best examined as the interplay among three processes: selection, opportunity structure, and time (see Rosenfeld, 1992, for a discussion of career processes as generally comprised of these elements). Selection effects include the cumulative biographical conditioning that individuals bring with them to succeeding contexts. Opportunity structures include structurally varied and proximate transition contexts such as schools, jobs, and marriages *and* their wider institutional and historical environments such as state policies relating to schools and their organization, employment practices that tie jobs and job rewards to credentials, citizenship obligations and entitlements and other political-economic conditions. Cross-national studies repeatedly document the importance of state policies related to education, labor, and social welfare for the level of variability or inequality in individual well-being and achievement (Burkhauser, Duncan and Hauser, 1994; Pampel, 1993; Hout in this volume). Wars, economic cycles or transformations, and natural disasters can also influence the distribution of resources and options at critical transition periods in lives and producing longlasting effects on achievement (Elder and O'Rand, 1995).

In addition, time acts as an independent force on the organization of the life course. The timing and ordering of transitions and durations in succeeding 'states' or contexts further organize the cumulation process. As such, cross-transition linkages comprise life pathways (Hogan and Astone, 1986) with continuous and discontinuous features stemming from this interaction and the temporal characteristics that further differentiate them.

Traditional Institutional Approaches

Cross-level analyses have been spurred on in the past two decades by the introduction and elaboration of the so-called "new structuralism" to stratification and social mobility research (Kerckhoff, 1994). The status attainment model of stratification, and its social psychological elaboration in the

Wisconsin model," dominated research on achievement and inequality from the late 1960's to the early 1980's. This exemplar examined the family origins-to-education-to-occupation distributions of individuals without explicit treatment of the normative structures in which they were embedded (Kerckhoff, 1976). Consequently, the explanatory framework had an individualistic bias that could not account for subgroup variations (such as those associated with race, gender and industrial location) in attainment. The structuralism introduced institutional covariates of individual distributions that attempted to account for these differences.

Normative domains such as educational systems (Kerckhoff, 1994), industries and labor markets (see Kalleberg and Bridges in this volume), and organizational opportunity regimes (Lawrence, 1984; Sørensen, 1986; Spilerman, 1977, 1986; and Kalleberg in this volume) were among the principal institutional contexts incorporated initially in stratification analyses as individual attributes. They were assigned values as global covariates at the individual level (i.e. individuals were assigned values representing structural contexts such as industry codes, labor market segments, neighborhoods) and included as predictors in structural models. More recently, macro-level variables in multilevel models are measured as context-specific aggregate indices (e.g. means or dispersion measures) of microlevel characteristics or as global variables not expressed in terms of individual characteristics and included in complex multi-equation systems or in dynamic models permitting time-varying covariates (DiPrete and Forristal, 1994; Mayer and Tuma, 1990).

Educational attainments have persistent, robust effects on later life outcomes across national contexts as well as in the U.S. But variations in national patterns have been observed because cross-level mechanisms vary. Two categories of mechanisms have been observed: (1) the interaction of individual traits with educational structures that vary across contexts and (2) the linkages among educational structures and subsequent achievement structures such as the workplace that vary across contexts. Educational tracking systems from elementary grades through transitions to jobs from school have structural effects on individual patterns of achievement, as several essays in this volume demonstrate (especially those by Gamoran, Alexander and Entwisle, Willms, and Hallinan). The educational career is a sequence of transitions stratified over time by a relatively orderly pattern of cumulative advantage or disadvantage within school contexts. Across school contexts heterogeneity and inequality are amplified by social class segregation further enhanced by differential opportunities for school choice. Finally, school-to-job transitions culminate what appears to be a narrowing opportunity structure for achievement where divergence rather than convergence is the dominant pattern.

Paradoxically, there is evidence that more loosely coupled school-to-job linkages may produce greater heterogeneity and inequality than tightly coupled systems. Kerckhoff's (1993) study of school tracking and the transition into the labor force in Great Britain provides strong multilevel evidence of the individual-school level interaction and the school-to-job linkage. And while Great Britain and the U.S. differ systematically in some aspects of tracking students into academic versus vocational tracks, the interface between school and job is relatively more ambiguous in these two countries than that observed in some other contexts, particularly Japan and Germany, leading to more variance in work and earnings trajectories in the former countries. Among the latter a tighter coupling between institutional contexts is evident, i.e. a more determinate track between curricular/ credential validation in the educational context and the individual's assignment in the workplace exists. Direct organizational placements are more formally established. And while the Japanese and German systems are different in many other respects, the tighter coupling of the educational and labor force contexts in these two countries appears to diminish the level of heterogeneity and inequality in the salary/wage sector following education. However, DiPrete and McManus report in this volume that comparison of U.S. and German earnings mobility patterns reveals higher levels of mobility in the U.S. In short, in the U.S., and to a lesser extent in the U. A., the tracks are not as direct (Shavit and Blossfeld, 1993). General curricula— even with ability tracking—appear to generate more ambiguous paths to jobs, especially in the absence of extended specialized educations, and perhaps to more rewarding, albeit more volatile, career earnings patterns.

In the employment context, work careers consist of job transition sequences that are anchored in initial inequalities stemming from social class, status group or education group membership, but are reoriented or deflected over time by the interaction of individual worker and organizational characteristics. Segmented labor markets provide differential opportunities for achievement. Internal labor markets are conceptualized as frameworks of cumulative advantage traditionally associated with higher educational or experiential credentials, larger employment establishments, promotional ladders, and wage and benefit structures encouraging long-term attachment patterns, while secondary and contingent labor markets are divergent frameworks of cumulative disadvantage (see Kalleberg).

Yet, we are learning that these labels may obscure considerable heterogeneity within these institutional contexts. Spilerman and Ishida's study of work careers in large insurance companies in the U. S. and Japan reports that promotional schedules defy easy or oversimplified views of fast-tracks or privileged ascents. For example, they question the generalizability of Rosenbaum's (1984) tournament model of careers in hierarchically organized employment contexts across cultural settings.

In addition, Kalleberg (in this volume) observes sufficient volatility in labor markets during the recent period of economic reorganization and globalization to inspire competing hypotheses regarding the polarization of labor market structures. The view that current trends are towards a bifurcated labor market structure in which some trajectories can be labeled as careers (i.e. as coherent job sequences with the accretion of human and social resources), while others cannot as a result of the temporal and substantive discontinuities between work episodes over the life course hindering the accumulation of human capital. Changing employment contexts in advanced industrial societies, and especially the U.S., are threatening to attenuate the education-career link even further as trends towards "flexible specialization take hold and gain more ground. The externalization of labor, the disappearance of the "lifetime job" with a single employer for growing segments of the workforce, and the reconstruction of compensations for work as we have known them (chiefly employee benefits) are adding more volatility and further decoupling in the education-workplace linkage (see Kalleberg in this volume).

Continued divergence appears to result from the interaction of workplace structures and workers' characteristics for midlife status achievement into retirement. Labor market duality, workplace mobility systems, rule structures and institutionalized timetables (Sørensen, 1986; Spilerman, 1986; Lawrence, 1986) are stratification systems that allocate rewards to jobs (workers) of differential value to the organization. Jobs (workers) of higher value are rewarded with wages and fringe benefits that provide incentives for workers to remain attached to the organization and to sustain positive trajectories of achievement. Jobs (workers) of lower value are rewarded less generously and thus encourage more mobility, heterogeneity and flatter trajectories of achievement. Multilevel approaches to these questions are beginning to link microlevel measures of individuals' career characteristics with employer-level indicators of organizational structure, employment policies, and other workplace characteristics to move towards a fuller cross-level approach (Kalleberg, in this volume).

A final measure of life course achievement is economic status at retirement. Diverging life course pathways within cohorts lead to increasing economic inequality (O'Rand, 1995). Gini coefficients of age group-specific economic (income) inequality in the U. S. show greater inequality among the elderly (age 60 and over) than any other adult age group (Crystal and Shea, 1990). Comparisons with other countries reveal a similar pattern of age-specific inequality, but also find country-level differences paralleling those found regarding school-job linkages (Hout in this volume), and class and earnings mobility (DiPrete and McManus in this volume). Political-economic structures, especially corporatist and social democratic welfare systems, are mediating environments that influence levels of inequality and mobility by regulating institutional linkages and by differentially redistributing resources to individuals following diverse careers (Pampel, 1993; Burkhauser, Duncan and Hauser, 1994).

Relational Approaches to Social Structure

While the traditional institutional approach to social structure emphasizes the influence of normatively organized domains of activity on career trajectories, another approach operationalizes structure as networks or systems of action (see Breiger, 1995, for a recent review). Here the achievement process emanates from the access to, matching, and exchange of resources among interconnected personal networks. Accordingly, educational and labor market contexts of achievement are viewed as more than socially-bounded and rule-driven domains; they are active systems of interpersonal relations that interact with normative systems and in many ways transcend them. They incorporate actors' perspectives more explicitly than traditional institutional approaches, yet avoid an individualistic bias by embedding these perspectives in relational systems with differential global characteristics. Thus, in the secondary school context, above and beyond curricular and ability groups, social ties operate as social capital for achievement. And in labor markets, workers' networks of intra- and inter-organizational ties have independent effects on careers that sometimes supersede those of formal institutional contexts.

The study in this volume by Bidwell and his associates on social networks and adolescent career development among 10th and 12th graders follows this argument. Adolescent networks are systems of resources that work to orient students' behaviors towards different achievement trajectories. Besides instrumentally useful resources, these networks provide social psychological systems of support since they serve as "audiences" for developing self concepts.

The relational structure of the labor market also differentiates careers above and beyond the constraints of organizational structures and individual resources. While the traditional institutional approach tends to emphasize the more formalized or rationalized linkages between normative domains, the relational approach prefers to examine fields of structured relationships among individuals that potentially cut across bounded domains. As such, it claims to characterize social action systems more directly and to preserve the perspectives of actors themselves. A recent argument presented by Coleman (1991) following this approach is critical of career analyses that characterize trajectories of individuals within systems rather than characterizing systems themselves. He conceives labor markets less as structures than as processes, specifically "matching processes." These processes consist of systems of action in which workers have resources and preferences for selected job resources at the same time that employers have preferences for selected worker resources (including educational credentials) and have job resources to offer workers. Matching is the product of the resources and preferences of the individual worker *relative to* 1) the resources of other workers in the market, 2) their interests in the job, and 3) the distribution of job resources. The matching algorithm is a minimizing function of the difference between the value of a worker's resources and the value of the job resources held by the worker (Coleman, 1991: 6).

In this vein, Baron and Pfeffer (1994), whose work on organizations has been central to the new structuralism in stratification research, have recently elaborated on the social psychology of organizations and inequality following a relational approach to structure. They argue that work organizations are "communities of fate," where processes of social comparison, matching, and evaluation are pervasive and consequential for individuals and for social structure alike. Work organizations are shaped by interactional and cultural processes permitting the micro-to-macro flow of influence.

Finally, a similar approach is taken by Burt (1992) who argues that relational approaches to structure provide the means for explaining relative individual autonomy (agency) as well as institutional constraint. His concept of "structural holes" is central to the hypothesis that in competitive arenas like labor markets the optimal positions are derived from having diverse ties to clusters which are themselves weakly tied. These structures of nonredundant ties increase the span of access to information and resources and optimize the worker's market power. Variations in access to weak ties differentiate career trajectories, benefiting those with contacts that are more open and inclusive. Burt's study of senior managers in the volatile environment of the high technology industry demonstrates the unique contribution of the relational approach in transcending the boundaries of traditional institutions to explain individual outcomes—as and well as the possibility of systemic effects following from actions of individuals.

Perhaps the complementarity of institutional and relational approaches for the study of career trajectories is most apparent in this volume in Barbara Heyns' interesting account of the social origins of entrepreneurship in Post-Communist Poland. Here the volatility of the transition from communism to a market economy reveals that social action with career outcomes occurs in deinstitutionalizing settings within fields of social relations, *but* that institutional origins have transcendent influences in the process.

Conclusions

The new structuralism has benefited from improved methodologies and rapidly growing comparative databases that permit the direct examination of cross-level effects. The new methodologies provide algorithms that match individuals with social structures and, in some instances, incorporate time explicitly to capture social processes. They can more directly assess individual and structural outcomes as functions of micro and macro level characteristics. The databases have improved over the past four decades in at least two ways: microdata sources have improved with longitudinal information on educational and work career sequences that are more and more representative. And, macrodata bases have expanded to match individual information to direct indicators of the contexts of their careers, including employment organizations, social networks, and cross-national environments.

Institutional and relational theories provide complementary frameworks for the examination of cross-level effects. They provide the conceptual tools to examine both institutional constraint and the relational bases of individual autonomy. Accordingly, they enable us to account for both the heterogeneity of individual careers and their patterned differences. Their new promise is to delineate the macro-to-micro and the micro-to-macro flow of effects in social processes.

References

Alwin, Duane F. 1993. "Aging, Personality and Social Change: The Stability of Individual Differences Over the Adult Life-Span." In *Life-Span Development and Behavior* edited by D. L. Featherman, R. M. Lerner and M. Perlmutter. Hillsdale NJ: Erlbaum.

Baron, James N. and Pfeffer, Jeffrey. 1994. "The Social Psychology of Organizations and Inequality." *Social Psychology Quarterly* 57: 190-209.

Blau, Peter S. 1960. "Structural Effects." *American Sociological Review*, 25: 178-193.

Breiger, Ronald L. 1995. "Socioeconomic Achievement and Social Structure." *Annual Review of Sociology* 21: forthcoming.

Burkhauser, Richard V., Duncan, Greg J., Hauser, Richard. 1994. "Sharing Prosperity Across the Age Distribution: A Comparison of the United States and Germany in the 1980's." *Gerontologist*, 34: 150-160.

Burt, Ronald S. 1992. *Structural Holes: The Social Structure of Competition*. Cambridge MA: Harvard University.

Coleman, James S. 1970. "Properties of Collectivities." In *Macrosociology: Research and Theory* edited by J. S. Coleman, A. Etzioni, and J. Porter. Boston: Allen and Bacon: 1-102.

Coleman, James S. 1991. Matching Processes in the Labor Market." *Acta Sociologica*, 43: 3-12.

Crystal, Stephen and Shea, Dennis. 1990. "Cumulative Advantage, Cumulative Disadvantage, and Inequality Among Elderly People." *Gerontologist*, 30: 437-443.

Dannefer, Dale. 1987. "Ageing As Intracohort Differentiation: Accentuation, the Matthew Effect and the Life Course." *Sociological Forum*, 2: 211-236.

Dannefer, Dale. 1988. "Differential Gerontology and the Stratified Life Course: Conceptual and Methodological Issues." *Annual Review of Gerontology and Geriatrics*, 8: 3-36.

Dannefer, Dale. 1991. "The Race Is To the Swift: Images of Collective Aging." In *Metaphors of Aging in Science and the Humanities*, edited by G. M. Kenyon, J. E. Birren and J. J. F. Schroots. New York: Springer: 155-172.

DiPrete, Thomas A. and Forristal, Jerry D. 1994. "Multilevel Models: Methods and Substance." *Annual Review of Sociology* 20: 331-357.

Easterlin, Richard. 1980. *Birth and Fortune*. New York: Basic Books.

Elder, Glen H., Jr. and O'Rand, Angela M. 1995. "Adult Lives in A Changing Society." Pp. 452-475 in *Sociological Perspectives on Social Psychology*, edited by K. Cook, G. Fine and J. S. House. Boston: Allyn and Bacon.

Giddens, Anthony. 1976. *New Rules of Sociological Method: A Positive Critique of Interpretative Sociologies*. New York: Basic.

Henretta, John C. 1992. "Uniformity and Diversity: Life Course Institutionalization and Late-Life Work Exit." *Sociological Quarterly*, 33: 265-279.

Hogan, Dennis O. and Nan M. Astone. 1985. "The Transition to Adulthood." *Annual Review of Sociology* 12: 109-130.

Huber, Joan. (Ed). 1991. *Macro-Micro Linkages in Sociology*. Newbury Park CA: Sage.

Kanter, Rosabeth M. 1977. *Men and Women of the Corporation*. New York: Basic.

Kerckhoff, Alan C. 1976. "The Status Attainment Process: Socialization or Allocation." *Social Forces*, 55: 368381.

Kerckhoff, Alan C. 1993. *Diverging Pathways: Social Structure and Career Deflections*. Cambridge University Press.

Kerckhoff, Alan C. 1995. "Institutional Arrangements and Stratification Processes in Industrial Societies." *Annual Review of Sociology*, 21: 323-47

Kohli, Martin. 1986. "Social Organization and Subjective Construction of the Life Course." In *Human Development and the Life Course: Multidisciplinary Perspectives*, edited by A. B. Sørensen, F. E. Weinert and L. R. Sherrod. Hillsdale NJ: Erlbaum: 271-292.

Kohli, Martin. 1988. "Ageing As A Challenge for Sociological Theory." *Ageing and Society* 8: 367-394.

Lawrence, Barbara S. 1984. "Age-Grading: The Implicit Organization Timetable." *Journal of Occupational Behavior* 5: 23-35.

Maddox, George L. 1987. "Aging Differently." *Gerontologist*, 27: 557-564.

Mayer, Karl U. and Schoepflin, Urs. 1989. "The State and the Life Course." *Annual Review of Sociology* 15: 187-209.

Mayer, Karl U. and Tuma, Nancy B. (Eds). 1990. *Event History In Life Course Research*. University of Wisconsin.

Merton, Robert R. 1968. "The Matthew Effect in Science." *Science* 159 (January 5): 56-63.

Mills, C. Wright. 1953. "Two Styles of Research in Current Social Studies." *Philosophy of Science*, 20: 266-275.

Modell, John. 1989. *Into One's Own: From Youth To Adulthood in the United States 1920-1975*. University of California.

O'Rand, Angela M. 1995. "The Cumulative Stratification of the Life Course." In *Handbook of Aging and the Social Sciences*. Fourth Edition, edited by R. Binstock and L. R. George. NY: Academic Press: forthcoming.

Pampel, Fred C. 1993. "Relative Cohort Size and the Easterlin Effect." *American Sociological Review*, 58: 496-514.

Riley, Matilda White. 1993. "The Coming Revolution in Age Structure." Working Paper R-110, Pepper Institute on Aging and Public Policy, Florida State University, Tallahassee FL.

Rindfuss, Ronald R. 1991. "The Young Adult Years: Diversity, Structural Change and Fertility." *Demography* 28: 493-512.

Rosenbaum, Joel. 1978. "The Structure of Opportunity in School." *Social Forces*, 57: 236-256.

Rosenbaum, Joel. 1984. *Career Mobility in a Corporate Hierarchy*. NY: Academic.

Rosenfeld, Rachel. 1992. "Job Mobility and Career Processes." *Annual Review of Sociology* 18: 39-61.

Sørensen, Aage B. 1986. "Social Structure and Mechanisms of Life Course Processes." In *Human Development and the Life Course: Multidisciplinary Perspectives*, edited by A. B. Sørensen, F. E. Weinert, and L. R. Sherrod. Hillsdale NJ: Erlbaum: 177197.

Spilerman, Seymour. 1977. "Careers, Labor Market Structure, and Socioeconomic Achievement." *American Journal of Sociology* 83: 551-593.

Spilerman, Seymour. 1986. "Organizational Rules and the Features of Work Careers." *Research on Social Stratification and Mobility* 5: 41-102.

Wilensky, Harold L. 1981. "Family Life Cycle, Work and the Quality of Life: Reflections on the Roots of Happiness, Despair and Indifference in Modern Society." In *Working Life* edited by B. Gardell and G. Johansson. New York: Wiley: 235-265.

2

Social Psychological Aspects of Achievement

Jeylan T. Mortimer
University of Minnesota

Understanding the social psychological predictors of attainment was a major preoccupation of status attainment research in the late sixties and seventies. Sociologists examined the social and behavioral antecedents of achievement aspirations, such as family socio-economic background, significant others' influence and academic performance, as well as the consequences of these attitudes for attainments (Sewell, et al, 1969; Sewell, et al., 1970; Hauser, 1971; Gordon, 1972). Clear links were demonstrated between educational and occupational origins (as indicated by fathers' achievements) and adolescents' aspirations. Parental encouragement and school performance largely mediated these effects (Kerckhoff, 1974; Hauser, 1971; Duncan, et al., 1972: Alexander, et al., 1975; Wilson and Portes, 1975).

This body of work, focused on adolescence and early adulthood in the United States, laid the groundwork for subsequent elaborations of the status attainment model which have much enriched our conceptualization and understanding of the social psychology of achievement. Social scientists have studied a wide array of achievement-related attitudes and motivations, diverse attainment outcomes, socialization processes, and subgroup differences. Cross-national studies have alerted researchers to structural divergences in processes of achievement-relevant socialization and allocation. Finally, investigators have extended this research tradition to examine the social psychological dynamics of achievement throughout the life course.

Expansion of the Psychological Precursors
and Attainment Outcomes

The early attainment researchers mainly focused on aspirations and more realistic "plans" with respect to future education and occupation. But as Spenner and Featherman's (1978) review of the literature on "achievement ambitions" showed, a much wider array of psychological dimensions are implicated in achievement. In this regard, sociologists have much to learn from cognate social science disciplines.

Economists speak of "tastes for employment" and the "propensity to work" or, conversely the "propensity for unemployment," the "taste for leisure" (Corcoran and Hill, 1980), and the "taste for vacation" (Coe, 1978) as sources of occupational outcomes. They draw attention to attitudes regarding the "reservation wage," that is "the minimum offered wage necessary to induce an unemployed person to take up employment" (Hui, 1991: 1341), finding, not surprisingly, that longer spells of employment are associated with higher minimally acceptable wage offers (Hui, 1991; Baker and Elias, 1991).

Psychologists point to work motivation, the need for achievement, expectations about the consequences of achievement-related behaviors, and perceptions of the opportunity structure. For example, in a factor analytic study, Feather (1986) reported two dimensions of orientation toward future job prospects among Australian secondary school students. The first, a value factor, included indicators of interest in work, job need, and job want. The second was an expectation factor which he called "unemployment disappointment." This construct reflects the degree of helplessness or pessimism about job prospects, including the level of confidence about finding a job, the difficulty of doing so, the amount of time it will take, and the sense of personal control regarding employment outcomes.

Self-conceptions as sources of achievement are of interest to psychologists as well as sociologically-oriented social psychologists (see Spenner and Featherman, 1978; Schwalbe and Gecas, 1988). Investigators have noted positive relationships between self-esteem and educational plans (Kerckhoff, 1974), as well as between self-esteem and occupational aspirations (Gordon, 1972). Spenner and Otto (1985), in their panel study of young people in Washington state, found that women with higher self-esteem, measured while still in high school, experienced fewer months of subsequent unemployment over the following thirteen-year period; however, there was no such effect for men.

Whereas self-esteem refers to the global sense of worth, another set of self-conceptions may be even more pertinent to achievement. Internal control orientation, mastery, self-efficacy and the sense of competence all reflect expectations about the likelihood of successful goal attainment.

Bandura (1988) summarizes a large body of research demonstrating the importance of self-efficacy for work-related behaviors. A study of a panel of 1,000 ninth-graders in St. Paul, Minnesota provides support for Bandura's formulation (see Call, et al., 1993). An attempt was made to determine the social psychological antecedents of educational success among youth who come from poor families (those whose family incomes fall below the poverty line). Four years after the study began, those poor youth who appeared to be on a "successful" educational trajectory were separated from those who were not. The "successful" youth had not dropped out of school, they had a "B" average or above, and they had taken some action to prepare for college admission (e.g., taken the Scholastic Achievement Test, talked to a counsellor about college, sent for, or submitted, a college application, or other concrete activities). There were no significant differences between the two groups in aspirations or plans for educational attainment, nor were there differences in their occupational aspirations. However, the more successful poor adolescents had a significantly higher sense of economic self-efficacy. Furthermore, there is evidence that self-rated confidence in finding a job is predictive of employment success after leaving secondary school (Feather and O'Brien, 1986; O'Brien and Feather, 1990).

Some social psychologists focus on occupational reward values (Rosenberg, 1957; Davis, 1964). A panel study of University of Michigan men (Mortimer, et al., 1986) showed that emphasis on extrinsic occupational values while still in college predicted employment stability and income attainment a decade following graduation. In addition to higher incomes, those seniors with higher extrinsic values—who placed greater emphasis on money, advancement, prestige and security—had less unemployment, involuntary part-time employment and underemployment, as well as fewer changes in career direction during the ten years following college graduation. Earlier interest in the intrinsic rewards of work predicted autonomy on the job a decade later; and people-oriented values—such as an interest in working with people and being of use to the society—fostered adult work that was high in social content. More recent research on high school students shows that their occupational values increasingly predict the features of their part-time jobs as they move through high school (Mortimer, et al., 1994). Ninth-grade occupational value orientations had no significant effects on tenth-grade work experiences. However, intrinsic values measured in the tenth grade had a positive effect on the opportunity to learn job skills in the eleventh; the pattern was replicated subsequently, between the junior and senior years. Moreover, intrinsic values measured in the sophomore and junior years significantly predicted subsequent opportunities to be helpful to others at work.

Of great interest from a social policy perspective are the attitudinal precursors of unemployment and career instability (Mortimer, 1994). For example, a measure of adherence to the "Protestant work ethic" was found to distinguish students who found jobs one year (Feather and O'Brien, 1986) and two years (O'Brien and Feather, 1990) after leaving Australian secondary schools. Greater perceived need for a job also characterized those who were more successful in finding work (Feather and O'Brien, 1986).

There is evidence that young people who are more distressed have greater difficulty in the job market after leaving school. Unemployed young people in Australia had lower life satisfaction and manifested greater stress, a less positive attitude, and more depressive affect two years earlier when they were still in school than those who found employment after leaving school (Feather and O'Brien, 1986; O'Brien and Feather, 1990). In another Australian study (Winefield and Tiggemann, 1985), young people who became unemployed also expressed more boredom and depression, and males who became unemployed expressed more loneliness, before leaving school.

Attainment researchers initially focused on educational attainment and occupational prestige early in the career as indicators of socio-economic status outcomes, and to a lesser extent, income. Achievement-related attitudes have recently been associated with particular labor market entry segments predictive of divergent occupational career lines (Ashton and Sung, 1991). Other studies have linked prior psychological attributes with a diverse array of other occupationally-relevant consequences whose significance extends throughout the work career—such as work autonomy (Mortimer, et al., 1986), job stressors (Shanahan, et al., 1991), substantive complexity of tasks and other structural imperatives of the job (Kohn and Schooler, 1983).

These examples illustrate the multitude of achievement-related attitudes and attainment-related outcomes that have been scrutinized by investigators from a wide array of social science disciplines. Understanding the sources of these diverse achievement-related motivations and attitudes constitutes a major challenge for future research.

The Socialization of Achievement Orientations

The relationships between social class and child educational and occupational outcomes have been found to be mediated by social psychological dimensions, such as the favorableness of the self-concept, the sense of control of the environment, and aspirations, as well as by educational performance (Kerckhoff, 1972). How do social class, gender, family composition, parent-child relationships, peer relations, and school experiences lead to the development of those attitudes and values that predict achievement? Gecas (1979) has documented linkages between social class and modes of parental control, power relationships in the family, and communication between parent and child. These differences in parent-child relations fostered achievement-related psychological advantages or disadvantages in children. Kohn (1969, 1981) speculated that class differences in parental values with respect to self-direction and conformity limit intergenerational mobility. That is, emphasis on conformity among blue collar workers would promote values and behaviors in children that are adaptive for similar work, but would not equip them with the self-directed orientations and behaviors facilitative of success in managerial and professional roles. Feather (1986) found that high school students of higher social class origin believed that unemployment was attributable to more internal causes, and this belief was negatively related to helplessness and pessimism.

However, early studies examined the socio-economic precursors of educational and occupational aspirations, under the assumption that the status of the family of origin was fixed. Given growing attention to *intra*generational mobility, the faultiness of this assumption has become increasingly apparent. That is, parental socio-economic status may change during the periods of childhood and adolescence, a time when important vocational socialization is taking place (Featherman and Spenner, 1988). Family socio-economic mobility may foster redirection in children's trajectories of achievement.

We know little about the sources of occupational values, though there is some evidence that they are transmitted intergenerationally through close and communicative parent child relations that promote identification and modelling. The closeness of the father-son bond fosters intrinsic values in professional families and extrinsic values in business families (Mortimer and Kumka, 1982). Supportive relations with fathers also stimulate higher levels of anticipated work involvement (Mortimer, et al., 1986). Ongoing research suggests that the link between socio-economic background and occupational reward values emerges during the high school years. Work values become more strongly linked to socio-economic origins, in a manner characteristic of adults, as students mature. That is, socio-economic background has no significant impact on boys and girls' occupational values in the 9th grade. However, by the senior year it had significant positive effects on intrinsic values (Mortimer, et al., 1994).

It is widely assumed that the influence of high school track placement (e.g., academic, vocational, commercial, etc.) and ability grouping on achievement orientations is mediated by socialization processes, especially teacher-student and peer relationships. An opposing, though not necessarily contradictory, point of view is that students learn of their likely occupational destinations through observation of these self-placements, as well as the fates of their similarly-situated predecessors; they form aspirations accordingly (see Gamoran, this volume). Though such socialization and allocative mechanisms probably work in tandem, understanding their relative importance, or the conditions that make one or the other process more salient, would elucidate important social psychological dynamics of achievement.

Adolescents' own work experience may also be implicated in the social psychological process of achievement. An ongoing study of high school students in St. Paul, Minnesota, shows that positive work experiences—especially the opportunity to learn skills at work which are perceived as useful in the future—induce intrinsic occupational values (Mortimer, et al., 1994). At the same time, positive connections between school and work and advancement opportunity enhanced boys' sense of mastery (Finch, et al., 1991); girls' self-perceived efficacy increased when they reported that they were paid well. Feather (1986) similarly finds that eleventh grade students who had work experience prior to leaving high school had lower levels of helplessness and pessimism in relation to future job prospects. The positive association between adolescent part-time work and both employment and income in the years immediately following high school (Millham, et al., 1978; Freeman and Wise, 1979; Meyer and Wise, 1982: Mortimer and Finch, 1986) may be at least partially attributable to these salutary psychological outcomes. Study of the St. Paul youth's transition to adulthood may provide direct evidence with respect to such processes of social psychological mediation.

Finally, as Bidwell, Plank and Muller (this volume) point out, whereas investigators have extensively examined the influence of significant others—including parents, teachers, and peers—on aspirations, little is known about the ways in which the organization of adolescents' networks of associations influence aspirations as well as other orientations to achievement.

Subgroup Differences
in the Social Psychology of Achievement

In another kind of elaboration of the status attainment model, researchers are increasingly attending to subgroup differences in the process of attainment. Whereas early studies were often based on men, researchers increasingly inquired about gender-specific attitudinal predictors of attainment. Though employment is increasingly common among adult women, adolescent girls still encounter traditional values emphasizing the importance of appearance, popularity, marriage and parenthood which may interfere with achievement-related effort and occupational advancement. Bidwell et al. (this volume) present evidence that cohesive peer networks strengthen boys' ambitions, while reducing those of girls. Moreover, by observing the experiences of their mothers and other adult women, girls may become increasingly aware of the dilemmas and role conflicts involved in combining family life and work, as well as the sex-typed job market and other obstacles to women's achievement. High occupational attainments may come to be seen as incompatible with the achievement of familial goals. Though there has been much controversy about causal order, it is fairly well established that, for women, a high level of family involvement and larger family size are associated with lower levels of female socio-economic achievement (McLaughlin, et al., 1988).

Gender differences in educational and occupational plans and aspirations continue to be of interest. While early studies—in the sixties and before—showed that boys have higher achievement orientations than girls; studies in the seventies and eighties indicated no consistent gender difference. More recent research suggests that adolescent girls often surpass boys in the level of their aspirations. Study of a representative panel of adolescents drawn from the St. Paul public schools is consistent with this latter trend (Dennehy and Mortimer, 1993). It shows that, in the aggregate, girls have educational aspirations and plans, as well as occupational aspirations, that exceed those of boys. Moreover, their commitment to work in the future—that is, the importance which they attach to future work—is equivalent to that of boys. However, their sense of economic efficacy—their predictions about the likelihood of their actually being able to achieve their economic goals, such as owning their own home or having a job which pays well—is, on the average, significantly lower than those of boys (Dennehy and Mortimer, 1993). Consistently, economists find that women have lower reservation wages than men, a pattern that would depress their wages relative to men (Hui, 1991; Lynch, 1983; Jones, 1989).

Several studies demonstrate that girls have a weaker sense of self-efficacy than boys in general (Maccoby and Jacklin, 1974; Simmons and Blyth, 1987; Gecas, 1989: p. 305; Finch, et al., 1991). If, in fact, it is not so much aspirations that stimulate persistence in achievement-related behavior, but a real sense of efficacy and confidence that one's efforts are likely to be successful, girls may still be psychologically disadvantaged despite their high aspirations. Adolescent girls have also been found to have lower self-esteem than boys (Simmons and Blyth, 1987) and higher levels of depressive affect (Rutter, 1986), attributes which may also impede success in the job market.

Whereas these studies, like most in this field, generally report mean differences, by gender, in achievement-relevant attitudes and psychological traits, such may obscure important differences among women in orientations and planning strategies. To what extent do young women view their futures as contingent on future spouses, children, and others, diminishing their propensity to make firm plans given unpredictability in the needs and demands of others (Hagestad, 1992)? Geissler and Kruger (1992), in their qualitative study of German young women, note different models of "biographical continuity." Some women construct their future biographies with reference to career, focusing on obtaining professional qualifications and delaying marriage. Others, in contrast, expect to enact traditional female adult roles, emphasizing limited labor force participation and economic dependence on a husband. Still others consider job and family to be equally important. Such divergence in planning modes would certainly influence the intensity of achievement-related striving and the extent of future attainment.

Racial and ethnic differences in the social psychology of achievement are of considerable importance. Ogbu (1989) finds that despite high aspirations, black youth are easily discouraged in their attempts to achieve. Given the long history of racial discrimination in the United States, many black youth believe that they will confront obstacles in their quest for occupational and economic attainments even if they are successful in the educational system. Instead of pressing forward in the face of difficulties, their "folk culture of success" leads them to assume a somewhat fatalistic posture, "What's the use of trying?" In this way, Black youth are channelled away from schoolwork and toward behaviors that diminish the likelihood of legitimate employment success. Indicating the realism of these attitudes, Wilson (1987) and Sullivan (1989) document the absence of employment opportunities for young people in the inner city.

Much more attention needs to be directed to subgroup differences in the social psychology of achievement, and to the sources of these variations. Given continuingly rapid change in gender roles, there is need for careful monitoring of gender differences in achievement orientations and their consequences. What experiences determine whether girls will be oriented to careers or to more traditional gender roles? Moreover, little is known about the achievement orientations of minority groups other than Blacks. Are the achievement attitudes which predict attainments in the general population also characteristic of high-achieving Asian-Americans? And what about very recent newcomers, such as the Hmong, who exhibit high aspirations as well as factors mitigating against their achievement—familial poverty as well as early marriage and fertility in the adolescent generation (McNall, et al., 1994).

Structural Moderation of the
Social Psychological Dynamics of Attainment

There are differences in the process of attainment depending on the sector of the labor market, whether in the primary or core, or in the periphery or secondary sector (see Beck, et al.'s discussion of income attainment, 1978, in the U.S.; and Ashton and Sung's, 1991, assessment of young people's early careers in Britain). However, studies of labor market segmentation and attainment have generally ignored social psychological aspects of the attainment process. Kerckhoff (1989) suggests that the status attainment and labor segmentation models be integrated to develop a more balanced picture.

Comparative, cross-national studies of the social psychology of achievement would much contribute to our understanding of structurally-determined variability in the process. Whereas in the United States educational attainment is measured by years of formal schooling and the receipt of diplomas and degrees, of much greater importance in Britain is achievement in the complex system of "qualifications" (Kerckhoff, 1990). These are obtained through diverse experiences, including regular schooling, apprenticeship, on-the-job training, vocational or technical training and university-level education, and are certified by examination. Many students, especially men, who left school early with low-level qualifications, and who had been in the "less favored" secondary school locations, obtained additional qualifications through these opportunities. At the same time, "further education" is a relatively strong predictor of occupational prestige attainment measured at the age of 23. Thus, many British young people are able to compensate for their initial disadvantage in the highly stratified "sponsored" mobility system of regular schooling by participation in the "alternative route" (p. 160).

Kerckhoff (1993) finds structural sources of cumulative educational advantage in the British educational system. Some students move through high-achieving career lines, i.e., junior school high ability groups, elite secondary schools, and higher education. Others move from a junior school low ability group, to a low ability group in a comprehensive school, and terminate their education with no postsecondary courses. He concludes, "at each stage in the educational career...there were very strong effects of organizational structure on the achievements of the individual students, net of the effects of the students' social origins, personal characteristics, and past experiences and performances." (p. 200)

Kerckhoff's comparative studies of the transition to adulthood in Great Britain and the United States, though focused on structural differences, bring to mind several very interesting questions about psychological dynamics. What individual-level consequences—cognitive, affective, and behavioral—are fostered by "regular" and by "alternative" educational structures and allocative mechanisms? For example, placement in "lower-level" schooling in Britain (e.g., secondary modern as opposed to grammar schools) given the highly public nature of assignment, could detract from self-esteem, the motivation to learn and the expenditure of effort. School type (e.g., grammar school, comprehensive school, etc.) and ability grouping have significant effects on the level of educational qualifications eventually obtained, even when ability, as gauged by objective test as well as by self and teacher ratings, is controlled. Whether this results from variation in teachers' expectations, self-labelling and adjustment of aspirations or other processes, are questions remaining to be addressed. Moreover, one might investigate the psychological consequences of the "alternative route." Might this opportunity reduce the alienation produced by assignment to "lower level" secondary schools, or to lower ability groups, enhancing commitment to both "regular" and "further" education among those who are not destined to receive higher educational degrees?

There has been little attention to differences in culture, social structure, or the institutional linkages between school and work that could lead certain psychological dimensions to be more important for achievement in one context than another. Such studies would yield understanding of the interactions of structures and attitudes in predicting attainment outcomes. For example, the level of institutional connection between school and work could importantly moderate the effects of achievement orientations. The United States is characterized by loose institutional connections; Germany and Japan represent countries with tighter, more highly structured linkages (see Hamilton, 1990; Rosenbaum, et al., 1990). Because of clear institution-alized connections between particular schools and firms in Japan, the student's prior academic achievement and teacher recommendations are highly consequential for obtaining placement in high-quality jobs (Rosenbaum, et al., 1990). In such circumstances, psychosocial variables that influence school achievement could have greater relevance for early attainment outcomes among non-college youth than in the United States, where employers pay little attention to recent school leavers' academic performance, and schools have few resources to respond to requests for transcripts and other records, even when employers want them (Borman, 1991: 41).

These comparative analyses provide insight into possible structural bases of the problems of youth in the United States. Though social psychologists generally look to the microcontexts of development (e.g, the family, the school classroom, or the peer group) as the central determinants of achievement-related orientations, behaviors and outcomes, these cross-national studies draw attention to what might be important structural underpinnings of the much-heralded U.S. weaknesses in educational per-formance and economic productivity. The system of "further education" in Britain, like the institution of apprenticeship in Germany, and the struc-tured linkages between secondary schools and industrial corporations in Japan, provide clear economic incentives for the acquisition of job-related knowledge and skills prior to and/or following the completion of second-ary education. Comparable structures promoting non-college youth's continuing motivation to learn and to enhance their human capital are generally lacking in the United States. American non-college youth, in the years immediately after high school, drift between jobs whose skill levels are the same, or quite similar to, the jobs they were able to obtain when they were still in high school (Osterman, 1989). Nor are they likely to be enrolled in the kinds of highly focused, specialized programs (like the system of "further education" opportunities in Great Britain) after full-time labor force entry that increase their economic productivity. Not surprisingly, they have become increasingly disadvantaged economically and socially (W. T. Grant Foundation, 1988).

The Social Psychology of Achievement
through the Life Course

Most studies of the achievement process have focused on young people. Researchers typically survey aspirations, values, and other orientations of students prior to leaving full-time education. Educational sociologists focus on school-related determinants (such as tracking, ability grouping and external rewards) of intrinsic motivation and effort in school, which influence academic achievement and educational attainment (see chapters by Hallinan and Gamoran, this volume). Those interested in career decision-making have assessed the connection between students' values and occupational choices (Davis, 1964; Mortimer and Kumka, 1982; see also Heyns, this volume, for assessment of laissez-faire values and proprietorship aspirations among Polish business students.) Some investigators have followed youthful panel members over a period of time to ascertain the predictive capacity of these psychological attributes for educational and occupational attainments early, and sometimes later, in the work career (Mortimer, et al., 1986; Clausen, 1993).

In the early status attainment studies, aspirations were often measured at one point in time, and assumed to be relatively invariant over time. However, Kerckhoff's study (1974) suggested that adolescents form their educational and occupational aspirations during the high school years, and that aspirations were not as stable as assumed in the status attainment literature. Our study of adolescents in St. Paul found that both boys' and girls' educational aspirations and plans actually declined as they moved through high school (Dennehy and Mortimer (1993). The same pattern was true of their occupational aspirations. These decreasing levels of aspiration may indicate growing realism as adolescents become more aware of labor market realities. Another study indicates instability in aspirations in the years after high school as well. Rindfuss and his colleagues (1990), using National Longitudinal Survey data from 1972, the respondents' last year of high school, and follow-ups in 1973, 1974, 1976, and 1979, found that less than one quarter of the youth had the same occupational expectation at all time periods. We need to know much more about the sources of stability and change during this formative period. We also need more study of the processes of crystallization of achievement-related orientations as young people mature. At what point do persons become aware that there are intrinsic and extrinsic dimensions of work, each of which can be rewarding and that these rewards are differentially available in various occupational roles? Do these increasingly sophisticated conceptions of work induce change in occupational aspirations as young persons acquire more labor force experience?

Once a person has entered the workforce, employment and joblessness, as well as the quality of work (Mortimer et al., 1986; Kohn and Schooler, 1983), can influence diverse psychological attributes that influence subsequent occupational success. The early work career may be especially important in this regard, given that work orientations are in a particularly formative stage. If early jobs are unstable and unrewarding, workers may become alienated from work, develop poor work habits, and become less attached to the workforce (Corcoran and Hill, 1980: 40). Experiences of early joblessness could foster the development of psychological characteristics that affect the likelihood of future employment. There is evidence that unemployment fosters distress, self-blame and other psychopathology (Hamilton, et al., 1991; Kessler, et al., 1989) which could jeopardize subsequent success in the labor market. Unemployment also depresses the reservation wage (Hui, 1991). Frequent and/or persistent unemployment may cause workers to become discouraged, dropping out of the labor force because they believe that work is not available (DiPrete, 1981). Unemployment, in fact, may alter tastes, skills, and motivations in such a way that it is perpetuated over time (Baker and Elias, 1991).

Comparative historical studies of lives emphasize the increasing destructuration and individualization of the life course, as the duration, sequencing, and directionality of movement between historically age-graded status positions are becoming increasingly diverse and subject to manifold contingencies (see O'Rand, this volume; Modell, 1989). These trends make the linkages between school and work, as well as occupational career lines following completion of formal education, increasingly tenuous. Under such circumstances, it might be argued that social psychological factors become even more important in determining the achievement process, not only in the early stages of the life course, but throughout the socio-economic career. No longer can it be assumed that individuals, once securely placed on a lower rung of a success escalator, can ride smoothly toward the top, carried forward structurally via strong institutionalized career tracks. With a wider array of branching points, more prevalent reversals in the directionality of movement, and movements between such tracks (e.g., return to school for continuing training), individual motivation, volition, and effort may become increasingly salient. Thus, whereas research on the social psychology of mobility has been highly focused on adolescents and youth, future investigators might fruitfully extend the scope of "status attainment" studies to older people, examining human agency among middle-aged and older workers as determinants of career attainment later in the life course.

In light of the increasing diversification of career sequences, it is pertinent to investigate the manner in which success aspirations influence attainments as careers unfold. Clausen (1993) examines the attitudinal precursors in adolescence of life-long attainment, finding competence to be especially predictive. But are there any distinct social psychological antecedents of attainment for persons of different age? A teenager, upon leaving full-time schooling, might be motivated to find a job, at least in part, by a desire for independence and dissatisfaction with continued economic and other forms of dependency upon parents (Borman, 1991). In contrast, the older worker's job search and relocation attempts, and other achievement-related behaviors, may be more closely linked to family economic needs, the position of work in the "hierarchy of identities" (Stryker, 1985) and the level of investment in, and commitment to, the work role. What are the psychological antecedents of further mobility on the part of those who are mid-way on career ladders? Are there psychological dimensions which distinguish those who "plateau" relatively early in their careers, from those who continue to progress?

There has been relatively little study of the social psychological dynamics of achievement in middle age, when expected attainments do not materialize, or when unanticipated obstacles are encountered. What psychological factors promote early recovery from job loss and rapid reemployment? Hamilton, et al.'s quasi-experimental study of workers in four closing (and a control group of twelve non-closing) General Motors plants from 1987 to 1989 found that depression was a significant precursor of subsequent inability to locate a new job. Both unemployment and depression at wave 1 predicted unemployment at wave 2, one year after the plant closed; and unemployment and depression at wave 2 similarly predicted unemployment two years after the closing.

However, Kessler, et al (1989), on the basis of their study of a community sample in areas of Detroit with high unemployment rates, report that *greater* prior distress predicted reemployment of the unemployed over a one-year period (controlling age, sex, education, race, and marital status). The authors speculate that the more distressed unemployed workers may have engaged in more strenuous job search, encouraged by improving economic conditions.

Preexisting psychological orientations may influence the person's definition of the situation upon loss of a job. Unemployed workers may define themselves as unemployed members of the labor force and actively seek reemployment. Alternatively, they may view themselves as temporarily out of the workforce, and postpone seeking work – a more typical definition among workers in closing General Motors plants who had more seniority, were older, and female (Hamilton, et al., 1991). Many unemployed women withdraw from the labor market to pursue family-related objectives (Warr, et al., 1982). If the recent jobless see little prospect of finding a new job, they may become "discouraged workers" and drop out of the labor force entirely. Finally, if prospects are not bright, and if jobless workers are old enough, they may define themselves as retired.

It is reasonable to suppose that those with lower self-efficacy would be more likely to become "discouraged" workers (Banks and Ullah (1988: 118). Higher levels of depression and self-blame may also predict withdrawal from the labor force upon losing a job (Hoffman, et al, 1991: Table 6). In fact, not looking for a job may be one way to protect a fragile psyche, for Hoffman et al. (1991) show that to seek a job and not to find one increases depression. Jobless workers in their study who were "not looking" and did not find work were less distressed than the active but unsuccessful job seekers. Paradoxically, given the various possible definitions of the jobless situation, those who become unemployed could have higher self-efficacy than those who become discouraged or "retired."

Some have speculated that differences in job search behavior mediates the linkages between psychological variables and employment outcomes (Feather, 1986; Kessler, et al., 1989). But there has been little systematic study of this possible source of mediation. One study of unemployed Israeli workers (Shamir, 1986) found that among those who became reemployed, those with higher self-esteem made more use of individualistic, informal and active methods of job search, such as the use of personal contacts and direct application to the prospective employer. Those with lower levels of self-esteem were more likely to use impersonal methods, such as the labor exchange or employment services. They were also more willing to accept jobs that did not match their income and job content goals. Whereas such flexibility may be useful with respect to immediate employment prospects, it may have more negative long-term career implications.

The Causal Priority of Structure and Achievement Orientations

Some may question the causative role of achievement orientations in attainment, arguing that attitudes reflect likely career destinations, given socio-economic realities and existing opportunities, rather than determining the direction or extent of actual achievement (Roberts, 1968). In emphasizing socialization as the link between social origin and destination, the status attainment researchers tended to assume, implicitly if not explicitly, that the individual is relatively free to move within the social structure; social structural constraints on the attainment process were relatively ignored (see Kerckhoff, 1976, 1984). More recent work, such as those cross-national studies referenced above, emphasizes structural allocation, viewing attainment as resulting from structural limitations and selection criteria, and the individual as relatively constrained by the social structure. If opportunities determine achievement orientations (Ogbu, 1989; Kerckhoff, 1994), these psychological variables might merely mediate the effects of structural forces.

It is not easy to decide among such "causes," for the identification of antecedents, correlates, or predictors will depend on the particular point at which one enters the causal sequence. Taking "underclass" youth as a case in point, we know much about the economic, technological, demographic and other structural trends that have eroded youth employment opportunities. Youth in the inner cities often have few occupational role models and very limited job prospects. However, they do have chances to obtain income through hustling, crime, drugs, or welfare dependency. Educational and occupational aspirations, the motivation to seek jobs, and the sense of control over attainment are undoubtedly affected (Wilson, 1987; Sullivan, 1989; Banks and Ullah, 1988). Unsuccessful attempts to find paid work, accompanied by perceived or real discrimination, may only intensify pessimism and weaken the "propensity to work." Furnham (1985:109) speaks of a "destructive vicious circle" occurring when youth fail to find jobs: they experience stress and disappointment, lowered self-esteem and decline in expectations, all of which lessen the intensity and fruitfulness of subsequent job search. In view of this sequence, is it the psychological impediment, or the structure, which is at the "root" of the failure to succeed? This simple formulation of the question does not do justice to the complex, dynamic, interactive, and reciprocal interrelations of structural, psychological and behavioral phenomena in the achievement process. Future researchers need to attend to both structural and psychological variability to fully understand the processes of achievement throughout individual lives.

References

Alexander, Karl L., Bruce K. Eckland, and Larry J. Griffin. 1975. "The Wisconsin Model of Socioeconomic Achievement: A Replication." *American Journal of Sociology 81*:324-342.

Ashton, David N. and Johnny Sung. 1991. "Labor Markets and the Life Course Patterns of Young Adults in Great Britain." Pp. 23-42 in *The Life Course and Social Change*, edited by Walter. R. Heinz. Wannheim: Deutscher Studien Verlag.

Baker, Meredith and Peter Elias. 1991. "Youth Unemployment and Work Histories." Pp. 214-244 in *Life and Work History Analyses: Qualitative and Quantitative Developments*, edited by Shirley Dex. London: Routledge.

Bandura, Albert. 1988. "Organizational Applications of Social Cognitive Theory." *Australian Journal of Management* 13:275-302.

Banks, M. H. and P. Ullah. 1988. *Youth Unemployment in the 1980's: Its Psychological Effects*. London: Croom Helm.

Beck, E. M., Patrick M. Horan, and Charles M. Tolbert II. 1978. "Stratification in a Dual Economy: A Sectoral Model of Earnings Determination." *American Sociological Review* 43:704-720.

Borman, Kathryn M. 1991. *The First Real Job: A Study of Young Workers*. Albany: State University of New York Press.

Call, Katherine T., Jeylan T. Mortimer, Chaimun Lee, and Katherine Dennehy. 1993. "High Risk Youth and the Attainment Process." Paper presented at the annual meetings of the American Sociological Association.

Clausen, John S. 1993. *American Lives. Looking Back at the Children of the Great Depression*. New York: Free Press.

Coe, Richard D. 1978. "Absenteeism from Work." Ch. 5 in *Five Thousand American Families—Patterns of Economic Progress, Vol. VI, Accounting for Race and Sex Differences in Earnings and Other Analyses of the First Nine Years of the Panel Study of Income Dynamics*, edited by Greg J. Duncan & James N. Morgan. Survey Research Center, Institute for Social Research: University of Michigan.

Corcoran, Mary and Martha S. Hill. 1980. "Persistence In Unemployment Among Adult Men." Ch. 2 in *Five Thousand American Families—Patterns of Economic Progress, Vol. VIII, Analyses of the First Eleven Years of the Panel Study of Income Dynamics*, edited by Greg J. Duncan & James N. Morgan. Survey Research Center, Institute for Social Research: University of Michigan.

Davis, James A. 1964. *Great Aspirations: The Graduate School Plans of America's College Seniors*. Chicago: Aldine.

Dennehy, Katherine and Jeylan T. Mortimer. 1993. "Work and Family Orientations of Contemporary Adolescent Boys and Girls." Pp. 87-107 in *Men, Work, and Family*, edited by Jane C. Hood. Newbury Park, CA: Sage Publications.

DiPrete, Thomas. 1981. "Unemployment over the Life Cycle: Racial Differences and the Effect of Changing Economic Conditions." *American Journal of Sociology* 87:286-307.

Duncan, Otis D., Daniel L. Featherman and Beverly Duncan. 1972. *Socioeconomic Background and Achievement*. New York: Seminar Press.

Feather, Norman T. 1986. "Employment Importance and Helplessness about Potential Unemployment among Students in Secondary Schools." *Australian Journal of Psychology* 38:33-44.

Feather, Norman T. and Gordon E. O'Brien. 1986. "A Longitudinal Study of the Effects of Employment and Unemployment on School-Leavers." *Journal of Occupational Psychology* 59:121-144.

Featherman, David L. and Kenneth I. Spenner. 1988. "Class and the Socialization of Children: Constancy, Change, or Irrelevance?" Pp. 67-90 in *Child Development in Life Span Perspective*, edited by E. Mavis Hetherington, Richard M. Lerner, and Marion Permutter. Hillsdale, NJ: Lawrence Erlbaum Associates.

Finch, Michael D., Michael Shanahan, Jeylan T. Mortimer, and Seongryeol Ryu. 1991. "Work Experience and Control Orientation in Adolescence." *American Sociological Review* 56:597-611.

Freeman, Richard B. and David A. Wise. 1979. *Youth Unemployment*. Cambridge, Massachusetts: National Bureau of Economic Research.

Furnham, Adrian. 1985. "Youth Unemployment: A Review of the Literature." *Journal of Adolescence* 8:109-124.

Gecas, Viktor. 1979. "The Influence of Social Class on Socialization," Pp. 365-404 in *Contemporary Theories about the Family, Vol. I, Research-Based Theories*, edited by Wesley R. Burr, Reuben Hill, F. Ivan Nye, and Ira L. Reiss. NY: Free Press.

Gecas, Viktor. 1989. "The Social Psychology of Self-Efficacy." *Annual Review of Sociology* 15:291-316.

Geissler, B. and Helga Kruger. 1992. "Balancing the Life Course in Response to Institutional Requirements." Pp. 151-167 in *Institutions and Gatekeeping in the Life Course*, edited by Walter Heinz. Wannheim: Deutscher Studien Verlag.

Gordon, Chad. 1972. "Looking Ahead: Self-Conceptions, Race, and Family as Determinants of Adolescent Orientation to Achievement." *Rose Monograph Series*. Washington, DC: American Sociological Association.

Hagestad, Gunhild. 1992. "Assigning Rights and Duties: Age, Duration, and Gender in Social Institutions." Pp. 261-279 in *Institutions and Gatekeeping in the Life Course*, edited by Walter Heinz. Wannheim: Deutscher Studien Verlag.

Hamilton, Stephen F. 1990. *Apprenticeship for Adulthood: Preparing Youth for the Future*. New York: The Free Press.

Hamilton, V. L., Hoffman, W. S., Broman, C. L. & Rauma, D. 1991. "Aftermath: A Panel Study of Unemployment and Mental Health among Autoworkers." Unpublished paper.

Hauser, Robert M. 1971. *Socioeconomic Background and Educational Performance. Rose Monograph Series*. Washington, DC: American Sociological Association.

Hoffman, W. S., V. L. Hamilton, C. L. Broman, and D. Rauma. 1991. "Unemployment, Depression, and Self-Blame Among Autoworkers." Paper presented at the annual meetings of the American Sociological Association Annual Meeting.

Hui, Weng-tat. 1991. "Reservation Wage Analysis of Unemployed Youths in Australia." *Applied Economics* 23:1341-1350.

Jones, Stephen R. G. 1989. "Reservation Wages and the Cost of Unemployment." *Economica* 56:225-246.

Kerckhoff, Alan C. 1972. "Socialization and Social Class." Englewood Cliffs, NJ: Prentice Hall

Kerckhoff, Alan C. 1974. "Ambition and Attainment: A Study of Four Samples of American Boys." *Rose Monograph Series*. Washington, DC: American Sociological Association.

Kerckhoff, Alan C. 1976. "The Status Attainment Process: Socialization or Allocation?" *Social Forces* 55:368-381.

Kerckhoff, Alan C. 1984. "The Current State of Social Mobility Research." *The Sociological Quarterly* 25:139-153.

Kerckhoff, Alan C. 1989. "On the Social Psychology of Social Mobility Processes." *Social Forces* 68:17-25.

Kerckhoff, Alan C. 1990. *Getting Started: Transition to Adulthood in Great Britain*. Boulder: Westview Press.

Kerckhoff, Alan C. 1993. *Diverging Pathways. Social Structure and Career Deflections*. New York: Cambridge University Press.

Kerckhoff, Alan C. 1994. "Social Stratification and Mobility Processes: The Interaction Between Individuals and Social Structures." Pp. 476-496 in *Sociological Perspectives on Social Psychology*, edited by Karen Cook, Gary A. Fine, and James S. House. New York: Allyn and Bacon.

Kessler, Ronald C., J. Blake Turner, and James S. House. 1989. "Unemployment, Reemployment, and Emotional Functioning in a Community Sample." *American Sociological Review* 54:648-657.

Kohn, Melvin L. 1969. *Class and Conformity: A Study in Values.* Homewood, IL.: Dorsey.

Kohn, Melvin L. 1981. "Personality, Occupation, and Social Stratification: A Frame of Reference." Pp. 267-297 in *Research in Social Stratification and Mobility*, edited by Donald J. Treiman and Robert V. Robinson. Greenwich, CT: JAI Press, Inc.

Kohn, Melvin L. & Carmi Schooler. 1983. *Work and Personality: An Inquiry into the Impact of Social Stratification.* Norwood, New Jersey: Ablex.

Lynch, Lisa M. 1983. "Job Search and Youth Unemployment." *Oxford Economic Papers 35(Supplement):*271-282.

McLaughlin, Steven D., Barbara D. Melber, John O.G. Billy, Denise M. Zimmerle, Linda D. Winges, and Terry R. Johnson. 1988. *The Changing Lives of American Women.* Chapel Hill, NC: The University of North Carolina Press.

McNall, Miles, Timmothy Dunnigan, and Jeylan T. Mortimer. 1994. "The Educational Achievement of the St. Paul Hmong." *Anthropology and Education Quarterly* 25:1-22.

Maccoby, Eleanor E. and Carol N. Jacklin. 1974. *The Psychology of Sex Differences.* Stanford: Stanford University Press.

Meyer, R. M. & David A. Wise. 1982. "High School Preparation and Early Labor Force Experience." Pp. 277-347 in *The Youth Labor Market Problem: Its Nature, Causes, and Consequences*, edited by Richard B. Freeman and David A. Wise. Chicago: University of Chicago Press.

Millham, Spense, Roger Bullock and Kenneth Hosie. 1978. "Juvenile Unemployment: A Concept Due for Re-Cycling?" *Journal of Adolescence* 1:11-24.

Modell, John. 1989. *Into One's Own. From Youth to Adulthood in the United States 1920-1975.* Berkeley and Los Angeles, CA: University of California Press.

Mortimer, Jeylan T. 1994. "Individual Differences as Precursors of Youth Unemployment." Pp. 172-198 in *Youth Unemployment and Society*, edited by Anne C. Petersen. New York: Cambridge University Press.

Mortimer, Jeylan T. and Michael D. Finch. 1986. "The Effects of Part-Time Work on Self-Concept and Achievement." Pp. 66-89 in *Becoming a Worker*, edited by Kathryn Borman and Jane Reisman. Norwood, New Jersey: Ablex.

Mortimer, Jeylan T. and Donald Kumka. 1982. "A Further Examination of the 'Occupational Linkage Hypothesis.'" *The Sociological Quarterly* 23:3-16.

Mortimer, Jeylan T., Jon Lorence and Donald Kumka. 1986. *Work, Family, and Personality: Transition to Adulthood.* Norwood, New Jersey: Ablex.

Mortimer, Jeylan T., Seongryeol Ryu, Katherine Dennehy, Ellen Efron Pimentel, and Chaimun Lee. 1994. "Part-Time Work and Occupational Value Formation in Adolescence." Revision of paper presented at the 1992 American Sociological Association Annual Meeting. Pittsburgh.

O'Brien, Gordon E. and Norman T. Feather. 1990. "The Relative Effects of Unemployment and the Quality of Employment on the Affect, Work Values and Personal Control of Adolescents." *Journal of Occupational Psychology* 63:151-165.

Ogbu, John U. 1989. "Cultural Boundaries and Minority Youth Orientation Toward Work Preparation." Pp. 101-140 in *Adolescence and Work: Influences of Social Structure, Labor Markets, and Culture*, edited by David Stern and Dorothy Eichorn. Hillsdale, New Jersey: Lawrence Erlbaum.

Osterman, Paul. 1989. "The Job Market for Adolescents." Pp. 235-256 in *Adolescence and Work: Influences of Social Structure, Labor Markets, and Culture*, edited by David Stern & Dorothy Eichorn. Hillsdale, New Jersey: Lawrence Erlbaum.

Rindfuss, Richard R., Elizabeth C. Cooksey and R. L. Sutterlin. 1990. *Young Adult Occupational Achievement: Early Expectations Versus Behavioral Reality*. Paper presented at the World Congress of Sociology. Madrid, July.

Roberts, K. 1968. "The Entry into Employment: An Approach Towards a General Theory." *Sociological Review* 16:165-84.

Rosenbaum, James E., Takehiko Kariya, Rick Settersten and Tony Maier. 1990. "Market and Network Theories of the Transition from High School to Work: Their Application to Industrialized Societies." *Annual Review of Sociology* 16:263-299.

Rosenberg, Morris. 1957. *Occupations and Values*. Glencoe, Illinois: Free Press.

Rutter, Michael. 1986. "The Developmental Psychopathology of Depression: Issues and Perspectives." Pp. 3-30 in *Depression in Young People: Developmental and Clinical Perspectives*, edited by Michael Rutter, Carroll E. Izard & Peter B. Read. New York: Guilford Press.

Schwalbe, Michael L. and Viktor Gecas. 1988. "Social Psychological Dimensions of Job-Related Disability." Pp. 233-271 in *Work Experience and Psychological Development Through the Life Span*, edited by Jeylan T. Mortimer & Kathryn M. Borman. Boulder: Westview Press.

Sewell, William H., Archibald O. Haller, and Alejandro Portes. 1969. "The Educational and Early Occupational Attainment Process." *American Sociological Review* 34:82-93.

Sewell, William H., Archibald O. Haller, and George W. Ohlendorf. 1970. "The Educational and Early Occupational Status Attainment Process: Replication and Revision." *American Sociological Review* 35:1014-1027.

Shamir, Boaz. 1986. "Self-Esteem and the Psychological Impact of Unemployment." *Social Psychology Quarterly* 49:61-72.

Shanahan, Michael J., Michael D. Finch, Jeylan T. Mortimer, and Seongryeol Ryu. 1991. "Adolescent Work Experience and Depressive Affect." *Social Psychology Quarterly* 54:299-317.

Simmons, Roberta and Dale Blyth. 1987. *Moving into Adolescence: The Impact of Pubertal Change and School Context*. New York: Aldine.

Spenner, Kenneth I. and Luther B. Otto. 1985. "Work and Self-Concept: Selection and Socialization in the Early Career." Pp. 197-235 in *Research in Sociology of Education and Socialization, Vol. 5*, edited by Alan C. Kerckhoff. Greenwich, CT: JAI Press.

Spenner, Kenneth I. and David L. Featherman. 1978. "Achievement Ambitions." *Annual Review of Sociology* 4:373-420.

Stryker, Sheldon. 1985. "Symbolic Interaction and Role Theory." Pp. 311-378 in *Handbook of Social Psychology, Vol. I*, edited by Gardner Lindzey & E. Aronson. New York: Random House.

Sullivan, Mercer L. 1989. *Getting Paid: Youth, Crime and Work in the Inner City*. Ithaca: Cornell University Press.

Warr, Peter, P. Jackson, and M. Banks. 1982. "Duration of Unemployment and Psychological Well-Being in Young Men and Women." *Current Psychological Research* 2:207-214.

Wilson, Kenneth L. & Alejandro Portes. 1975. "The Educational Attainment Process: Results from a National Sample." *American Journal of Sociology* 81:343-363.

Wilson, William J. 1987. *The Truly Disadvantaged: The Inner City, the Underclass, and Public Policy*. Chicago: University of Chicago Press.

Winefield, Anthony H., and Marika Tiggemann. 1985. "Psychological Correlates of Employment and Unemployment: Effects, Predisposing Factors, and Sex Differences." *Journal of Occupational Psychology* 58:229-242.

William T. Grant Foundation. Commission on Work, Family, and Citizenship. 1988. *The Forgotten Half. Pathways to Success for America's Youth and Young Families*. Washington, D.C.: The William T. Grant Foundation.

3

Building Conceptual
and Empirical Bridges
between Studies of Educational
and Labor Force Careers

Alan C. Kerckhoff
Duke University

There tend to be two groups of researchers who deal with social stratification processes, one group working on educational processes, the other group working on labor force processes. There is only very limited communication between those two groups, and we are far from an adequate understanding of the combined effects of those two stratification processes and how they are related to each other.

If we consider the bodies of literature those two groups of scholars have produced, it is possible to identify at least six nested levels of analysis of the factors that contribute to the distribution of a cohort of individuals into locations in a society's stratification system:[1] individual attributes (e.g., ambition, ability), interpersonal relationships (e.g., family and peer group resources, value definitions, encouragement), educational settings (e.g., internal school organization, curriculum, teaching style), occupations (e.g., skill level, autonomy), work settings (e.g., firm size, internal labor markets, service industries), nation states (e.g., socialist, corporatist, capitalist).

It is not possible to deal with all six in the present discussion, however. I will focus on the last four—educational settings, occupations, work settings, and nation states in order to develop some general ideas about stratification processes as they vary across societies. I will focus on the socially provided channels of attainment as a means of identifying societal variation. In doing so, I will suggest the outlines of a map of stratification processes that may be useful in further comparative studies.

The educational system has appropriately been referred to as "the sorting machine" for society (Spring 1976), but I want to broaden that metaphor to include both educational and labor force sorting processes. This broader metaphor will help to make two features of stratification processes more salient. One is the critical significance of the socially provided structural locations whose hierarchical order constitutes the substance of what we mean by "stratified." The other is the fact that societal institutions actively contribute to distributing ("sorting") a cohort into those stratified locations. This is not to minimize the importance of the role played by individual actors and their intimate social relations (which Mortimer and Bidwell et al demonstrate in their contributions to this volume), but only to make salient the active role of institutional actors.

If we conceive of stratification processes as those which generate the distribution of a cohort into hierarchically arranged positions in the society, given their origins in that same set of positions, we see that those stratification processes shape the life course careers of the cohort members. That is, the sorting processes serve to shape the origin-destination trajectories of the cohort members, and the institutionally provided structural locations define the alternative trajectories that are possible. Those trajectories are paths through sets of structural locations encountered at successive stages of the life course, and which individuals follow which trajectories is determined by the intersection of individual and institutional actions.

The very concepts of careers and trajectories, if they are to be at all useful in social science research, must be based on the postulate that there are varying probabilities of movement from a given location at one stage to several possible locations at a successive stage. That is, it should be possible to identify "career lines," or most frequently traveled pathways through the multiple locations across life course stages (Gaertner 1980; Spilerman 1977; Spenner, Otto, and Call 1982).

Our research has tended to separate the analysis of careers and career lines in schools from the analysis of those in the labor force. We need to bridge those two separate approaches by conceptualizing stratification processes as occurring throughout the life course (as O'Rand suggests in this volume). To do so means to view careers and career lines as lifetime trajectories which result from stratification processes occurring in both educational and labor force settings. It also means that we seek to understand the probability of linkages between locations (steps in trajectories) not just within schools and within the labor force but also between them. We can use the concepts of career, career line and trajectory as tools to generate a map of stratification processes throughout the life course.

I will begin by focusing on the structural features of educational systems and how they may affect the process of social stratification. I will use a comparative perspective to point up the peculiar features of the American educational system and how those features may be related to stratification processes. I will then turn to some structural features of the labor forces of industrial societies, again with an emphasis on how the American labor force structures differ from those in other industrial societies. And, finally, I will speculate a bit about ways in which these features of educational and labor force structures may be related to each other and how their varied associations across societies may help to produce variations in stratification processes and in the trajectories cohorts follow in different societies.

Educational Structures and Stratification Processes

Some recent comparative work has focused on differences in the educational systems of industrial societies and on the effects of those differences on the distribution of individuals in the societies' stratification systems (Allmendinger 1989; Maurice, Sellier, and Silvestre 1986; Muller and Karle 1992; Raffe and Tomes 1987). Although all educational systems sort students into hierarchical categories, they differ in the ways they go about doing it and in the nature of the hierarchies they produce.

The educational systems vary in several important ways: (1) the degree of stratification of the system (i.e., the proportions of a cohort that are able to move to successively higher attainment levels), (2) the degree of centralized control of the system and the uniformity of its programs and products, (3) how differentiated the educational credentials are, (4) the educational system's "capacity to structure" the flow of students into the labor force (i.e., the match between educational credentials and occupational categories), (5) the degree and kind of institutional linkage between educational and labor force institutions – there may be very little linkage (as in France), there may be a direct linkage (as in Japan [Rosenbaum, Kariya, Settersten, and Maier 1990; Spilerman and Ishida in this volume]), or the linkage may be due to a credentialing system that depends heavily on apprenticeships and other types of labor force experience (as in Germany [DiPrete and McManus in this volume]).

The U.S. educational system is essentially unique among industrial societies. In terms of the five dimensions of variation just noted, it differs from most systems in other industrial societies in the following ways: (1) It is much less stratified; more American students stay in school at higher attainment levels than do students elsewhere. (2) It is highly decentralized, and there is a great deal of variation among both the programs offered at any particular educational level and the "quality" of the students who complete those programs. (3) The American system offers only very general credentials (a high school diploma or a college degree) while most European systems offer a much wider range of differentiated credentials. (4) As a result, most European systems have a much greater "capacity to structure" the flow of students into the labor force; there is a tighter fit between educational credentials and occupational categories in Europe than in the U.S. (5) There is less formal linkage between schools and employers in the U.S. than in almost any other industrial society. Students generally leave school and seek jobs on their own.

The educational systems of all industrial societies use structural distinctions to organize their students into groups or units receiving differentiated curricula. In most European societies specialized secondary schools are used to accomplish this purpose (e.g., the Hauptschule, Realschule, and Gymnasium in Germany), but there may also be differentiated programs within the schools. American schools are much less likely to be differentiated in this way, although the increasing use of magnet schools is a move in that direction, and organizational units within schools (ability groups, tracks) are generally found.

Curricular distinctions within schools are even more important in the stratification process in the U.S. than in most other industrial societies just because there are few other kinds of stratifying mechanisms used by the educational system. Students' locations in those differentiated structural positions are necessarily based on institutional decisions, if for no other reason because of organizational constraints (Hallinan 1992). The decentralized (local) control of schools in this country leaves that decision-making process more open to what Bidwell and Quiroz (1991) refer to as "client power" (parental intervention) than are similar decisions in societies with more centralized control of the schools. It seems likely, then, that such decisions will reflect the social status of students' parents (Lareau 1989; Useem 1992; Willms in this volume). In any event, the internal organizational distinctions serve to increase the spread of academic performances of students as Gamoran and Alexander and Entwisle discuss in their contributions to this volume.

Although they have received less systematic attention in the literature on the stratifying effects of educational institutions, variations in the academic programs in post-secondary institutions undoubtedly serve to further increase that spread. These variations are of two kinds, among kinds of institutions (technical institutes, community and junior colleges, four-year colleges, universities) and among the "quality" levels within each of these (Ivy League, small state university).

These characteristics of our educational system lead it to produce a set of "graduates" (of either high school or college) who are highly varied in their educational qualities. Yet, these highly varied "products" of our school system are relatively undifferentiated in terms of the formal credentials they obtain.[2] There are four large amorphous categories of products of the American educational system—high school drop-outs, high school graduates, college drop-outs (who far outnumber high school drop-outs!) and college graduates.

If we think of this outcome in terms of career trajectories, it is apparent that a number of relatively refined location distinctions within the educational system (defined in terms of ability groups, tracks and so on) seem to lead to a very delimited set of "terminal" locations. Educational careers may be traceable through structural locations in elementary school, between elementary and secondary school, and between secondary and post-secondary schools, but the end states are not formally highly differentiated.

The Education-Occupation Linkage

When we follow American students' careers after they complete their schooling, it is also apparent that the credentials they obtain are seldom directly linked to kinds of jobs. There are few obvious education-occupation connections. Overall, there is a very loose coupling between American educational and labor force institutions, although it may be possible to identify linkages between the very general educational credentials and fairly gross occupational categories (e.g., high school drop-outs and college graduates are not very often found in the same occupations).

This very loose education-occupation linkage in the U.S. is undoubtedly one of the reasons for the division of labor between those studying education and those studying the labor force. For the majority of American students, the educational system provides little, if any, direct preparation for labor force participation. Most American students leave school with neither occupationally-relevant preparation nor credentials. Specific job skills are learned after leaving school. Or at least after leaving the only kind of school Americans see as "worth counting."[3] Work skills are learned either on-the-job or through part-time courses at technical institutes or community colleges. It is unusual for either on-the-job training or post-secondary vocational training courses to lead to nationally recognized occupationally-linked credentials.[4]

For most American students, then, the educational system "passes the buck" to employers or to the students themselves to provide opportunities to learn needed job skills. Employers are concerned that employees learn the skills needed on particular jobs, however, and there is no felt need for their programs of on-the-job training to teach general skills that can be used elsewhere. And, of course, there is almost never any formal, nationally recognized certification of employer-provided training.

This is a very different school-work relationship than is found in most other industrial societies, and it means that the overall stratification process and career trajectories are different in the U.S. than elsewhere. Maurice et al. (1986) provide an insightful analysis of the differences between the

German and French systems of education as they relate to stratification processes, and Allmendinger (1989) adds further understanding by comparing the German and American systems. These authors point out that the German educational system's highly differentiated structure and occupationally-relevant credentials has a strong "capacity to structure" the flow of students into the labor force, while the French and American systems are very weak in this respect. Part of the greater capacity to structure in Germany (and in Austria [Haller, Konig, Kraus, and Kurz 1985]) is due to the frequent combination of school and work after leaving full-time school, through apprenticeships or other programs that systematically combine work and study.

Maurice, et al. go on to show how, in contrast to the German case, the very general credentials of French students lead to a relatively random distribution of students into the labor force. That, in turn, leads to a great deal of job changing in the early work careers, and heavy dependence on seniority in the process of career mobility. We are left with a sense of a significant discontinuity in the careers of French young people that is not nearly as common in Germany. Many of these same differences are reported by Allmendinger in her comparison of Germany and the U.S.

In many European countries most students leave school and obtain a full-time job relatively early, but they continue to study part-time in pursuit of formal, nationally recognized occupationally-relevant credentials. For instance, the basic education-occupation linkage in Great Britain is not as loose as in France and the U.S. (Kerckhoff 1993). The combination of specialized secondary school examinations and non-university post-secondary programs leading to nationally recognized occupationally-relevant credentials makes the careers of young Britons almost as orderly as those in Germany and more so than in either France or the U.S.

Most young Britons leave full-time school at an early age, and their educational credentials are not very predictive of their initial labor force placements. However, there is an increasingly tighter "fit" between educational and occupational credentials during late adolescence and early adulthood in Great Britain because educational credentials gained after leaving regular school provide access to specialized kinds of jobs (Winfield, Campbell, Kerckhoff, Everett, and Trott 1989). Although the overall degree of social mobility in the U.S. and Great Britain is highly similar, the career pathways by which the mobility is produced are quite different.

Labor Force Structures and Stratification Processes

These comparative works provide clear evidence of differences in the structures of the educational systems of industrial societies, and they suggest ways in which those education structures are linked to sorting processes in the labor force. In fact, some of this literature seems to imply that the differences in the sorting process in the labor force are simple derivatives of the differences in the educational systems, that any societal differences in career patterns can be attributed to educational, not labor force, differences.

However, to interpret the literature that way would be to overlook the great degree of interpenetration of educational and work experiences in most industrial societies. Educational and labor force processes are not nearly as wholly separate as in the U.S. Such an interpretation would also imply that labor force structures do not vary among industrial societies,[5] and there is growing evidence that they do (Kalleberg 1988). If nothing else, it is important to recognize that industrialized societies vary in the relative sizes of economic sectors (Carroll and Mayer 1986) and occupational groups (Terway 1987) and in their distributions of occupations by status levels (Ishida 1993). To the extent that the shapes of careers differ in different parts of the labor force, these differences alone would lead to overall societal variation in career patterns.

There are also societal differences in the basic demographics of the labor force. Because of the lower proportions in higher education and the widespread tendency to combine work and schooling, many more young people are in the labor force full-time in most European countries than in the U.S. The proportion of older people in the labor force also varies since retirement ages and retirement benefits differ across societies (O'Rand and Spilerman and Ishida in this volume). In addition, the participation of women in the labor force varies widely both overall and by age and marital status, and degrees and kinds of occupational segregation by gender vary across societies (Sorrentino 1990; Spilerman and Ishida in this volume).

Other societal differences also undoubtedly lead to varied distributions of career patterns. Differences among socialist, corporatist and capitalist societies are the most obvious and broadly relevant ones (Erikson and Goldthorpe 1987; Esping-Andersen 1990; Treiman and Yip 1989; Zagorski 1984). But, even among capitalist societies, labor unions are much stronger in some societies than others (Goldthorpe 1984), and varied clarity of differentiation among levels of occupations probably affects available career paths (Haller et al. 1985).

As with the educational system, the American labor force pattern is rather different from those of other industrial societies. There is a higher proportion of the labor force in service industries and occupations, fewer youthful workers, more women in the labor force, and weaker unions in the U.S. than in most other industrialized societies. These general structural features of societies' labor forces are undoubtedly linked to the dynamics of careers, but we have very limited knowledge of those relationships. Tracing careers through these varied structural arrangements requires longitudinal data from multiple societies, and those data have not been widely available until quite recently. With the increasing availability of such data, it should be possible to make more systematic and informative comparisons.

One of the difficulties in making progress in this way even when adequate data are available is the fact that much of the conceptualization of labor force structure has been either too refined or too gross to trace career patterns through it. Some of the most intriguing conceptualizations of labor force structure concern either broad industrial sectors (Zucker and Rosenstein 1981) or the internal organization of positions within firms. Concepts such as internal labor markets (Althauser 1989), vacancy chains (Chase 1991) and the degree to which vacancies are "open" or "closed" (Sorensen and Tuma 1981) are all valuable contributions, but they are most useful in tracing patterns of movement within firms (Rosenbaum 1984; Spilerman and Lunde 1991), and it is difficult to extrapolate from such studies to national patterns of career trajectories.

However, it should be possible to use the logic of these approaches to labor force analysis in developing overarching conceptualizations of careers and career lines through educational and labor force structures. There have been very few efforts to use the concepts of careers and career lines in studies of labor force mobility. Those studies that have used them have generally focused on movements within restricted occupational categories (Gaertner 1980; Spilerman 1977), and efforts to expand their use to the full range of occupations in the labor force (Spenner et al. 1982) have demonstrated how complex the overall picture is. It is apparent that to carry out analyses of careers and career lines in the labor force we need a set of categories that fall between those defined by jobs in internal labor markets and industrial sectors but that the full set of occupations is overly refined.[6]

At least two possible approaches have been suggested in previous literature. One approach is suggested by Sorensen (1977) who used occupational prestige scores rather than individual occupations as units of analysis. It is thus possible to identify moves within the labor force in terms of a single hierarchical dimension whose units can be adjusted to be at whatever level of refined differentiation desired (e.g., only deciles might be distinguished and thus only ten labor force locations need be considered).

A second approach is used by Haller et al. (1985) in their comparative study of Austria, France and the U.S. They construct a 23-category typology of occupational/sectoral groupings (such categories as higher employees, production; skilled workers, craft industries; unskilled workers, building trades) and map worker movements between them over time. This second approach is closer to that used in most studies of careers and career lines, and I will use it as an example of a promising approach.

Haller et al show that the occupational categories are linked together during the labor force careers of men in the three societies. There are very different flow patterns among them between first and later jobs. This is in part a result of different distributions of the three labor forces across occupational categories (e.g., many more agricultural workers in Austria and France, more skilled workers in Austria, more managers in the U.S.).[7]

While the analyses Haller et al report are necessarily limited due to the two-point definition of careers and the age range of the samples, they show some striking societal differences. For instance, there is essentially no flow between unskilled and semiskilled work positions and skilled work positions in Austria but heavy flows in France and the U.S. Also, there is much greater movement across industrial sectors in the U.S. than in either of the other countries.

The Haller et al study shows the feasibility of charting career lines between categories and of identifying major societal differences. That is the basis for suggesting that that study be used as a model. Whether the same categories of occupations are used would depend on the analyst's purpose, but the general approach is promising. It may be, for instance, that the social class categories proposed by Erikson and Goldthorpe (1992) or Wright (1985) or some other set of categories might be preferred.

Charting the flows of workers across such a set of categories during their labor force careers is becoming increasingly possible as large national data sets reporting work careers become available. Both individual careers and prominent career lines can be defined in these terms. The logic of concepts such as internal labor markets and open and closed positions will also be useful in discussing the patterns identified. In addition, it should be possible to link up these labor force careers and career lines with careers and career lines in educational institutions, although additional classification and analysis problems will need to be dealt with when that is done. I will suggest in the next section some ideas for such an analysis for the U.S., and in the final section I will suggest an approach to comparative analyses.

Educational and Labor Force
Stratification Processes in the U.S.

The literature reviewed above suggests a way to approach the conceptual problem of linking educational and labor force stratification processes. Two dimensions of linkage are suggested. The first is the degree to which educational institutions provide credentials that have a direct bearing on individuals' occupational qualifications. The second is the degree to which educational and labor force institutions collaborate in shaping the school-to-work transition. The U.S. evidently has an exceptionally weak linkage whichever of these two dimensions we consider.

The very weakness of the linkage in the U.S. seems to lead to a set of stratification processes that may be unique, at least in their overall configuration. The extended period of education and the generic nature of our educational credentials have two important implications. First, the system essentially rules out of any serious competition for good jobs those who do not obtain the only basic credential we offer, the high school diploma. This is a sizable category (about 15% of recent cohorts) of very young "failures" who are hardly considered to be "employable" in an economy that accepts a 6% unemployment rate as "normal". At the other end of the continuum, there is a category of "winners" (college graduates) who are almost guaranteed access to the better jobs (about 25% in recent cohorts). In the middle, we have the majority, an amorphous category of high school graduates and college drop-outs, whose adult positions are highly problematic.

Especially for that large middle category, experience after school becomes all-important in determining their adult locations in the stratification system. Even after labor force entry, however, the American system seems to provide a less uniform set of experiences than in most other societies.

Careers appear to be more orderly and predictable in, say, Germany or Japan than in the U.S. (DiPrete and McManus and Spilerman and Ishida in this volume). In most other industrial societies labor force entry points seem to lead to a more limited set of career lines that provide orderly career patterns than in the U.S., especially during the early years in the labor force. The American system seems to be especially "open" or unstructured in both educational and labor force stratification processes.

Yet, recent American studies of both educational and labor force stratification processes have increasingly emphasized structured sorting processes. In educational settings, we have shown that grouping of students between schools, between classrooms and within classrooms has significant effects on their later levels of academic success (Alexander and Entwisle and Gamoran in this volume). Although we do not provide them with different kinds of credentials, our internal sorting processes significantly affect both their academic achievements (i.e., grades and test scores) and their academic attainments (i.e., high school and college diplomas). I have argued elsewhere (Kerckhoff 1995) that these internal sorting mechanisms are especially important in the American system just because it offers so few and such generic educational credentials. Awarding credentials tends to be an either-or matter, and the internal sorting mechanisms appreciably alter the distributions of probabilities of obtaining the credentials.

Similarly, American studies of labor force processes have emphasized such structural features as industrial sectors, internal labor markets, vacancy chains, and so on (Althauser 1989; Chase 1991; Hodson and Kaufman 1984). It is at least possible that those structural features are actually more important in the American case than elsewhere just because our system "passes the buck" from the schools to the firms to sort out the amorphous school system products into stratification levels. It may be that these labor force sorting processes are typically American processes. Or more generally, the significance of such labor force sorting processes may vary depending on the extent to which the sorting has already been carried out by the educational system. This is at least a hypothesis worth investigating.

American analysts may face more challenging conceptual and analytic problems than those in other industrial societies because the very decentralized nature of our educational and labor force systems makes some of the linkages between the two systems especially difficult to identify. There may be important but varied kinds of coupling that link American educational and labor force institutions. If we can identify these kinds of linkage, we may see more order in the school-work relationship than is initially apparent.

For instance, in some American communities there may be close links between employers and schools that resemble those found more generally in Japan. Well-established employers in some American communities may have an on-going relationship with the local high schools to insure a continuing supply of competent workers. Such a relationship would not "structure" the flow of students into the labor force in the same way as in Germany, but it could provide a much more orderly transition from school to work than seems generally to occur in this country. We could expect that such a relationship would also have a feedback effect on what happens in the school. In particular, it would probably help keep many non-college-bound students motivated to do well in high school.

The same kind of relationship might exist between some employers and local community colleges or technical institutes. In such cases, the college or institute curricula could have a greater "capacity to structure" the flow of students into the labor force than seems generally to be found in this country. Employers might seek out potential employees who have successfully completed particular kinds of courses. Unfortunately, our knowledge of vocational post-secondary institutions is very limited. We need to do a great deal more to understand this ubiquitous but seemingly unstandardized element of our educational system. We have essentially ignored it because it is so difficult to "measure" its credentials and their effects on mobility. But, if at least half of the non-college bound high school graduates (Lewis, Hearn, and Zilbert 1993) and many college drop-outs take such post-secondary courses, the courses almost certainly affect at least some of their job prospects and career patterns. And if most of those who take these courses are part of wholly local labor pools, the fact that the credentials have little or no national currency may not be as important as it initially would seem to be.

Another hypothesis worth investigating is that post-secondary vocational courses constitute a mechanism that feeds internal labor markets. Most of the literature on internal labor markets is concerned with patterns of movement within firms, and it tends to emphasize firm-specific skills and on-the-job training (Althauser 1989). However, there are also occupational internal labor markets in which general skills and training are more clearly involved, and post-secondary vocational courses may be more important there than in in-firm internal labor markets.

Even in cases in which specialized training is called for and nationally recognized credentials are available, the transferability of skills in the labor force may depend on the actions of the employer. For instance, Finlay (1983) has shown how it is possible for some groups of employers to limit the transferability of even widely recognized credentials by limiting new hires to those without the formal credentials when new openings occur and not providing access to the formal credentials by such unqualified employees.

Courses at community colleges or technical institutes could be an integral part of the functioning of even in-firm internal labor markets if employers sponsor the course-taking of those employees who are chosen to move up in the firm's hierarchy of jobs. Or, the courses might function indirectly in either in-firm or occupational internal labor markets if employers give preference in the job queue to those who have already had certain kinds of courses. The relevance of such courses in the functioning of internal labor markets might also vary depending on the kind of firm (e.g., large or small) or the industry (e.g., service or manufacturing) involved.[8]

Our knowledge about how internal labor markets operate is not adequate to make very confident statements about these matters, especially with respect to training courses that have only local significance. However, even regular educational credentials appear to be valued in different ways by different American industries, as Bridges' contribution to this volume shows. Similar differences undoubtedly exist with respect to vocational courses and credentials.

If these speculations about the varied relevance of educational and labor force structures for American career patterns have any merit, they suggest that there may be some gain in looking for the conditions of that variation. Recent research and theorizing have shown that the effects of school structure varies depending on the kind of school involved (Gamoran in this volume) or the kind of community context within which it functions (e.g., the amount of "client power" it has to contend with [Bidwell and Quiroz 1991]). Similarly, recent research and theorizing about labor force structures have strongly suggested that such structures as internal labor markets are found more often in some kinds of firms and occupations than others (Althauser 1989).

We need to assemble more systematic data on these kinds of variation so that we can better conceptualize the kinds of contexts within which sorting structures are likely to be important and within which they have varying kinds of effects. We probably already have in hand sufficient information to warrant generating some preliminary hypotheses, but it will take a concerted effort to systematize that information.

An Approach to Comparative Analysis

Almost all comparative analyses discussed above have suggested that the American case has unusual characteristics that should affect the shapes of school-work careers and, thereby, the society's stratification processes. The school-work linkage appears to be weaker in the U.S. than in almost any other industrial society. Any attempt to trace individual career patterns across those two institutional domains in the U.S. leads to an impression of great variation. The discussion in the previous section was focused on possible ways to search for some order in that variation.

If we assume a comparative rather than a wholly American perspective, however, it may be possible to achieve additional insights into the roles of educational and labor force organizations in shaping careers and, thereby, shaping the overall process of societal stratification. One way to do this is to consider the U.S. as an (or the) extreme example of "loose" structuring of careers and other industrial societies as contrasting examples of kinds and degrees of "tighter" structuring.

The literature reviewed in this paper indicates a systematic linkage between the kinds of educational and labor force sorting processes found in industrial societies. Those societies in which relatively refined sets of educational credentials are awarded have less job changing during the early years in the labor force and less variation in work career mobility patterns. Germany and the U.S. are often noted as contrasting cases in these respects. In addition, those societies in which there is a well-established relationship between educational and labor force institutions seem to have more orderly and less varied work career mobility patterns. Japan and the U.S. are often noted as contrasting examples in this respect. There also appears to be a general linkage between central control of education and a more diversified set of nationally recognized educational credentials, although France seems to be an exception. Finally, the Haller et al research suggests that clearer work career patterns can be found in societies with high proportions of the labor force in agriculture and with a "professionalization of manual work" (reflected in Austria in the significance of the apprenticeship system).

These characteristics seem to epitomize societies with tight structuring of careers. They can form the basis for a set of tentative hypotheses about careers and career lines in industrial societies. At the most general level, they suggest that school-work careers should be more orderly and career lines more easily identified in societies in which there is central control of the educational system, a set of nationally recognized occupationally relevant educational credentials, regularized school-employer relationships, and professionalization of manual work.

If we assume that the U.S. has a looser career structuring than most other industrial societies, we would expect more early job changing and more variation in work career patterns (i.e., fewer clear career lines) in the U.S. than almost any other industrial society. The literature reviewed above is at least consistent with that expectation. In addition, however, it may be possible to derive a number of more refined hypotheses on the basis of these general observations. In an attempt to stimulate greater interest in comparative career analysis, I would like to suggest a few of these and encourage others to do the same. Some of those I suggest have already received some support in previous research, but all would require additional investigation. Underlying most of them is the basic assumption that there is general societal recognition of the degree to which careers are tightly or loosely structured and that students' and workers' attitudes and behaviors reflect that fact.

For several reasons, these hypotheses can be viewed as premature. To test them in any systematic way, it would be necessary to place the societies dealt with on the loose-tight continuum and to judge the relative importance of the definitive criteria I have suggested, tasks that remain to be done. Also, in all cases, the implicit phrase "other things equal" is implied, and that is bound to raise additional questions, not dealt with here, about what "other things" need to be included in that proviso. However, it may be preferable to be premature than to ignore the potential value of such an effort. As a beginning, I suggest the following:

(1) In societies in which careers are tightly structured, students should have clearer and more "realistic" expectations of their educational and occupational futures relatively early in life. That is, their expectations should be closer to what systematic analyses of career patterns would lead outside observers to predict. An analysis of the educational expectations of thirteen year olds in England and the U.S. (Kerckhoff 1977) is consistent with this hypothesis, since it showed greater realism in England. However, it also provided evidence of greater realism in the U.S. by late adolescence.

(2) If young people in societies with tightly structured careers have more realistic views of the future, we might expect those who are destined for relatively low outcomes to more fully accept those outcomes than their counterparts in societies with loosely structured careers. Again using England and the U.S. as examples of societies with relatively tightly and loosely structured careers, respectively, analysts have reported a greater commitment to egalitarian attitudes and a greater tolerance of "irregular" mobility patterns in the U.S. (Robinson and Bell 1978; Turner 1966). However, studies have also reported disaffection with the educational system by some low-performing adolescents in both societies (e.g., Stinchcomb 1964; Willis 1977). How representative those cases are, however, is not clear.

(3) There should be less intergenerational mobility in societies with tightly structured careers because the earlier individuals enter career lines, the greater the effects of social origin on career entry portals is likely to be. It is frequently reported that the effect of social origin on educational success declines as students move through the levels of education (Shavit and Blossfeld 1993; Hout in this volume), so the tighter the linkage between early and later positions in the educational system (and then in the labor force), the less social mobility there should be.

(4) Internal labor markets should play a more salient role in the careers of workers in societies with loosely structured careers. Research that reports more within-firm advancement in France than in either Germany or England (Marsden 1986; Maurice et al 1986) is at least consistent with this hypothesis (see also Kalleberg and Lincoln 1988; Loveridge 1983; Stark 1986).

Conclusion

The most general point in this chapter is that we need to know more than we do about the ways in which educational and labor force institutions operate together to shape individual careers and, in so doing, serve to stratify the members of the society. One suggestion—derivable from Maurice, et al., Allmendinger, and others—is that educational institutions are relatively more important in some societies and labor force institutions are relatively more important in others. It seems likely, however, that the situation is even more complex than that.

Especially in the United States, there seems to be the need for two additional kinds of analysis. First, we have not yet adequately indexed the role of educational institutions because we have almost wholly ignored a major part of the post-secondary experiences of our population—courses taken in community colleges and technical institutes. We have ignored these courses in large part for methodological reasons—we don't know how systematically to take them into account. But they undoubtedly make a great deal of difference in the sorting processes in this society and we need to specify their role.

Second, we have yet to do an adequate job of accounting for the kinds of linkage between educational and labor force institutions. We have effectively treated those linkages as if they do not exist because they are not sufficiently regularized to justify using them in a consistent manner in our analyses. It seems likely that there is a variety of types of linkage and that the several types will be found in different kinds of contexts. We need to attempt to identify the kinds of contexts in which the several types of linkages most frequently appear.

We also need to think through more carefully than we have thus far the theoretical implications of our usual views of the ways structural effects come about in educational and labor force contexts. There are two basic differences between our ideas about the nature of structural effects in those two settings. First, most structural arrangements we study in schools are seen as purposely established to affect the achievement levels of the students. We may believe that they do not always accomplish their purpose, but they are seen as attempts to influence student outcomes. In contrast, the labor force structures we most often study are seen as having been designed to increase the effectiveness of the firms. To appreciate the possible significance of that difference, it may help to imagine how our educational system might be affected (and how our theories of structural effects would need to be altered) if all of a school's operating resources were determined by the collective performance of its students.

Second, explanations of the effects of structural arrangements in the two settings focus on very different kinds of processes. In schools, the structures are seen as directly affecting students' achievements through curricula, teaching styles, social definitions, and student motives. In contrast, in the labor force, differences in worker outcomes are seen as the indirect result of firm or industry organizational constraints and cost-benefit considerations. In addition to these being quite different conceptualizations, both of them may be overly narrow.

The most basic point about the American case is that the decentralized control of education and the relative autonomy of employing organizations have produced a highly varied set of educational outcomes and education-occupation relationships, and we need to devote some time and energy to searching for some order in what appear to be highly disparate stratification processes. In doing so, we will profit from using a comparative perspective. It will provide clues as to possible alternative ways of structuring stratification processes, and it will make us more sensitive to the unique features of the American case.

Notes

1. I am indebted to David Grusky for helping me recognize this way of organizing the literature on stratification processes.

2. One of the results of the lack of differentiated credentials is a strong emphasis in the U.S. on where students go to school or college.

3. It is very difficult to obtain reliable information about the courses taken or the credentials obtained in post-secondary programs in community colleges and technical institutes. For instance, in the 442 page publication of the National Center for Education Statistics, "The Condition of Education 1994," there is no mention of these kinds of courses. The only index entries under "technical" and "vocational" are concerned with high school and regular college courses.

4. The kinds of credentials Althauser and Appel discuss in this volume are an exception, in that they are nationally standardized and recognized. But they are credentials for semi-professional occupations, and they are not typical of credentials earned through post-secondary vocational courses.

5. That implicit assumption of uniformity of labor force structures is consistent with much of the comparative literature on occupational mobility. There is evidence of a common hierarchical order of occupations (Treiman 1977) as well as similarity in the amount of intergenerational mobility in industrial societies (Ganzeboom, Treiman, and Ultee 1991). However, inter-societal uniformity in mobility patterns is increasingly being questioned (Ganzeboom, Luijkz, and Treiman 1989; European Sociological Review, Vol. 8 No. 3 [December 1992]; Hout in this volume), and greater attention is being directed toward understanding intersocietal differences.

6. In an attempt to link educational locations with labor force locations, I have used a four-part classification of industries (the cross-classification of core-peripheral with service-production (Kerckhoff 1993), but it proved to be overly crude. A more refined scheme is needed.

7. They also acknowledge a classification problem. Since so many Austrian men enter the labor force as apprentices, they used the men's first job after the end of the apprenticeship as their first job. This essentially classifies apprenticeships as a form of education. That special feature of the Austrian data and their way of handling it clearly reflect the differences already discussed between stratification regimes in which there is an interpenetration of educational and work experiences (such as Austria and Germany) and those in which the two are almost completely separate (such as the U.S.) The countries' methods of recording workers' positions in the labor force also reflect such differences. In U.S. census data, apprentices are classified as "operatives." If British data were included, comparative analysis would be even more difficult because the British classify apprentices in the occupations for which they are training.

8. There could be a direct link between kinds of firms and the courses workers take in that some employers may openly encourage and even financially support course-taking. Or there could be an indirect linkage. For instance, it may be that when there are employers in the community who reward course-taking, there is more public understanding of the potential value of such courses, and people take them on their own initiative.

References

Allmendinger, Jutta. 1989. Career Mobility Dynamics - A Comparative Analysis of the United States, Norway, and West Germany. Berlin: Max-Planck Institut fur Bildungsforschung.

Althauser, Robert P. 1989. "Internal Labor Markets." Annual Review of Sociology 15: 143-61.

Bidwell, Charles E., and Pamela Quiroz. 1991. "Organizational Control in the High School Workplace: A Theoretical Argument." Journal of Research on Adolescence 1: 211-29.

Carroll, Glenn R., and Karl Ulrich Mayer. 1986. "Job-Shift Patterns in the Federal Republic of Germany: The Effects of Social Class, Industrial Sector and Organizational Size." American Sociological Review 51: 323-41.

Chase, Ivan D. 1991. "Vacancy Chains." Annual Review of Sociology 17: 133-54.

Erikson, Robert, and John H. Goldthorpe. 1987. "Commonality and Variation in Social Fluidity in Industrial Nations. Part II: The Model of Core Social Fluidity Applied." European Sociological Review 3:145-66.

_____. 1992. Constant Flux: Comparative Analysis of Social Mobility in Industrial Nations. Oxford: Clarendon Press.

Esping-Andersen, Gosta. The Three Worlds of Welfare Capitalism. Princeton, NJ: Princeton University Press.

Finlay, W. 1983. "One Occupation, Two Labor Markets: The Case of Long-Shore Crane Operators." American Sociological Review 48: 306-15.

Gaertner, Karen N. 1980. "The Structure of Organizational Careers." Sociology of Education 53: 7-20.

Ganzeboom, Harry B. G., Rudd Luijkx, and Donald T. Treiman. 1989. "Intergenerational Class Mobility in Comparative Perspective." Research in Social Stratification and Mobility 8: 3-84.

Ganzeboom, Harry B. G., Donald J. Treiman and Woot C. Ultee. 1991. "Comparative Intergenerational Stratification Research: Three Generations and Beyond." Annual Review of Sociology 17: 277-302.

Goldthorpe, John H. 1984. "The End of Convergence: Corporatist and Dualist Tendencies in Modern Western Societies." Pp. 315-43 in J. H. Goldthorpe (ed.) Order and Conflict in Contemporary Capitalism. Oxford: Oxford University Press.

Haller, Max, Wolfgang Konig, Peter Kraus, and Karin Kurz. 1985. "Patterns of Career Mobility and Structural Positions in Advanced Capitalist Societies: A Comparison of Men in Austria, France and the United States." American Sociological Review 50: 579-603.

Hallinan, Maureen T. 1992. "The Organization of Students for Instruction in the Middle School." Sociology of Education 65: 114-27.

Hodson, R., and R. L. Kaufman. 1984. "Economic Dualism: A Critical Review." American Sociological Review 47: 272-39.

Ishida, Hiroshi. 1993. Social Mobility in Contemporary Japan. Stanford, CA: Stanford University Press.

Kalleberg, Arne L. 1988. "Comparative Perspectives on Work Structures and Inequality." Annual Review of Sociology 14: 203-25.

Kalleberg, Arne L., and James R. Lincoln. 1988. "The Structure of Earnings Inequality in the U.S. and Japan." American Journal of Sociology 94 (Supplement): 121-53.

Kerckhoff, Alan C. 1977. "The Realism of Educational Ambitions in England and the United States." American Sociological Review 42: 563-71.

_____. 1993. Diverging Pathways: Social Structure and Career Deflections. New York: Cambridge.

_____. 1995. "Reforming Education: A Critical Overlooked Component." Forthcoming in Maureen T. Hallinan (ed.), Restructuring Schools: Promising Practices and Policies. New York: Plenum.

Lareau, Annette. 1989. Home Advantage: Social Class and Parental Intervention in Elementary Education. London: Falmer Press.

Lewis, Darrell R., James C. Hearn, and Eric E. Zilbert. 1993. "Efficiency and Equity Effects of Vocationally Focused Postsecondary Education." Sociology of Education 66: 188-205.

Loveridge, R. 1983. "Sources of Diversity in Internal Labour Markets." Sociology 17:44-62.

Marsden, D. 1986. The End of Economic Man?: Custom and Competition in Labour Markets. New York: St. Martin's Press.

Maurice, Marc, Francois Sellier, and Jean-Jaques Silvestre. 1986. The Social Foundations of Industrial Power: A Comparison of France and Germany. Cambridge, Mass.: MIT Press.

Muller, Walter, and Wolfgang Karle. 1992. "Social Selection in Educational Systems in Europe." European Sociological Review 8: 233-54.

Raffe, David, and N. Tomes. 1987. The Organisation and Content of Studies at the Post-Compulsory Level: Country Study: Scotland. OECD Educational Monograph. Paris: OECD.

Robinson, Robert V., and Wendell Bell. 1978. "Equality, Success, and Social Justice in England and the United States." American Sociological Review 43: 125-43.

Rosenbaum, James E. 1984. Career Mobility in a Corporate Hierarchy. New York: Academic Press.

Rosenbaum, James E., Takehiko Kariya, Rick Settersten, and Tony Maier. 1990. "Market and Network Theories of the Transition from High School to Work: Their Application to Industrialized Societies." Annual Review of Sociology 16: 263-99.

Shavit, Yossi, and Hans-Peter Blossfeld (eds.). 1993. Persistent Inequality: Changing Educational Attainment in Thirteen Countries. Boulder, CO: Westview Press.

Sorensen, Aage B. 1977. "The Structure of Inequality and the Process of Attainment." American Sociological Review 42:965-78.

Sorensen, Aage B. and Nancy B. Tuma. 1981. "Labor Market Structures and Job Mobility." Research in Social Stratification and Mobility 1:67-94.

Sorrentino, Constance. 1990. "The Changing Family in International Perspective." Monthly Labor Review 41-58.

Spenner, Kenneth I., Luther B. Otto and Vaughn R. A. Call. 1982. Career Lines and Careers. Lexington, Mass.: Lexington Books.

Spilerman, Seymour. 1977. "Careers, Labor Market Structure, and Socioeconomic Achievement." American Journal of Sociology 83:551-93.

Spilerman, Seymour, and Tormond Lunde. 1991. "Features of Educational Attainment and Job Promotion Prospects." American Journal of Sociology 97: 689-720.

Spring, Joel. 1976. The Sorting Machine. New York: David McKay.

Stinchcombe, Arthur L. 1964. Rebellion in a High School. Chicago: Quadrangle Books.

Stark, David. 1986. "Rethinking Internal Labor Markets: New Insights from a Comparative Perspective." American Sociological Review 51: 492-504.

Terwey, M. 1987. "Class Position and Income Inequality: Comparing Results for the Federal Republic of Germany with Current Research in the USA." International Journal of Sociology 17: 119-71.

Treiman, Donald T. 1977. Occupational Prestige in Comparative Perspective. New York: Academic Press.

Treiman, Donald T., and Kam-Bor Yip. 1989. "Educational and Occupational Attainment in 21 Countries." Pp. 373-94 in Melvin L. Kohn (ed.), Cross-National Research in Sociology. Newbury Park, CA: Sage.

Turner, Ralph H. 1966. "Acceptance of Irregular Mobility in Britain and the United States." Sociometry 29:334-52.

Useem, Elizabeth L. 1992. "Middle Schools and Math Groups: Parents' Involvement in Children's Placement." Sociology of Education 65: 263-79.

Willis, Paul. 1977. Learning to Labor: How Working Class Kids Get Working Class Jobs. New York: Columbia University Press.

Winfield, Idee, Richard T. Campbell, Alan C. Kerckhoff, Diane D. Everett, and Jerry M. Trott. 1989. "Career Processes in Great Britain and the United States." Social Forces 68: 284-308.

Wright, Eric O. 1985. Classes. London: Verso.

Zagorski, Krysztof. 1984. "Comparisons of Social Mobility in Different Socio-Economic Systems." Pp. 13-41 in Manfred Niessen, Jules Peschar, and Chantal Kourilsky (eds.), International Comparative Research: Social Structures and Public Institutions in Eastern and Western Europe. Oxford: Pergamon.

Zucker, Lynne G. and Carolyn Rosenstein. 1981. "Taxonomies of Institutional Structure: Dual Economy Reconsidered." American Sociological Review 46:869-84.

PART TWO

Educational Contexts
and Processes

The papers in Part II help us understand how educational settings and processes generate a cumulative dispersion of student performances, a major contributor to social stratification. The first two papers deal with the formal organization of students within schools. In the first of these, Adam Gamoran reviews the state of our knowledge about the effects of organizing students in such categories as ability groups and tracks. The general pattern he reports is for those in "high" groups to gain academically from that placement but for those in "low" groups to fall back academically. Such placements also affect the attitudes and expectations of students and their significant others. Since placements tend to persist over time, they apparently have cumulative effects on outcomes. Gamoran reviews several theoretical approachs to interpreting these effects, and he recognizes the probable importance of both symbols (the social meaning of locations in school structures) and institutional practices (teaching styles, curricular offerings).

Karl Alexander and Doris Entwisle follow Gamoran's general review with a report on the effects grouping by ability in first grade have on outcomes in middle school. Their detailed data come from a longitudinal study of students in Baltimore inner city schools. They include in their definition of "organizational differentiation" not only ability groups and tracks but also special education classes and retention in grade. All of these make classes more academically homogeneous, and all of them have identifiable effects on outcomes in sixth grade. This fine-grained study provides clear evidence that some students experience a downward spiral, not only in their academic performance, but also in their attitudes toward school and their academic self-images.

The third paper in Part II, by Charles Bidwell, Stephen Planck, and Chandra Muller, takes what O'Rand refers to in Chapter One as a "relational approach" to understanding students' careers. They show how the friendship networks of high school students mediate the effects of schools, families and neighborhoods on students' aspirations and attitudes as well as their participation in school and work activities. The networks are viewed as sources of both information and normative definitions and sanctions, and they help us to interpret the effects of school, family and neighborhood.

The last two papers in Part II are concerned with kinds of educational reforms and their effects on equity and student achievement. J. Douglas Willms examines what happened when Scottish parents had a choice of schools for their children to attend. He asks whether the practice increased the desegregation of social status groups, as some supporters of the practice have predicted? His data come from Scotland, but the observed patterns are probably not unique to that country. As many have predicted, requests for particular schools in Scotland initially came heavily from middle class parents, and the schools most frequently requested were largely in high status areas. The overall pattern across a ten-year period of school choice was an increase in the segregation of middle class students, most clearly seen in large urban areas. School choice clearly did not reduce social status segregation.

In the final paper in Part II, Maureen Hallinan notes that proposals for school reform are frequently generated by concern with broader social issues — with value conflicts, economic problems and so on. She argues that there should be one primary basis for evaluating proposed reforms, their expected effect on student learning, because that is the basis of educational achievement and later occupational placement. After analyzing the three primary contributors to student learning (ability, effort, and opportunities to learn), she discusses several reform proposals (such as magnet schools, doing away with curriculum tracks, and school-to-work programs) in terms of both the forces that brought them forward and their probable effects on student learning and achievement. She points out that even reforms with non-learning goals can have positive (or negative) effects on student learning.

These five papers deal with several mechanisms and processes that either directly or indirectly affect the distribution of academic achievement. In the papers by Gamoran and by Alexander and Entwisle the mechanisms are the internal organizations of schools and the categorical differentiations among students. Bidwell et al. show how networks of peer relations serve to mediate the influences of schools, families and communities on student attitudes and behaviors. And Willms and Hallinan discuss the ways in which policy decisions can and do alter academic settings and student performances. Together, these papers suggest the array of sources of influence on educational stratification.

4

Educational Stratification and Individual Careers

Adam Gamoran
University of Wisconsin, Madison

My aim in this chapter is to describe and assess research on the stratified structure of educational systems. I am primarily concerned with studies of the impact of varied experiences within schools on cognitive and status outcomes. I will not address the full spectrum of work in the status attainment tradition—that is, research on the determinants of educational and occupational success—but will concentrate on the subset of this literature which examines stratification *within* levels of schooling, and the effects of these hierarchies on the progress of individuals through the educational system. Clearly, research on status attainment has provided an essential stimulus to studies of stratification in school systems, and I will take note of how theoretical developments and empirical directions in the status attainment tradition have influenced work on stratification within school systems. In addition, I will show that research in this area has three important characteristics that have earned it substantial attention within the sociology of education: It is cumulative, in that studies tend to build on one another, leading to substantial growth in knowledge; it is comparative, with studies from several other countries complementing work done in the United States; and it is policy-relevant, stimulated by and contributing to debates about how schooling should be organized.

Effects of Stratification in Schools:
Socialization, Allocation, and Legitimation

Sociologists have long recognized that persons who accumulate more years of schooling attain higher status as adults (e.g., Sorokin 1927). At each level of schooling, however, considerable variation in status attainment remains. At one time the conventional wisdom held that the main reason for this disparity was inequality among schools: students who completed their years of study at a "good" school were better off than those who had gone to a "bad" school, other things being equal. By the early 1970s, however, it was clear that this explanation was largely inadequate: Differences among schools had little impact on variation among students, with other conditions held constant (Coleman et al. 1966; Mosteller and Moynihan 1972; Jencks et al. 1972; Averch et al. 1972).

One important reaction to this finding was the decision to consider variation in students' experiences *inside* schools. Because student outcomes varied much more within schools than between them, it made sense to look at the connection between within-school differences in schooling and student outcomes. Seminal contributions to this effort include studies by Heyns (1974) and Alexander and McDill (1976), who showed that curriculum tracking in high schools was associated with variation in educational results. Students enrolled in a college preparatory curriculum were more likely to plan on attending college, to earn high grades, and to score high on tests.

These were not the first survey studies of curriculum tracking, but they were the first to estimate effects of tracking holding constant differences in students' abilities prior to tracking. They reflected and contributed to both the school-effects and the status attainment traditions. Both studies relied on a conceptual model of the school as a socializing agency, in which college-track membership provided a context for social interactions that led to higher expectations and higher test scores. By the end of the 1970s, however, two important theoretical articles had added new views of the school in the attempt to understand the role of schooling in status attainment: Kerckhoff (1976) emphasized the *allocative* role of the school, and Meyer (1977) focused on the school as a *legitimizer*.

Kerckhoff (1976) reinterpreted the association between social-psychological processes and attainment. He argued that changes in status ambitions associated with schooling reflected students' responses to status classifications and resource allocations rather than interactions that students experienced in school:

> In the school setting, for example, teachers make decisions when assigning grades, dividing a class into reading groups or other functional units, or singling out individual students for special attention....These decisions not only provide the individuals involved with information about themselves and their probable future, but they also create socially significant classifications on the basis of which others will respond to them differentially. In short, the decisions segmentalize the population of students into categories whose attainment probabilities are different. The same kinds of decisions are made by counsellors...(p. 374-375).

This conceptual framework redirected the attention of sociologists towards allocative processes occurring in schools, and their impact on outcomes for students.

A year later, Meyer (1977) argued that both socialization and allocation could be subsumed under a theory of education as a legitimizing institution. For Meyer, schooling affects status attainment by creating rules and understandings in which persons in some categories are elevated above others. An educational system not only allocates persons to positions; it also plays a key role in providing the authority and legitimacy that defines the hierarchy to which those persons are allocated.

For the most part, subsequent research has not led to the rejection of one view (socialization, allocation, or legitimation) over another. Instead, scholars have examined all three aspects of the role of schooling in status attainment. Studies of stratification in school systems—including work on specialized schools, curriculum tracks, ability-grouped classes, and within-class ability groups—have drawn on all three of these perspectives, although usually without explicitly contrasting them in the context of a single study. Thus, theoretical developments in status attainment research in the 1970s set the agenda for work on stratification in school systems occurring over the next two decades.

Stratification and Socialization in Schools

Studies that emphasize socialization as a key mechanism rely on elements of the allocation and legitimation perspectives to set the stage for differential socialization. A prime example comes from writers who present effects of tracking on expectations, attitudes, or achievement, and describe these as the outcome of varied socialization across tracks: alongside the attention to socialization for varied outcomes, these authors recognize the importance of allocation processes in determining how students are divided into the different tracks. Only a few writers acknowledge this explicitly (e.g., Alexander, Cook, and McDill 1978; Gamoran and Mare 1989; Kerckhoff 1990), but the view is implicit in all such studies. Moreover, research in this area accepts the importance of external norms in assigning legitimacy to the stratified structure of school systems, thus setting the broad context for grouping and tracking (Gamoran and Berends 1987). In this sense, then, studies of status attainment as socialization invariably draw on allocation and legitimation theories. Still, research in the socialization tradition is distinctive in its assumption that varied outcomes are produced not by the mere allocation to varied positions, but by socializing experiences that occur within the different schools, tracks, and groups.

Grouping, tracking, and achievement. Many writers have shown that students assigned to higher-status ability groups and curriculum tracks gain more knowledge and skills, as measured by standardized achievement tests, compared to students in lower tracks (Oakes, Gamoran, and Page 1992). Several recent studies explore the socializing experiences that yield such achievement differences; these studies emphasize variation in classroom instruction across high, middle, and low groups and tracks. In elementary schools, Barr and Dreeben (1983), Rowan and Miracle (1983), and Gamoran (1986) observed that the faster pace of instruction for high-ability reading groups contributed to achievement advantages over the course of a year. At the secondary level, students in college-preparatory programs take more academic courses, and especially more advanced academic courses in math and science, and these experiences foster achievement gains (Gamoran 1987; Sebring 1987). Teacher surveys suggest that honors math and science classes in middle schools add to achievement in part by introducing students to more problem-solving activities (Hoffer and Gamoran 1993), and an observational study indicated that greater attention to serious academic content gave honors English students an edge over their regular- and remedial-class counterparts (Gamoran et al., in press).

In an important review, Slavin (1990) issued a challenge to sociological studies showing increasing achievement gaps among students assigned to high- and low-status classes. Slavin examined a large body of work on the effects of ability-grouped classes in secondary schools, and concluded that inconsistencies in estimated effects of grouping, which centered around zero, meant that grouping has no effects on achievement. Not only were the effects zero on average, Slavin argued, but high-group students did not gain, and low-group students did not lose, as a consequence of their varied positions in the hierarchy. Slavin offered two explanations for why studies of high and low tracks tend to show increasing inequality: First, he allowed that broad curriculum tracking—that is, assignment to separate programs which dictate diverse arrays of courses—might have cumulative effects on achievement not apparent in narrower studies of ability grouping. Second, he argued that observed effects of ability grouping in non-experimental studies reflected selection bias—that is, effects were caused by unexamined differences among students in varied classes, rather than by differences among the classes themselves.

I have offered a different interpretation for inconsistencies in research on ability grouping (Gamoran 1993). My view is that small-scale naturalistic and experimental studies are likely to differ in the way grouping is implemented; in particular, they may differ in how instruction is allocated to varied classes. In some experiments, teachers may have provided the same instruction to all classes; this would likely result in no apparent effects of grouping. In other studies, teachers may have worked hard to remediate those in low-ability classes, but still other cases may exist in which better instructional resources were directed towards high-ability classes. My interpretation is actually consistent with Slavin's (1990, p. 491) general conclusion that "unless teaching methods are systematically changed, school organization has little impact on student achievement." On average, in the real world, research indicates that instructional content and methods do vary systematically, favoring those in high-status classes and working against those at the bottom of the hierarchy (Gamoran and Berends 1987; Murphy and Hallinger 1989; Oakes, Gamoran, and Page 1992). For this reason, I maintain, naturalistic studies of representative samples are more likely than small-scale experiments to show increased inequality associated with ability grouping.

My conclusion is supported not only by observational evidence, but also by the only two studies of ability grouping using national survey data that permit comparison of students in high- and low-ability classes to comparable students in mixed-ability classes. In a study of British secondary schools, Kerckhoff (1986) found that students in high-ability classes gained, and those in low-ability and remedial classes lost ground, relative to those in ungrouped classes. In the United States, Hoffer (1992) observed a similar pattern for junior high math and science achievement. Moreover, Hoffer (1992) replicated his math and science findings using a statistical model that adjusted for possible selection bias in estimates of track effects. Using the same technique, Gamoran and Mare (1989) reported that earlier studies that used rich controls for prior achievement and family background had not overestimated the effects of tracking.

These studies are consistent with the conclusion that variation in students' experiences in different groups and tracks contributes to inequality in cognitive outcomes. This conclusion rests primarily on a socialization perspective, though it relies on allocation and legitimation views to explain why the tracks exist and how students are assigned.

Tracking, expectations, and attitudes. Research on the effects of grouping and tracking on non-cognitive outcomes draws on the same conceptual framework, hypothesizing that varied socialization experiences lead to diversity in expectations and attitudes, while leaving explanations of the sorting process to allocation and legitimation perspectives.

A long tradition of research has established that assignment to college preparatory programs is associated with higher expectations for post-secondary schooling, compared with other high school experiences (see Gamoran and Berends 1987 for a review). Among students with similar test scores, those in higher tracks are more likely to expect to attend college. Berends (1992) has found the same pattern as early as ninth grade. Moreover, Berends observed that among students with similar test scores and expectations in eighth grade, those in honors classes are more likely to maintain high expectations than are students in regular and remedial classes during the transition to high school.

Research on attitudes towards school is more ambivalent. High-track students more often conform to the schools' demands while low-track students more often resist, but these differences may be a cause instead of a consequence of track assignment (Gamoran and Berends 1987). Waitrowski et al. (1983) found no changes in delinquency, self-esteem, or attachment to school as a consequence of assignment to a college-preparatory program. However, Vanfossen, Jones, and Spade (1987) observed a widening self-esteem gap between college-track and other students, and Berends (in press) found that non-college students reduced their engagement in school and increased their discipline problems, compared to otherwise similar college-bound students.

To the extent that stratification in schools results in varied non-cognitive outcomes, socializing experiences are said to play a key role. Teachers, guidance counselors, and peers communicate the meaning of differential assignments, helping to motivate high-track students and alienate those in lower tracks. British researchers have termed this the "polarization" process (Lacey 1970; Abraham 1989).

Cross-national corroboration of socialization research. Research on the differentiation of student attitudes and expectations is as much British as it is American (Gamoran and Berends 1987). Research on achievement is mainly American, but has been corroborated by important studies in other countries. Several draw on British data, including Kerckhoff's (1986) study of British secondary schools, described above. Similar findings have been obtained in Israel (e.g., Shavit and Featherman 1987), Taiwan (Hsieh 1987), and Thailand (Lockheed 1987).

International research has also shown that stratification *between* schools can exert substantial effects on achievement growth. For example, Kerckhoff (1986) demonstrated widening achievement gaps as a consequence of assignment to high-status grammar schools versus low-status secondary modern schools in Britain. Grammar school students also gained, and secondary modern students lost, relative to similar students in comprehensive schools that had heterogeneous student populations. Thus, findings for between-school stratification mirror those for within-school stratification. Comparable results were obtained for the comparison of academic and vocational high schools in Israel (Shavit and Williams 1985), and vocational, general, and pre-university secondary schools in the Netherlands (Eeden 1994). In the United States, specialized public schools have been too rare to make such comparisons feasible, and research on public and private schools has not yet emerged from controversy over whether private-school achievement advantages should be attributed to the schools, or to the students who attend private schools (see Jencks 1985 for a summary). Well-designed studies from other countries lend support to the conclusion that selective schools "add value" in the same way that high-status groups and tracks within schools contribute to achievement growth, over and above initial differences among students.

Stratification as an Allocation Process

I argued earlier that work in the socialization tradition implicitly acknowledges the value of an allocation perspective for explaining why different students end up in different schools, tracks, and groups. Yet the contribution of allocation research is not limited to this indirect impact.

Research emphasizing the allocative properties of school systems has drawn attention to direct ties between one's position in the status hierarchy from one year to the next, and from one level of schooling to the next. (By "direct ties," I mean effects of previous assignment on subsequent assignment that are independent of the presumed intervening mechanisms, e.g. achievement test scores.) Although this pattern has long been assumed to hold (e.g., Parsons 1959), empirical documentation is fairly recent. As of the early 1980s, Rosenbaum (1976) and Alexander and Cook (1982) had observed hints that track positions tended to persist from year to year, but only Yogev (1981), in a study of Israeli schools, demonstrated clear, direct ties between track assignment in one year and track assignment in the next. More recent work provides substantial support for the early findings. Gamoran (1989) observed that second grade reading group assignment depends in part on first grade positions. Pallas et al. (1994) also uncovered connections in reading-group assignment across the elementary school years. In similar fashion, Hallinan (1991, 1992) has documented the persistence of track positions from junior through senior high school.

In a study of a British birth cohort, Kerckhoff (1993) uncovered a high degree of consistency in status allocations from primary to secondary school, from secondary to tertiary education, and from schooling to the labor force. Persistent ties result not only from skill differences among students found in varied locations, but from long-term allocative effects of the status positions themselves: Even net of achievement, those in higher positions in primary school typically achieved higher rank at the secondary level, and those who were well placed in secondary school obtained greater qualifications than those less well located, net of earlier test scores. This pattern of direct allocative effects combined with indirect effects via socialization (i.e., test score gains) resulted in substantial *cumulative* effects on life chances that emerged over the course of the educational career.

In light of these findings, earlier research that attributed track effects on expectations to differential socialization may need to be reassessed. Instead of calling on socialization processes such as peer influences to explain how college-track youth come to hold higher expectations for themselves, a more parsimonious model would state that high school students correctly perceive that status designations have concrete bearing on their futures, and they adjust their expectations accordingly. This reinterpretation is just where Kerckhoff (1976) began almost 20 years ago, yet we still lack sufficient evidence to determine whether socialization is required to account for effects of tracking on expectations, or whether allocation alone is implicated. Still, we have made great progress in identifying the extent to which allocation persists from year to year and across levels of the school system, and we have solid evidence on the impact of status allocations.

Institutional Effects of Educational Stratification

Another way of interpreting outcome differences associated with the educational status hierarchy is that varied outcomes reflect symbolic meanings legitimized in the wider society. Gamoran (1986) hypothesized that first grade reading groups affect achievement by enhancing the motivation of high-group students and depressing engagement among low-group students; these processes were seen to occur not through socialization per se, but through anticipatory socialization as a consequence of perceiving the symbolic meaning of ability-group assignment; that is, as a self-fulfilling prophecy. The evidence, however, did not support the hypothesis (Gamoran 1986). Rather, the association between group rank and achievement was fully explained by differential instruction, leaving no effects to which anticipatory socialization might be attributed.

Recently, Pallas et al. (1994) tested Gamoran's (1986) hypothesis with more direct evidence on changes in students' expectations and self-concepts as a consequence of ability group assignment. The authors found no evidence of anticipatory socialization. However, they found support for institutional effects of a different type: Ability-group assignment affected teachers' and parents' expectations for student performance, net of students' actual performance levels. Thus, although the symbolic meanings of educational categories may be obscure to elementary school *students*, they may be more apparent and more consequential to parents and teachers. Since teachers, in particular, make recommendations and decisions about future placement, effects on teacher expectations may have long-term consequences for students.

Although institutional processes do not account for variation in elementary-school achievement, they may play a greater role at the secondary level. Gamoran and Berends (1987) argued that effects of high school tracking on achievement may reflect shared understandings that exist outside schools. These norms define some students as "college-bound," and, perceiving these symbolic designations, students adjust their efforts accordingly. No studies have yet considered the salience of institutional processes in affecting cognitive or status outcomes at the secondary level.

Socialization, Allocation, and Legitimation as Complementary Mechanisms

Taken as a whole, this body of work has made substantial progress in helping us understand the nature and effects of stratification in school systems. Assignment to selective schools, tracks, and ability groups contributes to achievement inequality in a variety of contexts. High school tracking also affects post-secondary expectations, and may influence more general attitudes towards schooling, though evidence on the latter point is less secure. Researchers have also demonstrated structural linkages from each point in the system to the next, showing that one's position in one year influences placement in the next, independently of performance.

Theoretically, the work indicates that socialization, allocation, and legitimation are complementary processes that work simultaneously to bring about these effects. It is not necessary to reinterpret socialization results as allocation effects, as Kerckhoff (1976) suggested; rather, allocation and socialization processes operate in concert. Aside from the question of changes in expectations, which cannot be unambiguously attributed to either socialization or allocation, one can trace the workings of each of the empirical connections described above and interpret them as fundamentally allocative or socializing processes. The clearest example of this is elementary school reading, where allocation is closely linked to previous test scores and ability-group positions, and learning is tightly connected to instructional conditions (Barr and Dreeben 1983; Gamoran 1986; Pallas et al. 1994).

Nor is it appropriate, in my view, to consider socialization and allocation as special cases of legitimation theory, as Meyer (1977) originally suggested. At most, this claim is supportable in the sense that the existence of status hierarchies within school systems is supported by normative understandings that are widely shared. As to the *effects* of stratification, however, most are more properly understood as the consequences of allocation or socialization. One exception brought to light so far is Pallas et al.'s (1994) finding that ability-group positions influence teachers' and parents' expectations for children in ways that go beyond differences in students' actual educational performances. Gamoran and Berends (1987) also hypothesized that effects of secondary-school stratification on achievement may result from institutionalized beliefs over and above instructional conditions, but this hypothesis has not been tested at the secondary level and has failed to hold at the elementary level (Gamoran 1986; Pallas et al. 1994).

In bringing together socialization, allocation, and legitimation perspectives, research in this area has moved into new theoretical territory. Recent writers have taken a longer-term view of the process and effects of educational stratification, evolving a new approach that promises to further develop and enhance our understanding of schooling and its effects.

A Career Perspective on Educational Stratification

After nearly two decades of research on short-term effects of stratification, researchers have begun to consider the system as a whole, and its effects on individuals as they traverse the length of the system. The educational career refers to the paths an individual follows over time from one structural position to the next (Kerckhoff 1990, 1993). In this conception, processes of legitimation, allocation and socialization are closely intertwined in creating structural positions, distributing persons among the positions, and establishing trajectories that tend to persist (though not invariably) over the life course. More than looking simply at the relation between one's position at a given point in time, and outcomes that follow immediately, the career perspective monitors the progress of individuals throughout the stratified structure of schooling and into the labor market.

In the context of a career perspective, however, some points in time and some positions in the structure may be more salient than others. Bidwell (1989) has argued that key thresholds, such as the transition from high school to college or the labor market, demand greater attention. In particular, Bidwell urges researchers to attend to the multiple meanings of educational transitions. He points to the relation between substantive and symbolic meanings of trained capacities; in the language I have been using, one could refer to these as the allocative, socializing, and legitimizing functions of educational structure. Successful passage through an educational transition (e.g., high school graduation) carries meaning in each of these domains. Hence, one may view an educational career as a sequence of transitions through the stratified educational system.

In a recent review, Pallas (1993) explicitly places schooling in the context of the life-course, viewing school participation as one of a series of stages though which individuals pass as part of the transition from youth to adulthood. Pallas shows that the structure of the educational system figures prominently in the sequence of life-course events for individuals. His conclusion is partly based on evidence that cross-national variation in educational structure is tied to differences in the timing of important transitions. For example, widespread availability of "further education" in Britain—that is, post-secondary schooling not at university level and generally pursued simultaneously with labor market participation—means that it is much more common in Britain than in the United States for persons to enter the labor force before completing their education (see also Kerckhoff 1990).

Research on stratification in school systems seems primed to follow this approach. Researchers who have been engaged in short-term analyses of grouping and tracking are now producing studies of long-term, cumulative effects (Kerckhoff 1993; Hallinan 1994; Hoffer 1994; Dauber 1994). Theoretically, these studies draw on the career perspective, recognizing that a persistent pattern of allocation and socialization carries implications that are more significant—both substantively and symbolically—than can be detected through analysis of short-term effects or even of single transitions in isolation. If Kerckhoff's (1993) analysis can be generalized, long-term effects are persistent and cumulative, so that what appear to be modest influences at a given point in time turn out to be substantial "deflections" over the life course.

An important caution for this line of work is that one must avoid an overly rational view of educational organization and allocation. For the sake of parsimony, there is a tendency to assume that assignment to schools and classes is an orderly, logical process, in which students' presumed educational needs are taken into account. This is not to say inequality is ignored – on the contrary, a variety of biases influence the assignment process, and these have been examined closely—but the assumption is that assignment occurs in an orderly fashion.

Case studies of schools show this view is far too simplistic. Particularly at the secondary level, student assignment is more a matter of scheduling and logistics than an issue of educational needs (DeLany 1991). Even at the elementary level, there is enormous overlap in student abilities among those assigned to groups of differing status, and it is not clear why so much overlap exists (Pallas et al. 1994). One possibility is that over time, the variance in student performance increases within each status level (e.g., within high groups, low groups, honors classes, regular classes, etc.). Yet students' positions in the hierarchy tend to persist despite their varied performances. Although some shifts in rank occur, these are not always at the margins, because of scheduling and other logistical constraints (Hallinan and Sorensen 1983; DeLany 1991). Consequently, overlap increases among students assigned to different levels.

This interpretation could be tested by asking whether the degree of overlap widens as students proceed through the school system. Is there more overlap in achievement among sixth grade than second grade reading groups? One might also assume that key transitions (such as the transition to high school) are used to reallocate students to reduce overlap, but case studies make one skeptical that this occurs (DeLany 1991; Gamoran 1992). For the career perspective on stratification in schools, this caution highlights the importance of considering the organizational context of stratification alongside the progress of individual careers.

Future Directions for Research on Educational Careers

By the end of this decade, we will have much more information about the long-term effects of stratification in schools, including more secure knowledge about the allocative role of schooling over an extended period, and its cumulative socializing impact. This much can be seen in work currently underway. Beyond that, more work is needed.

First, despite the progress made, we need still better information about the mechanisms through which the effects of stratification occur. Although evidence about the overall effects of stratification comes from a variety of countries, evidence on mechanisms is exclusively American. For example, outside the U.S., do effects of middle school ability grouping reflect instructional differences? It is possible that in other countries where group assignment is more formalized, effects of group assignment reflect symbolic status distinctions—i.e., allocation and legitimation—more than instructional or other socialization effects as in the United States. Hence, there is a need for comparative analysis of the mediating role of instruction in producing effects of selective schools, classes, and groups.

Second, although much is known about how educational stratification affects students between the ages of 6 and 18, we know much less about later and especially earlier periods. Yet the expansion of both pre-school and post-secondary education has coincided with increasing inequality of access to the types of schooling with the highest status (nursery schools at the pre-school level, and 4-year colleges at the post-secondary level) (Alsalam et al. 1992). Pre-kindergarten may be the most stratified domain of education at the present time, if one takes into account all the various types of external care for young children. Because there is much less public funding for education for pre-school-aged children compared with funding after age 5 (Head Start is the notable exception), family wealth is a strong predictor of the type of care and education children receive. Does stratification prior to kindergarten reinforce or reduce inequality in readiness for school? On the one hand, if pre-school is unequally allocated, for example along socioeconomic lines, then inequality may be reinforced. On the other hand, if variation in pre-school care is less unequal than variation in children's home lives, then disparities in school readiness may be reduced, despite the stratified nature of pre-school care. More research has been conducted on stratification at the post-secondary level (e.g., Brint and Karabel 1990), but this domain remains less scrutinized than K-12 education, yet it is highly stratified and deserves more attention from researchers concerned with stratification and inequality.

Third, more research is needed on the transition out of education and into the workforce. Studies of cumulative effects of grouping and tracking in the U.S. are limited to the educational system and do not move beyond it. In the future it will be essential to examine the impact of the stratified structure of schooling on life chances, taking into account not only educational opportunities but labor market participation, as a consequence of the experiences of schooling. For the British case, Kerckhoff (1993) has shown that educational careers have long-term consequences.

Fourth, sociologists working in this area could write more explicitly for policy-makers. Sociological research in this domain has made important policy contributions: Evidence on the salience of within-school variation in student achievement, on the association of student achievement with sociodemographic conditions that vary within schools, and on the linkages between stratification in schools and stratification in the wider society, all derive from work by sociologists. More explicit commentary on these findings for general audiences would raise the quality of discourse about such issues. A recent example is Hallinan's exchange with Oakes in *Sociology of Education* (1994). It is important that sociologists bring their evidence and insights more directly to the policy audience, in ways that address the choices that confront educational decision-makers.

Notes

This paper was written at the Consortium for Policy Research in Education (CPRE), Wisconsin Center for Education Research, University of Wisconsin-Madison. CPRE is supported by the Office of Educational Research and Improvement, U.S. Department of Education (grant no. OERI-R117G10007). Findings and conclusions expressed in this paper are those of the author and do not necessarily reflect the views of the supporting agencies.

References

Abraham, John. 1989. "Testing Hargreaves' and Lacey's Differentiation-Polarisation Hypothesis in a Setted Comprehensive." *British Journal of Sociology* 40:46-81.

Alexander, Karl L., and Martha A. Cook. 1982. "Curricula and Coursework: A Surprise Ending to a Familiar Story." *American Sociological Review* 47:626-640.

Alexander, Karl L., Martha A. Cook, and Edward L. McDill. 1978. "Curriculum Tracking and Educational Stratification." *American Sociological Review* 43:47-66.

Alexander, Karl L., and Edward L. McDill. 1976. "Selection and Allocation within Schools: Some Causes and Consequences of Curriculum Placement." *American Sociological Review* 41:963-980.

Alsalam, Nabeel, Laurence T. Ogle, Gayle T. Rogers, and Thomas M. Smith. 1992. *The Condition of Education, 1992.* Washington, DC: U.S. Department of Education.

Averch, H. A., S. J. Carroll, T. S. Donaldson, H. J. Kiesling, and J. Pincus. 1972. *How Effective is Schooling? A Critical Review and Synthesis of Research Findings.* Santa Monica, CA: RAND.

72

Barr, Rebecca, and Robert Dreeben. 1983. *How Schools Work*. Chicago: University of Chicago Press.

Berends, Mark. 1992. "Effects on School Orientations and Achievement in the Transition from Middle to High School." Unpublished Ph.D. thesis. Department of Sociology, University of Wisconsin-Madison.

Berends, Mark. In press. "Educational Stratification and Students' Social Bonding to School." *British Journal of Sociology of Education*.

Bidwell, Charles E. 1989. "The Meaning of Educational Attainment." *Research in Sociology of Education and Socialization. Vol. 8, 1989: Selected Methodological Issues*, edited by Krishnan Namboodiri and Ronald Corwin. Greenwich, CT: JAI Press.

Brint, Steven, and Jerome Karabel. 1989. *The Diverted Dream: Community Colleges and the Promise of Educational Opportunity in America, 1900-1985*. New York: Oxford University Press.

Coleman, J., E. Campbell, C. Hobson, J. McPartland, A. Mood, F. Weinfield, and R. York. 1966. *Equality of Educational Opportunity*. Washington, DC: U.S. Government Printing Office.

Dauber, Susan. 1994. "Tracking and Transitions through the Middle Grades: Channeling Educational Trajectories." Paper presented at the annual meeting of the American Sociological Association, Los Angeles.

DeLany, Brian. 1991. "Allocation, Choice, and Stratification within High Schools: How the Sorting Machine Copes." *American Journal of Education* 99:181-207.

Eeden, Pieter van den. 1994. "Educational Selectivity from the Multilevel Perspective." Unpublished manuscript, Department of Social Research Methodology, Vrije Universitat, Amsterdam, the Netherlands.

Gamoran, Adam. 1986. "Instructional and Institutional Effects of Ability Grouping." *Sociology of Education* 59:185-198.

Gamoran, Adam. 1987. "The Stratification of High School Learning Opportunities." *Sociology of Education* 60:135-155.

Gamoran, Adam. 1989. "Measuring Curriculum Differentiation." *American Journal of Education* 97:129-143.

Gamoran, Adam. 1992. "Access to Excellence: Assignment to Honors English Classes in the Transition from Middle To High School." *Educational Evaluation and Policy Analysis* 14:85-204.

Gamoran, Adam. 1993. "Alternative Uses of Ability Grouping in Secondary Schools: Can We Bring High-Quality Instruction to Low-Ability Classes?" *American Journal of Education* 101:1-22."

Gamoran, Adam, and Mark Berends. 1987. "The Effects of Stratification in Secondary Schools: Synthesis of Survey and Ethnographic Research." *Review of Educational Research* 57:415-435.

Gamoran, Adam, and Robert D. Mare. 1989. "Secondary School Stratification and Educational Inequality: Compensation, Reinforcement, or Neutrality?" *American Journal of Sociology* 94:1146-1183.

Gamoran, Adam, Martin Nystrand, Mark Berends, and Pauil C. LePore. In press. "An Organizational Analysis of the Effects of Ability Grouping." *American Educational Research Journal*.

Hallinan, Maureen T. 1991. "School Differences in Tracking Structures and Track Assignments." *Journal of Research on Adolescence* 1:251-275.

Hallinan, Maureen T. 1992. "The Organization of Students for Instruction in the Middle School." *Sociology of Education* 65:114-127.

Hallinan, Maureen T. 1994. "Effects of Tracking on Achievement of Black and White Students: A Longitudinal Study." Paper presented at the annual meeting of the American Sociological Association, Los Angeles.

Hallinan, Maureen T., and Aage B. Sorensen. 1983. "The Formation and Stability of Instructional Groups." *American Sociological Review* 48:838-851.

Heyns, Barbara. 1974. Social Selection and Stratification within Schools. *American Journal of Sociology* 79:1434-1451.

Hoffer, Thomas. 1992. "Middle School Ability Grouping and Student Achievement in Science and Mathematics." *Educational Evaluation and Policy Analysis* 14:205-228.

Hoffer, Thomas. 1994. "Cumulative Effects of Curriculum Tracking on Student Achievement." Paper presented at the annual meeting of the American Sociological Association, Los Angeles.

Hoffer, Thomas, and Adam Gamoran. 1993. "Effects of Instructional Differences among Ability Groups in Middle-School Science and Mathematics." Paper presented at the annual meeting of the American Sociological Association, Miami.

Hsieh, H-C. 1987. "Ability Stratification in Urban Taiwanese Secondary Schools." *Bulletin of the Institute of Ethnology* 64:205-252.

Jencks, Christopher L. 1985. "How Much Do High School Students Learn?" *Sociology of Education* 58:128-135.

Jencks, C. L., M. S. Smith, H. Acland, M. J. Bane, D. Cohen, H. Gintis, B. Heyns, and S. Michaelson. *Inequality*. New York: Basic Books.

Kerckhoff, Alan C. 1976. "The Status Attainment Process: Socialization or Allocation?" *Social Forces* 55:368-381.

Kerckhoff, Alan C. 1986. "Effects of Ability Grouping in British Secondary Schools." *American Sociological Review* 51:842-858.

Kerckhoff, Alan C. 1990. *Getting Started: Transition to Adulthood in Great Britain*. Boulder, CO: Westview.

Kerckhoff, Alan C. 1993. *Divergent Pathways: Social Structure and Career Deflections*. Cambridge: Cambridge University Press.

Lacey, Colin 1970. *Hightown Grammar*. Manchester: Manchester University Press.

Lockheed, Marlane E. 1987. *School and Classroom Effects on Student Learning Gains: The Case of Thailand*. World Bank Education and Training Series, Discussion Paper No. EDT 98.

Meyer, John 1977. "The Effects of Education as an Institution." *American Journal of Sociology* 83:55-77.

Mosteller, Fredrick, and Daniel P. Moynihan, Editors. 1972. *On Equality of Educational Opportunity*. New York: Vintage.

Murphy, Joseph, and Philip Hallinger. 1989. "Equity as Access to Learning: Curricular and Instructional Treatment Differences." *Journal of Curriculum Studies* 21:129-149.

Oakes, Jeannie, Adam Gamoran, and Reba N. Page. 1992. "Curriculum Differentiation: Opportunities, Outcomes, and Meanings." Pp. 570-608 in *Handbook of Research on Curriculum*, edited by Philip W. Jackson. Washington, DC: American Educational Research Association.

Pallas, Aaron M. 1993. "Schooling in the Course of Human Lives: The Social Context of Education and the Transition to Adulthood in Industrial Society." *Review of Educational Research* 63:409-447.

Pallas, Aaron M., Doris E. Entwistle, Karl L. Alexander, and M. F. Stluka. 1994. "Ability-Group Effects: Instructional, Social, or Institutional?" *Sociology of Education* 67:27-46.

Parsons, Talcott 1959. "The School Class as a Social System: Some of its Functions in American Society." *Harvard Education Review* 29:297-313.

Rosenbaum, James E. 1976. *Making Inequality: The Hidden Curriculum of High School Tracking*. New York: Wiley.

Rowan, Brian, and Andrew W. Miracle, Jr. 1983. "Systems of Ability Grouping and the Stratification of Achievement in Elementary Schools." *Sociology of Education* 56:133-144.

Sebring, Penny A. 1987. "Consequences of Differential Amounts of High School Coursework: Will the New Graduation Requirements Help?" *Educational Evaluation and Policy Analysis* 3:258-273.

Shavit, Yossi, and David L. Featherman. 1988. "Schooling, Tracking, and Teenage Intelligence." *Sociology of Education* 61:42-51.

Shavit, Yossi, and Richard Williams. 1985. "Ability Grouping and Contextual Determinants of Educational Expectations in Israel." *American Sociological Review* 50:62-73.

Slavin, Robert E. 1990. "Achievement Effects of Ability Grouping in Secondary Schools: A Best-Evidence Synthesis." *Review of Educational Research* 60:471-499.

Sociology of Education. 1994. "Exchange." (Contributions by M. T. Hallinan and J. Oakes.) *Sociology of Education* 67:79-91.

Sorokin, Pitirim A. 1927. *Social Mobility*. New York: Harper.

Vanfossen, Beth E., James D. Jones, and Joan Z. Spade. 1987. "Curriculum Tracking and Status Maintenance." *Sociology of Education* 60:104-122.

Waitrowski, Michael D., Stephen Hansell, Charles R. Massey, and Donald L. Wilson. 1982. "Curriculum Tracking and Delinquency." *American Sociological Review* 47:151-160.

Yogev, Avraham. 1981. "Determinants of Early Educational Career in Israel: Further Evidence for the Sponsorship Thesis." *Sociology of Education* 54:181-195.

5

Educational Tracking during the Early Years: First Grade Placements and Middle School Constraints

Karl L. Alexander
Doris R. Entwisle
The Johns Hopkins Univerisity

In line with the early educational stratification perspective, in which the school-to-work transition and persistence in the educational system through and beyond high school were the predominant concerns (e.g., Hauser, 1970), research on tracking thus far has focused mainly on curriculum differentiation at the upper grade levels, and then mainly on individual attainment outcomes, like test scores, marks and aspirations. Tracking systems as structural constraints on the *student career* are just beginning to command attention. Research on track mobility at any level of schooling is sparse; sparser still are studies that examine placement patterns *across* levels of schooling. Kerckhoff's (1993) *Diverging Pathways* is the most comprehensive treatment of these issues presently available. Tracking a cohort of British youth from elementary school into young adulthood, Kerckhoff's analysis shows that track placements and other structural features of school organization constrain later placements and performance outcomes all throughout the schooling process, from the early primary grades into the postsecondary level. Recently, several analyses have begun to address these matters in the U.S. too (Gamoran, 1992; Hallinan, 1992; Hoffer, 1992; Stevenson, Schiller and Schneider, 1994), but all focus on tracking at the upper grade levels, in middle school and beyond. This neglect of early tracking in U.S. research is unfortunate, as educational "sorting and selecting" in the early primary grades no doubt sets the stage for much that follows (e.g., Entwisle and Alexander, 1993).

The present paper describes tracking patterns in first grade, when the process commences, and how they articulate with initial program place-ments in middle school. It thus begins to explore structural constraints that originate in children's very first encounters with educational tracking. The data come from our Beginning School Study (BSS), which since 1982 has been monitoring the academic progress and personal development of 790 youngsters who began first grade that year in 20 Baltimore City public schools. The sampling of schools spans the range of socioeconomic levels in the City system, as well as different school integration contexts, with whites, relatively well-to-do neighborhoods and integrated schools oversampled to sustain strategic comparisons. Within schools students were selected randomly from 1981-82 kindergarten rosters, with supple-mental sampling in the fall to pick up new entrants. All first grade classrooms are covered in the final "beginning school cohort." The project now is in its twelfth year. Soon we will know how many of the study youngsters are on-time twelfth graders, but almost certainly it will be well under half. According to interview data obtained from 82% of the original 790 in the spring of Year 11, just 48% at that point were eleventh graders. Fifteen percent (N = 99) had already dropped out and another third were a year or more behind (22.4% in tenth grade; 12.4% in ninth grade; one still in eighth grade).[1] These youngsters all started out together as first graders in the fall of 1982, but over the years much has happened to move them onto different educational pathways.[2] It is reasonable to suspect that educational tracking has played a role.

The Several Dimensions of Early Tracking

Although tracking comes in many guises,[3] research tends to address the issue piecemeal. Typically a single form of tracking, like ability grouping, is examined in isolation from the others. Indeed, some of the more common forms of tracking in the primary grades usually aren't even thought of as such -retention and Special Education placements, for example. Following Oakes (1992), and before her Sørensen (1970; 1987), we favor a broad construction of tracking as inhering in the organizational differentiation or students. Ability grouping in the primary grades, curricular distinctions in the middle grades and high school, Special Education programs and retention all regroup students, reduce heterogeneity in the instructional unit (the goal of virtually all systems of tracking), and confer distinctive organizational identities. Ability grouping is the form of early tracking most often studied from an educational stratification perspective, but there are important parallels that cut across all these forms of tracking. Like assignment to low instructional groups, retention and Special Education placements usually are based on assessed ability or correlates thereof. Given the achievement-oriented ideology that pervades the educational system, they almost certainly carry negative connotation. Repeaters are separated from their same-age peers and depart from the normal timetable of grade progressions. Special Education typically occurs outside regular classes and also often has the effect of throwing children off schedule. This asynchrony makes repeaters and Special Education students conspicuous and thus vulnerable to negative labelling.

Reading Groups in First Grade

According to McPartland, Coldiron and Braddock (1987), more than 90% of elementary schools use within class ability grouping for reading in first grade. Within class grouping (as distinct from between class grouping) benefits pupils of some or all ability levels (Kulik and Kulik, 1987; Slavin, 1987), but the conditions that allow positive effects to materialize and whether benefits occur for both reading and math are disputed Archambault, 1989).[4] In reviewing research on grouping in the primary grades, for example, Slavin (1987) found too few methodologically sound studies to permit conclusions for reading, but since reading is the area of the curriculum that relies most often on small group instruction this leaves the matter very much open (only about 25% of schools use small groups in math – see McPartland, Coldiron and Braddock, 1987). Beyond the question of how grouping affects performance, where both sentiment and evidence are mixed, there also is concern about the stigma that supposedly attaches to low group membership (e.g., Rist, 1970).

Small instructional groups help teachers deal with practical problems of classroom management. Even in schools that group entire classes by ability or readiness tests, further grouping often occurs inside the classroom. Splitting a class of 30 into three or four groups of about the same level of readiness simplifies lesson planning and makes it easier to meet individual students' needs. Grouping, in this sense, is an "organizational response to an organizational problem" (Dreeben, 1984: 83). In consequence, grouping arrangements often are broadly similar from place to place regardless of school context or student characteristics, like the distribution of ability levels in the class (Hallinan and Sørensen, 1983).

As an organizational imperative, instructional grouping creates "bottom dog" groups made up of a third to a fourth of the class wherever it is used. This helps explain why conventional social and demographic "risk factors" (i.e., family SES level; race/ethnicity), ordinarily powerful predictors of educational outcomes, have practically no bearing on group placements (Haller, 1985; Haller and Davis, 1980; Pallas, Entwisle, Alexander and Stluka, 1994; Sørensen and Hallinan, 1984).[5]

Grade Retention

There are no good national data on grade retention, but retention rates in many localities are quite high. According to data compiled by Shepard and Smith (1989) for 14 states for the 1985-86 school year, grade-specific retention rates in the 7% - 8% range are common. These data are consistent with off-time rates at the end the elementary years of fifty percent or more, which national data show in many urban areas with large poverty level and minority enrollments (Bianchi, 1984). In Shepard and Smith's data, retention rates consistently are highest in first grade, *averaging* 11% for the 13 states with first grade data. Eight of the 13 states had first grade retention rates above 10%. By way of comparison, the *highest* figure in grades two through six was a little over 8%. In Baltimore too retention at the elementary level is highest in first grade. Both the 1982 BSS data and system-wide data for the 1989-90 school year (Kelly, 1989) put the first grade rate at over 16%.

For some time sentiment in the research community regarding retention has been almost universally negative. In 1971, for example, Abidin, Golladay and Howerton referred to retention as "an unjustifiable, discriminatory and noxious educational policy," the 1991 meeting of the American Educational Research Association held a symposium entitled "Retention: Processes and Consequences of a Misguided Practice," and quotes like the following abound (House, 1989:210): ".... the evidence is extensive and unequivocal. It includes test scores, surveys, personality and emotional adjustment measures, case studies—everything from elaborate statistical analyses to asking students how they feel. Almost everything points in the same direction—retention is an extremely harmful practice."

Such sweeping pronouncements almost certainly overstate the case for the kinds of outcomes most often considered in evaluations of retention (e.g., marks, test scores and attitudes). Studies do not weigh in consistently against retention (see, for example, Pierson and Connell, 1992; Peterson, DeGracie, and Ayabe, 1987; Reynolds, 1992), and our own assessment (Alexander, Entwisle and Dauber, 1994) over the elementary and middle school years finds mainly positive, not negative, effects of single retentions for all these criteria.[6] But what of retention as a structural constraint on children's later schooling? Despite concerns that repeating a grade closes off opportunities later, evidence on the issue is almost entirely circumstantial.

Early retention consistently predicts later dropout and most dropouts are in non-academic tracks (Cairns, Cairns and Neckerman, 1989; Fine, 1991; Stroup and Robins, 1972; Lloyd, 1978), so there certainly are indications of retention's relevance for tracking patterns across the student career. However, the only direct evidence of such linkages comes from the NELS-88 data. Stevenson, Schiller and Schneider (1992) find, for example, that elementary school repeaters are less likely than other youngsters to take high level courses in middle school and high school, even after adjusting for background factors and test scores. This pattern is consistent with the mobility constraint idea; unfortunately, the NELS-88 data rely on retrospective reports of children's prior promotion histories and this particular analysis also used self-reports to determine both middle school and high school curriculum placements. Thus, while early retention probably limits curricular options later, so far there is little solid evidence to this effect.

Special Education

From the mid-seventies to the early nineties the number of children of all ages receiving Special Education services increased from 3.7 million to 4.8 million, or from about 8% to just over 12% of 3 to 21 year-olds (Office of Special Education Programs, 1991; Viadero, 1992). Moreover, despite P.L. 94-142 and the mainstreaming movement, most Special Education students continue to receive services outside regular classrooms (Office of Special Education, 1991). Nevertheless, with few exceptions (e.g., Carrier, 1986; Mehan, 1992; Mehan, Hetweck and Meihls, 1985; Mercer, 1974) Special Education still has received little attention as an educational "track."

According to the Office of Special Education Programs (1991), between 1976-77 and 1989-90 students classified as learning disabled increased from 24.9% of the total receiving services to 50.0%, by far the largest percentage increase registered in any of the standard placement categories (e.g., mental retardation, serious emotional disturbance, speech or language impairments, hearing impairments, etc.). Learning disabilities are defined by a marked discrepancy between ability and performance, but often the category is a catch-all, with screening frequently done simply through test scores (Singer, Palfrey, Butler and Walker, 1989). Criteria for distinguishing between low-achieving and learning disabled children are ambiguous and practices vary greatly from place to place (e.g., Algozzine and Ysseldyke, 1983; Reynolds, 1984). Minority youngsters are greatly overrepresented among the educationally mentally retarded and in some other Special Education categories, raising equity questions that seem invariably to arise in the context of tracking (e.g., Heller, Holtzman and Messick, 1982).

As with ability grouping and retention, assessments of traditional Special Education programs tend to be critical (e.g., Madden and Slavin, 1983; Leinhardt and Pallay, 1982). Again, however, practically nothing is known about how Special Education placements tie in with other forms of tracking. This holds both for short-term issues, like how placements overlap, and for longer term issues, like how early placements limit opportunities later.

Early Tracking in the BSS

First Grade Placements

As shown in Table 5.1, just over 16% of the BSS cohort was held back at the end of first grade, a figure in line with city-wide statistics; 13% received Special Education services in their first *or* second school years;[7] and when children are classified according to whether they were in the lowest group in their classroom, in the highest group, or in an intermediate level group,[8] 22% were located in the lowest.[9] In the rightmost columns, low and high placements are tallied across these three facets of early tracking. Most youngsters (almost 70%) are spared low placements altogether, but sizeable minorities are placed low in one (17%), two (9%), and all three (5%) areas.

These low placements are our main concern. The literature on ability grouping, retention and Special Education tend to treat them as isolated in children's experience. In the real world, though, they often combine. Figure 5.1 shows how they overlap in the case of first grade repeaters. There are 88 such youngsters in the BSS whose Special Education standing and reading group level also are known. Seventy-seven percent were in low reading groups, 45% of whom also received Special Education services (equivalently, a third of the 88 were assigned to Special Education *and* in low reading groups). The corresponding figures for children promoted at the end of first grade were in the 10% - 12% range (see lower chart in Figure 5.1). Just a fifth of the retainees were spared both other low placements versus more than 80% of the promoted group.

Overall, then, almost 80% of first grade repeaters had multiple low placements. So too did 61% of children in low reading groups and 56% of those receiving Special Education services. The specific configurations are presented in Figure 5.2 (where high placement patterns also are displayed). Here "Low" means held back, receiving Special Education services and being in the lowest reading group. Conversely, "high" means promoted, not receiving Special Education services and assignment to the class's highest reading group. Retention and Special Education are dichotomies, so "low" also means "not high." In other words, reading group level is what distinguishes the two classifications.

Over half of the 30% placed low in first grade (194 of the 630 with data on all three measures) had just one low placement—26% in low reading groups, 10% retained and 19% receiving Special Education services. The three "interventions" in these instances are separable, which is how they are treated in most of the literature—one facet of tracking in isolation from the others. However, about 14% of the total and just under half of those with low placements occupied two or three low track "slots." The main pattern combines low reading group with grade retention, but there also are

TABLE 5.1   First Grade Track Placements: Reading Group Level, Special Education, Retention, and Tallies of Low and High Placements

1. *Reading Group*		# Low Placements[a]		# High Placements[b]	
Lowest	22.1% (132)	0	69. 2% (436)	0	5. 6% (35)
Intermediate	38.3% (228)	1	17.0% (107)	1	15.4% (97)
Highest	39.6% (236)	2	9.2% (58)	2	43.3% (273)
		3	4.6% (29)	3	35.7% (225)
2. *Special Education*					
Yes	13.3% (105)				
No	86.7% (685)				
3. *Retained*					
Yes	16.2% (128)				
No	83.8% (662)				

[a]Includes lowest reading group, retained and receiving Special Education services.

[b]Includes highest reading group, not retained and not receiving Special Education services.

promoted children who were in low reading groups and received Special Education services and others who were in Special Education and held back but not in low reading groups. The numbers involved are small in these instances, but the patterns we assume are reliable, so system-wide in the BCPS, and nation-wide in places like Baltimore, a great many children are touched by all these experiences, singly and in combination. Indeed, almost 15% are tracked low in all three areas: placed in a low reading group, assigned to Special Education and held back at year's end.

These patterns bring to light some of the complexity of early tracking. For example, problems associated with low track placements might compound as the number of such placements increases. If this is the case, then research on retention, or on grouping, or on Special Education will understate how *tracking per se* impacts students in the early grades.[10] Of course, effects also could be offsetting, or some combinations of placements could be more

FIGURE 5.1   First Grade Tracking Patterns: Repeaters
and Promoted Children Compared

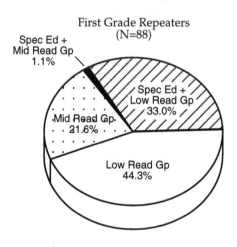

First Grade Repeaters
(N=88)

Spec Ed +
Mid Read Gp
1.1%

Spec Ed +
Low Read Gp
33.0%

Mid Read Gp
21.6%

Low Read Gp
44.3%

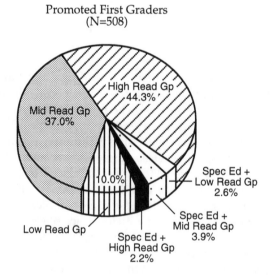

Promoted First Graders
(N=508)

High Read Gp
44.3%

Mid Read Gp
37.0%

10.0%

Spec Ed +
Low Read Gp
2.6%

Low Read Gp

Spec Ed +
Mid Read Gp
3.9%

Spec Ed +
High Read Gp
2.2%

FIGURE 5.2   Low and High First Grade Tracking Patterns

First Graders with Low Placements
(N=194)

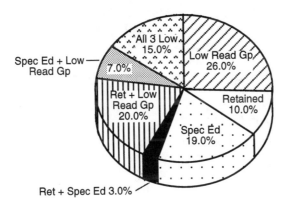

First Graders with High Placements
(N=595)

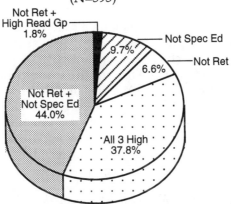

problematic than others. To address such issues, research will have to begin examining the *tracking system* in its totality.

The lower chart of Figure 5.2 shows the other side of first grade tracking. Over 90% of the cohort (595/630) registered at least one "not low" placement. More than a third of this group, it turns out, was favorably situated with respect to all three tracking criteria: these youngsters were in high reading groups, were not held back and did not receive Special Education services. Another 40+%, while not in high reading groups, nevertheless managed to avoid both retention and Special Education. Hence, even in Baltimore public schools, which enroll mainly poor and minority youngsters, most children are *not* tracked low early on. These youngsters all moved on to second grade to realize whatever benefits follow a *high* track history -promoted on schedule, top reading group and no identification with Special Education.

Placements Beyond First Grade

Table 5.2 examines the overlap in first grade placements in more detail. It also shows the patterning of later retentions and encounters with Special Education. Using data from school records, retention and Special Education services are monitored through sixth grade, the first year of middle school;[11] however because of retention and other setbacks, not everyone makes it to sixth grade on the same timetable. The data in Table 5.2 take into account when that transition was made, and so overlap the transition to middle school for everyone. Nine youngsters, or under 2%, skipped a grade in elementary school and were sixth graders after five years; 61% (N=352) were on-time sixth graders; 32.3% (N=185) were in sixth grade in their seventh school year; and 4.7% (N=27) took eight years to make it to sixth grade.

Table 5.2 reveals large, patterned differences associated with all three dimensions of first grade tracking, long-term as well as short-term. The left-side panel covers children's retention histories. Almost 3/4ths of the children in low first grade reading groups were held back at some point, over half in first grade. Additionally, through sixth grade 35% were retained *a second time*. In comparison, none of the high reading group youngsters repeated first grade, 88% had smooth promotion histories and just 6 (2.5%) were double repeaters by middle school. The intermediate level reading group youngsters' overall retention rate and double retention rate both were between the high group-low group extremes.[12] The mapping onto retention of children's relative reading group rank in first grade thus not only is orderly, *but extends all through the primary grades*.

Special Education and retention also are linked throughout the primary grades. Special Education students, more likely to repeat first grade, also had a somewhat higher retention rate in grades 2 - 6 than did children who

TABLE 5.2 Overlap in Early Track Placements: First Grade Through Sixth Grade

	First Retention			Any 2nd Ret	Special Education*			
	Never Ret	Ret 1st Grade	Ret Grs 2-6		Never In	Assign in Grs 1 or 2	Assign in Grs 3-6	Receive Services in Gr 6
1. First Grade Reading Group								
Lowest	27.3% (36)	51.5% (68)	21.2% (28)	34.9% (46)	43.9% (58)	40.9% (54)	15.2% (20)	50.9% (43)
Middle	56.1% (128)	8.8% (20)	35.1% (80)	11.0% (25)	79.4% (181)	11.8% (27)	8.8% (20)	15.7% (27)
Highest	87.7% (207)	—	12.3% (29)	2.5% (6)	91.9% (217)	5.9% (14)	2.1% (5)	6.0% (10)
2. Special Education Year 1 or 2								
Yes	27.6% (29)	44.8% (47)	27.6% (29)	31.5% (33)	—	100.0% (105)	—	60.9% (42)
No	67.6% (463)	11.8% (81)	20.6% (141)	9.8% (67)	87.3% (598)	4.1% (28)	8.6% (59)	13.5% (64)
3. Retained 1st Grade								
Yes	—	100.0% (128)	—	44.5% (57)	35.9% (46)	46.9% (60)	17.2% (22)	56.3% (49)
No	74.3% (492)	—	25.7% (170)	6.5% (43)	83.4% (552)	11.0% (73)	5.6% (37)	12.5% (57)

*Note: The "Years" (rows) versus "Grades" (columns) distinction is meaningful for Special Education. The first classifies children according to their placements in Project Years 1 and 2. The second classifies children according to their grade level – first, second, third, etc. More children are identified as receiving Special Education services in "Grades 1 or 2" than in "Years 1 or 2" because for the repeaters the "Grade 1 or 2" period spans as many as four years.

were not in Special Education at the beginning[13] and were much more likely to be held back a second time (31.5% versus 9.8%). First grade repeaters also were at greater risk: 44.5% of them were held back a second time compared to just 6.5% double retention among children promoted at the end of first grade (a fourth of whom were held back after first grade).

The right-side panel of Table 5.2 shows similar patterning with respect to Special Education services beyond first grade. Youngsters in low reading groups and first grade repeaters who made it out of first grade without being assigned to Special Education still were more likely *later* to receive services than were children not tracked low initially. More than half those who had low placements in first grade received Special Education services in sixth grade and this holds for all three varieties of first grade tracking. In comparison, the *highest* figure for children not tracked low in first grade was 15.7%, for those in middle reading groups.

Summary: Early Tracking in First Grade and Beyond

To this point we have looked in detail at three dimensions of early tracking: reading group placement, retention and assignment to Special Education. Most youngsters in the Beginning School Study were spared low placements in all three areas of tracking, but in first grade 30% were low in at least one area. Moreover, for many children two or more of these placements overlapped, and the compounding of low placements extended beyond first grade. Children placed low in one area in first grade were more likely also to occupy other low slots in first grade, but even when multiple low placements were avoided initially the risk of being placed low later, through sixth grade, was elevated. Educational tracking thus begins early, involves several dimensions of tracking, touches a great many children in various combinations and for many children has repercussions all through the primary grades. The question addressed next is whether those repercussions extend to curriculum tracking in middle school.

Tracking in the Middle Grades

Curriculum differentiation in the middle grades signals the onset of tracking as conventionally understood. At that point, students begin taking different subjects (e.g., English versus reading) and the same subjects are taught at different levels, often with little overlap in content. In math, advanced students may take pre-algebra, while others still are working on number skills; in the language curriculum, high level students often take a foreign language and may move on to literary criticism and creative or expository writing, while children in lower level classes are limited to remedial reading, rules of grammar, vocabulary building and the like.

Until middle school, children's options in principle remain open even if they have fallen behind. In high school, though, many upper level courses have prerequisites, and curricular decisions in the middle grades are the waystations to them. Children placed in general math in middle school or at the start of high school will not take Calculus in twelfth grade, nor will children taking functional reading be able to enroll in Advanced Placement English literature. The curriculum in the upper grades levels in the main academic subjects is sequenced and hierarchical, so unless the groundwork has been laid in middle school students are effectively cut off from high level options (e.g., Gamoran, 1992; Oakes, 1988; Oakes, 1989/90; Stevenson, Schiller and Schneider, 1994). We suspect that tracking constraints also extend "down" into the early primary grades where, we have seen, "hidden" forms of tracking touch many children's lives. In this section, we examine how first grade track placements articulate with middle school course placements in the language arts program (reading and English), math and foreign languages.

Program Placements in Sixth Grade

BCPS schools mainly follow a k-5, 6-8, 9-12 grade organization, with middle school beginning in sixth grade. English displaces reading as the "regular" language arts curriculum in Baltimore's middle schools, but in sixth grade most BCPS students (about 3/4ths) take both reading and English, a common pattern nationwide (Epstein and MacIver, 1990). All reading courses are remedial and/or Special Education, while the English program distinguishes among "remedial," "regular" "Enriched" and "Advanced Academic" courses. The remedial English curriculum (e.g., "English with Reading/Writing Emphasis") is intended for students who fail the City's reading and writing proficiency tests. It concentrates on paragraph construction, rules of grammar and the like, while Enriched and Advanced Academic students study "characterization, literary devices and authors' purposes," "... writing in a variety of genres, and some lower level skills of debate and defense" (quoted from BCPS course descriptions). Enriched classes are available in all middle schools; Advanced Academic in 11 of 27, including two city-wide magnet schools.

The math program also distinguishes remedial, regular and advanced courses, the latter involving a pre-algebra/algebra sequence. These distinctions are used in most but not all middle schools. For example, in one school attended by some of the BSS youngsters there are no sixth grade classes as such. Instead, students are placed in math and English based on their assessed readiness. Course "levels" in this school (5 in English and math) are distinguished according to level of difficulty and differ in student composition. A sixth grader in a higher level course that enrolls mainly seventh and eighth graders would be considered "advanced," while Level 4 and 5 courses are "low" regardless of students' grade level. Even in this

FIGURE 5.3 Sixth Grade Course Placements by English Level

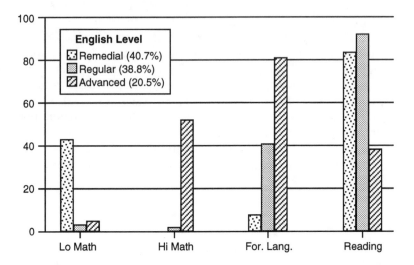

school, then, it is possible to approximate the "remedial" - "regular" "advanced" distinctions used generally throughout the City system.

Foreign language instruction is available in all middle schools, but not all students begin a foreign language in sixth grade. In some schools, for instance, students taking reading or remedial English are not allowed to take a foreign language. Since foreign language study in the middle grades has been found to influence program placements in high school (e.g., Alexander and Cook, 1982; Rosenbaum, 1976), these restrictions could be consequential later. There is no counterpart of "remedial" in the foreign language program, but in some schools "honors" courses are distinguished from "regular" ones. However, not many BSS youngsters take high level foreign language courses, so the comparisons that follow simply distinguish "any" foreign language from "none."

Table 5.3 describes sixth grade course level placements in English and math (low; regular; high), both from the last quarter available on transcripts,[14] and whether or not the student took reading or a foreign language at any point in the year. Almost 3/4ths of the cohort took remedial reading, 41% were in low level English, 20% in low level math and almost 2/3rds did not take a foreign language. Low level placements thus are commonplace, and it probably will come as no surprise that they tend to align across areas of the curriculum. As displayed in Figure 5.3, for example, students in Enriched and Advanced Academic English are the ones most often exempted from remedial reading: just under 39% of the 98 youngsters in upper level English courses took reading, as against 84% of the 194 students in low level English and 92.4% of those in regular English. These youngsters also were more likely than the others to begin a foreign language in sixth grade (81% compared to 9% of those in low level English classes and 41% of those in regular classes) and to be taking high level math (52% versus under 2% of regular and low level English students).[15]

Figure 5.4 shows how these placements overlap or combine across all four areas of the curriculum, much as was done in Figure 5.2 for the three facets of first grade tracking. Although the tracking distinctions used here are completely different than those in first grade, the idea at both points is to characterize students' relative standing in the then relevant hierarchies of organizational differentiation. Comparing just the sample splits in Figures 5.2 and 5.4, we see many fewer high placements in sixth grade than in first (90+% in first grade vs. 220/477, or 46% in sixth grade) and more low placements (30% vs. 88%).[16] It thus appears students' placements have deteriorated from one level of schooling to the next, at least in the aggregate, although it remains to be determined whether the predominant forms of tracking at the two levels are at all comparable in terms of psychological salience and practical import.[17]

These are important issues, with potentially far reaching ramifications. For example, children's school engagement, as reflected in their school performance, liking of school, and academic self-image, all typically spiral downward over the years. The reasons for this distancing of youth from things academic are not well understood, but some research implicates challenges encountered in acclimating to organizational arrangements in the middle grades, including the system of tracking (for overview see Eccles and Midgley, 1990; Eccles, Midgley and Adler, 1984).

Here we see that more children experience more low placements in sixth grade than in first, and this alone could set them back if it shakes their confidence and assaults their sense of self. But differences in the *character of tracking* could further compound children's difficulties. As typically implemented, curriculum differentiation in the middle grades is akin to whole class ability grouping. Broad scope, exclusive and highly visible, this is one of the most divisive kind of grouping arrangements (e.g., Slavin, 1987; Sørensen, 1970).

From the upper chart in Figure 5.4, we see that almost 15% of the BSS sixth graders with low placements were low "across the board." Other young-sters had just one (21.7%), two (27.0%) or three (26.8%) low placements,[18] with various language arts configurations dominating the patterns. The isolated low placement most often is reading (21.7%); another frequent pattern had reading trading off with foreign language study (27.0%), and another combined reading with remedial English at the expense of foreign language study (22%). Low math placements, in contrast, were both less

FIGURE 5.4   Low and High Sixth Grade Tracking Patterns

Sixth Grade Low Placement Patterns
(N=419)

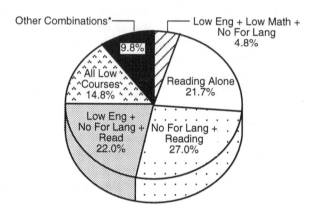

Other Combinations*

Low Eng + Low Math +
No For Lang
4.8%

9.8%

All Low Courses
14.8%

Reading Alone
21.7%

Low Eng +
No For Lang +
Read
22.0%

No For Lang +
Reading
27.0%

* Includes all patterns with
2.5% or less of the sample

Sixth Grade High Placement Patterns
(N=220)

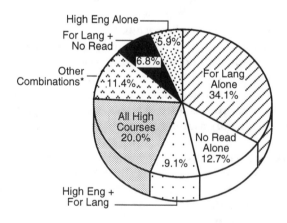

High Eng Alone

For Lang +
No Read

Other
Combinations*

5.9%

6.8%

11.4%

For Lang
Alone
34.1%

All High
Courses
20.0%

No Read
Alone
12.7%

9.1%

High Eng +
For Lang

* Includes all patterns with
5% or less of the sample

common and less concentrated.

High placements altogether were relatively rare, as more than half the sample had *no* high sixth grade placements. At the same time, almost a fifth of the cohort was placed high in two or more areas, so some youngsters still managed to wind up with upper level concentrations (or, equivalently, to avoid low level ones, e.g., reading). For example, 93% of the students in high level math also were in high level English, 90% took a foreign language and just 12.3% took reading.[19] Altogether, almost 10% of the cohort was high in all four areas, which in Figure 5.4 we see accounting for a fifth of those with any high placements.

That children's course levels tend to align across areas of the curriculum is not surprising. For one thing, children with strong academic records in one area tend to be strong in other areas as well. Administrative consider-ations also play a role. Most schools, for example, use just a few "templates" in scheduling classes. Block scheduling, in which pupils move as a group from class to class, simplifies planning but has the effect of placing children in the same track for all or most of their academic subjects. But administra-tive actions can also force crossing levels. In Baltimore there are no remedial math courses keyed to proficiency tests akin to "English with Reading/ Writing Emphasis" in the language arts area. Instead, remedial courses in math all are Special Education, so marginal students are more likely to wind up in low level English than in low level math.

Structural Constraints from First Grade into Middle School

We now consider the overlap of sixth grade course-taking patterns with first grade track placements. This is done in Table 5.4, area by area and in terms of low placements. Though individual course-taking configurations are too sparsely populated to sustain comparisons, by tallying low and high sixth grade placements we at least can determine whether constraints associated with early tracking compound as the number of low first grade placements increases.

Associations between first grade tracking and sixth grade placements are significant for all areas of the middle grades curriculum save reading.[20] The largest Etas,[21] in the .3 - .4 range, mainly involve placements in math and the tally of low placements across all four areas, but the tie between reading group level in first grade and English level in sixth grade also is in this range.

While these relationships are only modest to mid-range, the enrollment patterns that underlay them often are strikingly different. For example, two-thirds of first grade repeaters were in low level English in sixth grade compared to just over a third of promoted first graders, a difference of 32.3 points revolving around first grade retention. Larger still is the 35.2% absolute difference (61.5% - 26.3%) comparing children in high and low first grade reading groups.

TABLE 5.3 Sixth Grade Course Placements: English Level, Math Level, Reading Enrollment, Foreign Language Enrollment, and Tallies of Low and High Level Placements

English		Math		Reading		Foreign Language		# Low Level Courses[a]		# High Level Courses[b]	
Low Level	40.7% (194)	Low Level	20.2% (97)	Taking	74.0% (375)	Taking	33.9% (172)	0	12.2% (58)	0	53.9% (257)
Regular	38.8 (185)	Regular	68.0 (327)	Not Taking	26.0 (132)	Not Taking	66.1 (335)	1	23.3 (111)	1	24.7 (118)
High Level	20.5 (98)	High Level	11.9 (57)					2	26.8 (128)	2	7.8 (37)
								3	24.7 (118)	3	4.4 (21)
								4	13.0 (62)	4	9.2 (44)

[a]Includes low level English, low level math, taking reading, and not taking a foreign language
[b]Includes high level English, high level math, not taking reading, and taking a foreign language

At the high end, advanced sixth grade placements were rare among youngsters tracked low in first grade, especially first grade repeaters, just two of whom were in high level sixth grade English, one in high level math. By way of comparison, of the youngsters promoted the first time through first grade, a fourth as sixth graders were in high level English and a seventh were in high level math. Children in low reading groups in first grade or in Special Education were not excluded from high level courses in sixth grade to the same extent as first grade repeaters, but such placements still were relatively rare for them. For example, the *absolute* difference comparing high and low first grade reading groups in terms of sixth grade high level English enrollments (38.0% - 12.8% = 25.2%) is close to that between retained and promoted youngsters (22.4%).

Table 5.4 thus shows the relevance of children's tracking experiences in first grade to sixth grade placements area by area. The rightmost columns show additionally that placements *across* the four areas also map onto first grade tracking. Children in Special Education in first grade, for instance, on average took 0.9 more low level courses and 0.5 fewer high level courses as sixth graders than did their cohortmates not in Special Education, and a similar pattern holds for the other facets of first grade tracking. Since first grade track placements overlap substantially, this does not necessarily mean that all three dimensions of early tracking contribute uniquely to sixth grade coursetaking patterns, but at the zero-order level connections involving all three—retention, Special Education and reading group level—are significant, with most in the .20 - .35 range.[22]

Finally, the last entries (bottom panel) in Table 5.4 show how sixth grade curricular placements map onto the tally of low first grade placements. If, as might be suspected, the consequences of early tracking compound across types of tracking, then the likelihood of being placed low in sixth grade should increase as the number of low first grade placements increases. With the exception of reading, this seems to be the case. Indeed, youngsters low on all three early tracking measures consistently fared worst in sixth grade.[23] However, those with *two* low first grade placements, compared to the low groups on each of the *individual tracking measures*, generally do not have either the highest percentage of low sixth grade placements or the lowest percentage of high sixth grade placements. In most instances there is at least one other group—sometimes repeaters, sometimes members of low first grade reading groups, sometimes children assigned to Special Education—with more extreme percentages.

These are small differences, but they signal some of the complexities that arise as one begins to look broadly at systems of tracking. Tallies of low and high placements, as used here, usefully summarize children's general standing as it overlaps individual tracking hierarchies, but it appears some placements matter more than others, at least for some areas of the middle

TABLE 5.4 Overlap of First Grade and Sixth Grade Track Placements

First Grade Placements	Sixth Grade Course Levels and Coursetaking Patterns									% Taking For Lang	% Taking Reading	# Low Courses	# High Courses
	English Level				Math Level								
	% Low	% Reg	% High	(N)	% Low	% Reg	% High	(N)	(N)	(N)	(N)	(N)	(N)
Special Education													
Yes	62.5	29.7	7.8	(64)	53.1	42.2	4.7	(64)	15.7 (70)	72.9 (70)	2.8 (64)	0.5 (64)	
No	37.3	40.2	22.5	(413)	15.1	71.9	12.9	(417)	36.8 (437)	74.1 (437)	1.9 (413)	1.0 (413)	
Eta	.18***				.28***				.15***	.01^{NS}	.24***	.13**	
Retained													
Yes	67.0	30.7	2.3	(88)	50.6	48.3	1.1	(89)	9.6 (94)	81.9 (94)	2.9 (88)	0.3 (88)	
No	34.7	40.6	24.7	(389)	13.3	72.4	14.3	(392)	39.5 (413)	72.2 (413)	1.8 (389)	1.0 (389)	
Eta	.28***				.35***				.25***	.09^{NS}	.36***	.23***	

Reading Group

Lowest	61.5	25.6	12.8	(78)	50.0	43.6	6.4	(78)	19.3 (83)	73.5 (83)	2.7 (78)	0.6 (78)
Inter-mediate	43.1	46.4	10.5	(153)	16.7	77.6	5.8	(156)	25.1 (167)	79.0 (167)	2.2 (153)	0.6 (153)
Highest	26.3	35.8	38.0	(137)	7.3	70.8	21.9	(137)	44.8 (145)	65.5 (145)	1.6 (137)	1.4 (137)
Eta	.28***	.33***			.38***				.23***	.14^NS	.35***	.30***

Low Placements

0	32.3	42.6	25.1	(263)	9.4	75.9	14.7	(266)	39.1 (279)	73.5 (279)	1.8 (263)	1.0 (263)
1	41.0	41.0	18.0	(61)	27.9	63.9	8.2	(61)	29.0 (69)	68.1 (69)	2.1 (61)	0.8 (61)
2	70.0	22.5	7.5	(40)	50.0	45.0	5.0	(40)	14.0 (43)	76.7 (43)	2.9 (40)	0.5 (40)
3	77.8	22.2	0.0	(18)	77.8	22.2	0.0	(18)	0.0 (18)	83.3 (18)	3.4 (18)	0.2 (18)
Eta	.28***				.41***				.23***	.07^NS	.37***	.19**

Significance levels: *p ≤ .05 level; **p ≤ .01 level; ***p ≤ .001 level grades curriculum. We also suspect that placement configurations will have different consequences depending on exactly how they fit together organizationally and administratively. In other words, research needs to be sensitive to nonadditivities or conditional relationships when trying to sort out effects involving multiple track hierarchies. These complications deserve fuller treatment than is possible here.

Discussion

Educational tracking exists in many forms at all levels of schooling. Research on curriculum differentiation in high school initially was framed in terms of over-arching programs: college preparatory, vocational, general, and such. Such global distinctions remain useful for some purposes, but coursetaking patterns increasingly cross these traditional lines of divide (DeLany, 1991; Garet and DeLany, 1988; Powell, Farrar and Cohen, 1985) and it has proven useful in recent research to examine instead placement practices and consequences in specific areas of the curriculum, like the language arts, math, or science. Doing so reveals that determinants of high level and low level course placements sometimes differ across subjects (Gamoran, 1992; Hallinan, 1992; Stevenson, Schiller and Schneider, 1994), that consequences of track level also differ (Hoffer, 1992), and that tracking arrangements themselves are sensitive to school organizational properties, instructional practices and classroom processes (Bryk and Thum, 1989; Kilgore, 1991; Kilgore and Pendleton, 1993; Lee and Bryk, 1988; Lee and Smith, 1993).

Progress on these many fronts is leading to a more mature, nuanced understanding of how tracking actually works. However, the disaggregated approach carries limits of its own and no doubt studies soon will begin "reaggregating" the curriculum, although not in the way it used to be done.[24] Looking at course placements piecemeal, as current practice encourages, neglects ties across areas of the curriculum that give tracking its systemic character. The traditional program distinctions lumped too much together, but a course level focus loses sight of program coordination, and so in its own way also obscures important aspects of tracking.

These same concerns apply to early tracking. Despite the pretense of a uniform curriculum, children's experience of schooling in the primary grades is far from uniform. There are any number of organizational and administrative practices at the school and classroom level that use supposedly educationally relevant criteria to distinguish children from one another. These create new organizational identities, structure the daily routine, and build in differences where otherwise none might exist.

Ability grouping in the primary grades most clearly parallels curriculum differentiation at the secondary school as a mode of organizational differentiation (e.g., Rosenbaum, 1980; 1984), yet just as there are many different tracks in the upper grades, so too is early tracking multifaceted. Reading groups, retention and Special Education are three prototypical forms.

Achievement outcomes in the upper grades (e.g., test scores; dropout) can be predicted from early schooling markers (Cairns, Cairns and Neckerman, 1989; Ensminger and Slusarcick, 1992; Lloyd, 1978), so how children settle initially into the student role is of great consequence over the long haul. Elsewhere we have argued the importance of the beginning school transition as a critical period for children's schooling (Entwisle and Alexander, 1989; 1993). Some of the reasons for the crucible nature of early schooling involve considerations internal to the child (e.g., the rapid pace and changing nature of cognitive and affective development in the 6 - 8 age range). These reasons are widely recognized, but other reasons, less well appreciated, involve considerations internal to the school, including the largely buried systems of tracking that begin to channel children along different educational pathways right from the start.

This paper has described first grade tracking and how it ties in with coursetaking in sixth grade. Despite extensive literatures on all three of the "tracks" examined here, their overlap has been virtually ignored and this could be a serious oversight. About 30% of the BSS cohort were placed low on at least one of the three tracks; 14% were tracked low in two or more areas. Furthermore, low placements combined in just about all ways possible, and children placed low in first grade were at elevated risk later of being held back either for the first or second time or of being assigned to Special Education.

Many youngsters thus occupy low slots in the school's tracking hierarchies at the very start of their school careers. Though our research is Baltimore based, virtually all schools group in reading or other subjects so the problem is not limited to poor, urban areas. All these placements are intended to help children, and it should not be assumed their consequences are necessarily negative. Our inquires and those of others, for example, find slower than expected academic progress among children placed in low reading groups in first grade (e.g., Gamoran, 1986; Pallas, Entwisle, Alexander and Stluka, 1994), but for children in the BSS retention has mainly positive, not negative, effects (Alexander, Entwisle and Dauber, 1994).[25] Moreover, and of most immediate relevance, there are important issues involving early tracking that have received virtually no attention.

For one, whether particular tracking configurations have distinctive consequences is unknown, but our overview of first grade profiles identifies multiple tracks as a practical concern. Retention, Special Education and reading group standing are not isolated events in children's experience. They intersect in all sorts of ways. Though low standing in one area increases the odds of low standing in the others, placements across the three dimensions of first grade tracking are far from perfectly aligned: some repeaters are not in low reading groups or assigned to Special Education; despite children's being in low reading groups, many are promoted at year's end and do not receive Special Education services; there even are Special Education students with no other low track identities. For many children tracking messages thus are mixed, and this ambiguity could soften the impact of negative messages that revolve around their low track identification. On the other hand, multiple low track placements could prove to be an especially weighty burden.

A second open question is how early tracking ties in with tracking systems at the upper grade levels. Track placements constrain opportunities at the middle grades and beyond (e.g., Gamoran, 1992; Hallinan, 1992), but whether such constraints extend back to children's very first encounters with educational tracking remains to be determined. Most evaluations of early tracking examine consequences for school performance or in the socioemotional realm; however, tracking systems do not just change youngsters, they also channel them, opening doors for some, closing them for others (e.g., Oakes, 1988; 1989/90).

Structural constraints originating in tracking systems at the earliest grade levels are just beginning to command attention. Kerckhoff's recent study of within and between school tracking in Great Britain (1993), for example, discovered substantial "institutional inertia" in math placements from early elementary school (age 7) to late elementary school (age 11). Children in tracked math classes (about 30% of the total) were likely to be placed similarly on both occasions,[26] and structural connections across levels of schooling even were detectible at age 16, the last year of compulsory school attendance in Great Britain at the time (1974). Whether the same sort of "institutional inertia" also characterizes early tracking in the U.S., and whether facets of tracking other than ability group level are implicated, remain to be determined.

To our knowledge the data presented in the present paper are the first documentation of connections between early tracking and middle school curriculum placements that encompass several hierarchies of organizational differentiation at both levels of schooling. Descriptive detail was provided on the overlap of first grade retention, reading group level and Special Education with later retention, later receipt of Special Education services, and sixth grade (middle school) placements in English, reading, math and foreign languages. Overlap in placements from first to sixth grade was observed for all areas of the middle grades curriculum save reading.

While considerable additional work will be required before we can talk in terms of "effects" as distinct from "patterns," the orderliness seen here in placements stretching from the very start of elementary school into the middle grades is consistent with the view of tracking systems as comprising opportunity structures that advance the interests of some while impeding those of others. It is striking that actions taken in first grade could have consequences so far removed in time (6 - 8 years) and space (in middle school as the venue), but the persistence over time of hierarchies of inequality is one of the defining features of systems of stratification, and educational institutions are no more exempt from stratifying processes than are any of society's other institutions. The stratification embodied in early tracking thus far has been largely hidden from view, however, and its consequences still are not well understood.

Notes

Data collection for this research was supported by the W.T. Grant Foundation Grant No. 83079682 and National Institute of Child Health and Development Grant No. 1 R01 16302. The analysis was supported by National Science Foundation Grant No. SES 8510535 and National Institute of Child Health and Development Grants No. 1 R01 21044, 5 R01 23738, and 5 R01 23943; and by Grant No. R117D4005 from the Office of Educational Research and Improvement, U.S. Department of Education, to the Johns Hopkins University Center for Research on the Education of Students Placed at Risk. We thank the children, parents, teachers, principals and other school system personnel who have given us such splendid cooperation in all phases of this research.

1. Just over 1% (N=7) were accelerated. According to more recent data (through spring '95 or 13 years), about half the cohort has graduated high school, a fourth has dropped out and another fourth are still in school, putting them at least one year behind and thus at elevated risk of dropout.

2. For additional detail on these pathways through the first eight years of the cohort's experience, see Alexander, Entwisle and Dauber, 1994, Chapter 2.

3. Considering just ability grouping in the primary grades, one reviewer (Slavin, 1987) distinguishes seven different grouping arrangements.

4. Care also must be exercised not to generalize conclusions across different types of grouping arrangements (e.g., Reuman, 1989; Rowan and Miracle, 1983).

5. See Oakes, Gamoran and Page, 1992, for an excellent, comprehensive overview of these and other issues involving tracking at all levels of schooling.

6. See Karweit, 1992, for a balanced overview.

7. Spring reading group level is known for 596 members of the cohort. These data come from teachers. In the case of Special Education, data from the first two years are combined. We initially sampled regular classrooms, so hardly any youngsters were in separate classes the first year (just 2 of 790, as compared to 63, or 8%, in pullout-programs). This clearly is an undercount; and since assignments in a given year frequently are based on assessments made the previous spring, we reasoned that including second year placements in the tally would give a fairer reading of the early Special Education experience. The 13% figure includes children who received supplemental services from regular classes (i.e., pullout programs in reading and/or math) as well as those assigned to separate Special Education classes.

8. Thirty-four others were in classes that did not use small groups for reading,

and so could not be classified in terms of rank position. No information is available for the other 160 members of the cohort (20% missing data). These data come from 50 first grade teachers who responded to our inquiry about the group placements of the BSS youngsters in their classes.

9. This approach slides over distinctions in the middle ranks, but identifies children placed highest and lowest, where the signals that attach to group placements should be clearest. The most common arrangement was three groups, used by 29 of the 50 teachers. The next most common pattern was four groups, employed by 12 teachers. Four teachers used just two groups, while three used five groups. This distribution seems pretty typical of practices from the early eighties (e.g., Dreeben, 1984; Hallinan and Sørensen, 1983). Sixty percent of the study youngsters were in classes with three groups; a fourth were in classes with four groups. The other arrangements, including ungrouped classes, involved fewer than ten percent of the sample.

10. The reality of multiple low placements also complicates allocating responsibility when trying to assess how any one dimension of tracking affects children's schooling. Estimates of how reading group level affects achievement, for example, could be off unless effects associated with retention or Special Education are adjusted for.

11. This information is available only for children who remained in the BCPS the entire time, 72.5% of the total (N=573).

12. The same holds if the figures in Table 5.2 are recast in terms of "relative risk." There are 64 low group children who were not held back in first grade. These are the low group children "at risk" of first retention after first grade. Twenty-eight of them, or 43.8%, were held back in grades 2 - 6. This compares to 38.5% of the 208 middle group children who were not first grade repeaters.

13. Again, "relative risk" comparisons point in the same direction. Half the first grade Special Education children not held back in first grade are held back later (29/58) compared to 23.3% of those not in Special Education (141/604).

14. Some students transferred out during the year and sometimes courses were not taken for the full year. Referencing enrollments to the last available quarter maximizes case coverage.

15. Had we used math placements as the frame of reference, differences across other areas of the curriculum would have been even larger.

16. The same comparisons also can be seen in the low and high tallies reported in the rightmost columns of Tables 5.1 and 5.3.

17. Also, since we cover ability grouping in just one area, the first grade patterns likely understate low placements. We doubt that more complete coverage would alter the picture appreciably, however.

18. The "other combinations" total of just under 10% would add, at most, 2% to these totals. For example, 2.0% of the 419 were not taking a foreign language as their only low placement.

19. Math is more selective than English when it comes to high level placements, so all these figures are lower using English as the frame of reference. Still, the trend is similar (see Figure 5.3).

20. Seventy-four percent of the sample takes reading in sixth grade, so the distribution skew no doubt damps relationships involving reading.

21. Calculated from the cross-classifications that also are the source of the percentage distributions in Table 5.3, Eta is a measure of association analogous to the product-moment correlation but applicable to nominal and ordinal as well as interval level measurements.

22. Indeed, in most instances the associations, though attenuated, hold up even when controls are introduced. Two of the six partial correlations involving Special Education services (net of retention and reading group level) are significant at least at the .05 level (# low placements, .12; math level, .16); five of six involving retention status are significant (# low courses, .19; # high courses, .12; English level, .13; math level, .16; foreign language enrollment, .14); and five of six involving reading group level are significant (# low courses, .19; # high courses, .15; English level, .19; math level, .22; foreign language enrollment, .10).

23. This, though, is a small group (N=18 in Table 5.3) and their situation is extreme. Beyond their standing as members of low reading groups, first grade repeaters and recipients of Special Education services, their academic profile in first grade (test scores and marks) puts them far below all other groups. Under such extreme circumstances, sorting out the sources of their academic difficulties later on, including the reasons behind their low middle school placements, will be exceedingly difficult.

24. See Stevenson, Schiller and Schneider, 1994, for an example of the sort of approach we have in mind.

25. Even where the weight of evidence suggests generally adverse effects (i.e., for children in low ability groups), exceptions to the rule often can be found (e.g., Gamoran, 1993).

26. With sizeable, significant regression effects predicting later group level from earlier group level, net of a whole host of controls.

References

Abidin, R.R., W.M. Golladay, and A.L. Howerton. 1971. "Elementary School Retention: An Unjustifiable, Discriminatory and Noxious Policy." *Journal of School Psychology* 9:410-17.

Alexander, K.L. and M.A. Cook. 1982. "Curricula and Coursework: A Surprise Ending to a Familiar Story." *American Sociological Review* 47:626-40.

_____, D.R. Entwisle, and S. Dauber. 1994. *On the Success of Failure: A Reassessment of the Effects of Retention in the Primary Grades*. Cambridge, MA: Cambridge University Press.

Algozzine, B. and J. Ysseldyke. 1983. "Learning Disabilities as a Subset of School Failure: The Over-Sophistication of a Concept." *Exceptional Children* 50:242-46.

Archambault Jr., F.X. 1989. "Instructional Setting Features and Other Design Features of Compensatory Education Programs." Pp. 220-63 in *Effective Programs for Students at Risk*, edited by R.E. Slavin, N.L. Karweit and N.A. Madden. Boston: Allyn and Bacon.

Bianchi, S. 1984. "Children's Progress Through School: A Research Note." *Sociology of Education* 57:184-92.

Bryk, A.S. and Y.M. Thum. 1989. "The Effects of High School Organization on Dropping Out: An Exploratory Investigation." *American Educational Research Journal* 26:353-83.

Cairns, R.B., B.D. Cairns, and H.J. Neckerman. 1989. "Early School Dropout: Configurations and Determinants." *Child Development* 60:1437-52.

Carrier, J.G. 1986. "Sociology and Special Education: Differentiation and Allocation in Mass Education." *American Journal of Education* 94:281-312.

DeLany, B.D. 1991. "Allocation, Choice, and Stratification Within High Schools: How the Sorting Machine Works." *American Journal of Education* 99:181-207.

Dreeben, R. 1984. "First-Grade Reading Groups: Their Formation and Change." Pp. 69-84 in *The Social Context of Instruction: Group Organization and Group Process*, edited by P.L. Peterson, L.C. Wilkinson and M. Hallinan. San Diego: Academic Press.

Eccles, J.S. and C. Midgley. 1990. "Changes in Academic Motivation and Self-Perception During Early Adolescence." Pp. 134-55 in *From Childhood to Adolescence: A Transitional Period?* edited by R. Montemayor, G.R. Adams and T.P. Gulotta. Newbury Park, CA: Sage.

_____, C. Midgley, and T. Adler. 1984. "Grade-Related Changes in the School Environment: Effects on Achievement Motivation." Pp. 283-331 in *The Development of Achievement Motivation*, edited by J.G. Nicholls. Greenwich, CT: JAI Press.

Ensminger, M.E. and A.L. Slusarcick. 1992. "Paths to High School Graduation or Dropout: A Longitudinal Study of a First Grade Cohort." *Sociology of Education* 65:95-113.

Entwisle, D.R. and K.L. Alexander. 1989. "Early Schooling as a 'Critical Period' Phenomenon." Pp. 27-55 in *Sociology of Education and Socialization*, edited by K. Namboodiri and R.G. Corwin. Greenwich, CT: JAI Press.

_____ and K.L. Alexander. 1993. "Entry Into Schools: The Beginning School Transition and Educational Stratification in the United States." Pp. 401-23 in *Annual Review of Sociology*, vol. 19. Palo Alto, CA: Annual Reviews, Inc.

Epstein, J.L. and D.J. MacIver. 1990. Education in the Middle Grades: *National Trends and Practices*. Columbus, OH: National Middle School Association.

Fine, M. 1991. *Framing Dropouts: Notes on the Politics of an Urban Public High School.* Albany, NY: State University of New York Press.

Gamoran, A. 1986. "Instructional and Institutional Effects of Ability Grouping." *Sociology of Education* 59:185-98.

_____. 1992. "Access to Excellence: Assignment to Honors English Classes in the Transition to High School." *Educational Evaluation and Policy Analysis* 3:185-204.

_____. 1993. "Alternative Uses of Ability Grouping in Secondary Schools: Can We Bring High-Quality Instruction to Low-Ability Classes?" *American Journal of Education* 102:122.

Garet, M. and B.D. DeLany. 1988. "Students, Courses and Stratification." *Sociology of Education* 61:61-77.

Haller, E.J. 1985. "Pupil Race and Elementary School Ability Grouping: Are Teachers Biased Against Black Children?" *American Educational Research Journal* 22:456-83.

_____ and S.A. Davis. 1980. "Does Socioeconomic Status Bias the Assignment of Elementary School Students to Reading Groups?" *American Educational Research Journal* 17:409-18.

Hallinan, M.T. 1992. "The Organization of Students for Instruction in the Middle School." Sociology of Education 65:114-27.

_____ and A.B. Sørensen. 1983. "The Formation and Stability of Instructional Groups." *American Sociological Review* 48:83851.

Hauser, R.M. 1970. "Educational Stratification in the United States." Pp. 102-29 in *Social Stratification: Research and Theory for the 1970s*, edited by E.O. Laumann. New York: Bobbs-Merrill.

Heller, K.A., W.H. Holtzman, and S. Messick, eds. 1982. *Placing Children in Special Education: A Strategy for Equity.* Washington, DC: National Academy Press.

Hoffer, T.B. 1992. "Middle School Ability Grouping and Student Achievement in Science and Mathematics." *Educational Evaluation and Policy Analysis* 14:205-27.

House, E.R. 1989. "Policy Implications of Retention Research." Pp. 202-13 in *Flunking Grades: Research and Policies on Retention*, edited by L.A. Shepard and M.L. Smith. London: Falmer Press.

Karweit, N. 1992. "Retention Policy." Pp. 1114-18 in *Encyclopedia of Educational Research*, edited by M. Alkin. New York: Macmillan.

Kelly, S.P. 1989. "15,000 City Students Failed Despite Debate Over Promotions." *The Evening Sun*, 25 July, C1.

Kerckhoff, A.C. 1993. *Diverging Pathways: Social Structure and Career Deflections.* New York: Cambridge Press.

Kilgore, S.B. 1991. "The Organizational Context of Tracking in Schools." *American Sociological Review* 56:189-203.

_____ and W.W. Pendleton. 1993. "The Organizational Context of Learning: Framework for Understanding the Acquisition of Knowledge." *Sociology of Education* 66:63-87.

Kulik, J.A. and C.L. Kulik. 1987. "Effects of Ability Grouping on Student Achievement." *Equity and Excellence* 23:22-30.

Lee, V.E. and A.S. Bryk. 1988. "Curriculum Tracking as Mediating the Social Distribution of High School Achievement." *Sociology of Education* 61:78-94.

_____ and J.B. Smith. 1993. "Effects of School Restructuring on the Achievement and Engagement of Middle-Grade Students." *Sociology of Education* 66:164-87.

Leinhardt, G. and A. Pallay. 1982. "Restrictive Educational Settings: Exile or Haven?" *Review of Educational Research* 54:557-78.

Lloyd, D.N. 1978. "Prediction of School Failure from Third-Grade Data." *Educational and Psychological Measurement* 38:1911200.

Madden, N.A. and R.A. Slavin. 1983. "Mainstreaming Students with Mild Handicaps: Academic and Social Outcomes." *Review of Educational Research* 53:519-69.

McPartland, J.M., J.R. Coldiron, and J.H. Braddock. 1987. *School Structures and Classroom Practices in Elementary, Middle and Secondary Schools.* Report No. 14. The Johns Hopkins University, Center for Research on Elementary and Middle Schools.

Mehan, H. 1992. "Understanding Inequality in Schools: The Contribution of Interpretive Studies." *Sociology of Education* 65:1-20.

———, A. Hetweck, and J.L. Meihls. 1985. *Handicapping the Handicapped: Decision Making in Students' Careers.* Stanford, CA: Stanford University Press.

Mercer, J. 1974. *Labelling the Mentally Retarded.* Berkeley, CA: University of California Press.

Oakes, J. 1988. "Tracking in Mathematics and Science Education: A Structural Contribution to Unequal Schooling." Pp. 106-25 in *Class, Race and Gender in American Education,* edited by L. Weis. Albany, NY: State University of New York Press.

———. 1989/90. "Opportunities, Achievement and Choice: Women and Minority Students in Science and Mathematics." *Review of Research in Education* 16:153-222.

———. 1992. "Can Tracking Research Inform Practice? Technical, Normative and Political Considerations." *Educational Researcher* 21:12-21.

———, A. Gamoran, and R.N. Page. 1992. "Curriculum Differentiation: Opportunities, Outcomes and Meanings." Pp. 570-608 in *Handbook of Research on Curriculum,* edited by P.W. Jackson. New York: Macmillan.

Office of Special Education Programs. 1991. *To Assure the Free Appropriate Public Education of All Children with Disabilities: Thirteenth Annual Report to Congress of the Implementation of the Individuals with Disabilities Act.* Washington, DC: U.S. Department of Education.

Pallas, A.M., D.R. Entwisle, K.L. Alexander, and M.F. Stluka. 1994. "Ability-Group Effects: Instructional, Social or Institutional?" *Sociology of Education* 67:27-46.

Peterson, S.E., J.S. DeGracie, and C.R. Ayabe. 1987. "A Longitudinal Study of the Effects of Retention/Promotion on Academic Achievement." *American Educational Research Journal* 27:107-18.

Pierson, L.H. and J.P. Connell. 1992. "Effect of Grade Retention on Self-System Processes, School Engagement and Academic Performance." *Journal of Educational Psychology* 84:300-07.

Powell, A., E. Farrar, and D.K. Cohen. 1985. *The Shopping Mall High School.* Boston: Houghton-Mifflin.

Reuman, D.A. 1989. "How Social Comparison Mediates the Relation Between Ability-grouping Practices and Students' Achievement Expectancies in Mathematics." *Journal of Educational Psychology* 81:178-89.

Reynolds, A.J. 1992. "Grade Retention and School Adjustment: An Explanatory Analysis." *Educational Evaluation and Policy Analysis* 14:101-21.

Reynolds, M.C. 1984. "Classification of Students with Handicaps." *Review of Research in Education* 11:63-92.

Rist, R. 1970. "Social Class and Teacher Expectations: The Self-Fulfilling Prophecy in Ghetto Education." *Harvard Educational Review* 40:411-51.

Rosenbaum, J.E. 1976. Making Inequality. New York: Wiley.

———. 1980. "Some Implications of Educational Grouping." *Review of Research in Education* 8:361-401.

———. 1984. "The Social Organization of Instructional Grouping." Pp. 53-68 in *The Social Context of Instruction: Group Organization and Group Process,* edited by P.L. Peterson, L.C. Wilkinson and M. Hallinan. San Diego: Academic Press.

Rowan, B. and A.W. Miracle. 1983. "Systems of Ability Grouping and the Stratification of Achievement in Elementary Schools." *Sociology of Education* 56:133-44.

Shepard, L.A. and M.L. Smith. 1989. "Introduction and Overview." *Flunking Grades: Research and Policies on Retention*, edited by L.A. Shepard and M.L. Smith. London: Falmer Press.

Singer, J.D., J.S. Palfrey, J.A. Butler, and D.K. Walker. 1989. "Variation in Special Education Classification Across School Districts: How Does Where You Live Affect What You Are Labeled?" *American Educational Research Journal* 26:261-81.

Slavin, R.E. 1987. "Ability Grouping and Student Achievement in Elementary Schools: A Best-Evidence Synthesis." *Review of Educational Research* 57:293-336.

Sørensen, A.B. 1970. "Organizational Differentiation of Students and Educational Opportunity." *Sociology of Education* 43:35576.

_____. 1987. "The Organizational Differentiation of Students in Schools as an Opportunity Structure." Pp. 103-29 in *The Social Organization of Schools: New Conceptualizations of the Learning Process*, edited by M.T. Hallinan. New York: Plenum.

_____ and M. Hallinan. 1984. "Effects of Race on Assignment to Ability Groups." Pp. 85-103 in *The Social Context of Instruction: Group Organization and Group Processes*, edited by P.L. Peterson, L.C. Wilkinson and L.C. Hallinan. New York: Academic Press.

Stevenson, D., K. Schiller, and B. Schneider. 1994. "Sequences of Opportunities for Learning." *Sociology of Education* 67:185-198.

Stroup, A.L. and L.N. Robins. 1972. "Elementary School Predictors of High School Dropout Among Black Males." *Sociology of Education* 45:212-22.

Viadero, D. 1992. "Report Finds Record Jump in Special-Education Enrollment." *Education Week* 11:19.

6

Peer Social Networks and Adolescent Career Development

Charles E. Bidwell
Stephen Plank
The University of Chicago
Chandra Muller
The University of Texas, Austin

This paper explores how adolescents' egocentric peer friendship networks affect the process of career development. By career development, we mean the processes that induce change in a young person's beliefs and information about work, conceptions of self (especially as a worker), and expectations, aspirations, and decisions about education and employment.

Elsewhere in this volume, Gamoran, in agreement with Elder (1995), argues that the life course can be conceptualized fruitfully as a series of transitions that vary from one life to another, rather than as a fixed sequence of stages that is essentially invariant across lives. Lives can differ in the transitions they display, in the onset and duration of these transitions, and to some degree in the sequences that they form. O'Rand takes the same view of the life course and shows us how little we know about the processes through which life course transitions and their variation come about—fundamentally, the contributions of human agency and social institutions to these processes and the relationships of the volitional and institutional in lives being lived. Mortimer addresses these matters with specific reference to occupational attainment. She advocates a social psychological approach in which occupational histories are analyzed as outcomes of individual efforts to realize values and motives within a social structure of opportunities and constraints.

Our findings will address certain of these issues. They will provide evidence of ways in which young people's knowledge and beliefs about work, their participation in high school, and their educational and occupational plans vary with the form of their school-specific egocentric peer friendship networks and with the beliefs and activities that characterize these groups of friends.

With varying degrees of self-awareness and foresight, young people shape and direct their lives according to what they know and believe about themselves and about their immediate and future prospects. We conceive of friendship networks as among the prime social situations within which young people's lives unfold. Our findings will give some indication of these volitional elements in adolescent career development. They will also suggest that the peer networks that form in the school are small systems of communication and interpersonal influence that affect young people's occupational knowledge and beliefs, their conceptions of themselves, and their plans for education and work.

We will consider how the normative and behavioral content and the form of high school students' peer networks, along with the respondents' own centrality within them, affect their participation in the everyday activities of school and their longer-term knowledge, beliefs, and plans about education and jobs. We will provide evidence that these networks mediate relationships between young persons' career development and the broader institutional contexts of school and, to an extent, family.

Our study follows a long tradition of research on significant others (friends, parents, teachers) as mediating actors in processes of educational and occupational status attainment (e.g., Alexander and Campbell, 1964; Alexander, Eckland, and Griffin, 1975; Haller, 1982). This work has had a seminal influence on our thinking about the formation of educational and occupational plans and aspirations within the school context, by opening up the black box of the school. Most of this work has been on the high school, and it has shown the importance of interpersonal relationships as links between where students are located in a school's social and moral order and what they think about their educational and occupational prospects and how they evaluate them.

However, there is more to do. This research has not considered how educational or occupational plans and aspirations may form in the context of beliefs and information about work. In addition, it is essentially research on dyads, in which properties of networks are simple sums of dyadic properties. For example, in this approach, one might sum the occupational plans of a student's significant others to measure interpersonal influence on the student's own aspirations. However, dyads usually are embedded in structures of social ties, and these network structures can substantially strengthen or weaken dyadic influence on what people think and do.

Whether one thinks of social networks as in fact composed of dyads and cliques (e.g., Friedkin, 1993) or of structurally equivalent positions (e.g.,

Burt, 1992), these networks must be treated as multifunctional – social structures for communicating information, arrays of sentimental bonds that ground influence and persuasion, and intimate arenas for self-other reference that enable comparative self-evaluation. We will present findings about the first two of these functions—how access to information affects the range and accuracy of occupational knowledge, how exposure to persuasion affects values, beliefs, and participation in school, and how both information and persuasion affect educational and occupational ambition indirectly, via their more proximate direct effects on school participation.

Concepts and Propositions

Our conceptual framework is based on Simmel's (1950:40, 1971:41-140) analysis of the elements of primary social relations, especially his distinction between their form and content. It has evolved during the process of data analysis, so that the findings that we will report are not strict tests of a priori hypotheses.

Our argument rests on three assumptions about the consequences of egocentric social networks for what people believe, know, and do. The first assumption concerns network form. We construe network form broadly, to include both properties of the network structure and properties of the location of individuals within this structure. We will be concerned with two aspects of structure—network density and network closure. Density denotes the proportion of possible ties in a network that are in fact observed. Closure refers to the rate at which a network's members form ties with persons outside the network. We will consider one aspect of individual location in a network. This construct is centrality—the ratio of the rate at which a member (ego) receives interaction from others in the network (alters) to the aggregate rate at which the alters receive interaction from ego and all other alters.

We assume that network form can affect beliefs, knowledge, and behavior through its consequences for communication and persuasion. With respect to communication, the denser a network, the greater its communicative efficiency should be because as density increases, the number of incomplete pathways (communication blockages) in the network decreases. The more closed a network, the smaller the number of information items that can enter the network because as closure increases, the number of entry points from outside the network decreases. As a result, the more closed the network, the more information redundancy it should contain. Hence, relatively few items of information are acquired by any member, although what is acquired may be learned very well. Finally, the more central a member's location in a network, the greater the number of information pathways that reach this person. Therefore, the more central the member, the greater the number of items of information that this person should receive.

With respect to persuasion, we expect the primary persuasive effect of an interpersonal tie to occur as a result of the strength of the sentimental bond in the dyad. Density is a reasonable measure of the aggregate strength of an individual's ties to the members of his or her group. Therefore, we expect the members of a network to experience more persuasion in a network the greater its density. Closure may have some reinforcing effect on network persuasion by raising the salience of the network in its members' eyes.

Our second assumption concerns network content. Neither communication nor persuasion is content-free. In the one case, information is transmitted and, in the other, there is an effort by one member of a dyad to bring the other closer to some standard of belief or conduct. Therefore, we assume that what a network's members know, believe, and do will vary directly with the aggregate level and the distribution of knowledge, belief, and behavior in their egocentric networks. About the distribution of this content, information diversity should increase the range of any member's knowledge. Diversity of beliefs and behavior should increase the normative and behavioral options open to a member and consequently reduce the likelihood of compliance with any given norm or behavioral pattern.

To some degree any such relationships will result from homophilic selection. Nevertheless, they should also arise from communication or influence processes within existing networks, often to a substantial degree. In fact, the most interesting relationships that we will explore will be contingent relationships between network content and network form. The covariation of network content and individual knowledge, beliefs, or conduct should be strengthened or weakened by variation in the properties of network form that we have just discussed. These contingent effects will appear in our findings as statistical interactions of measures of network content and form, and we expect them to be the primary ways in which network form is associated with individual level measures of knowledge, belief, and behavior. There may be one exception to this proposition. If efficient network communication and relatively open network boundaries increase the volume and diversity of information in a network, network density and closure may have direct effects on the accuracy and amount of information that members acquire.

Our third assumption is about the time horizons of adolescent's peer relationships. We assume that by comparison with many adult social networks (e.g., colleague relationships at work, ties among neighbors or kin), these time horizons are short. Among young people, network membership and activities tend to change frequently with age and changing situations, so that the primary interests found in these networks are relatively transient (Hallinan and Tuma, 1978; Epstein, 1983). Consequently,

FIGURE 6.1   The Career Development Process

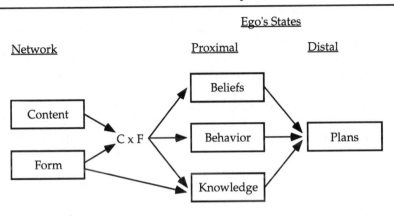

we expect the direct effects of our network variables (measures of content and the interactions of content and form) to be limited to behavior and knowledge and to present-oriented beliefs. We expect these networks to affect beliefs about the longer term, such as educational and occupational plans, only indirectly via their direct effects on the more proximal beliefs and on knowledge and conduct.

These expectations are summarized in Figure 6.1. In this diagram, the relationships between network form and content and longer-term plans are mediated by the young person's current sets of beliefs, job knowledge, and behavior in school. These proximal variables are themselves affected by the interaction of network form and content, with an additional main effect of network form on job knowledge.

Figure 6.1 contains no exogenous variables. We have not made predictions concerning relationships between network form or content and such exogenous variables as the subject's own ascriptive traits, his or her socioeconomic background, the size or student composition of the high school, or the subject's high school curricular track, year in school, or grade point average. These relationships are not our primary interest.

Data and Procedures

Research sites and samples

Our findings come from the first year of a multi-wave study of the adolescent and early adult life course. The primary focus of this study is on career development from the preadolescent years into the early years of full-time labor force participation. The principal contribution of this study will be made by analyzing developmental relationships between the subjects' evolving life courses and situational change at the immediate level of interpersonal social relations and at higher levels of social organization. (On the distinction between standard longitudinal analysis and developmental life course analysis, see Sampson and Laub, 1995.) Nevertheless, a preliminary examination of the first year's cross-sectional findings—here concerning associations between life course states and interpersonal ties—will be instructive.

Multi-wave data are being gathered in thirteen American public high schools and, for each high school, two feeder middle schools. In each of these high schools, the study drew samples at random of the 1992-93 10th and 12th grade student cohorts and in each of the middle schools of the 6th and 8th grade cohorts. The sampled students are to be followed with annual waves of measurement over at least five years (including those subjects who leave the original research sites).

These schools are located in twelve communities (in one of which two high schools and the corresponding middle schools are participating in the study). These communities vary widely in economic and population characteristics. Our data come from six of the thirteen high schools. We chose six sites in which we came closest to an adequate enumeration of the respondents' egocentric networks – at the minimum, a median enumeration rate of twenty percent. In fact, for the six schools in our sample, the median enumeration rate is 0.36. The mean is 0.35, with a standard deviation of 0.23. For the seven schools we have excluded, the median enumeration rate is 0.09; the mean is 0.13, with a standard deviation of 0.15.

Although we will analyze data from only six sites, these high schools differ markedly in socioeconomic composition and curricular emphasis. Two of the schools are those from the same large midwestern city. Here, Magnet High School recruits students city-wide, and, because there is a large applicant pool, it is highly selective academically. Students are chosen for this school on the basis of test performance, teachers' recommendations, and interviews. Magnet High enrolls about 900 students, of whom some 60 per cent are white and another 30 per cent African-American. The student body is diverse socioeconomically. About 90 per cent of its students take at least one Advanced Placement college preparatory course, and the school sends about three-fourths of its graduates to four-year colleges and universities, along with another 20 per cent to two-year colleges. Its four-year drop-out rate is less than five per cent.

In contrast, Roosevelt High School serves a local attendance area and enrolls about 1400 students, of whom about 60 percent are African-American students and 30 per cent white. About half of its students come from families below the Federal poverty line and about 60 per cent are from single parent families. However, dropping out of Roosevelt is comparatively rare (a four-year rate of some ten per cent). About 70 per cent of its graduates go to college, of whom about 50 per cent enroll in two-year institutions.

Forest View High School serves an inner-city student body in one of America's largest cities. Forest View has 1,200 students, of whom 60 per cent are Hispanic, 15 per cent African-American, and another 15 per cent non-Hispanic white. Some 90 per cent of these students are from below the poverty line and about three-fourths from single parent homes. The four-year drop-out rate in this school is 40 per cent, and of the graduates about 20 per cent attend four-year colleges and another 20 per cent two-year schools.

Middlebrook High School is located in an affluent suburb of a prosperous East Coast city. The high school district is somewhat diverse occupationally and ethnically, but the population is predominantly white and is composed mainly of upper-level professionals and managers. Middlebrook enrolls 1,700 students. About 70 per cent of these students are white, and the remaining students are racially diverse. Very few are from families in poverty.

This high school has an established tradition of academic excellence and sends about three-fourths of its graduates to four-year institutions. Its four-year drop-out rate is less than one per cent. Middlebrook has strong Advanced Placement and honors programs in each of the principal arts and sciences areas, located within a structure of strongly bounded curricular tracks (college prep, general, and vocational). Students here enjoy an extensive extra-curricular and athletic program, but the participants come overwhelmingly from the college prep track.

Grosse Chute High School is the central high school of an upper midwestern industrial city, with a population of about 200,000. This city is relatively prosperous, but it contains pockets of poverty and has an unemployment rate of about 15 per cent. Its population is predominantly white. The city's population composition is mirrored in Grosse Chute's 1,500 students. Ninety per cent are white, and 15 per cent come from families below the poverty line. The four-year drop-out rate is a bit under 15 per cent, but it is important to remember that many of these young people drop out to enter jobs or to marry. The school maintains a large, specialized vocational program that enrolls about a fourth of the students. Another fourth are enrolled in the college prep curriculum, but in contrast to those of some of the schools already described, Advanced Placement courses are limited in number and scope. Many of the vocational graduates continue in community college. About half of the college prep graduates attend four-year schools, the rest two-year colleges.

River High School serves a midwestern town of about 15,000 inhabitants. This town provides service to a surrounding farming area and is the home of a number of prosperous light industries. River High enrolls approximately 1,400 students, of whom 90 per cent are white. About 15 per cent come from homes below the poverty line. Very few are from single parent families. The four-year drop out rate is five per cent. This high school offers a comprehensive curriculum, with an active vocational component and a small college prep program. Its Advanced Placement coverage is spotty. Of its graduates, only about 10 per cent attend four-year colleges, while 50 per cent enroll in two-year schools (most of these a local community college). Of the remainder, the boys tend to go directly to work. Although some of the girls go to work, many choose to marry and remain out of the labor force.

Measurement

In the present study, we used three sets of data, each collected in a group questionnaire administration during the 1992-93 school year. We constructed measures of the respondents' schools and families and of their activities, beliefs, and educational and occupational plans from responses to items in a questionnaire that replicates portions of the NELS:88 survey of American high school students (Ingels, 1990). We built our measure of occupational knowledge from a fifteen-item battery in another questionnaire that is devoted to knowledge and images of work. This scale measures accuracy of knowledge about a range of white and blue collar jobs and job-related issues in the American occupational structure. It does not cover work in the informal economy. We describe these measures in greater detail in Appendix A.

To measure attributes of the respondents' egocentric friendship networks, we drew on nominations made by the members of our samples. Each of the respondents completed a form in which he or she listed the names of up to fourteen people in response to the question, "Who are the friends you usually hang around with?" In addition to listing the names, the respondent gave each nominee's gender and indicated whether the friend was a neighbor, classmate, co-member of an activity like a band or club, or something else (which was specified).[1]

The samples were stratified by gender and ethnicity and, in some of our schools, by level of academic performance (at the minimum honors vs. others). Thus, we have data that can be used to form chooser-chosen matrices for network analysis, accompanied by other data that can be used to derive measures of network composition.

We constructed simple measures of network size and structure. Our measure of network size is the number of alters nominated by the respondent from his or her school and grade. In lieu of a standard measure of network density, we will use a measure that we call cohesion. In our usage, cohesion is the proportion of alters in an egocentric network who nominated at least one other alter in this network as a member of *their own* egocentric friendship networks.

We decided to use this cohesion measure rather than a standard density

measure because we discovered that the distribution of alter-alter nominations was severely skewed. Relatively few alters in any of these networks
nominated more than one or two other alters, so that the ratio of possible to
observed one-way within-network ties is badly attenuated. Our cohesion
measure and this ratio, which is the standard density measure, are reasonably strongly correlated ($r = .63$).

Our measure of closure is the ratio of within-network ties originating
from the network's members to the total number of ties originated by these
respondents. Finally, our measure of centrality is somewhat different from
the most commonly used measures of centrality. We have defined a
respondent's (ego's) centrality as the quotient of two ratios. The ratio in the
numerator is ego's observed number of nominations received from the
alters in the egocentric network divided by ego's possible received nominations. Possible nominators are limited to persons who were nominated by
ego and who, in turn, responded to our questionnaire. The ratio in the
denominator is the average of the comparable ratios, calculated for each of
ego's nominated friends (alters). Possible nominations for each of the alters
are again limited to those from people in ego's network who responded to
our questionnaire.

Because our network measures are based on friendship ties to other
students within the respondent's school grade, we will lose some information about peer relations outside the school and grade as a context for career
development. However, we assume that the school grade for most high
school students encompasses the greater number of friendship choices.

Findings

Although we have made no predictions about the action of exogenous
variables, several variables that were indicators either of the respondents'
ascriptive traits or social origins or of their current school settings proved
to be substantially correlated with endogenous and dependent variables in
our models. Sets of these variables were treated as exogenous in our
models. Therefore, each of the series of models to be described below
consists of four blocks of variables. (See Appendix A for detailed information about these variables.) The first three blocks include the exogenous
variables. Block 1 contains the measures of ego's gender and level of
parental education. In one series of models, this block also includes measures of parental occupation and ego's own educational expectations. Block
2 is a series of dummy variables for ego's school site, serving as a proxy for
such school attributes as the composition of the student body and the degree
and kind of curricular specialization. Block 3 locates ego in this school,
either in relation to the distribution of student attainment—the respondent's
grade point average (GPA)—or in relation to the formal structure of the

school—year in school and self-reported high school track placement.

These blocks of exogenous variables are followed by measures of the content of ego's network (belief, information, or behavior), measures of network form, and terms for the interaction of content and form. We will report the Ordinary Least Squares (OLS) evaluation of these models.

Although our data are cross-sectional, we have some basis for inferences about the relative importance of selection versus communication and persuasion in the relationships we will observe between network form and content and ego's measured beliefs, behavior, and plans. When selection effects are strong, there should be correspondingly strong correlations between ego's belief, behavior, or plan and the corresponding mean for the alters in the network. In this case, expanding a model to include measures of network structure, like cohesion or centrality, and terms for the interaction of these variables with network content, should add little to the explained variance. At the same time, the size and statistical significance of the parameter estimates for the first and third blocks of exogenous variables, that is, the measures of ego's own traits, should be reduced. To the extent that these two criteria are satisfied, we will infer that selection effects are stronger than those of communication or persuasion. To the extent that adding terms for network structure and structure-content interactions increases a model's predictive power and to the extent that parameter estimates for the first and third blocks of exogenous variables are not reduced in size and significance, we will infer that communication or influence effects were relatively strong.

Participation in school

Tables 6.1 and 6.2 present the evaluation of models that predict behavior in school. Table 6.1 reports the findings for the number of extra-curricular activities engaged in (other than sports), while Table 6.2 contains the results for school trouble (our measure of the severity of the respondents self-reported infractions of school rules).[2]

These tables present a sharp contrast, according to the foregoing reasoning. Extra-curricular participation appears to have been substantially influenced within ego's network. However, although we find a significant association between ego's school trouble score and the alters' mean score, this relationship appears to have arisen chiefly from the selective formation of peer ties.

In Table 6.1, Model I reports the effect parameters for a model in which the predictors are our three blocks of exogenous variables. The results are straight-forward. Females are more likely than males to be involved in the non-sports extra-curriculum, as are respondents with better educated parents. By comparison with Grand Chutte respondents (the reference category), respondents from Magnet High School show an unusually high level of

TABLE 6.1   Models of Ego's Non-Sport Extracurricular Participation[a]

	I	II	III	IV
Intercept	-0.51	-0.59*	-0.28	-0.45
Female	0.34***	0.34**	0.37***	0.35**
Parent's Education	0.10***	0.09**	0.09**	0.09**
Forest View	-0.11	-0.06	-0.04	-0.05
River	-0.46*	-0.39*	-0.33	-0.35
Middlebrook	-0.35*	-0.20	-0.14	-0.18
Roosevelt	0.27	0.24	0.28	0.26
Magnet	0.59***	0.45*	0.40*	0.41*
GPA	0.41***	0.37***	0.36***	0.37***
Senior	0.43***	0.34**	0.36**	0.33**
College Prep Track	0.47***	0.41**	0.37**	0.40**
Voc/Tech Track	0.42	0.43	0.46*	0.42
Mean of Friends' # of Non-Sports		0.18***	-0.05	0.08
Cohesion			-1.36**	
Cohesion*Mean of Friends' # of Non-Sports			0.94***	
Centrality				-0.18
Centrality*Mean of Friends' # of Non-Sports				0.11*
Adjusted R^2	0.234	0.249	0.265	0.251

n = 653   * p < .05   ** p<.01   *** p<.001
[a]See Appendix A for descriptions of dependent and independent variables.

extra-curricular participation, while those from River High, the small town school with a restricted extra-curriculum, an unusually low level. It is more surprising to find that respondents from Middlebrook High also are comparatively less active participants in the extra-curriculum. However, other of our data show that the Middlebrook community was distinctive in the range of non-school activities available to high school youth, and many Middlebrook students take part in these programs. Finally, getting good grades, being in the college prep rather than the general track, and being a senior rather than a sophomore were each positively associated with extra-curricular participation.

In the remaining three models, we introduce measures of the egocentric networks. Adding these variables adds appreciably to the explained variance, while the effect parameters for the first and third blocks of exogenous variables are essentially unaffected. It is interesting to observe that the significant associations between school site and extracurricular

TABLE 6.2   Models of Ego's School Trouble[a]

	I	II	III	IV
Intercept	7.87***	5.87***	6.26***	6.00***
Female	-0.38	-0.27	-0.24	-0.22
Parent's Education	-0.07	-0.08	-0.08	-0.07
Forest View	0.32	0.11	0.08	0.11
River	- 1.88***	-1.37***	- 1.28***	- 1.32***
Middlebrook	-0.09	0.03	0.07	0.04
Roosevelt	-0.61	-0.49	-0.56	-0.51
Magnet	-1.46***	-1.03**	-1.00**	-0.98**
GPA	-1.09***	-0.88***	-0.85***	-0.87***
Senior	0.37	0.30	0.27	0.30
College Prep Track	-0.20	-0.10	-0.09	-0.09
Voc/Tech Track	0.82*	0.73	0.69	0.68
Mean of Friends' School Trouble		0.32***	0.26***	0.31***
Cohesion			- 1.68	
Cohesion*Mean of Friends' School Trouble			0.19	
Centrality				-0.18
Centrality*Mean of Friends' School Trouble				0.01
Adjusted R^2	0.202	0.253	0.256	0.252

n = 710   * p < .05   ** p<.01   *** p<.001
[a]See Appendix A for descriptions of dependent and independent variables.

participation are to a modest degree mediated by properties of the respondents' egocentric networks.

In Model II, we find a substantial association between the mean level of alters' and ego's participation. When we introduce the measures of network form—cohesion in Model III and ego's centrality in Model IV—we find significant interactions of network form and content.[3] In each case, the association between the aggregate activity level of the alters in the network and ego's activity becomes stronger the more cohesive the network and the more central ego's location in it.[4]

The parameter estimates in Table 6.2, for the prediction of school trouble, suggest a stronger influence of selection effects than those of the prior table. In Model I, the results again are sensible. The more trouble-prone respondents are least likely to be found in Magnet or River High and, within their schools, most likely to be in the vocational track. They tend to have low grades.

When the network measures enter the models (Models II-IV), the explained variance increases, but the only significant network correlate of ego's school trouble is the level of his or her friends' school trouble. The significant coefficients in the third block of exogenous variables, for GPA and vocational track placement, now weaken and, in the latter case, lose statistical significance. Neither of the modeled structural variables has a significant main effect, and neither interaction term (content by form) is significant. If our reasoning is correct, we can infer that involvement in school trouble to a substantial degree preceded friendship formation.

Job knowledge

Table 6.3 presents the parameter estimates for five models that predict the respondents' scores on our job knowledge scale. Job knowledge should be especially sensitive to exposure to information about jobs. For this reason, we constructed the models to represent the respondent's involvement in four information environments: the family, the school, locations within the formal structure of the school, and the egocentric peer network.

Model I contains the blocks of exogenous variables. This model has been expanded to include a series of dummy variables that classify the occupation of whichever of the respondent's parents is the family's principal breadwinner. These categories group the occupations according to substance as well as standing—more complex and less complex professional jobs (Professional II vs. Professional I), managerial, lower white collar, laborer, and other blue collar. In this model, lower white collar is the omitted category. We assume that these job categories are reasonably valid indicators of the focus and range of job information available in the family. Given the content of the job knowledge scale, one might expect the children from families of middling occupational standing to score unusually well, on the assumption that the content of the parental occupation was reflected in the content of job information current in the family. However, scores on the job knowledge scale depend substantially on a range of knowledge, and a family's range of information might be expected to increase in rough approximation to increases in occupational standing, as a function of differences in families' human capital resources.

Model II introduces the network mean on the dependent variable. Model III extends the representation of network content to include the respondent's report of the principal current interests and activities of the alters in his or her network—the academic and social factor scale scores—to determine whether the chief activities and interests of this group of friends would affect the availability of job information in the network and the respondent's sensitivity to this information. Models IV and V introduce, respectively, network cohesion and ego's centrality, each accompanied by the corresponding interaction term.

TABLE 6.3   Models of Ego's Job Knowledge Score[a]

	I	II	III	IV	V
Intercept	-0.58	-0.58	-0.80	-0.60	-0.53
Female	0.09	0.09	0.10	0.11	0.10
Parent's Education	0.05	0.05	0.05	0.05	0.06
Ego's Educational Expectations	0.06	0.06	0.08*	0.09*	0.08*
Professional I	-0.13	-0.13	-0.15	-0.13	-0.16
Professional II	0.28	0.27	0.22	0.21	0.21
Manager/Administrator	0.17	0.17	0.19	0.18	0.15
Laborer	0.10	0.10	0.07	0.08	0.04
Other Blue Collar	0.25	0.25	0.23	0.21	0.22
Forest View	-0.40	-0.37	-0.28	-0.33	-0.33
River	0.18	0.18	0.23	0.27	0.29
Middlebrook	0.20	0.19	0.17	0.13	0.16
Roosevelt	0.13	0.12	0.20	0.20	0.20
Magnet	0.65**	0.62**	0.65**	0.57*	0.55*
GPA	0.17*	0.17*	0.19*	0.19*	0.18*
Senior	0.36**	0.35*	0.36**	0.34*	0.37**
College Prep Track	0.43**	0.42**	0.45**	0.45**	0.43**
Voc/Tech Track	0.00	0.00	0.07	0.06	-0.01
Mean of Friends' Job Knowledge		0.03	0.03	-0.15	-0.18
Academic Factor			-0.24***	-0.23 ***	-0.23***
Social Factor			-0.01	0.01	0.01
Cohesion				-1.03	
Cohesion*Mean of Friends' Job Knowledge				0.77**	
Centrality					-0.24*
Centrality*Mean of Friends' Job Knowledge					0.22**
Adjusted R²	0.127	0.125	0.141	0.150	0.155

n = 552   * p < .05   ** p<.01   *** p<.001
[a]See Appendix A for descriptions of dependent and independent variables.

To the extent that we have been able to measure the information environment of the respondents' families, the parameter estimates for Model I suggest that these families were not effective information sources for these young people. Neither the type of parental job nor the level of parental education is a significant predictor. Nonetheless, we had expected parental jobs to affect both the focus and range of job information in the family.

Moreover, one would expect the variety of job information, and perhaps the frequency of family discussion about such matters, to be a positive correlate of parental education.

There is evidence that the school itself is a more effective environment for informing our respondents about jobs. Respondents from Magnet High scored exceptionally well on the job knowledge scale. In contrast to each of the other schools, including the curricularly demanding Middlebrook High, Magnet High enrolls a student body of highly diverse social origins without being intensively tracked. Thus, in Magnet High information about a diversity of jobs and work worlds could be communicated from one student to another without encountering the structural blockages induced by a tracked curriculum. Tracking, by contrast, undoubtedly imposes substantial limits on students' ability to interact with others whose backgrounds and experiences differ from their own.

Within the school, students who are high performers score better than others, as do seniors compared with sophomores (the latter finding no doubt reflecting maturational and experiential changes in the life course). Of greater interest, perhaps, we see that the same track boundaries that limit and segregate student interaction, thereby evidently defining distinctive job information environments. They do so irrespective of the school in which they are located. The college prep track, compared with either the general or the vocational or technical track seems to confer an information advantage. This advantage presumably has several sources—the range and explicitness of information treated in courses, in face-to-face interaction with teachers, counselors, and fellow students, and in the context of those extra-curricular activities, like debate or publications, that draw their participants chiefly from the college prep track.

In Model II, we introduce the average level of the network alters' job knowledge scores and in Model III the two factor scores in which the respondent describes the degree to which his or her network of friends is oriented in interests and activities to things academic or more heavily in the realm of adolescent sociability. Model III presents a perplexing finding, to which we will turn in a moment. Note first that simply having friends who are well informed about work does not in itself seem to confer an information advantage on the respondents (Model II). However, the parameter estimates for the content-form interaction terms in Models IV and V are significant. When these interactions are plotted (see Figures 6.2 and 6.3), the plots show that when network cohesion is low or when ego's location in the network is relatively peripheral, the relationship between the network job score mean and ego's mean is essentially zero. However, the more cohesive the network or the more central ego's location, the more strongly positive this relationship becomes.

These findings are consistent with our notion of information environ-

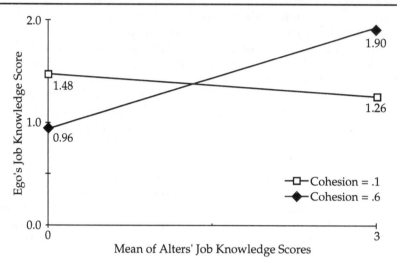

FIGURE 6.2 Mean of Alters' Job Knowledge Scores,
Ego's Job Knowledge Score, & Cohesion

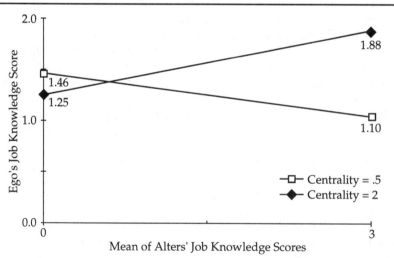

FIGURE 6.3 Mean of Alters' Job Knowledge Scores,
Ego's Job Knowledge Score, & Centrality

ments. They suggest that, along with the school and the track within the school, the egocentric network comprised a series of paths for communicating information about the work world. In this interpretation, the more cohesive the network, the more complete the set of paths and the fewer the communication barriers. Similarly, the more central ego's location, the greater his or her relative exposure to incoming messages. In short, both of the interaction terms suggest conditions affecting the efficiency of the egocentric network as an information system.

The greater efficiency of the more cohesive networks may also have arisen from the greater salience or persuasiveness of information coming from others whom ego trusted (as a function of positive sentiment), while our finding concerning centrality may indicate effects not only of communication, but also of status (e.g., the most informed in a group of the informed thereby gaining a central position). Our data do not allow us to disentangle the specific mechanisms involved in these associations, but communication almost certainly would prove to be prominent among them.

In any event, selection mechanisms to not appear to be the primary source of the association of network properties and job knowledge scores. In the models of Table 6.3, the block of network variables makes its own contribution to predictive power, while adding measures of network structure to Models IV and V does not alter the significant parameter estimates in the third block of exogenous variables.

It is difficult to understand the negative sign of the coefficients for Ego's Academic Factor Score found consistently in Models III through V. The negative coefficient does not appear to be artifactual. If the more academically oriented networks are those in which the greater amount and diversity of information circulates, an intuitively reasonable expectation, then this coefficient should be positive. Note that once this factor score enters the model, the coefficient for the respondent's own educational expectations, which is positive, becomes statistically significant, suggesting that friends' academic orientations depressed the job knowledge scores of even the more academically oriented respondents.

This finding might be interpreted as indicating a lack of information diversity in the more academically oriented networks, as a result of some distinctive narrowing or focusing of interests or experiences. However, a fairly wide range of interest and experience indicators available in our data did not show marked differences between the more and the less academically oriented networks. If anything, the members of the more academically-oriented groups of friends were somewhat more likely than others to participate across a spectrum of information-giving activities. Perhaps subtle interpersonal comparison processes were at work that we could not discern. In any event, this finding requires more investigation and, for the moment, remains a puzzle.

Educational and occupational plans

Table 6.4 reports our findings for the prediction of the respondents' educational plans. We obtained somewhat similar findings for the prediction of expected occupational attainment, looking ahead to age 30, but the predictive power of these models is very small. Therefore, we will limit our discussion to the prediction of educational plans.

We introduce the mean of the alters' educational plans in Model II. Then, following the conceptual framework that was summarized in Figure 6.1, we introduce three measures of the respondent's proximal in-school behavior—the number of extracurricular activities (other than athletics), the hours spent in these activities, and the school trouble score. Extra-curricular hours and school trouble proved to be significant predictors and first appear in Model III. In Model IV, we add the respondent's depiction of the academic and social orientations of the friendship group and in the remaining models the measures of network cohesion, ego's centrality, and the accompanying content-form interaction terms.

For the most part, these findings replicate those of earlier educational attainment research, showing the distinctive importance of social origins, school attainment, track placement, and the beliefs, activities, and aspirations of significant others among a student's peers for the student's own educational plans. However, with respect to these associations between ego's plans and network content, the configuration of coefficients and predictive power in this series of models suggests that strong selection effects were at work.

For us, the more interesting findings have to do with the apparent role of extra-curricular participation as a mediating variable linking the content of these students' friendship networks to their educational expectations. We found, in a series of models not reported here, that the number of hours that our respondents spent in the non-sports extracurriculum was significantly predicted by mean alter's hours of such participation, with a pattern in the estimated models suggesting that more than selection had been at work to produce this association. We undertook a path analysis predicting ego's educational expectations, in which, among the endogenous variables, the academic and social factor scores and alters' hours are prior to ego's hours. This analysis shows that about half of the total effect of alters' hours on ego's educational plans is indirect, via ego's extra-curricular hours. Most of the total association of the two factor scores with the dependent variable is direct. These results provide a tentative indication that certain network effects on the longer-term, more distal outlooks of our respondents arose from more proximal patterns of activity (and perhaps associated beliefs and information) induced within the context of peer friendship.

TABLE 6.4   Model of Ego's Educational Expectations[a]

	I	II	III	IV	V	VI
Intercept	4.90***	3.98***	4.40***	4.59***	4.58***	3.91***
Female	0.21	0.21	0.22	0.16	0.15	0.10
Parent's Education	0.11**	0.11*	0.09*	0.09*	0.09*	0.07
Forest View	-0.14	- 0.07	-0.11	-0.19	-0.19	-0.15
River	-0.22	-0.17	-0.19	-0.25	-0.26	-0.36
Middlebrook	0.52*	0.41	0.46	0.36	0.36	0.40
Roosevelt	-0.21	-0.18	-0.10	-0.20	-0.19	-0.17
Magnet	-0.04	-0.10	-0.11	-0.17	-0.17	-0.22
GPA	0.35***	0.32***	0.22*	0.20*	0.20	0.20
Senior	0.28	0.25	0.29	0.19	0.20	0.20
College Prep Track	0.91***	0.85***	0.75***	0.73***	0.73***	0.73***
Voc/Tech Track	-0.29	-0.22	-0.17	-0.16	-0.16	-0.07
Mean of Friends' Educational Expectations		0.15*	0.11	0.11	0.11	0.18*
Ego's School Trouble			-0.05*	-0.02	-0.02	-0.02
Ego's Hours of Extracurriculars			0.16**	0.14**	0.13*	0.13*
Academic Factor				0.26**	0.26**	0.25**
Social Factor				-0.18*	-0.18*	-0.19*
Cohesion					0.07	
Cohesion*Mean of Friends' Expectations					0.01	
Centrality						0.80
Centrality*Mean of Friends' Expectations						-0.08
Adjusted R²	0.201	0.209	0.228	0.247	0.244	0.257

n = 503   * p<.05   ** p<.01   *** p<.001
[a]See Appendix A for descriptions of dependent and independent variables.

Conclusion

For the most part, our findings are consistent with the conceptual argument with which we opened this paper and with the life course perspective that characterizes many of the other papers in this volume. So far as proximal, in-school behavior is concerned, we have observed a systematic interplay of form and content in the egocentric friendship networks of our respondents that strongly suggests the persuasive influence of cohesive social ties on conduct, perhaps in conjunction with the social controls of norm-setting and self-other comparison.

In our findings on job knowledge and its correlates, we have found no less suggestive evidence of the importance of the network as a communication system and of network form as a set of attributes affecting the system's efficiency. Striking here is the way in which this informal system appears to work side-by-side with the communication pathways provided by the more formal structures of school curricula and by local district and school policies governing tracking and the composition of the student body.

Our findings are tentative and our measurement, especially of the family context, is incomplete. However, there are suggestions in these data of a possible reduction in the importance of the family as a source of occupational information for high school youth, giving the school, in both its formal and informal social organization, a more central place. One must bear in mind the modest predictive power of this series of models, which probably indicates unmeasured within-school communication and the action of information sources external to our conceptual scheme. Nevertheless, if our findings are borne out, they will depict the high school as an array of formal and informal social structures that make it an important locus for interventions designed to increase the occupational information effectively available to young people.

The friendship network as a place where information is communicated and proximal behavior and, presumably, beliefs are influenced, and how these networks stand in relation to other clusters of social ties and the more macroscopic levels of social organization—formal organizations and institutions—are major ideas underlying our conceptual argument and major strands in our findings. Especially in our greater ability to predict proximal events than more distal outcomes, we can see how involvement in networks of ties to peers (and by implication to adults), rather than determining life course events or outcomes, provides repertoires of information, behaviors, and beliefs that the young person can use as he or she makes decisions about next steps in life. No doubt the richness and the content of these repertories is in good measure a matter of institutionally ordered opportunities and constraints—a major point of juncture between the institutional and volitional in the life course.

Notes

The research reported in this chapter was supported by a grant from the Alfred P. Sloan Foundation. The authors alone and not the Foundation are responsible for the contents herein. We are grateful for the research assistance of Daniel McFarland, Rebecca Sandefur, and Jennifer Schmidt. We are no less grateful for the critical comments of members of the Duke University Conference on Institution and Careers, the Sociology of Education Brown Bag Seminar at the Ogburn-Stouffer Center, University of Chicago and colleagues in the Department of Sociology, University of Massachusetts, Amherst.

1. In addition, the respondent reported the frequency of interaction with each nominee, which of them was a "best friend," and which of them was a source or object of advice. These data are not used in the present analysis.

2. We examined five other proximal outcomes. These were absenteeism from school, number of athletic extra-curricular activities, hours spent in extra-curricular activities (athletics and others separately), hours of unassigned reading, and hours spent doing homework. We observed some effects of network form and content, but the findings are less clear-cut than those presented in Tables 1 and 2.

3. We do not include cohesion and centrality in the same model because they are highly correlated ($r = .46$).

4. Although we hypothesized some effect of network closure and also thought it important to include network size in our models, neither variable had significant effects when these models were estimated. In addition, for some of our models (including the series for job knowledge shown in Table 3), we suspected that there might be a three-way interaction between cohesion, closure, and alters' mean job knowledge. However, the parameter estimates for this three-way interaction were not significant. In the light of the foregoing, we have removed network size and closure from each of the models that we discuss.

References

Alexander, C. Norman and Ernest Q. Campbell. 1964. "Peer Influences on Adolescent Educational Aspirations and Attainments." *American Sociological Review* 29:568-575.

Alexander, Karl N., Bruce Eckland, and Larry J. Griffin. 1975. "The Wisconsin Model of Educational Achievement." *American Journal of Sociology* 81:324-342.

Burt, Ronald. 1992. *Structural Holes*. Cambridge, Mass.: Harvard University Press.

Elder, Glen H., Jr. 1995. "Human Lives in Changing Societies: Life Course and Developmental Insights." In *Developmental Science: Multi-Disciplinary Perspectives*, edited by R. B. Cairns, G. H. Elder, Jr. and E. J. Costello. New York: Cambridge University Press.

Epstein, Joyce L. 1983. "Selection of Friends in Differently Organized Schools and Classrooms." Pp. 73-92 in *Friends in School: Patterns of Selection and Influence in Secondary Schools*, edited by Joyce L. Epstein and Nancy Karweit. New York: Academic Press.

Friedkin, Noah E. 1993. "A Formal Theory of Social Power." *American Sociological Review* 58:861-872.

Haller, Archibald O. 1982. "Reflections on the Social Psychology of Status Attainment." Pp. 3-28 in *Social Structure and Behavior*, edited by Robert M. Hauser, David Mechanic, Archibald O. Haller and Taissa S. Hauser. New York: Academic Press.

Hallinan, Maureen T. and Nancy B. Tuma. 1978. "Classroom Effects on Changes in Children's Friendships." *Sociology of Education* 51:270-282.

Ingels, Steven J., Samir Y. Abraham, Rosemary Karr, Bruce D. Spencer and Martin D. Frankel. 1990. *NELS:88 Base Year Student Component Data File User's Manual*. Washington, D. C.: National Center for Educational Statistics.

Sampson, Robert J. and John H. Laub. 1994. "A Life Course Theory of Cumulative Disadvantage and the Stability of Delinquency." In *Developmental Theories of Crime and Delinquency: Advances in Criminological Theory, Vol. 6*, edited by Terence P. Thornberry. New Brunswick, N. J.: Transaction Publishers.

Simmel, Georg. 1950. *The Sociology of Georg Simmel*. Edited and translated by Kurt H. Wolff. New York: The Free Press.

_____. 1971. *On Individuality and Social Forms*. Edited by Donald N. Levine. Chicago: University of Chicago Press.

Appendix A

Descriptions and Distributions of Variables

I. Descriptions of Variables

Dependent Variables

Non-Sport Extracurricular Participation — Ranges from 0 to 9, based on participation in each of nine categories of school-based, non-athletic activities.

School Trouble — Ranges from 0 to 24, based on degree of trouble experienced in each of six categories of school-related disciplinary problems.

Job Knowledge Score — Rasch score constructed from twelve true-false items about a wide range of jobs and work-related terms. The range of items includes topics especially relevant to blue-collar and craft jobs (e.g., "An apprentice is a new worker who is assigned to learn a trade from a more skillful worker"), as well as topics relevant to expert professions (e.g., "Most lawyers spend their working days in court rooms"). The informal economy is not represented in the scale.

Educational Expectations — From question, "As things stand now, how far in school do you think you will get?" Response categories are: 1=less than h.s. graduation; 2=h.s. graduation only; 3=less than 2 years of vocational, trade, or business school; 4=2 years or more of vocational, trade, or business school; 5=less than 2 years of college; 6=2 or more years of college; 7=B.A.; 8=M.A., or equivalent; 9=Ph.D., M.D., or equivalent.

Independent Variables

Female — Dummy variable with male as the excluded reference category.

Parent's Education — Education level of more highly educated parent (or the one present, if only one is present).

Response categories are 1=did not finish h.s.; 2=h.s. graduation or GED; 3=vocational school, junior college, or other 2-year school; 4=some college; 5=B.A.; 6=M.A., or equivalent; 7=Ph.D., M.D., or equivalent.

Professional I
Professional II
Manager/Administrator
Laborer
Other Blue Collar
— Series of five dummy variables representing the occupation of the family's principal earner (father, if present and employed; otherwise, mother). Professional I includes jobs such as accountant and registered nurse. Professional II includes jobs such as physician and lawyer. Manager/Administrator includes jobs such as sales manager and restaurant manager. Laborer includes jobs such as construction worker and farm laborer. Other Blue Collar includes jobs such as mechanic and beautician. The excluded reference category, Lower White Collar, includes jobs such as bank teller and dental technician.

Forest View
River
Middlebrook
Roosevelt
Magnet
— Series of five dummy variables representing five of the six schools, with Grosse Chute as the excluded reference category.

GPA — Ranges from 0.5 to 4.0, with 0.5 representing grades "mostly below D" and 4.0 representing "mostly A's."

Senior — Dummy variable with sophomore as the excluded reference category.

College Prep Track
Voc/Tech Track
— Pair of dummy variables with general track as the excluded reference category.

Mean of Friends'
  Number of Non-Sports
— See description of dependent variable, above. Mean based on friends for whom non-missing responses were available.

Mean of Friends'
  School Trouble
— See description of dependent variable, above. Mean based on friends for whom non-missing responses were available.

Mean of Friends' Job Knowledge Score	See description of dependent variable, above. Mean based on friends for whom non-missing responses were available.
Mean of Friends' Educational Expectations	See description of dependent variable, above. Mean based on friends for whom non-missing responses were available.
Academic Factor	First factor (eigenvalue=3.83) derived from a factor analysis of eleven items following the question, "Among the friends you hang out with, how important is the following?" Most heavily loading items are attending class regularly, studying, getting good grades, and continuing education past high school.
Social Factor	Second factor (eigenvalue=2.00) derived from a factor analysis of eleven items following the question, "Among the friends you hang out with, how important is the following?" Most heavily loading items are having a steady boyfriend/girlfriend and being willing to party and get wild.
Cohesion	Proportion of alters in ego's nominated network who nominated at least one other alter in this network as a member of their own friendship networks. Based on alters who responded to our questionnaire.
Centrality	Quotient of numerator and denominator, where denominator is the ratio of ego's observed to possible nominations received from the alters in the egocentric network. Denominator is the average of the comparable ratios, calculated for each of ego's nominated friends (alters). In both numerator and denominator, possible nominations received are limited to those from people in ego's network who responded to our questionnaire.

II. Distributions of Variables.

All distributions are for the sample used in Table 3 except for Non-Sport Extracurricular Participation and corresponding friends' mean (sample from Table 1), School Trouble and corresponding friends' mean (sample from Table 2), and Educational Expectations and corresponding friends' mean (sample from Table 4).

Dependent Variables

Non-Sport Extracurricular Participation	Mean= 1.78		Std. Dev.= 1.51
School Trouble	Mean= 3.43		Std. Dev.= 2.92
Job Knowledge Score	Mean= 1.38		Std. Dev.= 1.53
Educational Expectations	Mean= 7.22		Std. Dev.= 1.81

Independent Variables

Female	1	62.5%	0	37.5%
Parent's Education	Mean= 4.10		Std. Dev.= 1.87	
Professional I	1	11.2%	0	88.8%
Professional II	1	7.6%	0	92.4%
Manager/Administrator	1	13.6%	0	86.4%
Laborer	1	10.5%	0	89.5%
Other Blue Collar	1	31.9%	0	68.1%
Forest View	1	6.9%	0	93.1%
River	1	18.1%	0	81.9%
Middlebrook	1	23.9%	0	76.1%
Roosevelt	1	12.7%	0	87.3%
Magnet	1	21.6%	0	78.4%
GPA	Mean= 3.15		Std. Dev.= 0.80	
Senior	1	39.7%	0	60.3%
College Prep Track	1	51.8%	0	48.2%
Voc/Tech Track	1	6.2%	0	93.8%
Mean of Friends' # of Non-Sports	Mean= 1.59		Std. Dev.= 1.24	
Mean of Friends' School Trouble	Mean= 3.47		Std. Dev.= 2.37	
Mean of Friends' Job Knowledge Scores	Mean= 1.22		Std. Dev.= 1.19	
Mean of Friends' Educational Expectations	Mean= 7.26		Std. Dev.= 1.33	
Academic Factor	Mean= 0.07		Std. Dev.= 0.91	
Social Factor	Mean=-0.10		Std. Dev.= 0.97	
Cohesion	Mean= 0.31		Std. Dev.= 0.19	
Centrality	Mean= 1.17		Std. Dev.= 0.83	

7

School Choice and Community Segregation: Findings from Scotland

J. Douglas Willms
University of New Brunswick
and University of Edinburgh

Many educators, parents and politicians are optimistic that schemes designed to increase choice in schooling will bring about an improvement in America's schools. The early proponents of increased choice argued that the use of free market mechanisms would increase competition among schools and make schools more accountable to parents (Freidman 1962; Hirschman 1970). They proposed voucher schemes whereby parents would receive a voucher that they could apply to tuition costs at either a public or private school (e.g., see Coons & Sugarman 1978), or alternatively, tuition tax credits, which would allow parents to cover some of the costs of private schooling through tax deductions. The State of Minnesota has allowed such deductions for some time. Recently, mechanisms to increase choice within the public sector have been introduced in a number of states (see Clune & Witte 1990). These have taken a variety of forms such as "mini-schools" within schools, open enrollment policies, magnet schools, and controlled choice programs (Rassell & Rothstein 1993). Many of the mechanisms are intended to increase the diversity of school offerings and improve the match between school programs and parents' and students' preferences. Because increased choice means schools must compete for students, its proponents hope that school and classroom practices will improve and that higher academic standards will be achieved.

There are few critics of increased parental choice. It was endorsed by past Presidents Reagan and Bush, and by President Clinton. It has received widespread support from business-oriented conservatives, liberal policy scholars, the African-American community, and the Catholic Church (Dougherty & Sostre 1992). Its supporters argue that increased choice will give poor and disadvantaged families opportunities that have long been available to the white middle-class. But some educationists are concerned that increased choice may further elitism in schools: families with greater social and cultural capital will have greater ability to exercise choice, which will lead to greater inequalities along racial, ethnic, and social class lines (Levin 1980). Despite considerable discussion amongst researchers, there has been little empirical evidence on the effects of choice programs in the U.S. Some of the first analyses of data from the National Educational Longitudinal Study suggest that choice programs are not bringing about the intended gains in academic achievement (Schiller 1993); however, the effects are difficult to discern because there is such wide variation in types of choice programs in the U.S. (Plank *et al.* 1993).

In the U.K. legislation that enables parents to choose schools within the public sector has been in place for over a decade. The 1980 Education Act and the 1981 Education (Scotland) Act gave parents the statutory right to request places in schools outside their designated attendance areas. The legislation also required local education authorities (LEAs, called EAs in Scotland) to publish brochures for each school that reported the school's examination results. The brochures were also to describe policies concerning homework, uniforms, and school discipline, and to include information about the curriculum. The majority of placing requests have been made on behalf of children entering primary school, or transferring to secondary school. The Acts require education authorities to take these requests into account, and only under certain circumstances can they be rejected. During the first few years after the Acts were passed, nearly all requests were granted. The British experience is relevant to U.S. policy because in many respects the reform embodies the ideals of a free-market approach strived for by the American proponents of choice (e.g., see Chubb & Moe 1990).

Much of the empirical research on school choice has been conducted in the U.K., owing heavily to support from the Economic and Social Research Council. Scotland in particular has had an active research program, led by Michael Adler and his colleagues (Adler 1993; Adler & Raab 1988; Adler *et al.* 1989; Petch 1986) and furthered by the Centre for Educational Sociology (Echols *et al.* 1990; Willms & Echols 1992).

The Adler *et al.* (1989) study, based on interviews with over 600 parents, found that parents who exercised choice were motivated more by a desire to avoid the school in their attendance area than to find the optimal school for their child. The reasons parents gave for choosing a particular school tended to be associated with social factors such as disciplinary climate or a school's general reputation, or with practical consideration such as proximity. Few parents emphasized educational considerations such as teaching methods or examination results.

The Echols *et al.* (1990) study was based on a large nationally- representative sample of the cohort of pupils that entered secondary school in 1982, the first year that the legislation became operational. They found that better educated parents and those with higher levels of social class were more likely to exercise choice. Moreover, the schools they chose tended to have higher social class intakes and were more likely to be schools that had been founded before the turn of the century. Many of these older schools had formerly been selective grammar schools, and still include the term "academy" in their name. Willms and Echols (1992) later examined survey data describing the cohort that entered secondary school in 1984, and were able to match some of the pupils' responses with parent data from the Adler *et al.* sample. They found that parents who exercised choice chose schools with higher mean socioeconomic status than that of their assigned school. However, the chosen schools only marginally benefitted their children in terms of academic attainment and were not particularly effective or ineffective when compared with schools of similar SES intake.

Prior to the mid-sixties, Scotland operated a tri-partite system of secondary modern, comprehensive, and grammar schools. Selection into secondary schools was based primarily on teachers' accounts of pupil ability. During the late sixties and seventies, secondary schooling was reorganized along comprehensive lines, and by 1980, when legislation on parental choice was introduced, over 95% of Scottish pupils attended their neighbourhood comprehensive school. Reorganisation had the effect of reducing segregation and narrowing the gap in attainment between working- and middle-class pupils (McPherson & Willms 1987). Parental choice may be reversing this trend. Both the Adler group and the CES researchers expressed concerns that parental choice was causing an increase in segregation along social class lines, and that this in turn would increase the gap in educational attainment between children with middle- and working-class backgrounds. However, these effects could not be directly observed with cross-sectional data.

This study attempts to further the work by employing longitudinal data on schools and communities to address four questions concerning the effects of the parental choice legislation over the period 1982-1991. First, what is the incidence of parental choice in Scotland? Has demand increased as the reform has taken hold, and if so, has there been a decline in the proportion of placing requests granted? Second, has the relationship between choice behaviour and parental background remained stable over the ten-year period? This question is asked with regard to choice within the state sector, and the choice of independent schools. Third, have parents tended to choose schools with higher social class intakes? Fourth, have schooling systems in Scottish communities become increasingly segregated along social class lines, and if so, are increases in between-school segregation related to the incidence of parental choice?

Data and Methods

The data come from two sources. One is a set of policy documents prepared by The Scottish Office (1993, 1992; Scottish Education Department 1983, 1985, 1986, 1987a, 1987b, 1989, 1990). These documents describe the incidence of choice within the state sector from 1981 through 1991. The second source is the Scottish Young People's Surveys (SYPS) of 1985, 1987, 1989, and 1991. The target populations for the cohort element of these surveys were all pupils who started their fourth year of secondary school in a Scottish secondary school, either public or private, in the preceding academic year. Thus, the majority of the pupils covered by these surveys entered secondary school in 1980, 1982, 1984 and 1986. Pupils were administered a questionnaire covering various topics regarding their school experience, family background, educational attainment, and post-school destinations. In the last three of these surveys, half of the questionnaires included questions pertaining to whether the pupils had attended a non-designated school as a result of parental choice. Achieved sample sizes for the four surveys were as follows: 1985, N=6501; 1987, N=6360; 1989, N=5581; and 1991, N=4450. Further details of the surveys are reported by Lamb, Burnhill and Tomes (1988).

Many of the analyses in this study are simply descriptive, and are portrayed through simple line graphs and histograms. But the questions concerning the effects of choice across communities are more complex. One of the central features of this analysis is that communities, schools, and pupils are treated as the units of analysis in a multilevel model. Because nearly all of the movement across school catchment boundaries or to the private sector occurs in communities with two or more schools, the effect of choice on segregation can be best observed at the community level. The analysis estimates the extent of among-school segregation in each of 54 Scottish communities using three separate segregation indices, described below. The multilevel model is then used to test whether levels of segregation have been increasing in these communities, and if so, whether increases are associated with the incidence of choice. Because the extent of choice varies among the fifty communities, and over time, we have a powerful design for testing whether choice is related to these indicators, both cross-sectionally and longitudinally. In this respect, the study is unique in that it examines differences among "multi-school communities" in a multilevel framework, with time as one level of the analysis.

Definition of Variables

Social Class. The occupations of pupils' fathers were classified into the seven categories of the Registrar General's social-class categories: Professional, Intermediate, Skilled Non-Manual, Skilled Manual, Partly Skilled, Unskilled, and No Occupation or Unclassified (Office of Population Censuses and Surveys 1970). This scale has been used extensively in British educational and sociological research.

Parental Education. This measure comprises information on the number of years of formal schooling completed by the pupils' mothers and fathers. It has three levels: both parents schooled to age 15 years or less; one or both parents schooled to age 16 years, but neither to 17 years; one or both parents schooled to 17 years or more. Where only one parent was reported by the pupil, the classification was based on that parent. The Scottish schooling system has always allowed pupils to achieve certification in the terminal school examinations at around age 17; therefore, the highest level of this variable can be considered a proxy for the attainment of this certification.

Socioeconomic Status. A statistical composite of fathers' occupation, mothers' education, and number of siblings was derived through a principal components analysis of the pupils' reports on these measures for 1991 SYPS data. The same scaling was then applied to calculate an individual-level SES score for each pupil in each cohort. Pupils' individual-level SES scores were aggregated to the school and community levels to estimate mean school and community SES.

Community. The same definition of community employed by McPherson & Willms (1987) was used to classify schools into communities across the four cohorts. They defined community in three stages:

> First, all schools, including private schools, were allocated to places as defined by the Registrar General, Scotland (RGS 1967). Second, all places served by more than one school were then identified. Third, if the schools in that place served all pupils in that place, and only those pupils, the place was defined as a multiple-school community. In setting this definition, only data on school location and catchment were used, and not details of individual pupils' home addresses. Where a school in one place served pupils living in another place, the places were concatenated until a set of places was identified such that it was the minimum set within which the schools served all pupils in that set, and only those pupils. This set was also then defined as a multiple school community. (p. 517)

With this definition of community, virtually all pupils in the community had no effective choice other than to attend a school in that community. Very few pupils in single-school communities exercised choice. For example, in the 1990/91 data, 20% of the pupils attended schools in single-school communities, but only 29 (6.8%) of the 424 pupils who were attending non-local schools were in single-school communities.

Segregation. I employ three measures of segregation. Two of these are based on the distribution of pupils with parents from middle- and working-class backgrounds. In these analyses "middle class" comprises the top two categories—professional and intermediate occupations. One index is the dissimilarity index, which indicates the proportion of pupils with middle class backgrounds that would have to change schools in order to achieve an even distribution across schools of pupils from middle- and working-class backgrounds. The second index, the isolation index, indicates the extent to which middle class pupils are exposed only to each other, and thus isolated from pupils with working class backgrounds. This index differs from the dissimilarity index in that a minority group could be unevenly distributed across schools, but if it were a relatively small group, it would not necessarily be isolated from members of the majority group. The third index, the correlation ratio, indicates the proportion of variance in individual level SES that is among schools. This index is useful here in that it facilitates comparisons with earlier work, and with SES segregation in other countries. All three indices are standardized such that they vary from zero to one. Massey and Denton (1987) describe these indices in greater detail.

Results

The Extent of Parental Choice

The incidence of placing requests for Scotland rose from just over 1% in 1980/81 to about 2.5% by 1985/86, and rose only slightly thereafter. By 1990/91, 3% of the secondary pupil population had placing requests made on their behalf. However, the percentages differ markedly among Education Authorities (EAs). As one would expect, the incidence tends to be higher in EAs serving urban areas. Glasgow has had the largest proportion of placing requests over the last four years, with 5% making requests in 1990/91. Renfrew, which includes the conurbation comprising Paisley, and Lothian, which includes Edinburgh, also had considerably higher percentages than the national average. Grampian, which includes Aberdeen, is somewhat of an exception: it had a 4% incidence in 1986/87, but by 1990/91 the level had dropped to about 2%.

The majority of requests at the secondary level were made on behalf of pupils who were entering their first year of secondary school (referred to as S1). Figure 7.1 shows the number of requests for entry at S1, expressed as a percentage of the S1 pupil population. The incidence for Scotland rose from 8% in 1983/84[1] to over 10% in 1987/88, and remained steady at levels between 10% and 11% to 1990/91. The provisional estimate for 1991/92 is 11.8% (The Scottish Office 1993). Thus, by the beginning of the 1990's, more

FIGURE 7.1   Requests Upon Entry as a Percentage of the S1 Pupil Population

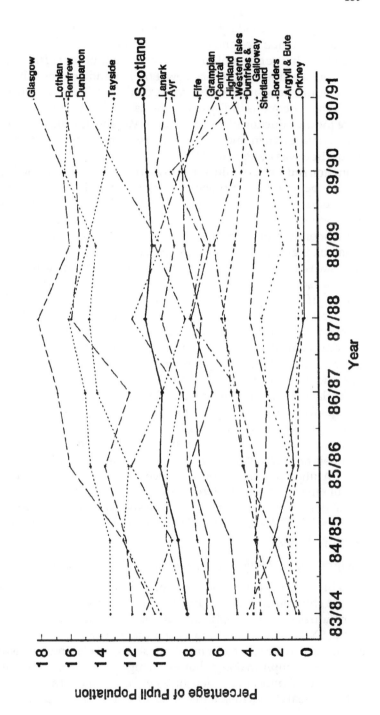

than 10% of the secondary school pupils were attending a school other than the school in their designated catchment area.

The 10% figure does not adequately show the impact of the legislation for many of the authorities. In Glasgow, Lothian, and Renfrew, about 15 to 18% of the pupils have had requests made on their behalf during the last half of the decade. Requests in Tayside were also higher than the national figures since the introduction of the legislation. Moreover, Adler *et al.* (1989) found that within Lothian and Tayside, there were some city areas where the proportion was more than 50%.

In Scotland, an EA could refuse to grant a request if it deemed compliance would "be seriously detrimental to the order or discipline of the school or to the educational well-being of the pupils there," or if compliance meant that a school must appoint another teacher, or significantly extend or alter the school. [See Section 28A(3)(a) of the 1980 Education (Scotland) Act.] What distinguishes Scottish legislation from the Act covering England and Wales was that an EA could only refer to conditions at the receiving school, whereas south of the border an LEA could deny a request if compliance would affect the provision of efficient education or the efficient use of resources (Adler 1990). Demand-side provision in Scotland was initially stronger than that of England and Wales also because of the appeal procedure. In both cases a parent could appeal a refusal to a committee; in England and Wales the appeal committee's decision was final, but in Scotland a parent could appeal a refusal from the committee to the courts. In Scotland, when an appeal is upheld, the EA must review the cases of all parents who have similar circumstances, regardless of whether they have had an appeal refused (Adler 1990).

In the first two years following the legislation, nearly all requests in Scotland were granted. But by 1983, some Scottish EAs began "capping" the enrolments of popular schools. Between 1982/83 and 1990/91 the national rate of refusals has climbed from around 3% to nearly 14%. Glasgow, which has had the highest percentage of requests, also had the highest percentage of refusals—17.4%. Lothian and Dunbarton also had refusal rates above the national average.

Social Class and Educational Background of Choosers

Table 7.1 shows the social class and educational backgrounds of parents whose children attended a private school or a state-funded school other than the designated school in their attendance area. Over the period covered by the SYPS data, there was a steady increase in the proportion of pupils attending private schools or non-local state schools, and the distribution of the type of pupil making choices changed. In 1985, there were strong, statistically significant relationships between choice of a private school and fathers' social class (chi-square=378.3, df=6, p < .01) and parental education

TABLE 7.1 Percentage of Students in Private Schools and Chosen State-Funded Schools, by Year, and by Fathers' Occupation and Parents' Education

	1985		1987			1989			1991		
	Private School	(n)	Private School	Non-Local State School	(n)	Private School	Non-Local State School	(n)	Private School	Non-Local State School	(n)
Social Class of Father											
Professional Occupations	18.2	(279)	18.7	10.6	(173)	28.2	7.7	(157)	21.6	10.1	(262)
Intermediate Occupations	9.1	(1232)	10.8	6.2	(632)	11.6	8.3	(564)	10.9	9.9	(1036)
Skilled Non-Manual Occupations	3.9	(386)	4.1	7.9	(200)	3.6	8.5	(176)	3.6	9.6	(289)
Skilled Manual Occupations	0.6	(2094)	0.7	5.7	(1000)	0.3	9.1	(739)	0.9	9.8	(1246)
Partly Skilled Occupations	0.3	(824)	0.6	4.1	(327)	0.5	9.0	(300)	0.8	11.6	(474)
Unskilled Occupations	0.3	(240)	0.0	4.7	(95)	0.0	5.9	(93)	0.0	9.6	(147)
No Occupation or Unclassified	2.1	(914)	1.5	5.6	(489)	1.7	8.8	(509)	3.6	12.3	(688)
Chi-Square[1] (df=6)	378.3**		208.7**	16.3*		290.7**	1.6		286.2**	5.1	
Level of Parents' Education											
One or both to 17 Years or more	14.9	(965)	16.9	8.1	(510)	16.6	8.9	(512)	15.3	9.1	(1006)
One or both to 16 Years only	2.9	(1661)	2.7	6.0	(885)	3.7	9.2	(892)	2.8	11.7	(1605)
Both to 15 Years or Less	0.6	(3583)	1.0	5.3	(1575)	0.9	8.2	(1138)	1.3	10.1	(1532)
Chi-Square (df=2)	468.2**		246.5**	11.0**		186.9**	2.3		270.4**	2.6	
All Pupils	3.4	(6209)	4.2	6.0	(2970)	5.1	8.7	(2542)	5.3	10.5	(4143)

[1]The chi-square tests displayed in the private school columns are tests for independence of the 2 by 7 contingency table of private/state-funded by social class, and the 2 by 3 contingency table of private/state-funded by level of education. Similarly, the chi-square tests displayed in the non-local state school column apply to comparisons of local to non-local state-funded schools. * p< .05, ** p< .01.

(chi-square=468.2, df=2, p < .01). The majority of pupils who attended private schools were of middle class backgrounds, or had at least one parent schooled to 17 years or more. These relationships for choice into the private sector did not change significantly between 1985 and 1987. Recall that the 1987 data describe the first cohort that entered secondary school under the parent choice legislation. For that cohort the relationships between choice of a non-local state school and fathers' social class and parental educational were similar to the distributions for choice of private schools.[3] The relationships were not as strong (for fathers' social class, chi-square=16.3, df=6, p < .05; for parental education, chi-square=11.0, df=2, p < .01), but there was clearly greater propensity to exercise choice among higher social class and better educated parents.

By 1989 there were two noteworthy changes. First, the pattern of choice within the state sector changed, such that there were roughly equal proportions choosing from each social class group, and for groups with similar levels of education. Second, there was a steady increase in choice of the private sector, rising from 3.4% in 1985 to 5.3% in 1991. The relationship between choice of the private sector and parental background remained strong and statistically significant (for fathers' social class, chi-square=290.7, df=6, p < .01; for parental education, chi-square=186.9, df=2, p < .01). The increase in choice of the private sector did not stem from increased proportions of working class pupils; rather, it stemmed from two factors. First, there were rising levels of social class between 1985 and 1991; for example, the proportion of pupils from professional occupations rose from 4.5 to 6.3%, and the proportion from intermediate occupations rose from 20 to 25%. Second, despite the change in the social class distribution, the proportion of pupils from professional and intermediate backgrounds choosing the private sector did not decrease; indeed, it increased slightly from 18.2% to 21.6% for professional occupations, and from 9.1% to 10.9% for intermediate occupations.

Socioeconomic Status of Chosen Schools

Previous analyses of the Scottish data suggested that parents chose schools with disproportionately high levels of mean pupil SES (Echols *et al.* 1990; Willms & Echols 1992). Willms & Echols (1992) compared the mean SES of the pupils' designated school with the chosen school they attended, for a sample of 195 pupils that were part of the Adler *et al.* (1989) sample. They found that on average the chosen schools had a mean SES that was 0.25 of a standard deviation higher than their designated schools. The size of the difference varied among the three regions studied. The SYPS data do not identify the pupils' designated schools; thus, in this study I cannot estimate differences in mean SES between designated and chosen schools. Instead, I estimate the discrepancy between the SES of the chosen school and the

TABLE 7.2: Differences between the Mean SES of Chosen Schools
and the Mean SES of the Community

	Mean Difference	Standard Error	N
1987			
School Mean SES minus Mean SES of all Schools in the Community (including Private)	.041	.035	172
School Mean SES minus Mean SES of State-Funded Schools in the Community	.127**	.339	172
1989			
School Mean SES minus Mean SES of all Schools in the Community (including Private)	.007	.290	207
School Mean SES minus Mean SES of State-Funded Schools in the Community	.101**	.282	207
1991			
School Mean SES minus Mean SES of all Schools in the Community (including Private)	.032	.215	395
School Mean SES minus Mean SES of State-Funded Schools in the Community	.107**	.215	428

mean SES of the community. Mean SES of the community is calculated in two ways: one that includes both state-funded and private schools, and one that includes only the state-funded schools. The results are reported in Table 7.2.

The results indicate that the mean SES of the chosen state-funded schools do not differ significantly from the mean SES of the communities in which they are located, when private schools are included. Observed differences are small—less than .05 of a standard deviation—and statistically insignificant. However, the mean SES of the chosen state-funded schools are about .10 to .13 of a standard deviation higher than the mean SES of the community, when only state-funded schools are considered. There does not appear to be any change in this effect over the period covered by the SYPS data. We can conclude that parents choosing within the state sector disproportionately chose schools with higher mean SES than other state-sector schools.[4]

Changes in Community Segregation

The two previous analyses showed that there was a small increase in the proportion of parents choosing private schools, and that parents who chose private schools tended to be of higher educational and social class background. The analyses also revealed that those choosing state-funded non-local schools disproportionately chose high SES schools. Taken together, these two findings suggest that parental choice may be causing an

TABLE 7.3   Parameter Estimates for HLM Regression Models Explaining
Levels and Annual Changes in Community Segregation Indices

	Model 1		Model 2	
	Estimate	(SE)	Estimate	(SE)
Dissimilarity Index				
Average Level of Segregation	.2467**	(.0233)	.2453**	(.0233)
Annual Increase in Segregation	.0085	(.0047)	.0058	(.0064)
Proportion Exercising Choice			.0909*	(.0433)
Isolation Index				
Average Level of Segregation	.3225**	(.0159)	.3225**	(.0159)
Annual Increase in Segregation	.0089**	(.0029)	.0044	(.0045)
Proportion Exercising Choice			.0489	(.0358)
SES Segregation Index				
Average Level of Segregation	.0971**	(.0164)	.0971**	(.0164)
Annual Increase in Segregation	.0070*	(.0030)	.0044	(.0046)
Proportion Exercising Choice			.0283	(.0367)

*$p<.05$
**$p<.01$

increase in the extent of among-school SES segregation in local communities. Table 7.3 provides estimates of the effects.

Model 1 shows estimates of the average intercepts and average slopes for the within-community regressions of the segregation indices on year. Year was coded 0 for 1985, 2 for 1987, 4 for 1989 and 6 for 1991, such that the intercept represents that average value of the index among the 54 communities for 1985. The estimate for the dissimilarity index is 0.2482, which indicates that approximately one-quarter of the middle class pupils would have had to change schools to achieve an even distribution of pupils across all schools. The estimated annual increase was 0.0085 per year (statistically significant at $p<.10$, but not at $p<.05$). Using this figure, the estimated change in the dissimilarity index for the period 1985 to 1991 is therefore (6 x 0.85=) 0.05; that is, an increase from 0.25 to 0.30. Thus, to achieve an even distribution of middle and working class pupils, an additional 5% of all pupils would need to change schools. To place the values of these segregation indices in context for the American reader, the Dissimilarity Index for Blacks in 1988 in San Francisco was .235; in Los Angeles it was .530 (see Rumberger & Willms 1989).

The estimate of the average isolation index across the 54 communities was 0.3250, and the average annual increase was 0.0089 (statistically significant, $p<.01$). This indicates that approximately three-eighths of the middle-class pupils were exposed only to each other, and thus isolated from working-class pupils. The significant annual increase indicates that over the

FIGURE 7.2   Average of Segregation Indices for Scottish Communities

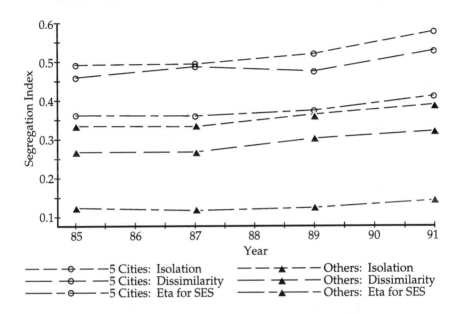

period 1985 to 1991 there was a tendency for middle class pupils to become more isolated in schools that were predominantly middle-class.

The last measure of segregation, which is calculated using our composite measure of SES, indicates the proportion of variance in SES that is among schools. The average level of segregation on this measure was .0971, with an estimated annual increase of 0.0070 (statistically significant, p<.05).

The estimates of the segregation indices and their annual change varied across the 54 communities. Some of this variation is attributable to sampling error; with these data it is not possible to achieve accurate estimates of the indices for the smaller communities (see Willms & Paterson 1995). However, it is possible to achieve reasonably accurate estimation of the indices for the larger communities, and for the smaller communities combined. Figure 7.2 displays the changes in the average of each of the segregation indices for Scotland's five largest cities (Glasgow, Edinburgh, Paisley, Aberdeen, and Dundee) and for the other 49 communities. For the five largest cities, taken together, all three indices increased over the period. The figure shows that segregation increased for both large and small communities alike, and that the biggest increase was for the isolation of middle class pupils in the five large cities.

Figure 7.3 displays the increases in the isolation index for each of the five cities. Isolation increased between 1985 and 1991 in all of these cities,

FIGURE 7.3   Isolation of Middle Class Pupils in 5 Scottish Communities

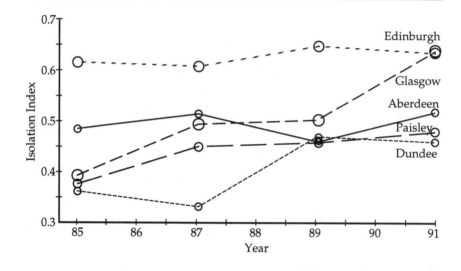

without exception. However, the change in Edinburgh, which had the highest level in 1985, was small. Aberdeen's index also changed only slightly. The changes in Glasgow, Paisley, and Dundee, however, were substantial. The change in Glasgow, Scotland's largest city, is particularly alarming: it rose from .392 in 1985 to .637 in 1991. The 1991 level of isolation is higher than the extent that Blacks were isolated in any of the six major school districts in California in 1988.

Changes in the SES segregation index provide some indication of the importance of the changes in Glasgow. McPherson & Willms (1987) documented a small but steady decline in the segregation index for Glasgow between 1977 and 1985, using data from the "school-leaver" element of the SYPS. Their estimates of SES segregation for Glasgow were 0.37 (1977), 0.35 (1981) and 0.33 (1985). The estimates calculated in this study for Glasgow, using the cohort element of the SYPS were: 0.39 (1985), 0.44 (1987), 0.44 (1989), and 0.56 (1991).

The second model in Table 7.3 examines whether the changes in the segregation indices over the period for each community were related to the proportions of pupils exercising choice. If choice were causing an increase in segregation, we would expect to observe larger annual increases in the segregation indices in communities where there was a higher incidence of choice. For all three indices, the annual rate of increase is partially explained by the extent of choice in the community. For the dissimilarity index, the incidence of choice accounted for nearly all of the annual increase in segregation. For the other two indices, the incidence of choice accounted for about one-half of the annual increase. The coefficient for the proportion exercising choice is statistically significant for the dissimilarity index (p<.05). For the other two indices, the coefficients are in the expected direction, but are not statistically significant. One limitation of this analysis is that the power of statistical tests at the community-level depends mainly on the number of communities, not the number of pupils, and with only 54 communities, the power to detect significant effects is limited.

Conclusions

Legislation in the early 1980s that enabled parents to choose schools outside of their designated attendance areas brought a type of "open enrollment" system to British schools. This study examines some of the effects of that reform on the provision of secondary schooling in Scotland. The analysis employs documents from the Scottish Office and data from four of the biennial Scottish Young Peoples' Surveys. One survey covered the cohort of pupils that transferred to secondary school one year before the reform became operational, and three surveys covered the cohorts that transferred to secondary school during the first, third and fifth years after the choice plan was in place. This study examines the extent that the reform has taken hold and its effect on school segregation in local communities.

The incidence of parents making requests for non-local schools climbed rapidly during the first five years of the reform, and then levelled off. Approximately 10 to 12% of the pupils transferring to secondary school have placing requests made on their behalf. As the incidence of requests increased, the proportion of requests refused also increased. During the first few years of the reform, only about 2 to 4 percent of the requests were refused, but by 1990/91, the refusal rate had reached nearly 14%. In some education authorities, it was considerably higher. Many of the refusals stemmed from the "capping" of popular schools that had reached maximum capacity.

The findings suggest that during the first few years of the reform, the right to choose was exercised mainly by parents from middle-class backgrounds. But as the reform took hold, a larger proportion of parents from working class backgrounds exercised choice. These changes were accompanied by an increase in the proportion of pupils opting to leave the public sector for private schools. The analysis shows also that parents disproportionately chose schools that served pupils with above-average levels of socioeconomic status.

The extent of segregation of middle- and working-class pupils was estimated for each year for the 54 Scottish communities that had at least two secondary schools. The analysis shows that between-school segregation along social class lines was increasing substantially during the period when the choice reform was proceeding. Differences among three types of segregation indices examined suggest that one of the main tendencies has been for middle class pupils to increasingly become segregated in a small number of schools within each community.

The extent of segregation and its rate of increase varied substantially among communities. Because of this variation, and because the incidence of choice varied among communities, the analysis could test whether the incidence of choice was related to the annual increase in segregation, using pupils, schools, and communities as levels of analysis in a multilevel model. The incidence of choice in a community was positively related to the annual increase in segregation, and when entered into the model explained about half of the annual increase in segregation. However, with only 54 communities, the relationship between choice and increase in segregation was not statistically significant.

This study cannot state definitively that choice legislation *caused* an increase in school segregation. Apart from the power of the analysis, there are a number of threats to the internal validity of such a claim. One problem is that the incidence of choice is greater in larger communities, and larger communities tend to have greater between-school segregation. During the period studied, it is possible that residential segregation increased, particularly in the cities. The social class structure changed during that period, with higher proportions of parents in middle class occupations. Levels of parental education also differed across the four cohorts studied, with the most recent cohorts having higher levels. Thus there could have been several forces other than increased parental choice that brought about the increase in community segregation. Nevertheless, the findings provide strong evidence that choice is not helping to reduce between-school segregation in Scottish communities. While some of the proponents of free-market approaches to education argue that choice mechanisms will improve opportunities for pupils from poorer backgrounds, the Scottish experience refutes this argument. If anything, pupils from working class backgrounds are being isolated in schools with less favourable contexts.

Although the American and Scottish schooling systems are very different, Scotland's experience with choice has implications for districts implementing choice plans and other reforms in the U.S. In many respects, Scotland provides a natural experiment on the effects of choice. Legislation on choice became operational in Scotland in 1982, and at that time nearly all pupils were attending schools in their designated attendance areas, with less than 4% attending private schools (McPherson & Willms 1987). Also, there was considerable uniformity in school goals, curricula and principles of organization (McPherson & Raab 1988). Because of this uniformity, the effects of market reforms are more easily discerned than in many schooling systems in the U.S. Also, because Scotland's starting point was close to fully comprehensive (i.e., non-selective), and because the choice legislation was far-reaching, the Scottish experience may provide an "upper bound" on what might be expected of similar reforms in the U.S. Of course the findings are of importance in their own right, to Scottish educators in particular, and to the sociology of education in general.

The two principal strategies for reforming U.S schools in the 1990s are to increase parental choice and to "restructure" schools, mainly by giving parents, teachers, and principals greater autonomy. One of the lessons from Scotland is that school reformers need to pay attention to the effects of these reforms on the entire school "community". A number of studies worldwide have shown that the collective properties of a school have an effect over and above the effects of pupils' individual backgrounds (see Willms 1992, for a review). Thus the performance of a school is contingent on the types of pupils attending it. When a pupil with an advantaged background transfers from a low- to a high-SES school, the contextual effect is strengthened for the chosen school and weakened for the school the child left. Unlike the markets for consumer products where all buyers can shift from one brand to another, it is not possible for all pupils to attend a school with a high social class intake. If choice and greater autonomy are to strengthen the hand of schools that are already advantaged, without safeguards to ensure equality, we will likely see widening disparities between the advantaged and disadvantaged.

Notes

This paper was prepared for the 1994 Annual Meeting of the American Educational Research Association. I am grateful to the Nuffield Foundation for funding the project, 'Standards, Tests and Parental Choice' which supported work on the paper, to the United Kingdom Economic and Social Research Council for its support of the Designated Research Centre at the Centre for Educational Sociology and to the Canadian Social Science and Humanities Research Council.

1. Figures for 1981/82 and 1982/83 were not available.

2. The SYPS estimates of choice within the state sector for Scotland are within about one-half of one percent of the figures reported by The Scottish Office. These differences may be attributable to error resulting from pupils who answered "not sure" to the SYPS question about choice, or due to sampling error.

3. This finding was reported earlier by Echols *et al.* (1990) for the 1987 cohort.

4. The discrepancy between the SES of the community and the SES of the chosen school probably underestimates the extent to which those choosing schools increased the SES of their school. For the 1989 data, Willms and Echols (1992) estimated differences between chosen school and designated schools for three authorities. They reported differences of 0.30 for Lothian, 0.10 for Tayside, and 0.21 for Fife, which are much larger than the discrepancies between community SES and chosen school SES— 0.10, 0.07, and 0.03 for these three authorities in that year.

References

Adler, Michael. 1993. "An Alternative Approach to Parental Choice." Pp. 183-98 in *Briefings for the National Commission on Education*. London: Heinemann.

Adler, Michael. 1990. "Rights as Trumps: The Case of Parental Choice of School in Scotland." *Education and the Law* 2: 67-72.

Adler, Michael, Allison Petch, and Jack Tweedie. 1989. *Parental Choice and Educational Policy*. Edinburgh: Edinburgh University Press.

Adler, Michael and Gillian M. Raab. 1988. "Exit, Voice and Loyalty: The Impact of Parental Choice on Admissions to Secondary Schools in Edinburgh and Dundee." *Journal of Education Policy* 2:155-179.

Coons, John E. and Stephen D. Sugarman. 1978. *Education by Choice*. Berkeley, CA: University of California Press.

Dougherty, Kevin J. and Lizabeth Sostre. 1992. "Minerva and the Marketplace: The Sources of the Movement for School Choice." *Educational Policy* 6:160-179.

Echols, Frank H., Andrew F. McPherson, and J. Douglas Willms. 1990. "Parental Choice in Scotland." *Journal of Educational Policy* 5:207-222.

Friedman, Milton. 1962. *Capitalism and Freedom*. Chicago: University of Chicago Press.

Hirschman, Albert O. 1970. *Exit, Voice, and Loyalty: Responses to Decline in Firms, Organizations, and States*. Cambridge, MA: Harvard University Press.

Lamb, Joanne M., Peter Burnhill, and Hilary Tomes. 1988. *SYPS 1987: Technical Report* (Edinburgh: Edinburgh University, Centre for Educational Sociology).

Levin, Henry M. 1980. "Educational Vouchers and Social Policy." Pp. 103-32 in *Care and Education of Young Children in America* edited by Ron Haskins and James J. Gallagher. Norwood, NJ: Ablex.

McPherson, Andrew F., and J. Douglas Willms. 1987. "Equalisation and Improvement: Some Effects of Comprehensive Reorganisation in Scotland." *Sociology* 21:509-539.

Office of Population Censuses and Surveys. 1970. *Classification of Occupations*. London: HMSO.

Petch, Allison. 1986. Parental Choice in Elementary School. *Research Papers in Education* 1:26-47.

Plank, Stephen, Kathryn S. Schiller, Barbara Schneider, and James S. Coleman. 1993. "Effects of Choice in Education." Pp. 111-34 in *School Choice: Examining the Evidence* edited by Edith Rasell and Richard Rothstein. Economic Policy Institute: Washington, D. C.

Registrar General, Scotland (RGS). 1987. *Annual Estimates of the Population*. Edinburgh, HMSO.

Rasell, Edith and Richard Rothstein (Eds.). (1993). *School Choice*. Washington, DC: Economic Policy Institute.

Schiller, Kathryn. 1993, February. "Schools of Choice and Student Achievement." Paper presented at the Sociology of Education Association Annual Meeting, Asilomar, CA.

Scottish Education Department. 1983. "Placing Requests in Education Authority Primary and Secondary Schools." (Statistical Bulletin No. 9/B6/1983). Edinburgh: Government Statistical Service.

Scottish Education Department. 1985. "Placing Requests in Education Authority Schools." (Statistical Bulletin No. 2/B6/1985). Edinburgh: Government Statistical Service.

Scottish Education Department. 1986. "Placing Requests in Education Authority Schools." (Statistical Bulletin No. 5/B6/1986). Edinburgh: Government Statistical Service.

Scottish Education Department. 1987a. "Placing Requests in Education Authority Schools." (Statistical Bulletin No. 2/B6/1987). Edinburgh: Government Statistical Service.

Scottish Education Department. 1987b. "Placing Requests in Education Authority Schools." (Statistical Bulletin No. 9/B6/1987. Edinburgh: Government Statistical Service.

Scottish Education Department. 1989. "Placing Requests in Education Authority Schools." (Statistical Bulletin No. 1/B6/1989). Edinburgh: Government Statistical Service.

Scottish Education Department. 1990. "Placing Requests in Education Authority Schools." (Statistical Bulletin No. 3/B6/1990). Edinburgh: Government Statistical Service.

Scottish Office. 1992. "Placing Requests in Education Authority Schools." (Statistical Bulletin No. Edn/B6/1992/13). Edinburgh: Government Statistical Service.

Scottish Office. 1993. "Placing Requests in Education Authority Schools." (Statistical Bulletin No. Edn/B6/1993/13). Edinburgh: Government Statistical Service.

Willms, J. Douglas. 1986. Social Class Segregation and its Relationship to Pupils' Examination Results in Scotland. *American Sociological Review* 51:224-241.

Willms, J. Douglas. 1992. *Monitoring School Performance: A Guide for Educators.* Lewes: Falmer.

Willms, J. Douglas and Frank H. Echols. 1992. Alert and Inert Clients: The Scottish Experience of Parental Choice. *Economics of Education Review* 11:339-350.

8

Educational Processes and School Reform

Maureen T. Hallinan
University of Notre Dame

Schools serve three main public functions in society: political, economic and social (Spring, 1991). The political function involves training students to be good citizens, preparing students for political leadership, transmitting political beliefs and ideologies, and maintaining power and stability. In a democratic society, schools aim to preserve freedom and teach students about their political and civil rights and responsibilities. In a totalitarian society, schools can be instruments of oppression and political control.

The economic function of schools is to contribute to a country's economic growth and technological development. The school is seen as the training place for future workers; schools prepare students for participation in the labor market. Through schooling, students are sorted by ability and interest, and prepared for future employment.

The social function of schools requires preparing students to live in community, to reduce social tensions and conflicts and to work toward social justice. Schools teach students moral values and social responsibility in order to insure societal stability and community development. Often schools are expected to play a role in social improvement, by directly dealing with social problems such as drugs, alcoholism, crime, violence, unemployment, and teenage pregnancy.

In addition to these public functions, schools serve private functions. Goodlad (1984) identifies these functions as vocational, social, intellectual and personal. Vocational goals are to train students for jobs, social goals are to prepare students for life in society, intellectual goals are to inculcate knowledge and develop student abilities, and personal goals are to foster student talents, responsibilities and freedom of expression.

The public and private goals of education generally coincide. The structures and processes that occur in school tend to facilitate the attainment of both communal and individual goals. At times, however, public and private goals conflict. Authorities may differ from individual citizens with respect to priorities, standards, and methods of attaining goals. Interested groups also may differ in the emphasis they place on the various public goals of education. Demands for school reform often stem from differences of opinion among public officials and between public authorities and private citizens about which school goals are being met and how schools are succeeding or failing.

Pressure for school reform, as evidenced in the current reform movement, generally occurs during a period of significant social change. The late 1980's and early 1990's typifies such a period. Dramatic economic, social and demographic upheaval characterizes this period, creating considerable social turmoil. During unsettled times, public opinion tends to shift, producing changes in attitudes and revealing value conflicts. Some values receive particular attention and are translated into policies and programs by individuals and groups. Pressure then is exerted on the schools to make changes that are consistent with these public shifts in values.

Several recent reforms can be directly linked to efforts to inculcate specific values in the school. For example, Democratic and Republican politicians recently have disagreed sharply about religious and moral values. As a result, school prayer has become an issue of public concern. Similarly, in the 1980's, a growing interest in remaining technologically competitive in a broadening world economy has pressured schools to be instruments of economic growth and development by providing students with the skills required for a changing labor market. Today, as a result of an increased public concern about personal safety, many school reform programs aim to reduce drug and alcohol abuse, high school drop-out rates, absenteeism and crime and violence in the schools.

The basis for the pressure to reform schools is the widespread view that the public school is a major instrument of social change. This perspective results from the belief that schools can solve social problems. The formation and expansion of the public school system in the nineteenth and twentieth centuries reflect the deeply rooted faith of Americans in the role of education as an instrument of social mobility and societal advancement.

The reform movement also is sustained by political considerations. Bowles and Gintis (1976) argue that the source of social ills, such as racism, sexism, poverty, crime and violence, lies deeply embedded in the structures of American society. If these problems were addressed at their roots, considerable societal disruption and conflict would result. It is far less disruptive to rely on the slow process of socialization that occurs in schools to shape the attitudes and behaviors of future citizens, than to address these issues directly. At the same time, educators see a causal relationship between deficiencies in the public school system and negative student behavior (Mortimer, this volume), leading to greater immediacy to the reform movement.

Since a call for school reform typically reflects value conflicts in society, it is imperative to understand the motivation driving a particular reform in order to estimate its potential to improve student learning. For example, the contemporary call to "detrack" schools, that is, to replace homogeneous ability grouping with heterogeneously grouped classes, is really an effort to remove social inequities in the schools. Advocates of detracking claim that detracking decreases racial and socio-economic segregation, and provides socially disadvantaged students with better opportunities to learn (see debate between Hallinan and Oakes, 1994).

School Reform and Student Learning

The paramount goal of schools, which should take precedence over all others, is to increase student knowledge. Every other goal, public and private, is an extension of this fundamental purpose of schooling. All reform efforts ultimately should be directed toward improving student learning. The danger of reform plans that stem from deep societal value conflicts is that strong attachment to a set of values and a sense of urgency about institutionalizing them may distract from the primary importance of the reform as a means to promote student learning. Many reform plans seem to be designed not with student learning in mind, but rather with a focus on other, often laudatory, goals. These reforms often are remarkably successful in achieving their purpose but do little to advance student achievement.

Since student learning should be the primary goal of every reform effort, the success or failure of a particular reform must be determined on this basis. To evaluate a reform, it is essential to identify the motivation of the reformers and to determine whether their motivation is consistent with and/or promotes student learning. The greater the growth in student learning, the more successful the reform. Even if secondary public or private goals are met, the reform is an educational failure if it does not improve student learning.

To evaluate the potential of a reform to increase student learning, the links between the conditions of the reform and student outcomes should be made explicit. It is essential to specify the connections between organizational, pedagogical or curricular change and the processes that govern learning. Unless the reform has a direct, positive influence on these processes, it will not improve learning and cannot be considered an educational success.

Determinants of Student Learning

Learning is a dynamic process that occurs over time; it is described as a change in an individual's knowledge, skills or values. The learning of interest here is that which occurs when students are exposed to instruction and the curriculum. It is the type of learning that produces academic achievement and that influences a student's educational attainment and future occupation. The more general norms and values that students learn in school, while important for their personal development and social responsibility, are not of concern here.

Sorensen and Hallinan (1977) present a model of the learning process that identifies three key elements—ability, effort and opportunities for learning—and that specifies the mechanisms that govern the relationship among these elements. The variation among students in the amount they learn in school is determined by variation in one or more of these three variables.

The first element in the learning model is ability. Typically, ability has been viewed as a stable, innate characteristic that defines a student's potential to learn. Ability has been conceived narrowly, referring to a specific set of cognitive processes, such as deduction, inference and memorization that are measured by IQ tests. Kerckhoff (1993) points out that the term ability suggests continuity of performance and certain boundaries or limitations that a person cannot transcend.

Recently, theorists (e.g. Gardner, 1993; Sternberg, 1990) have expanded the definition of ability to include such traits as creativity, logic, artistic talent, and physical manipulation. At the same time, educators have achieved a better understanding of learning styles, recognizing that some students are primarily visual learners, other auditory learners and still others learn best through physical involvement. Finally, research has shown that ability is not a fixed characteristic but rather is influenced by one's context and opportunities to learn. As a result of these developments in learning theory, ability is now seen as a broad, dynamic trait that has both inherited and acquired components.

The second element in the learning model is effort. Like ability, effort is determined by both individual and contextual variables. Personal characteristics that affect effort include need for achievement, parental pressure, ambition, energy, and motivation. Among the contextual variables that affect effort are peer pressure, role models, social reinforcements, and prevailing norms and values. Thus, variation in student learning is affected by two broad sets of individual variables—those determining ability and those determining effort.

Besides the individual traits of ability and effort, the learning process is comprised of opportunities to learn. Students cannot acquire knowledge unless they are exposed to it, regardless of their ability and effort. The amount of information presented to students is determined by the instructional process. Teachers transmit information to students, who internalize some degree of what is presented. The nature and content of the instructional process affects the amount that students learn.

These three basic characteristics—ability, effort and opportunities for learning—are the primary determinants of learning. Each of these components of learning is a function of other factors that affect their magnitude. For example, a student's social class, parent's education, race or ethnicity, gender, and family background, affect a student's ability level and effort, while school characteristics, such as per-pupil expenditure, organizational differentiation and size, and teacher characteristics, such as mobility, training and pedagogy, influence a student's opportunities to learn. Variation in one or more of these variables produces variation in the amount a student learns. Differences across students in ability, effort and opportunity explain variation in learning across students and over time.

The three primary determinants of learning, ability, effort and opportunity, should be the ultimate focus of all educational reform efforts. These variables, and the broader set of variables that influence them, must be the target of change in a reform that aims to improve student learning.

Change in Ability, Effort and Opportunities for Learning

Change in ability, effort or opportunities to learn produces change in a student's knowledge. An increase in one or more of these determinants of learning should increase the amount a student learns. However, it is unlikely that these variables have an additive effect on learning. An additive model implies that high levels of ability or effort can compensate for few opportunities to learn. In actuality, learning cannot occur without the opportunity to learn, regardless of ability and effort. Hence, a proper specification of the relationship among these three elements of the learning process is an interactive model. Sorensen and Hallinan (1977) propose a differential equation model to express the interaction among these variables and their effect on student learning. An understanding of how to increase ability, effort and opportunities to learn will provide the foundation for successful reform programs.

Ability

Since ability is, in part, inherited, it may represent the aspect of the learning process that is least amenable to change. Nevertheless, situational factors are known to have an impact on ability. Intellectual stimulation, exposure to knowledge, engagement in intellectual pursuits, and development of various cognitive skills, increase cognitive functioning and expand and deepen the ability to learn. An intellectually rich family life, a stimulating school atmosphere, opportunities to learn in and outside of school, travel, and hobbies, are likely to have a positive effect on a person's ability and increase future learning capacity.

Kerckhoff (1993) argues that a reconceptualization of the concept of ability is needed to avoid the self-fulfilling prophecy of students labeled as high ability producing high achievement while those viewed as low ability producing low achievement. A broader definition of ability and an acknowledgement of the various dimensions of intelligence could be a major factor in motivating students to achieve in areas that attract them and in which they have talent and skills. This involvement in the learning process could increase their ability to learn.

Effort

Effort is seen primarily as a function of motivation which, in turn, is determined by personal characteristics and situational variables. Most personal characteristics are genetically determined and remain fairly stable over a lifetime. An individual's curiosity, anxiety, sociability, and need for achievement, approval, and status, are shaped in early childhood and typically change little over time. Each of these characteristics affects how much a person values learning, and thus how much one is motivated to learn. The value attached to learning is a function of the rewards it provides. Certain personality characteristics make learning more intrinsically rewarding to some students than to others. For example, those who are intellectually curious or who have a high need for achievement, are likely to derive greater satisfaction from learning.

For students who are less intrinsically motivated, an external reward system can provide attractive reinforcements for studying. The components of a broadly based reward structure include tangible and intangible rewards. These would include grades, awards, prizes, status, esteem and social recognition. The more meaningful these rewards are to a student, the more effort the student will expend to attain them. However, the accessibility of the rewards is a critical factor in inspiring motivation and effort. When grades are assigned only for level of achievement, less able students who are unable to attain high levels of achievement become discouraged and abandon the effort to compete. When grades are assigned for growth in achievement, all students have a chance to succeed and the reward system serves to motivate everyone to improve their performance.

The value a student attaches to status, esteem or social recognition, depends on the basis of the status system. If a school has a strong academic orientation, then school authorities, parents and students alike are likely to value academic achievement and assign status to those who succeed academically. The desire to attain status, then, is likely to motivate students to study in hopes of attaining adult and peer respect for achievement.

However, if a student attends a less academically oriented school, or is a member of a peer group that does not value academic achievement, then other bases for status will be defined. These may have little or no effect on student motivation to learn or, indeed, may have a negative effect on academic effort. Consequently, to increase a student's effort to learn, an external reward system is needed that is both consistent with a student's values and that provides social rewards for academic effort.

Opportunities to Learn

The most controllable element in the learning model is opportunities to learn. Opportunities arise from three sources: the organizational differentiation of the student body, instructional pedagogy and the curriculum. Each of these factors can be manipulated in ways that have a direct impact on student learning.

a. Organizational Differentiation. One of the most noticeable features of American schools is the way students are organized for instruction. Dreeben and Barr (1988) state that schools perform a series of transformations of the composition of their student population by forming grades, classes, and instructional groups within classrooms. The aim of these transformations is to increase the efficiency and effectiveness of instruction. The most common basis for assigning students to instructional units is age and ability. Students are assigned to grades primarily on the basis of their age. Within grade, they often are assigned to classrooms and other instructional groups on the basis of ability. Within class ability grouping tends to be practiced at the elementary level and across class ability grouping or tracking is common at the middle and secondary level. Other bases for assigning students to groups include gender, language ability, and career interests. Increasingly more popular are heterogeneously grouped classes, formed in the belief that cognitive diversity can promote learning for all students, particularly those of lower ability.

Research has not revealed a direct effect of type of grouping on student learning. However, methods of grouping students have been associated with variance in instruction and pedagogy, which, in turn, affect student achievement. Kerckhoff (1993) claims that formal social structures, such as ability groups, systematically change student characteristics and alter educational outcomes. He documents the cumulative effects of school organization on achievement and occupational attainment, demonstrating significant long-term consequences of these effects.

In addition to grouping effects on student learning, the composition of a group influences within-group social processes that have an impact on student effort. Pupils assigned to the same group develop a set of norms that govern effort and level of achievement. Groups also form a comparative reference which affect a student's academic self-confidence and aspirations.

The greater a student's self-confidence and the higher the student's academic and career aspirations, the greater the motivation and effort to learn.

The organizational differentiation of a school determines the composition of a student's instructional unit. Compositional characteristics affect opportunities to learn through their influence on instructional pedagogy and the content of the curriculum. Student characteristics also engender social processes that affect student motivation and learning. Hence, opportunities to learn are channelled through organizational differentiation.

b. Instructional Pedagogy. The quantity and quality of instruction represent the most important opportunities for students to learn. The greater the quantity of instruction and the higher its quality, the more information students are exposed to and the greater their opportunity to increase their knowledge. Barr and Dreeben (1983) have shown that the greater the rate of instruction in reading groups, the higher the scores of first grade students on reading tests. Wiley (1976) demonstrated that the longer the school year, the higher the achievement test scores. Heyns (1978) showed that students who receive more instruction by attending summer school significantly raise their achievement levels the following academic year.

Quality of instruction varies by teacher characteristics and pedagogical techniques. Some teachers, by nature, are more engaging, authentic, and challenging to students than others. Teacher training programs can improve a teacher's ability to communicate to a certain extent.

More amenable to change are the pedagogical techniques employed by teachers. Two basic ways of instructing students are teacher-led instruction and student-centered instruction. Teacher-led instruction is characterized by the teacher's being the center of communication, providing information, directing discussion, and monitoring student input and behavior. The primary modes of communication include lectures, question and answer sessions, recitations, and discussion. Proponents of teacher-led instruction claim that it insures that students receive information in an orderly way, and allows mistakes to be corrected immediately. Critics argue that students are less interested in learning and that they participate less directly in the instructional experience.

An important feature of teacher-led instruction is the potential impact of the teacher's communication patterns on students' opportunities to learn. The interaction of teachers and students may be influenced by teacher reactions to students who vary in personal characteristics. Considerable research demonstrates how teacher style differs by the gender, race, ethnicity, and, to a lesser degree, social class of the students (Fennema and Peterson, 1987; Grieb and Easley, 1984; Good, 1970). Teachers tend to spend more time with boys, initiating more contacts with them, correcting, praising, and encouraging them, while also socializing and joking with boys more frequently than with girls. As a result, boys are instructed in a more supportive environment, both academically and emotionally, than girls, who seem to suffer benign neglect. Similarly, some studies show that white students receive more praise for academic performance than black students who receive more directives regarding behavior. These differential communication patterns affect students' attitudes toward school, self-esteem, achievement and educational aspirations. By favoring one demographic group over another, a teacher's pedagogical technique increases opportunities for some students to learn, relative to their peers.

Student-centered instruction occurs primarily in peer instructional groups. Stodolsky (1984) identifies five types of peer instruction: completely cooperative, cooperative, helping obligatory, helping permitted and peer tutoring. Minor differences exist among these groups, but they all stress student initiative in the learning process and focus on individual and group responsibility for learning. Students are seen as the primary resources for learning, and student interaction is the basic mode of instruction. Research (Slavin, 1987; 1990) indicates that students who work in peer instructional groups attain higher developmental skills than those working alone, likely a result of the discussion, argumentation and multiple perspectives that characterize these groups. Peer instructional groups also have been shown to improve social relations among students, particular those with different backgrounds or social characteristics. Improved sociability leads to more positive attitudes toward school, which likely affects students' motivation and effort to learn.

c. Curriculum. The content of the curriculum determines what is taught, rather than how it is taught. The choice of curriculum content ordinarily is determined by district and state educational authorities. Currently, there is a move toward establishing a national curriculum, in conjunction with the movement toward national assessment. Even in the absence of a national curriculum, however, considerable similarity is found across school districts and states in the courses that are offered to elementary, middle and secondary school students. Indeed, Meyer, Kamens and Benavot (1992) argue that there is a general worldwide consensus about the main elements of the curriculum. The central elements of the curriculum seem to be literature, mathematics, social studies, citizenship and morality. Most of the cross-cultural variance in curriculum content stems from political and cultural differences. Curricular variation in the United States is often accounted for by such factors as the inclusion of regional geography and history in social studies courses.

Most of the variation in curricular content that students experience is attributed to differential placement in courses within the school. The nature of the curriculum to which a student is exposed is determined, almost completely, by the track to which the student is assigned. In high school, students take Advanced, Honors, Regular or Basic courses. The top three levels of courses are college preparatory. They contain liberal arts, mathematics, and science courses, as well as some skill courses, such as keyboarding and computer science. Students tend to use the same text book, regardless of level, but the more advanced students cover more material in the text, or use supplementary materials, and receive a faster rate of instruction, than those in the Regular classes. More independent study is incorporated into the higher ability courses as well. Students in the high or average tracks aim for an academic diploma on graduation, which has somewhat rigorous course and sequence requirements. Students in the Basic courses, on the other hand, take fewer academic courses, aim only for a general diploma, tend to use more simplified text books, and take a preponderance of vocational and applied courses. Consequently, the curriculum to which students in Basic courses are exposed is markedly different from their peers in the academic track.

Two important questions arise concerning the curriculum, making it the target of educational reform. The first question is what changes in the curriculum are needed to reflect changes in American society. One major reform effort is directed toward including a multicultural perspective in the curriculum that would act as a corrective for a prior overemphasis on the influence of Western Europe on world change and development. The Rainbow Curriculum (Agard-Jones, 1994; Bird, 1993) recently implemented in New York City is an example of this effort. This program was controversial from the start, representing values that conflicted with those of many parents, educators and other citizens. The Board of Education was forced to withdraw the program after only two years of trial.

The second question about the curriculum is whether it should differ for students who vary in certain characteristics. Some school authorities favor an academic curriculum for higher ability students to prepare them for college, and a vocational curriculum for lower ability students to prepare them for the labor market. Others argue that all students should receive a basic liberal arts education, supplemented by vocational or other specialized training. Moreover, failing to take certain college preparatory courses at a particular grade level limits a student's access to future courses and may preclude their admission to many colleges. To insure that students' opportunities to learn are maximized, students need experienced counseling to guide their course selection. They are best served by decisions that provide the greatest ongoing accessibility to the curriculum.

Educational Reform and Student Learning

In 1983, the National Commission on Excellence in Education, appointed by President Reagan, issued the influential report, *A Nation at Risk*. This report documented serious inadequacies in the American public school system. Alarmed by the findings of this report, the public became motivated to improve the schools. Several reform plans were formulated in the subsequent decade. Some of these reforms succeeded in increasing student achievement, while others failed either to gain support or to improve student learning.

The success or failure of any educational reform is related to the goal of the reform and the means employed to attain that goal. If the specific goal of a reform is student learning, and the means used to attain that goal involve positive intervention in the learning process, the reform likely will be successful. The University of Chicago School Mathematics Project (1988, 1989) is just one example. This curriculum was designed at the University of Chicago by a group of researchers and educators, aimed at improving students' mathematics ability and achievement. The new curriculum provided a conceptual approach to mathematical concepts, required that the students develop higher-order thinking skills, emphasized applications as well as theory, and provided illustrations and examples that were salient to the age and interests of the students being taught. The reform increased students' mathematical fluency, strengthened their belief that they could do mathematics, and increased their opportunities to learn by an improved curriculum and more relevant instructional techniques. As a result, the reform is producing dramatic improvements in students' mathematics test scores.

Even if a reform has a political or social goal, rather than an academic one, if it relies on improving learning to attain its goal, the reform is likely to be a success. A popular reform in the 1980's was the creation of magnet schools. In addition to the regular curriculum, magnet schools offered specialization in the arts or sciences or some other area. The primary goal of this reform was to increase the racial and ethnic integration of the schools on a voluntary basis, in order to avoid forced integration through mandatory bussing. This goal was not directly related to student learning. However, to attain integration, the schools needed to attract an ethnically and racially diverse student body. Consequently, the curriculum in these schools was carefully designed to meet the educational needs of a broad spectrum of students. The result was that magnet schools quickly became popular and attracted large enrollments. The goal of integration was accomplished by improving opportunities to learn in these schools. The outcomes were greater student involvement, and, as indicated by test scores, improved learning.

On the other hand, if an educational reform has a non-educational goal and employs means that have little to do with the learning process or that hinder it, the reform is likely to fail in terms of student learning. For example, efforts to establish community-based control of schools failed in many school districts, most notably Chicago and Brooklyn, New York, because the aim of the reform was to change power bases. In attempting to achieve that aim, little attention was paid to altering educational processes in the schools.

Several significant educational reforms presently are being advocated and considered for adoption in public schools across the country. These reforms include parental choice of schools; performance-based instruction; national assessment and a national curriculum; local school autonomy; shared decision-making for parents and teachers; restructuring teacher training programs, teacher certification and professional mobility; required exit examinations for graduation from high school; lengthening the school day and school year, and establishing year-round schooling; detracking; student-centered instruction and cooperative learning; and redistribution of statewide funding for education. While all of these changes are purported to improve educational outcomes, it is rare that advocates of the reform make direct linkages between the proposed reform and the learning process. Consequently, the considerable energy that often is expended in promoting these programs often is misdirected to features of the programs that have little or no direct effect on student learning. The goals of each of these reforms must be clearly articulated and the way the innovation or intervention will affect the learning process must be made explicit in order to estimate the likelihood of the reform's success.

For illustration, two contemporary educational reforms will be examined. The first of these reforms involves curricular innovation and the second is the plan to detrack schools. The extent to which these reforms are likely to increase student ability, effort or opportunities to learn will be the basis of the analysis.

a.Curriculum Reform. Public response to societal changes in the United States has made the curriculum the object of numerous plans to reform the schools. One of the social forces that accounts for the current interest in the curriculum is social reaction to the changing population composition of the United States. The demographic characteristics of this country have changed dramatically in recent decades, resulting in a shift from a fairly large, white majority of Western European ancestry, to a smaller white majority and increasingly larger non-Caucasian, ethnic and racial minorities. This greater population diversity has evoked pressure to broaden and diversify the curriculum to meet the language, social and academic needs of the students. Minority groups have demanded a more multicultural curriculum that acknowledges and credits the contributions of minorities to the growth of Western civilization.

In New York City, the Rainbow Curriculum (Agard-Jones, 1994; Bird, 1993) was one response to this pressure. Educators developed and adopted a curriculum that emphasized multiculturalism, civil liberties, sex education, and language development. Since serious value conflicts regarding the curriculum were never really resolved, the program failed to receive community support and was terminated two years after it was adopted. Consequently, its effect on student learning is difficult to evaluate. Nevertheless, the initial reaction of many minority families was positive. They claimed that the new curriculum had greater relevance to their children than the one it replaced and judged that it increased student interest in school and their motivation to learn. In this case, a reform that was politically motivated, promised to have a positive impact on learning through its direct effect on student motivation and effort.

Another type of curriculum reform was a response to the economic recession of the 1980's. Increased unemployment, lower salaries and fewer job opportunities, coupled with a high drop-out rate from secondary school and an increase in crime and violence among youth, focused attention on schools as a means of solving these social problems. Until recently, the schools had provided little direct training for the work world (Kerckhoff, this volume). Now, teachers, parents, students, and employers are beginning to examine the link between schooling, employment and income as a means to economic growth and societal improvement. As a result, a number of reforms were directed at preparing students for technical or service positions in the labor market. These reforms aim to improve the curriculum primarily for lower ability students. Businesses are forming alliances with schools to provide leadership, funding and expertise in training students for entry level jobs in their organizations.

Nearly every state in the nation is adopting reforms directed at increasing the marketability of non-college bound students. One such program, entitled "Take Schools that Work", was developed by the Southern Regional Education Board and has been implemented in nineteen states. It emphasizes both academic studies and vocational-technical training. Instead of being assigned to the highly disparaged general education track, students involved in this program prepare for careers, college, or both. In mathematics, science, English and social studies classes, teachers address real-life situations and apply abstract concepts to concrete situations. Variations on this program include post-high school education in a community college or technical school, in preparation for a career of the student's choice. The school provides a warranty on the student's transcript that attests to the student's competence.

A similar and equally popular program is the Tech Prep curriculum that already exists in a large number of states. The most recent state to adopt this program is Indiana, in which the curriculum traditionally offered in the basic track will be replaced by the Tech Prep curriculum beginning in the 1994-95 school year. Tech Prep is a performance-based program designed to provide students with essential academic and technical foundations to enable them to gain employment or pursue further education after high school graduation. It involves business, industry and labor in the planning delivery and evaluation of the curriculum. The Tech Prep curriculum is designed around learning activities that emphasize problem solving, critical thinking skills, teamwork and cooperative learning skills. It also provides core courses in mathematics, science, language arts, economics, and computer literacy.

While "Take Schools that Work", Tech Prep, and similar curriculum innovations are fairly new, examination of the mechanisms that link the goals of the programs to the expected outcomes provide insight into the likelihood of their success. The primary goal of these reforms is to prepare students for the labor market, although they do include liberal arts courses in the belief that these represent a useful knowledge base for employment. The new curriculum is carefully designed with students' abilities in mind and is directed toward meeting their learning needs. It integrates abstract and applied knowledge and reinforces what is learned through student performance. The curriculum appears to represent a greater learning opportunity for students than that presented in the traditional general studies curriculum. If appropriate pedagogy accompanies the improved curriculum, it is likely that these curricular reforms will increase student effort. Moreover, the emphasis on performance may increase students' ability by expanding the ways in which they learn. In general, educational reforms such as these, that redesign the curriculum to better meet the learning needs of students, have considerable potential to promote student learning.

b.Detracking. A second reform that is gaining considerable popular support is the plan to detrack schools. Tracking, or the assignment of students to courses on the basis of their ability, is practiced in most middle and secondary schools, at least for mathematics and English instruction. Relying on a substantial body of empirical research (Gamoran, 1986, 1994; Sorensen and Hallinan, 1986; Oakes and Lipton, 1992), critics argue that tracking disadvantages low ability students by providing them with inferior instruction both in quality and quantity. Gamoran, in this volume, points out that tracking has allocative and legitimizing, as well as socializing, effects on students, all of which act to disadvantage the low ability pupil.

Reformists are urging school authorities to detrack schools, that is, to replace homogeneous grouping with heterogeneous grouping. Their rationale is that heterogeneous grouping improves the instruction offered to low ability students and provides them with a more challenging academic climate. Several major education groups, including the National Governors' Association, the Carnegie Council on Adolescent Development, and The College Board, have endorsed detracking as a means to improve student achievement.

A second goal of detracking is to eliminate the racial and social class segregation that accompanies homogeneous grouping. Given the current correlation between race, social class and academic ability, tracking results in a disproportionate number of white students being assigned to high academic tracks and black and lower class students being placed in the lower tracks. Since detracking creates more integrated instructional groups, it has been endorsed by the NAACP Legal Defense fund, the ACLU, the Children's Defense Fund, and the U.S. Department of Education's Civil Rights Division.

The success of a detracking plan depends on how the plan is implemented. In some schools, tracking is simply replaced by heterogeneous grouping, under the assumption that detracking automatically improves students' opportunities to learn. In these cases, teachers often are overwhelmed by the teaching demands created by a heterogeneously grouped class. This is not surprising, since tracking originally was established to facilitate instruction by reducing the diversity of student abilities. Anecdotal evidence indicates that simply detracking students without other modifications in program and pedagogy produces little improvement in learning and, in many cases, further obstructs the academic progress of lower ability students.

In other schools, detracking is accompanied by change in the culture of a school. Oakes and Lipton (1992) argue that tracking is embedded in a set of norms and beliefs about how students learn and what they should learn. These beliefs are built on closely held societal values. For detracking to be successful, it must be accompanied by changes in teachers' attitudes and expectations about student learning, including how learning occurs, how diverse are student abilities, the extent to which learning ability can be increased, and what knowledge is critical for students.

Besides being embedded in a set of norms and values, current tracking systems have political underpinnings. The political dimension of tracking is associated with status differences, expectations and consequences for academic and occupational outcomes. Consequently, tracking is related to the distribution of school resources, opportunities, and credentials that are valued in society. An unequal distribution of these valued goods is particularly troublesome when it encompasses race and class differences. For detracking to be successful, school faculties need to identify and address these political dimensions of tracking and reach a consensus that will motivate the detracking innovation.

Little research is yet available that systematically examines the effects of detracking on student learning. Anecdotal evidence and an understanding of the learning process suggest that simply replacing tracking by detracking has little impact on student ability or effort, and does little to increase students' opportunities to learn. Detracking may achieve a political or social goal, but fail in terms of improving student learning. However, if detracking is accompanied by changes in the curriculum and instructional pedagogy, the likelihood of success is greatly increased. With improved curriculum and methods of instruction, opportunities to learn may be provided through an integrated, thematic curriculum, cooperative learning approaches, a variety of assessment techniques, long-term projects, use of teacher aides, and various other strategies that make the learning process more authentic, interesting and relevant.

Conclusions

The aim of most educational reforms is to better prepare students for their political, economic, and social roles in society. Reform plans tend to mirror society's underlying values and reflect changes in that value system over time. The most controversial reforms generally are responses to conflicting values and conceptions about the role of school in society.

While it is nearly impossible to determine whether a particular educational reform has an impact on one of the general public goals of schooling, the impact of the reform on the intervening process of student learning is easier to determine. If a school reform facilitates or promotes student learning, it is likely, in the long-run, to have a positive impact on more global functions of education.

Reforms influence student learning when they are linked directly to the learning process. If a reform expands a student's ability or capacity to learn, or motivates a student to expend more effort in studying, then it has a positive impact on the primary determinants of learning. If a reform improves pedagogy, the curriculum, or the organization of students for instruction, then it increases students' opportunities to learn. By having an impact on one or more of these factors, reforms can achieve the most important purpose of schooling, namely, to improve student learning. Whether reforms attain other political, economic or social ends, in a direct or indirect way, is more difficult to measure. However, the likelihood that an educational reform will attain one or more of these social goals increases to the extent that the reform improves student learning.

Numerous educational reforms currently are being promoted in American schools. It is critical to analyze each reform to determine whether and in what way the reform affects the learning process. Advocates of a particular reform often speak eloquently about its lofty goals and about how well the innovation is attaining those goals. But unless a reform directly increases learning for all students, it cannot be called an educational success, regardless of what other ends it attains. Global goals of education are difficult to attain and the progress of a reform toward meeting those goals is difficult to ascertain. It is both easier and more meaningful to define the success of a reform simply in terms of whether it results in an increase in student learning.

Notes

The author is grateful for funding for this research from the U.S. Department of Education, Office of Educational Research and Improvement, Grant #008610960 and from the National Science Foundation, Grant #R117E1011139.

References

Agard-Jones, Leslie. 1994. "Going over the 'rainbow' curriculum for multicultural education." *Education Digest* 59(7):12.

Barr, Rebecca and Robert Dreeben. 1983. *How Schools Work*. Chicago, IL: University of Chicago Press.

Bird, Warren. 1993. "Rainbow curriculum loses momentum." *Christianity Today* 37(4):68.

Bowles, Samuel and Herbert Gintis. 1976. *Schooling in Capitalist America*, New York: Basic Books.

Dreeben, Robert and Rebecca Barr. 1988. "Classroom composition and the design of instruction." *Sociology of Education* 61:129-142.

Fennema, Elizabeth and Penelope Peterson. 1987. In Berliner, D.C. and B.V. Rosenshine, eds. *Talk to Teachers*. "Effective teaching for girls and boys: the same or different?" pp.111-125. New York: Random House.

Gardner, 1993. *Multiple Intelligences: the theory in practice*. New York: Basic Books.

Gamoran, Adam. 1986. Instructional and institutional effects of ability grouping. *Sociology of Education* 59:185-198.

Good, Thomas L. 1970. "Which pupils do teachers call on?" *Elementary School Journal* 70:190-98.

Goodlad, John I. 1994. *A Place Called School*. New York: McGraw Hill.

Grieb, H. and J. Easley. 1984. In Steincamp, M. and M. L. Maehr (Eds.) *Women in Science; Volume 2: Advances in Motivation and Achievement*, "A primary school impediment to mathematical equity; can studies in role-dependent socialization." Greenwich, CT: JAI Press, Inc. pp.317-362.

Hallinan, Maureen T. 1994. "Tracking: from theory to practice." *Sociology of Education* 67(2):79-84.

_____."Further thoughts on tracking." *Sociology of Education* 67(2):89-91.

Heyns, Barbara. 1978. *Summer Learning and the Effects of Schooling*. New York: Academic Press.

Kerckhoff, Alan C. 1993. *Diverging Pathways: Social Structure and Career Deflections*. Cambridge: Cambridge University Press.

Meyer, John, David Kamens and Aaron Benavot, with Yun-Kyug Cha and Suk-Ying Wong. 1992. *School Knowledge for the Masses: World Models and National Primary Curricular Categories in the Twentieth Century*. Falmer Publishing Company.

National Commission on Excellence in Education. April 1983. *A Nation at Risk: The Imperative for Educational Reform*. Washington, DC., U.S. Government Printing Office.

Oakes, Jeannie. 1994. "More than misapplied technology: a normative and political response to Hallinan on tracking." *Sociology of Education* 67(2):84-89. And "One more thought." p.91.

Oakes, Jeannie and Martin Lipton. February 1992. "Detracking schools: early lessons from the field." *Phi Delta Kappan* 448-454.

Slavin, Robert. 1987. "Ability grouping and student achievement in elementary schools: a best-evidence synthesis." *Review of Educational Research* 57:293-336.

_____. 1990. "Ability grouping in secondary schools: a best-evidence synthesis." *Review of Educational Research* 60(3):471-499.

Sorensen, Aage B. and Maureen T. Hallinan. 1977. "A reconceptualization of school effects." *Sociology of Education* 50:273-289.

_____. 1986. "The effects of ability grouping on growth in academic achievement." *American Educational Research Journal* 23(4):519-542.

Spring, Joel. 1991. *American Education: An Introduction to Social and Political Aspects.* New York: Longman Publishing Group.

Sternberg, Robert J. 1990. *Metaphors of the Mind: Conceptions of the Nature of Intelligence.* New York: Cambridge University Press. Stodolsky, Susan. 1984. In Peterson, Penelope, Louise Cherry Wilkinson and Maureen T. Hallinan (Eds.) *The Social Context of Instruction.* "Framework for studying instructional processes in peer work groups." Orlando: Academic Press. pp. 107-124.

University of Chicago School Mathematics Project (UCSMP). 1989. K-6, Evanston, IL: Everyday Learning Corporation. 1988. 7-12, Glenview, IL: ScottForesman.

Wiley, David. E. 1976. In *Schooling and Achievement in American Society.* Sewell, William H., Robert Hauser and David Featherman (Eds.) "Another hour, another day: quantity of schooling, a potent path for policy." New York: Academic Press.

PART THREE

Education and Labor Force Linkages

The division of labor that has developed over the past two decades between those who study schools and those who study the labor force has left the linkage between those two institutional settings less well-analyzed than it needs to be. The four papers in Part III provide some indication of the potential value of further work on this issue, although they go about analyzing the linkage in very different ways.

In the first paper, William Bridges seeks to clarify the role of educational certification in determining workers' earnings in the United States. To do this, he focuses on the importance for workers of "credentialism," the tendency of firms to reward the symbolic value of educational credentials rather than, or in addition to, the actual trained capacities the credentials represent. Using a broad conceptualization of types of industries and an analysis of pay levels associated with levels of educational attainment and credentials obtained, he shows that industries vary in these respects. He concludes that "credentialism" is more often found in industries in which the required skills are not obtained through formal training. In particular, industries dominated by male workers (especially in the financial sector) are more likely to provide rewards for the symbolic value of credentials. Bridges then speculates about the future prospects of such added rewards in light of on-going changes in the labor force.

The second paper, by Thomas DiPrete and Patricia McManus, also deals with the earnings returns to education, but it does so within a comparative framework. Building on earlier theory and research that shows a tighter education-occupation linkage in Germany, they show that education as such (once occupation is controlled) has a stronger effect on earnings in the U.S. than in Germany, although even in Germany direct effects of education are apparent. They also show that earnings are more directly affected by vocational credentials in Germany, while continued tenure with a single employer is more important in the U.S. As a result of these differences in the education-occupation linkage (tight in Germany, loose in the U.S.), earnings trajectories are also more uniform in Germany. The variations in the U.S. data are consistent with Bridges' observations in the previous paper. These two papers not only help to clarify the importance of education-occupation linkages, they also cast light on the varied relationships of both of those kinds of attainment with earnings.

The other two papers in Part III shift the focus from a very broad analysis of overall labor force patterns to very restricted portions of the labor force, but the role of educational credentials in the division of labor and in the lives of workers remains in the forefront. In the first of these, Robert Althauser and Toby Appel consider the two-tiered structure of several allied health occupations, the tiers being separated in ways often associated with dual labor markets — different education and credential prerequisites, wage differentials, blocked mobility between tiers, and (theoretically) a separation of tasks. The advantages of the upper tier workers are legitimized by both their superior credentials and the presumed task specialization. However, there is actually a great deal of overlap between the tasks performed by workers in the two tiers. This raises the question of whether (or how) the two-tiered structure can persist under these conditions. Althauser and Appel speculate that its persistence may depend on other structural elements such as hospital administrations and professional organizations.

In the last paper in Part III, Barbara Heyns also discusses the education of a particular part of the labor force, but her focus is on the institutions in which these prospective workers obtain their preparation. She analyzes the backgrounds, values, attitudes and expectations of business school students after the fall of communism in Poland. In a period of sweeping political and economic changes, the relationship between education and labor force outcomes is at best problematic. Educational programs that are clearly linked to those changes attract students with atypical attitudes and values, and the tension between the old and the new can be seen in their views of the future — the country's and their own. Heyns focuses especially on the tension between the role of women in the communist system and in the newly emerging free market economy.

These four papers make it clear that the school-work linkage is an important but a highly varied one, dependent on the characteristics of the social and cultural contexts in which it is situated. Bridges shows differences by industry in the labor force returns to education credentials within the U.S., and DiPrete and McManus analyze such differences between societies. Althauser and Appel describe instances in the U.S. in which educational credentials appear to be used to legitimate different levels of pay even when the tasks performed are highly similar. And, Heyns uses the case of Poland to show how societal change makes it difficult for students (and in this case especially women students) to estimate the best use they can make of the newly established credentials they obtain.

9

Educational Credentials and the Labor Market: An Inter-Industry Comparison

W.P. Bridges
University of Illinois at Chicago

An ongoing debate exists about why education enhances individuals' success in the labor market. Without sacrificing the inherent complexity of the issues, Bidwell (1989) provides a succinct statement of the range of possible answers:

> I have suggested that in present-day bureaucratic societies educational attainment has several meanings. It may denote components of trained capacity for job performance, ancillary bodies of information about the work world, or secondary status characteristics. Each of these denotations, in turn, may be substantive or symbolic, and the symbolic aspect may be either formal (certificates earned) or informal. (133)

In this paper, I investigate how one symbolic manifestation of education, credentialling, varies across industrial labor markets in the US economy. The underlying premise of this analysis is that education can play a different role in different labor market contexts. For example in some settings, those with more education may be more highly rewarded because of the trained capacity they have acquired. In other situations, those with higher levels of formal schooling may do better because of their greater exposure to and knowledge of high status culture. Credentialling, the facet of education studied here, is defined as the preoccupation of employers with employees having crossed one or more educational status thresholds.

Although a complete catalog of the possible ways in which education contributes to socio-economic success is beyond the scope of this paper—and unnecessary in light of Bidwell's thorough analysis—a few words are in order concerning some of the main positions which have been advanced.

The human capital/marginal productivity theory remains perhaps the dominant explanation (see Becker 1958 in economics, Featherman and Hauser 1978 in sociology). Put simply, formal schooling teaches individuals productivity-enhancing knowledge and skills which are demanded by employers. (In Bidwell's framework, this view corresponds to the cell defined by the intersection of the "substance" and "trained capacity" conceptual dimensions.) The cultural capital theory of education associated with Bordieu 1977, Dimaggio and Mohr 1985, and others, also holds that education is important because of *what* it teaches, but in this case what is imparted by schooling is familiarity with elite culture and the ability to fit in at an appropriate level in the larger status order.

Counterposed to these "substantive" views of schooling are theories which stress the importance of education as a symbol. Although Bidwell's scheme leaves room for six possibilities here (trained capacity vs. work world information vs. secondary status characteristics each symbolized formally or informally), not all of these possibilities seem very plausible empirically. In our view, meaningful distinctions can be drawn between two types of symbolic theories: (1) those closest to human capital theory, e.g., signalling or screening theory, in which more schooling is seen as an indicator of some latent desirable, but unobservable, trait[1] (Spence 1974; Stiglitz 1975, Spilerman and Lunde 1991); and (2) those which stress the importance of education not as a symbol of unobserved productive capacity, but as a symbol of conformity to the structure of the educational mertiocracy itself.

Symbolic theories of education are often, but not always, linked to the idea that credentialism produces discontinuities in the relationship between education and socio-economic outcomes. What matters is formal recognition of completion of blocks or integral units of educational attainment. Once again, Bidwell's analysis is informative. "As occupational allocation moves to the center of status allocation and becomes increasingly formalized with respect to evidence of trained capacity, the allocation system takes on a *threshold structure in which occupations are stratified according to minimum educational requirements.*" (1989: 123 *emphasis added*) The development of an industrial-educational system in which the crossing of normatively defined threshold points becomes valued in its own right, regardless of what it signifies in terms of trained capacity, is the essence of what, for the purposes of this paper, will be labelled "credentialism."

Although the emergence of a credential system can be traced to entrance requirements for well-established occupational specialties, recent developments in labor market research suggest that a focus on occupations *per se* may be too limiting. First, it is necessary to recognize that jobs (defined as a bundle of tasks within an organization) are often more meaningful units, particularly within internal labor markets, than occupations (Baron and

Bielby 1986; Althauser and Kalleberg 1971). Many individuals occupy positions and form identities around organization-specific roles which have only vague counterparts in external labor markets (Williamson 1975; Bridges and Villemez 1991). Second, the enforcement of educational requirements and the use of educational symbols in hiring, promotion, and compensation decisions are, in varying degrees, the prerogative of employers and their organizations. For example, a detailed and interesting account of one employer's struggles with the adoption of more stringent educational standards is contained in DiPrete's account of the post-World War II Federal Civil Service (1989, 137ff). In sum, when attention is focussed on the symbolic meanings of education, it seems logical to ask about the characteristics of those parties, i.e. employers, who elicit, receive, and act on the symbols in question.

Considering those symbolic theories that see education as an indicator of latent productivity, i.e., screening and signalling theories, one can make an additional distinction. On one side are those approaches which provide a clear neo-classical, marginalist account of the meaning of educational attainment. For example in Spence's view, greater amounts of schooling indicate the possession of productivity-related habits and traits which are inherently unobservable. However, individuals with the desired traits confront lower costs in acquiring the requisite symbol or signal, i.e., more years of schooling, and acquire more of it. Thus, employers who select on the basis of more years of completed education are choosing individuals who are less bothered by the difficulty of sustained, disciplined attention to more or less complex cognitive tasks. I argue that this logic easily conforms to a continuous and smooth relation between socio-economic outcomes and educational attainment. That is, whatever latent traits education is indexing may very well be distributed in the population in a relatively continuous fashion so that employers could rationally discriminate between an applicant with one year of college completed and one with two years.[2]

Other theories of education as an indicator of a latent productivity trait take a slightly different turn. Berg for example states:

> Education is often presumed also to be a continuous variable, approximately the same marginal differences in the economic values are assumed to exist between, say, any two successive years of high school. And researchers assume this despite the recurrent finding that diplomas and degrees command a price in the labor market that goes well beyond the marginal increment of learning that may be achieved between the third and fourth year of high school or college (1971, 26)

And in explaining the reasons for this attention to completed blocks of schooling he reports on interviews with business leaders in which:

> The college degree was consistently taken as badge of the holder's stability and was apparently a highly prized characteristic of young recruits. Most of the respondents made it perfectly plain that the content of the college program

mattered a good deal less than the fact of successful completion of studies." (1971, 75)

In short, the use of education as a symbol of unobserved productive capacity is consistent with both continuous and discontinuous reward functions for years of completed schooling.

However, both of these theories are different from a view of education which sees it less as a symbol of latent productivity, and more as a marker of degree holders' conformity to meritocratic culture. Thus, Michael Faia in "Selection by Certification" is attentive to the possibility that credentialling results from "irrational" or non-economic behavior on the part of employers and is explicitly concerned with locating discontinuities or abrupt shifts in labor market outcomes associated with the possession of formal certificates. Figure 9.1 locates these different versions of the symbolic meaning of education along a continuum that ranges from those theories alleging that education signifies unobserved productivity to those alleging that it signifies cultural conformity.

Empirical Studies of Credentialling

Much, but not all, of the empirical investigation of educational credentialism has been colored by a polemical tone in which the central research aim is to discredit the reigning "technical/rational" or human capital view of the functions of education. This ideological strain is readily apparent in Collins' 1979 volume, *The Credential Society*, where the opening chapter is titled, "The Myth of Technocracy." In presenting an alternative to the "technological function theory" of education, Collins embraces a diffuse notion of credentialism which draws water from the same well as the related "cultural capitalism" argument. Education matters insofar as it can be interpreted as an indicator of "cultural socialization" whether or not it indexes superior technical skills.

At the same time, Collins presents a slightly more nuanced view of the issues. In particular, he develops a set of empirical predictions about the use of educational requirements based on the notion that they play a key part in allowing organizations to maintain control through normative mechanisms rather than through instrumental or coercive means. As a consequence, he examines whether educational requirements are higher in "public trust" organizations than market oriented ones and finds a positive result. He also investigates the conditions under which business administration credentials are required for prospective managers finding that these degrees are particularly sought after in, "...(a) an extremely marketing-conscious manufacturing group [food, fabricated metals, printing]; (b) a public-relations-conscious transportation and utilities group [air and water transportation, gas and electric services]; and (c) the administrators of large

FIGURE 9.1   Theories of Educational Symbolism

	(Unmeasured Productivity)		(Cultural Conformity)
	◀──────────────────────────────────▶		
Theory/Theorist:	Signalling/ Spence	Screening/ Berg	Ritualism/ Faia
What Education Symbolizes:	Low Cost of Learning	Stability/ "Stick-to-it-iveness"	Conformity to Cultural Norms
Relation Between Education/Reward:	Continuous	Discontinuous	Discontinuous

scale service organization [hospitals and schools]." (1979, 35) Finally, he suggests that educational credentials increase in importance when anti-discrimination laws make overt ascriptive and status-based selection more difficult.[3] For present purposes, what is important in Collins' work is not his definition of credentialism, which leans more toward cultural capital than the "educational ritualism" at issue here, but his suggestions about both the fact and sources of variation in credentialism across different segments of the labor market.

A different, but no less polemical, stance is taken by Michael Faia (1981), although the target of his criticism is human capital and rational choice economics rather than functionalist sociology. Unlike Collins, however, he is not particularly interested in examining variation among employers or types of employers in the use of education as a credential. In general, his findings show that controlling for years of schooling, those who hold college and high school diplomas fare better in occupational prestige terms than those without them. Once occupation is controlled, however, he uncovers only minimal direct effects of certificates on income.

In contrast, Spilerman and Lunde (1991) offer a relatively non-ideological assessment of the role of formal certificates.[4] They attempt to find effects of earned degrees which would be consistent with what they term "a variant of the 'signal thesis' " (p 695). What they have in mind is that degrees are "overweighed" as signals at the outset of a hiring transaction—meaning that employers, in using certificates, attempt to measure latent productivity, but do so erroneously. Thus, they initially reward people with degrees beyond the level which they should, and later, employers correct their mistakes as the worker's true productivity becomes evident. However, their data do not bear out this supposition as they do not find the expected negative interaction effects of possession of a degree and seniority on promotion rates, which is their dependent variable. Instead, certificates seem to exert an influence which is more consistent with the "skill acquisition" thesis, than with the credentialism thesis. Furthermore, because their data all come from a single firm (and hence, single economic sector), they do not address the question of contextual variation in credential effects.

The perspective on credentialling adopted here incorporates more elements of the arguments presented by Collins and Faia than of those presented by Spilerman and Lunde. Like Faia, I am interested in capturing a more purely symbolic orientation toward education than is implied by Collins' proto-cultural-capital argument or Spilerman and Lunde's rational choice argument. While it goes perhaps too far to insist that employers who require and reward completion of blocks of educational units do so for irrational reasons, my definition of credentialism does emphasize that this behavior has a ritualistic or ceremonial component to it which may not get corrected as time passes. These aspects of organizational practice have been repeatedly recognized in the recent past, beginning with the essay by Meyer and Rowan (1977) and culminating in the so-called "neo institutional" perspective on organizational behavior (DiMaggio and Powell 1983, Edelman 1990, Zucker 1987).

However, like Collins, I am concerned with exploring variation in the occurrence of credentialling by examining different types of employment settings. The purpose of this endeavor is first to test whether the use of education as a symbolic credential is or is not constant across different parts of the economic landscape. Assuming that it is not, the second goal is to explore some preliminary hypotheses about what characteristics of economic settings may contribute to this usage. Finally, it is necessary to incorporate into the analysis, Bidwell's conception of blocks of educational completion or educational status thresholds. In describing how one might operationalize the signalling theory, he states, "If the signalling value of education arises primarily from the symbolic aspect of the threshold structure, then the relationship between educational and occupational attainment should approximate a stair-step function in which the more powerful effects correspond to the transition points in the structure..."(1989, 127) Although his reading of signalling theory is open to debate (see note 3), the linkage between education as a symbolic commodity and the stair-step functional form provides a useful tool for our subsequent analysis.

Hypotheses

The screening theory discussed above implies that a focus on blocks of completed education will be more likely in skilled than unskilled jobs.

However, what is central to this theory is that the skills be those which are difficult to measure or determine at the initiation of the employment relationship. Thus, our first hypothesis is that industries with a higher proportion of jobs which require difficult-to-measure skills will rely on certificates rather than reward continuous years of schooling.

Implicit in some critiques of the use of education as a hiring criterion is the idea that fixation on formal certificates devalues the market currency of those with more useful knowledge obtained in the "real world" or on the job itself. Following this logic, my next hypothesis is that industries with higher rewards for long periods of work experience will be less likely to use education as a credential than those with lower rewards for work experience.

As suggested earlier, the kind of credentialism at issue here is tantamount to a ritualistic use of education in employment decisions. Following a logic similar to that of Spilerman and Lunde (1991), I hypothesize that jobs which require skills that are learned in school will tend *not* to reward education in a credentialist manner. Or stated somewhat differently, the more "school-based" trained capacity matters, the less freedom employers have to indulge their tastes for the ceremonial, as opposed to the substantive, aspects of education.

Attention to the ceremonial meanings of education is also quite compatible with the so-called new institutionalist paradigm in organizational analysis which explains the adoption of various employment practices, e.g., promotion ladders, equal opportunity offices, personnel departments, etc., as attempts to secure organizational legitimacy by adopting culturally approved models of employment procedures. However, which organizations are most likely to be influenced by which institutional environments depends largely on the kind of employment practice under consideration. There have been many studies of employment outcomes and practices ranging from due process guarantees (Edelman 1990), to salary classification structures (Dobbin, et al. 1993), to gender and racial income disparities (Beggs 1993) which have used 'proximity to the public sector' as one indicator of susceptibility to normative pressures. That is, legal and state linked pressures are determinative when the practices in question symbolize 'fairness'. However, other governance structure elements, in particular internal labor markets and personnel departments, were found by Baron et al. (1988) to be more prevalent in service industries, "...which depend heavily on process (rather than outcome) measures of performance," and, "...formalize operating procedures to increase their own perceived legitimacy." The institutional pressures in this case seem to arise less from overt government intervention, and more from conformity with society-wide norms about distributive justice. That is, if reward distributions cannot be justified on the basis of measured differences in performance, the allocative structures which produce them can at least be presented as procedurally formalized and consistent.

In the case of educational credentialism, I will investigate several sources of institutional pressure. Thus, my next hypothesis is that industries more proximate to the public sector will be more likely to rely on educational credentials than those further removed. This prediction is motivated by the observation that education itself, at least in the US, is closely tied to the state, which serves as both a source of funding and a source of licensing for its practitioners. An alternative institutional hypothesis is that educational credentials are more heavily utilized by service industries and other sectors with outputs which are difficult to measure than by industries where products are tangible or more easily measured, as in the manufacturing or utility industries. A final institutional hypothesis reflects the findings of Collins pertaining to the demand for business degrees in "market conscious" and "public relations conscious" industries. That is, I predict that industries which are more sensitive to their public images will be more attentive to having properly credentialed work forces than those less attuned to these concerns.

Of course, bureaucracy itself has long been linked with the idea of procedural formalism or "red tape" and educational credentials are easily seen as a kind of unnecessary formality. Berg, for example, speculates that the, "nonrational use of formal credentials ... might be taken as a significant symptom of "bureaupathology." (1971, 175)[5] Thus, my next hypothesis is that industries with greater concentrations of bureaucratic organizations will rely more readily on educational credentials.

Finally, there is the matter, which Collins has also raised, of the degree of inclusion of minority and other groups historically devalued in American culture. The prediction here is that greater openness of an industry's labor force to black employees and to female employees will be associated with greater reliance on educational credentials. Although this proposition could be defended in several ways, the most compelling argument is that degrees, certificates, or titles provide a basis of status enhancement which offsets the perceived status deficiencies associated with being black or female.

Data and Methods

Educational credentialling

The underlying premise of the argument presented above is that the operation of a credentialling regime will produce sharp discontinuities in the function which relates rewards to education, and that these discontinuities will correspond to culturally recognized status thresholds in the educational system. There are at least two ways of looking for such discontinuities.

One is derived from Bidwell's depiction of the resulting reward structure as following a "stair-step" function. The second is to search for reward shifts associated with the possession of degrees and certificates. Although the first method motivates the procedures which are developed in this paper, it is worth considering the alternative method in some detail since it has much intuitively to recommend it.

Consider first the arguments raised by Faia, who employs dummy variables for "Respondent's Highest Earned Degree" in various regression analyses of occupation and income on education. Arguing against using thresholds in years of completed schooling he writes:

> The correlations between primary/secondary schooling and high school graduation (.49) and between college schooling and bachelor's- or graduate-level certification (.55 and .66, respectively) indicate that schooling and certification variables are conceptually and statistically distinct, and that there is substantial danger in using four years of college as a proxy for graduation (as in Jencks et al. 1979). Respondents holding the bachelor's degree as the highest degree have had anywhere from 14 to 20+ years of schooling. In addition, academic certification in Western societies is typically celebrated by elaborate ceremonies amounting to a rite of passage that rivals baptisms, bar mitzvahs, initiations, engagements, weddings, retirements, and funerals in its social poignancy. (1981, 1101)

Unfortunately, his arguments are not as persuasive as they first appear. For example, while the correlations he reports seem low, there are statistical, as well as substantive reasons for them not to be much higher.[6] More importantly, there are problems with his methodology which make the effects of the "highest degree" dummy variables difficult to interpret. Essentially, his procedure is to introduce the dummy variables for educational credentials into a model which already includes controls for years of education (actually a non-linear effect for years of education). The effects of the degree levels are then to produce shifts in intercepts depending on the highest degree earned. (See Figure 9.2) That this procedure is open to varying interpretations can be seen more easily by means of a simple comparison as in Table 9.1. The differences in degree status after controlling for years of schooling can be discerned by reading across the rows of this table. One of the meanings of having a higher or lower credential than would be expected by the number of years of schooling is that one is perceived as an over- or under- achiever for a given number of years of school. Thus, rather than reflecting a fetishism of degrees on the part of the population of employers, a positive effect of degree status controlling for years of schooling might just as easily indicate a preference in favor of over-achievers, e.g., those who have achieved certificates by spending fewer years in schools compared to those who have failed to amass enough graduation credits. In short, although initially plausible, the dummy variable methodology of Faia is not without problems.

FIGURE 9.2   Faia's Model of Educational Credentialism

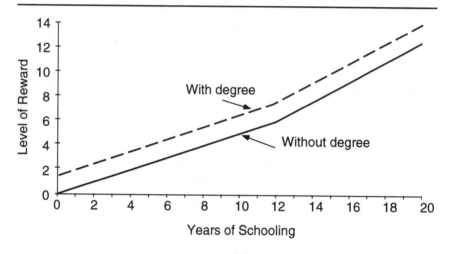

TABLE 9.1   Typology of Degree Recipients by Years of Schooling

| Years of Schooling | High School Degree | | College Degree |
	No	Yes	Yes
1 to 11	Dropouts	Skipped grade/GED	Child prodigy
12 to 15	Not enough credits	"Regular grad"	Accelerated BA
16 or more	Null?	Not enough credits	"Regular grad"

As an alternative to this approach, the method used here explicitly incorporates the idea of a discontinuous, stair-step function relating education to outcome. To assess whether an industry is responding to credentials rather than continuously varying levels of achievement, the "stair-step" functional form is directly compared to other functional forms and its superiority, or lack thereof, is evaluated by means of a test of statistical significance. In other words, the question is not whether the threshold credential model fits; it is how well it fits compared to the likely alternatives. In Figure 9.3 and Figure 9.4, I show the credential model I have specified and two of the alternative models it is tested against.

The alternative model in Figure 9.3 is a modification of the bilinear spline function utilized by Featherman and Hauser to capture differing returns to education at different levels of the education system. Their interpretation of a similar model, one that includes different slopes for education before

FIGURE 9.3   Stair-step Credential vs. Spline Functions of Educational Reward

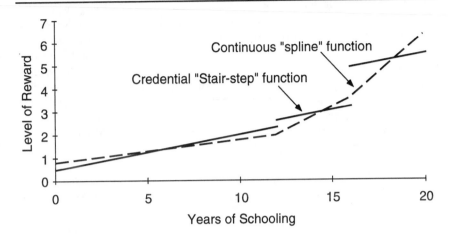

FIGURE 9.4   Stair-step Credential Models with Correct and Low Thresholds

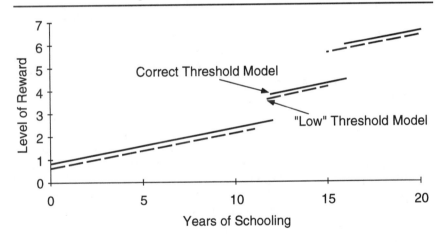

and after grade 12, is that ... "the additional premium for college is consistent with standard economic interpretations that the college-educated are more productive or trainable than others workers." (1978, 261) Thus, this continuous, piece-wise regression model can be taken to represent the human capital or "technological function" theories which are anathema to Collins and Faia.

A few moments reflection, however, should convince the reader that these two models are not easily compared to one another using conventional statistical tests. That is *each* of the alternative models contains terms which are not included in the other—a situation known as non-nested alternative models in the statistical literature. Recently, however, some appropriate methods for this situation have been brought to the attention of sociological audiences. (Weakliem 1992; Halaby and Weakliem 1993) Building on earlier statistical work (Cox 1961, Pesaran 1974), they introduce tests which can be used to determine whether each of the two non-nested alternatives significantly outperforms the other. In fact, Weakliem (1993) presents two different tests which he demonstrates to be asymptotically equivalent, the "N test", derived by Pesaran and used in Weakliem and Halaby's income models, and the "P test", developed by Davidson and Mackinnon (1983). With either of these tests, four basic outcomes are possible: (1) the alternative model—the spline regression function in this instance—can reject, i.e., outperform the null model—the credential model, but not vice-versa; (2) the null model can reject the alternative, but not vice versa; (3) both can mutually reject each other; and (4) neither can reject the other. In this analysis, I run separate income regressions (described below) within each of the Census detailed industries and identify those cases in which, as in (2) above, the credentialling model rejects the spline model. The test used here is the P test which is somewhat less computationally intensive than the N test.[7]

There are two other alternatives against which the credentialling model of Figure 9.3 is evaluated, one of which is shown in Figure 9.4. The alternative model has the same basic, discontinuous form as the credentialling model, with one important difference—the threshold points are located one grade level below the culturally defined thresholds of 8, 12, and 16 years used in the credentialling model. The logic of this test is that the credentialling model is more than a simple test of discontinuity in a reward function, but incorporates the added restriction that the discontinuity must occur at culturally meaningful points. Again, cases in which the null model rejects the alternative, but not vice-versa, are taken as evidence in favor of the credential hypothesis within an industry. A third set of comparisons is also made which are similar to those of Figure 9.4 except that the cutpoints are located one grade level above the thresholds incorporated in the credentialling model.

Before describing the data which are used to estimate these models, I should mention some of the weaknesses and limitations of the technique used here. As Bidwell astutely points out, the threshold structure of American education is not as simple as what is represented in these figures. The most important complication, which has been impossible to introduce here, is that the system of educational credentials differentiates horizontally as one moves progressively higher beyond secondary education and college. This is particularly true as one considers the interrelation of educational credentials and occupational entry requirements. However, the topic here is between-industry variation in educationally credentialling and the fact that occupation-related credentials are not fully detected here is not particularly troubling. A second pitfall is that there is some slippage between years of completed education and the possession of degrees and diplomas, although not nearly so much as Faia claims. Because of limitations in the data used, some error is inherent in estimating the presence of credential effects.[8]

Data: Education Regressions Within Industries

The basic source of data for the within-industry regressions is the 1% Public Use Microdata Sample (PUMS) from the 1980 US Census of Population. The advantage of this sample is that it contains enough observations to provide a suitably large number of cases within each industry. These data have been repeatedly used in other labor market studies and provide measures of many of the variables which are necessary for present purposes. Because the subsequent analysis will involve comparing the results of significance tests across different industries, samples of a constant size, i.e., 1500 elements, were drawn from each of the 3-digit industries identified in the Census.[9] Individuals were excluded from the industry regressions if (a) they were not wage and salary workers; (b) their industry affiliation was not reported; or (3) they worked less than 1 week in 1979.

The following variables were extracted and, where necessary, recomputed for use in the income regressions. The dependent variable was wage and salary income in 1979. The individual's total work hours in 1979 were estimated by multiplying the usual hours worked per week times the number of weeks worked in the year. Three work experience variables were used in the basic regressions. The first two were derived from the standard transformation used to estimate work experience from Census data, i.e. the individual's age minus highest grade attended minus 6. This was entered in quadratic form as experience and experience squared. The third work experience measure was a work interruption dummy variable based on a question about the respondent's work activity five years ago (a question used in the 1980 Census, but not repeated in 1990). Individuals with at least five potential years of work experience were scored 1 on this dummy variable if they were not working in 1975, all others were scored zero. Sex was coded 1 if respondents were female and 0 if they were male. Dummy variables were also included for race (1=black) and Spanish origin (1=Mexican, Puerto Rican, Cuban, or Other Spanish). In addition, control variables were added for ability to speak English (0=only speaks English to 4="Not at all"), and for non-metropolitan residence (1=outside SMSA).

Education was, of course, treated in varying ways in the different specifications described above. Although each equation included a term ranging from 0 to 20 corresponding to the respondent's highest grade completed, the meaning of this term varies depending upon the other education terms included. In the spline, or varying slopes, specification, the coefficient for the overall education term indexes the slope of income on education in the lowest education group, 12 years or less. In the credential or "stair-step" specifications, the coefficient for the overall education term indexes the change in income per year of education within each threshold block, where the slopes are assumed constant.

Data: Credential Regressions Across Industries

To investigate our hypotheses about the varying use of education as a credential across employers, several variables needed to be measured at the industrial level. First, each industry's labor force was characterized by two demographic variables: the proportion of female employees and the proportion of black employees. These were calculated from the same sample used for the within-industry regressions.

Two variables representing rewards for work experience were derived from the within-industry regression coefficients of income on experience and experience squared. Although the general form of the income-experience functions were the same in all industries, the familiar inverted U-shape, the specific forms of these functions differed in two ways across the industries under consideration. First, some were flatter than others, indicating a lower "total" return to experience over the life course. (A main tenet of human capital theory is that female workers are more likely to be found in work settings which offer less return to experience.) The curves also differed in a second way, however, which was the location of the "turning point" in the income returns to experience. That is, in some industries "skill depreciation" sets in at later ages than in other industries. To the extent that educational credentials favor the young over the old, we would expect that the "turning point" measure would be negatively correlated with credentialism across industries.[10] It is important to keep in mind that the dependent variable at issue in this paper is not simply the return to education, but how much better a discontinuous education specification performs compared to a continuous one.

Required skills for each industry were aggregated from two CPS supplement interviews which were conducted in January of 1981 and January of 1983. Each employed respondent was asked to indicate whether the job which he or she now held required skills obtained outside of the current employing organization. The two variables used here are (1) the proportion of respondents who said that their jobs required skills obtained from formal company training in a previous position, and (2) the proportion of respondents who said that their jobs required skills obtained from formal schooling. If credentials are being used as an aid in the process of selecting employees into jobs where skills are required, these variables would be expected to be associated with credentialling in a positive direction. On the other hand, if credentialling is tantamount to a ritualistic use of education, these variables would be expected to be negatively associated with it.[11]

To investigate the three institutional hypotheses, several other variables were taken into account. For some institutional variables, data were extracted from the US Commerce Department, Bureau of Economic Analysis file, "The Detailed Input-Output Structure of the US Economy, 1977". To capture the influence of consumer market orientation within each industry, advertising expenditures in millions of dollars by the industry were included.[12] For the second dimension of labor market institutionalization, susceptibility to government influence, the percentage of all purchases which were made by government bodies from each industry were used as an indicator.[13] In addition, a dummy variable coded "1" for industries in the "Public Administration" sector was included. As a first approximation to representing the institutional factor of having a "non-tangible" product, dummy variables for the "Finance", and "Service" sectors were also included as predictors. Finally, as a rough indicator of industry bureaucratization, a measure of average firm size in each industry was utilized.[14]

Findings

Table 9.2 summarizes the results of the three separate non-nested model tests across the 230 industries included in this analysis. As noted, four types of outcomes are possible with each of these tests. Evidence in favor of the credentialling model occurs when the comparison model is taken as the null hypothesis, and the credentialling model "rejects" or outperforms it. Industries with this outcome are classified in category (row) 4 of this table. The opposite case exists when the alternative model performs better than the credentialling model, and these outcomes are tabulated in row 1 of Table 9.2. Inconclusive results occur when both or neither model rejects the other. Industries in one of these situations are tabulated in rows 2 and 3.

As expected, the credentialling model does not apply to all segments of the labor market. Depending upon the alternative model considered, it is significantly better in between 26% and 53% of the industries. As a test of the agreement among the different tests of credentialling, cross-tabulations were constructed on these three variables after the two middle outcomes, i.e., those representing inconclusive results, were combined. (see Table 9.3) Although there is not perfect correspondence among these different tests, the level of agreement is reasonably high.

Before attempting to explain this between-industry variation in educational credentialling, it is worthwhile examining the actual income regressions from two industries that differ on these dimensions. Sample within-

TABLE 9.2: Outcomes of Non-nested Tests of Threshold-Credential Model
Across 230 Industries: US Census Data 1980

		MODELS BEING COMPARED		
		Credential vs low threshold model	Credential vs high threshold model	Credential vs differing slope model
	Outcomes of Non-Nested Tests	% of Industries	% of Industries	% of Industries
1	Alternative model rejects credential model	7.4	17.0	37.4
2	Neither model rejects other	36.1	13.5	20.0
3	Both models reject other	3.9	35.2	17.0
4	Credential model rejects alternative	52.6	34.3	25.7
	Total*	100.0%	100.0%	100.1%
	Number of cases	(230)	(230)	(230)

* Totals do not add to 100% because of rounding

industry regressions are shown in Tables 9.4 and 9.5. Results from a "credentialized industry", Pulp, Paper and Paperboard Mills, are shown in Table 9.4. (Following earlier work, e.g. Halaby and Weakliem, a cutoff value of 2.50, rather than 1.96, is used as a criterion for rejecting one model in favor of another.) This industry satisfies all of the three non-nested tests shown in Table 9.2: The "P" statistic for the credential model compared to the differing slope model is 5.85 (the reverse test has a value of 1.76); for the credential model compared to the "low threshold model" the statistic is 5.60 (the reverse test has a value of 0.04); and for the credential model compared to the "high threshold" model, the value of the statistic is 7.70 (the reverse test has a value of 0.84). Consistent with expectations, the effect of the overall years of education variable nearly disappears when the credential discontinuities are taken into account in model 2. (The difference in slope and difference in intercept parameters have been coded in such a way that the coefficients for each term represent the *change* in the size of the effect from the previous level. In Model 2, for example, there is an upward shift of $1700 in earnings at 12 years of schooling and another upward shift of $8500 at 16 years of schooling.) The effects of the other variables in the model are also largely consistent with expectations. There are wage penalties associated with being female and with being Black—although

TABLE 9.3: Consistency of Non-nested Tests of Threshold-Credential Model Across 230 Industries: US Census Data 1980

	Alt. model rejects cred. model	Inconclusive result	Cred. model rejects alt.	Total
Low Threshold as Alternative	*High Threshold as Alternative*			
Alt. model rejects credential model	41.2%	35.3%	23.5%	100.0% (17)
Inconclusive result	26.1%	47.8%	26.1%	100.0% (92)
Credential model rejects alternative	6.6%	51.2%	42.2%	100.0% (121)
Gamma =.412, p<.001				
Low Threshold as Alternative	*Different Slope Model as Alternative*			
Alt. model rejects credential model	100.0%	0.0%	0.0%	100.0% (17)
Inconclusive result	45.7%	45.7%	8.7%	100.1% (92)
Credential model rejects alternative	22.3%	35.5%	42.2%	100.0% (121)
Gamma =.669, p<.001				
High Threshold as Alternative	*Different Slope Model as Alternative*			
Alt. model rejects credential model	82.1%	15.4%	2.6%	100.1% (8)
Inconclusive result	34.8%	52.7%	12.5%	100.0% (108)
Credential model rejects alternative	19.0%	25.3%	55.7%	100.0% (114)
Gamma=.686 p<.001				

TABLE 9.4: Within Industry Regression in Sample Credential Industry: Pulp, Paper, and Paperboard Mills Census Industry 160 (Number of Cases=1500)

	Model 1		Model 2		Model 3	
	b	t	b	t	b	t
Intercept	-15786.0	-10.42*	-5664.3	-2.80*	-7938.8	-4.08*
Hours Worked	6.46	16.74*	6.00	15.72*	6.23	16.28*
Experience	585.1	11.38*	615.0	12.21*	632.8	12.33*
Experience Sqrd	-8.22	-7.20*	-9.52	-8.44*	-9.84	-8.50*
Work Interruptions	-2445.1	-2.69*	-2746.1	-3.08*	-2736.4	-3.04*
Black	-2996.3	-3.91*	-3484.5	-4.64*	-3350.9	-4.42*
Latino	-257.7	-0.13	-905.2	-0.46	-1047.0	-0.53
English Problems	-1048.5	-1.74	-1700.6	-2.85*	-1612.2	-2.67*
Female	-5189.2	-8.69*	-4966.2	-8.49*	-5034.4	-8.53*
Non-metro	-435.4	-1.00	-113.4	-0.26	-144.2	-0.33
Education	1311.4	13.46*	362.5	2.00*	601.2	4.02*
Intercept Changes						
At 12 Years			1745.3	2.19*		
At 16 Years			8525.6	8.28*		
Slope Changes						
At 12 Years					1306.5	5.12*
At 16 Years					905.2	1.19
R-sqd Adj	.441		.465		.455	

*t significant, p<.05

none with being Latino—and earnings are lower for those with work interruptions, those with difficulty speaking English, and those working fewer hours.

Table 9.5 shows the wage patterns for the Membership Organization industry in which the credential model does not uniquely outperform the alternative models on any of the non-nested tests. The "P" statistic for the credential model compared to the differing slope model is -.60 (the reverse test has a value of 6.71); for the credential model compared to the "low threshold model" the statistic is 1.51 (the reverse test has a value of 2.11 and neither model rejects the other on this test); and for the credential model compared to the "high threshold" model, the value of the statistic is .34 (the reverse test has a value of 4.50). There are also some slight differences in the effects of many variables. The effect of poor English skills is not significant in this industry, and there is no significant decrement in earnings associated with Latino ethnicity, with being Black, or with having a work interruption.

TABLE 9.5   Within Industry Regression in Sample Non-Credential Industry: Membership Organizations- Census Industry 881 (Number of Cases=1500)

	Model 1		Model 2		Model 3	
	b	t	b	t	b	t
Intercept	-6505.9	-4.75*	-7334.3	-3.67*	-2290.0	-1.00
Hours Worked	5.27	16.97*	5.31	16.96*	5.22	17.03*
Experience	389.0	8.98*	398.9	9.15*	386.7	8.97*
Experience Sqrd	-6.33	-6.95*	-6.51	-7.11*	-6.51	-7.13*
Work Interruptions	-1185.3	-1.72	-1176.8	-1.70	-1142.7	-1.68
Black	-1098.7	-1.43	-1192.5	-1.55	-1123.0	-1.48
Latino	-236.5	-0.13	-282.4	-0.16	-117.7	-0.078
English Problems	687.4	1.17	662.2	1.13	370.8	0.64
Female	-5361.4	-11.09*	-5180.0	-10.51*	-5074.6	-10.52*
Non-metro	-2244.7	-3.50*	-2222.6	-3.46*	-2170.8	-3.43*
Education	757.6	8.31*	900.1	4.88*	414.7	2.12*
Intercept Changes						
At 12 Years			-1524.9	-1.72		
At 16 Years			-78.6	-0.08		
Slope Changes						
At 12 Years					-148.6	-0.53
At 16 Years					2868.9	6.35*
R-sqd Adj	.435		.436		.452	

*t significant, p<.05

Living in a non-metropolitan setting does, however, diminish one's income in this industry.

While these regression results illustrate the differences between industries with greater and lesser degrees of credentialling, they also introduce a cautionary note into the subsequent analysis. The non-nested tests here detect relatively superior performance in a model even when the underlying difference in variance explained is very modest. (see Tables 9.4 and 9.5) Thus, at this phase of the analysis, we conclude that educational credentialism is relatively widespread, that it varies in occurrence across different segments of the economy, but that it may not be a social force of overwhelming empirical importance. Of course, to the extent that variations in credentialism can be explained, they are worth pursuing in more detail.

As a step in this direction, Tables 9.6 and 9.7 present results which are relevant to our preliminary hypotheses. There are three dependent variables in these tables, one for each of the non-nested tests on which the credential model can be compared to its rival. Each variable is scored 0, if the alternative model outperforms the credential model, 1 if the results are inconclusive, and 2 if the credential model outperforms the alternative. This scoring scheme is appropriate for the hypotheses under consideration, particularly when the differing slope and differing intercept models are being compared, in so far as low scores are consistent with a human capital interpretation and high scores with a credentialling interpretation. However, because the distribution of this variable is rather skewed, OLS regression is bypassed in favor of a technique which is better suited to this ordinal dependent variable-ordered probit analysis (Winship and Mare, 1983). The coefficients have been estimated in such a way that positive values mean that an industry with higher values on the independent variable are more likely to have higher credential scores. Table 9.6 contains the full range of predictor values relevant to our hypotheses, and Table 9.7 presents trimmed models with only those sets of variables which have significant partial effects.

Starting with the hypotheses about the presence of black and female workers, there is little evidence in favor of our initial hypothesis. While the proportion of black workers has an effect in the hypothesized direction, it never approaches statistical significance. Moreover, there is quite strong evidence in favor of the proposition that industries with higher concentrations of male, not female, workers tend to reward them in a credentialist fashion.

Evidence in favor of the institutional effects is best described as mixed. First, having a governmental entity as a customer has little to do with how an industry responds to educational attainment. Second, when the industry is a governmental entity, there is a significant tendency for education to be used in a *non*-credentialized manner—a finding consistent with Berg's observations in the early 70's. Third, the coefficient for expenditures on advertising also has the wrong sign and is not very large in any case. Fourth, in those instances when service industries differ systematically from other groupings, they, too, tend to reward education in a continuous, rather than a step-wise fashion. Fifth, average firm size in an industry also appears unrelated to credentialism, casting doubt on the bureaucratic ritualism hypothesis. On the other hand, industries in the financial services sector are strongly predisposed toward educational credentialling. In light of the patterns for other service industries, however, it is necessary to ask whether this stems from this sector producing an intangible product, or results from some other reason.

There are also only weak effects associated with the experience variables. Industries where experience continues to payoff well into a worker's career, i.e., those with late turning points, are those which eschew stepwise reward functions in favor of continuous ones; that is they behave in a non-credentialist fashion. The same is true, although not significantly so, for

TABLE 9.6   Between Industry Predictors of Educational Credentialism:
Ordered Probit Analysis. N=227.

	ALTERNATIVE HYPOTHESES TO EDUCATION STEP FUNCTION					
	Varying Slopes		Low Cut Points		High Cut Points	
	Coeff.	Chi-Sq	Coeff.	Chi-Sq	Coeff.	Chi-Sq
Intercept 1	-2.96	18.79*	-2.88	17.92*	-2.39	13.38*
Intercept 2	-1.82	7.39*	-1.31	3.93*	-.900	1.98
Experience Turning Point	-.032	3.69†	-.020	1.52	-.020	1.75
Total Return to Experience	-1.71e-6	2.27	6.0e-7	.284	-8.2e-7	.550
Female	-1.60	9.41*	-.319	.368	-1.11	4.68*
Black	1.34	.484	1.59	.642	2.26	1.41
Requires Skill from previous job	-3.27	3.53†	-3.41	3.90*	-3.99	5.61*
Requires Skill from School	-1.15	2.07	-.375	.223	1.07	1.90
Expenditure on Advertising	-7.7e-4	3.72†	-9.9e-4	7.70*	-2.7e-4	.613
Missing Advertis. Data	.059	.030	-.378	1.15	.525	2.40
Average Firm Size	7.2e-3	1.49	8.3e-3	1.70	6.9e-4	.014
Missing Firm Size Data	.039	.042	-.251	1.69	-.212	1.30
Pct of Purchases by Gov't	-.016	2.45	-.017	2.77†	.010	1.15
Missing Gov't Data	.217	.567	.169	.342	.303	1.19
Public Administration	-1.39	5.75*	.104	.040	-.375	.569
Finance	2.50	15.62*	1.18	3.38†	2.11	9.51*
Service	-.094	.109	-.579	3.97*	-.529	3.56†
Model Chi-Square	59.26	(15)	37.31	(15)	34.18	(15)

* Chi-Square significant, p <.05
† Chi-Square significant, p <.10

industries with high total returns to experience. Thus, the speculation that credentials and experience are alternative criteria for allocating employment rewards is tentatively supported in this analysis.

Perhaps the most interesting results in these tables, though, relate to whether jobs in the industry require skills which are obtained from formal

TABLE 9.7 Between Industry Predictors of Educational Credentialism: Trimmed Ordered Probit Analysis. N=227.

| | ALTERNATIVE HYPOTHESES TO EDUCATION STEP FUNCTION | | | | | |
| | Varying Slopes | | Low Cut Points | | High Cut Points | |
	Coeff.	Chi-Sq	Coeff.	Chi-Sq	Coeff.	Chi-Sq
Intercept 1	-3.08	21.98*	-2.25	88.95*	-1.66	46.42*
Intercept 2	-1.96	9.25*	-.731	13.68*	-.203	.822
Experience Turning Point	-.031	3.76†	——	——	——	——
Total Return to Experience	-1.57e-6	2.52	——	——	——	——
Female	-1.57	9.29*	——	——	-.881	4.59*
Requires Skill from previous job	-3.33	3.95*	-2.73	2.99†	-3.83	5.98*
Requires Skill from School	-1.42	4.78*	-.288	.219	.501	.625
Expenditure on Advertising	-7.0e-4	3.30†	-8.5e-4	6.23*	——	——
Missing Advertis. Data	.124	.403	-.389	4.01*	——	——
Public Administration	-.968	3.49†	——	——	——	——
Finance	2.47	16.82*	.814	1.90	1.73	7.37*
Service	——	——	-.838	12.75*	-.507	4.84*
Model Chi-Square	54.58	(9)	27.82	(6)	25.73	(5)

* t significant, p <.05
† t significant, p <.10

training in previous jobs or require skills which are taught in school. In both instances, and particularly in the case of skills obtained through formal on-the-job training, there are negative relationships with the use of education as a credential. In other words, in those jobs where skills obtained through formal training are important, education tends to be rewarded in a relatively continuous fashion, not in a step-wise fashion. What is important about this result, however, is that these data show that both tendencies operate simultaneously in the economy. Certain industries fit the human capital account of why schooling matters: their jobs require skills obtained from formal training and they reward years of education in a relatively smooth and continuous fashion. Other industries fit the opposite pattern: they are less likely to be concerned about skills which are associated with formal learning experiences and they reward education in discrete blocks.

Conclusions

This paper started with the premise that educational credentialism, as an example of cultural symbolism, implied the necessity of examining the characteristics of those social actors, i.e. employers, who are the audience for the symbols in question. Rather than postulating a constant cultural tendency to attend to the symbolic side of educational achievement, I hypothesized that different parts of the economic structure would show greater and lesser proclivities in this direction. In addition, extant theories of labor market organization were used in a preliminary attempt to explain patterns in between-industry response to educational achievements.

The results were strongly supportive of the argument's basic premise. There are measurable and consistent differences between types of employers in how they respond to various levels of educational achievement, and these differences conform to the definition of credentialling derived from earlier work. While the explanation of these between-industry patterns is perhaps in a more formative state, the outlines of an emergent explanation can be detected.

In general, hypotheses derived from the institutional paradigm are not consistent with these data. Instead, industries which use education in a credential-like manner are also those in which skills obtained from formal training are not required. These results also revealed a tendency for credentialism to hold sway in industrial settings numerically dominated by men and in the financial services sector. These patterns suggest there may be a strong element of traditionalism in educational credentialism. The financial services sector remains among the most culturally conservative groupings in our society, and with recent increases in the proportion of females in the labor market, industries with higher proportions of men seem appropriately characterized as more traditional. If this is the case, one might predict that even the limited extent of educational credentialling found in this analysis, and in several others, will become scarcer as time goes by.

Notes

I am grateful for the assistance of J. Beggs in helping with access to machine-readable data sources; to L. Biggs for advice on certain computations; and to the members of the UIC Social Organization thesis seminar for general comments. Helpful suggestions were also provided by M. Hout , C. Bidwell, and S. Spilerman.

1. These theories differ as to whether the latent productivity traits in question are achieved in school or are inherent in individuals. From the point of view of the present paper, this distinction is not particularly relevant.

2. Bidwell sees matters differently, arguing that signalling theory's propensity to construe education as a symbol means that it has an inherent tendency to posit discontinuities in the function which relates success to schooling. (127)

3. His evidence for this proposition is that in a sample of California employers those who had made the greatest efforts at racial integration were those with the highest educational requirements. How this should be interpreted is not immediately obvious. Is the role of high educational requirements akin to "status" insurance for the organization's public image whereby members of culturally devalued groups can be safely incorporated only if they meet "stringent" standards? Or, is the point that organizations for their internal control functions require a certain amount of "cultural exclusivity" in their hiring practices which will be satisfied one way or another?

4. This is supplemented in their analysis with consideration of the role of college quality and the role of majoring in a business subject. Spilerman and Lunde do find evidence that attendance at a more selective college and pursuit of a major in business both act as "credentials", in the productivity signalling sense of the word. Unfortunately, measures of these factors are absent in the data which we use.

5. He observes this to be true in the private sector, but not, ironically, in the public sector.

6. Consider, for example, the reported correlation of .49 between Faia's "primary/secondary" years of education variable and having "high school graduation" as one's highest educational credential. As is well known, the maximum correlations for variables with restricted ranges, a dichotomy like high school graduation is an extreme example, tend to be less than one, with the degree of attenuation depending on the correspondence in the marginal distribution of the variables under examination.

As an experiment, I calculated the maximum possible correlation between Faia's "primary/secondary" education variable and the "high school graduation" variable on the assumption that all those, and only those, with 12, 13, 14 or 15 years of schooling had a high school degree as their highest level of certification. (Faia's reported departures from perfect correlation are supposed to reflect the fact that some people finish high school with less than 12 years in school, and that some with 12 to 15 years of school do not have a high school diploma as their highest degree— either because they failed to finish high school or because they have already finished college). The primary/secondary variable was coded in the same manner as Faia's, i.e. as a spline variable with a minimum of 0 and a maximum of 12. The distribution of education was taken from the 1980 PUMS file used in the subsequent analysis. The correlation coefficient between primary/secondary schooling and high school graduation under these conditions of "perfect association" is .525. In other words, Faia's correlation is 93% of its maximum value assuming complete association.

7. Both tests were conducted on a subset of industries and the conclusions reached on the basis of each test were identical.

8. Probably, we underestimate such effects since the data probably include more people with too many years of education for their degree status than vice versa. If so, these people will have negative residuals in the credential model, but will perhaps fall closer to the regression line in the spline models.

9. Two industries with less than 100 observations, "Not specified professional equipment manufacturing" and "Not specified electrical and hardware products wholesaling" were dropped from the analysis. The analysis reported here does include data from 16 industries with between 284 and 1000 incumbents, and another

30 industries with between 1000 and 1500 incumbents.

10. The two measures were calculated as follows:

The total return measure was the area under the income - experience curve (ignoring the portion constant across industries) calculated at 50 years of experience. The specific calculation was:

$$\text{TotRet} = \left[\frac{b}{2}x^2 + \frac{c}{3}x^3\right]_0^{50}$$

The turning point measure was defined as:

$$\text{TurnPt} = -\frac{b}{2c}$$

where   b=coefficient for experience
        c=coefficient for experience squared

11. To better probe the signalling hypothesis, it would be desirable to have additional data. For example, industries in which employers agreed with the statement, "It is difficult to tell ahead of time who will work out on this job" should be those which rely on credentials as a signal. Unfortunately, these measures are not available for a broad cross-section of industries.

12. Within the manufacturing sector, the transportation and utility sector, and the service sector, missing values were replaced by the within-sector means. In the wholesale and retail trade sectors in which detailed industries were not covered in the Input-Output table, missing values were replaced by the overall mean. Again, a dummy variable was included in the regressions to index those cases where means were substituted.

13. Here, too, means were substituted for missing cases and a "missing case" dummy variable was entered as a control variable.

14. The basic data are those used by Beggs (1994) and were originally coded from the 1977 and 1982 economic censuses. For industries where the economic census data were unavailable, values were estimated using the following procedure: In the Annual Demographic File of the Current Population Survey, respondents report the number of people working for their employer. These estimates were aggregated to the industrial level and for those cases where both the economic census and CPS aggregates were available, the former were regressed on the latter. The resulting prediction equation was then used to estimate missing cases on the economic census measure from the aggregated CPS figures. A dummy variable was created to indicate which cases had been estimated in this way and it was also entered into the final analyses.

References

Althauser, Robert, and Arne Kalleberg. 1981. Firms, Occupations, and the Structure of Labor Markets: A Conceptual Analysis. In *Sociological Perspectives on Labor Markets.*, ed. Ivar Berg. New York: Academic Press.

Baron, James N., P. Devereaux-Jennings, and Frank R. Dobbin. 1988. "Mission Control? The Development of Personnel Systems in U.S. Industry." *American Sociological Review* 53:497-514.

Becker, G. 1964. *Human Capital*. New York: Columbia University Press.

Beggs, John J. 1994. The Effects of the Institutional Environment on Inequality. Unpublished manuscript. Department of Sociology. Louisiana State University.

Berg, Ivar. 1971. *Education and Jobs: The Great Training Robbery*. Boston: Beacon Press.

Bidwell, Charles E. 1989. "The Meaning of Educational Attainment." *Research in the Sociology of Education and Socialization* 8:117-38.

Bielby, William T., and James N. Baron. 1986. "Men and Women at Work: Sex segregation and statistical discrimination." *American Journal of Sociology* 91:759-99.

Bourdieu, Pierre. 1977. Cultural Reproduction and Social Reproduction. In *Power and Ideology in Education.*, ed. J. Karabel and A. H. Halsey. New York: Oxford University Press.

Bridges, William P., and Wayne J. Villemez. 1991. "Employment Relations and the Labor Market: Integrating Institutional and Market Perspectives." *American Sociological Review* 56:748-64.

Collins, Randall. 1979. *The Credential Society*. New York: Academic Press.

Cox, D. R. 1961. Tests of Separate Families of Hypotheses. In *Proceedings of the Fourth Berkeley Symposium on Mathematical Statistics and Probability.*, ed. J. Neyman. Vol. 1. Berkeley: University of California Press.

Davidson, Russell, and James G. MacKinnon. 1983. "Some Non-nested Hypothesis Tests and the Relations Among Them." *Review of Economic Studies* 49:551-65.

DiMaggio, Paul, and John Mohr. 1985. "Cultural Capital, Educational Attainment and Marital Selection." *American Journal of Sociology* 90:1231-61.

DiMaggio, Paul J., and Walter W. Powell. 1983. "The Iron Cage Revisited: Institutional Isomorphism and Collective Rationality in Organizational Fields." *American Sociological Review* 48:147-60.

DiPrete, Thomas. 1989. *The Bureaucratic Labor Market: The Case of the Federal Civil Service*. New York: Plenum Press.

Dobbin, Frank, John R. Sutton, John W. Meyer, and W. Richard Scott. 1993. "Equal Opportunity Law and the Construction of Internal Labor Markets." *American Journal of Sociology* 99:396-427.

Edelman, Lauren. 1990. "Legal Environments and Organizational Governance." *American Journal of Sociology* 95:1401-40.

Faia, Michael. 1981. "Selection by Certification." *American Journal of Sociology* 86:1093-1111.

Featherman, David L., and Robert M. Hauser. 1978. *Opportunity and Change*. New York: Academic Press.

Halaby, Charles N., and David L. Weakliem. 1993. "Ownership and Authority in the Earnings Function: Non-nested Tests of Alternative Specifications." *American Sociological Review* 58:16-30.

Meyer, John, and Brian Rowan. 1977. "Institutionalized Organizations: Formal Structure as Myth and Ceremony." *American Journal of Sociology* 83:364-85.

Pesaran, M. H. 1974. "On the General Problem of Model Selection." *Review of Economic Studies* 41:153-71.

Spence, Michael A. 1974. *Market Signaling*. Cambridge, Mass.: Harvard Univ. Press.

Spilerman, Seymour and Tormod Lunde. 1991. "Features of Educational Attainment and Job Promotion Prospects." *American Journal of Sociology*. 97:689-720.

Stiglitz, J. 1975. "The Theory of 'Screening', Education, and the Distribution of Income." *American Economic Review* 65:283-300.

Weakliem, David L. 1992. Comparing Non-nested Models for Contingency Tables. In *Sociological Methodology, 1992.*, ed. Peter Marsden. Vol. 22. Oxford: Basil Blackwell.

Williamson, Oliver. 1975. *Markets and Hierarchies.* New York: Free Press.

Winship, Christopher, and Robert Mare. 1984. "Regression Models with Ordinal Variables." *American Sociological Review* 49:512-25.

Zucker, Lynne G. 1987. "Institutional Theories of Organizations." *Annual Review of Sociology* 13:443-64.

10

Education, Earnings Gain, and Earnings Loss in Loosely and Tightly Structured Labor Markets: A Comparison between the United States and Germany

Thomas A. DiPrete
Duke University
Patricia A. McManus
Indiana University

The Link between Education and Earnings

Education is positively associated with earnings in all industrialized countries. The human capital explanation for this connection is that education provides skills, that skills are costly to obtain, and that the market therefore pays a return to these skills. Sociologists and institutional economists recognize the connection between education and earnings to be more complex than this skill-focused explanation suggests, for several well-known reasons. Whereas at least some skills are common to all countries at a given level of technological development, the way these skills are combined in the education process tends to show more cross-national variation. Furthermore, the credentials provided by the educational system show substantial cross-national variation, and the process by which individuals convert skills and credentials into job incumbency also differs by country. Finally, earnings are a function not merely (some would argue not even primarily) of one's skills, but also of one's occupation, and particularly of one's job. In short, the connection between earnings and skills is mediated by the processes that link earnings with jobs and occupations and that link people with jobs.

Much of the early sociological study of the linking processes between education and occupation involved measuring the effect of education on the attainment of occupational status. More recently, it has involved the study of how firms and corporate occupational bodies link or do not link training with the educational system. Sociology has also recently been concerned with the related question of how educational and training certification structure opportunities for occupational access and occupational mobility. Differences in the process by which individuals get access to occupations and change occupations is of course what scholars mean (at least in part) by the term "labor market structure." Thus, the new literature goes beyond either the human capital approach to education (education $\longrightarrow$ skills $\longrightarrow$ earnings) or the status attainment tradition (education $\longrightarrow$ occupational attainment) in focusing on the specific mechanisms by which individuals obtain and change jobs. These new studies in effect address the question: how does labor market structure create a linkage between education and labor market outcomes?

One important finding of the recent literature concerns the level of linkage between education and work institutions. Scholars have argued that education-work linkages are relatively tight in many continental countries and also in Japan (though the structure is quite different), while the linkages are relatively loose in the United States (e.g., Rosenbaum et. al. 1990). This assertion can be taken in two different senses. First, the process of matching individuals and jobs is relatively unsystematic in the United States. Workers jump from job to job at the start of their career learning about and evaluating their opportunities before they finally find a job that is suitable to their abilities and skills. In contrast, the school-to-work transition is more orderly in many other industrialized countries: the more standardized credentials make clear which occupation a particular individual is trained for, and the process of acquiring a suitable job thus occurs relatively quickly. Second, the statement that school to work linkages are weak in the United States can be taken to mean that even after the more lengthy American early career sorting process is concluded, the outcomes associated with a particular level of educational attainment or with a particular educational certificate or degree are more variable in the U.S. This variability exists because the more loosely structured American system does not prevent workers from obtaining jobs for which their education is not an obvious match to the extent found in more rigid systems.

The early career implications of tight or loose linkages between education and work have been thoroughly researched (Rosenbaum et al. 1990). Empirical investigations of how the school-to-work linkage affects the relationship between education and subsequent career experience, however, are less complete. Yet, the prediction about this relationship that follows from the above characterization of the school-to-work linkage is rather apparent. If linkages between education and job are tight in the early career, then one would expect education's subsequent impact on career processes to be mediated by initial placement. Subsequent outcomes should largely be a function of one's occupational and job position. This is particularly true if more structured labor markets create tighter links between occupation or job and rewards, as some scholars have found (Haller 1987). In contrast, individual resources should continue to affect career outcomes in more loosely structured labor markets, even when positional resources are controlled. The contrast between countries with weakly and strongly linked institutions should be even stronger in relatively turbulent economic periods—such as we are currently experiencing in the industrial world—because individual resources become still more important in loosely structured, turbulent labor markets. In other words, the looser linkages between education and early job placement in the United States should lead to stronger direct linkages between education and career dynamics in the United States than in countries where labor markets (and particularly the school to work transition) are more structured.

This paper explores this inference by analyzing education's role in career earnings change in two countries: Germany and the U.S. Differences between the German and American educational systems and their linkages to the world of work have been extensively discussed in the literature, and need not be repeated in full here (e.g., König and Müller 1986, Mayer et al. 1989; Blossfeld et al. 1989). Two differences need to be emphasized. First, the connections between education or training and the world of work are more systematic in Germany than in the U.S., because the German system produces standardized education and training credentials that are a prerequisite for most skilled jobs. Second, job-specific training is occupationally based in Germany, while in the U.S. a great deal of job-specific training is provided within firm-based internal labor markets as well as within occupations: the American system generates earnings trajectories that tend to rise both with years of tenure in a firm and with years of tenure in an occupation (DiPrete and McManus 1993).

Differences between the German and American labor markets lead to the following specific hypotheses. [1] We expect the direct effect of education to be stronger in the United States, because individual resources matter more in a society where the institutional "glue" that collectivizes life chances is stronger. [2] We expect the indirect effect of education (through occupation) to be stronger in Germany because of the tighter linkage between education/training and work. [3] In contrast to Germany, where training affects earnings largely through credentials and through the occupation to which these credentials provide access, the influence of training on labor market outcomes is revealed in the U.S. as effects of tenure in the firm or tenure in the occupation. The cross-national difference thus contrasts the effects of incumbency in a particular status and tenure in that status.

While data limitations prevent us from comparing historical periods, cross-national differences in these regards should be particularly strong in the 1980s relative to earlier times because of the partial breakdown of American internal labor markets that link individual outcomes together, and the consequent growing importance of individual level resources in determining labor market outcomes. The cross-national contrast should also be especially strong in recessions for the same reason: during recessions the internal labor markets that collectivize outcomes become weaker, and individual resources become a stronger predictor of outcomes. Our data do allow us to evaluate this second prediction.

Data and Methods

German data are from the English-language version of the German Socio-Economic Panel (GSOEP) and cover the six-year period from 1985 to 1991.[1] Given the recency of the German reunification, we restrict our attention to the West German sample, though we take account of reunification in the interpretation of the West German results.[2] American data for 1985-1991 are taken from the Panel Study of Income Dynamics (PSID). We divided this six year period into two three-year segments, and analyze three-year earnings mobility from 1985-1988 and then from 1988-1991. The first period is one of relative prosperity in both countries, while the second period is the start of a recession in both countries. The second period also encompasses the German reunification.

Results in this paper are computed for men only who were in one of the following two categories: [1] 18-61 years of age and employed in 1985, and sample respondents in the years 1985-1988, or [2] 18-61 years of age and employed in 1988, and sample respondents in the years 1988-1991. The males in the German sample, when weighted, constitute a representative sample of the western German population, including the foreign population resident in West Germany. The males in the PSID, when weighted, are representative of American male heads of households in 1968. Because much of our interest is in population comparisons, we use weighted PSID samples for our cross-national comparisons of earnings mobility (heads who are not descendants of original 1968 PSID sample families are given zero weights in the PSID). In our multivariate analyses designed to interpret cross-national differences, we use the full (unweighted) PSID sample.

We describe elsewhere (DiPrete and McManus 1995) the procedure we used to estimate earnings mobility. Briefly, we constructed a measurement model for earnings in Germany and in the U.S., in order to remove from measured earnings mobility that portion which is due to measurement error in the earnings reports at the two points in time between which mobility is measured. The German latent earnings variable is based on the following two measures:

[1] GEARN1: The respondent's answer to the question: "How high were your [gross] earnings last month?" It includes overtime but not holiday or back pay.

[2] GEARN2: The retrospective report from the following year survey of average gross monthly earnings for months in which the respondent received earnings. Respondents are asked to report earnings including sick-pay and compensation payments (but excluding bonuses such as holiday money), payments for training, self-employed earnings and earnings from second jobs.

We then constructed a similar measurement model for the PSID sample based on the following two measures:

[1] PEARN1: The total labor earnings in a calendar year as reported in the following PSID survey, divided by 12.

[2] PEARN2: The projected main job earnings for a calendar year computed from the wage per hour on the main job as reported in that year, the number of weeks worked on main jobs that year as reported in the following year's survey, and the average hours per week on main jobs in the calendar year as reported in the following year's survey.

We corrected the earnings data in both countries for inflation. We used CPI-U (The U.S. City Average for all Urban Consumers) for the US, and *Preise und Preisindizes für die Lebenshaltung* for Germany. In both the German and the American measurement model, we specified the metric of the latent earnings variable to be the same as the first of the two earnings measures (GEARN1 or PEARN1).

Results

We describe elsewhere (DiPrete and McManus 1995) the major differences in earnings mobility in the two countries. Briefly stated, Germany had substantially greater earnings growth during this period than did the United States. Furthermore, Germany had less variance in earnings outcomes. While part of the greater turbulence in the American results is due to the greater levels of job mobility found in the U.S., much of the earnings dynamics occurs within occupations and within jobs in the same firm. Here we focus on the effects of education and training on these earnings dynamics.

As a baseline against which to interpret later analyses, we first compare the relationship between education level and the log of 1985 monthly earnings for Germany and the United States. In this baseline model, we specified earnings to be a function of age, education and training.[3] Because the educational systems of the two countries differ, we used different educational benchmarks in the German and American analyses. For the

United States, we made the following mutually exclusive distinctions: (1) less than high school, (2) high school completion, (3) college attendance, and (4) college completion and post-graduate education. In Germany, we similarly distinguished four mutually exclusive educational levels (1) those who had not completed German lower schooling (*Hauptschule, Realschule*), including those with no degree, foreigners with a degree below the college level, and Germans who report "another" degree below the university level (*Anderer Abschluß*) other than those included in one of the categories below; (2) those who had completed lower intermediate schooling (*Hauptschulabschluß, Mittlere Reife, Realschulabschluß*), (3) those who had completed upper-intermediate schooling (*Fachhochschulreife – Abschluß einer Fachoberschule* or an *Abitur – Hochschulreife*), and (4) those who had completed technical school or university (*Hochschulabschluß, Fachhochschule, Universität, Technische/Sonstige Hochschule* or university degree from outside Germany). Educational level is measured every year in the GSOEP. In the PSID, the educational level of all household heads was measured in 1985.

In addition, we measured additional work-related training. For Germany we used the following three categories: (1) those who had completed an apprenticeship or vocational school (*Lehre, Berufsfachschule, Handelsschule, Schule des Gesundheitswesens*), (2) those who completed *Fachschule*, and (3) those with other vocational training (*Sonstige Ausbildung*). The United States does not have the extensive vocational training system found in Germany, but the PSID includes the following question: "Did you receive any other degree or a certificate through a vocational school, a training school, or an apprenticeship program?" We included the answer to this question as a variable in our analyses.

We next specified a more elaborate regression that included the baseline variables as well as variables which might mediate the effects of education, namely occupation, industry, tenure with current employer, and (in Germany) whether the worker had a term or an indefinite employment contract.[4] Given the relatively small samples found in panel data, we limited our occupational controls to modified EGP categories (Ganzeboom, Luijkx, and Treiman 1989), and used semi/unskilled manual work as the omitted category. Industry was measured using a common four-sector taxonomy, which we further elaborated for the manufacturing/mining sector.[5]

Table 10.1 shows the results from the baseline earnings model. These results demonstrate that education has a powerful influence on earnings in both the U.S. and Germany. The effects of college completion vs. intermediate-level schooling were very similar in the two countries (0.548-0.173 = 0.375 in Germany, and 0.784-0.372= 0.412 in the United States). Two differences between the U.S. and Germany are notable. First, training had a big impact on earnings in Germany. A worker with lower-intermediate education (*Hauptschulabschluß, Realabschluß*) who com-

TABLE 10.1   Effects of Education and Training on Log Earnings Germany
and the United States, 1985, Males only

Variable	Germany Coefficient	T-Ratio
Intercept	4.939	59.252
Age	.068	15.465
Age^2	-.001	-13.653
Lower School	.127	8.594
Middle School	.173	5.105
University	.548	25.483
Vocational Training	.095	6.904
Fachschule	.247	9.568
R^2	.28	
	United States	
Intercept	9.833	60.119
Age	.083	9.428
Age^2	-.001	-7.574
High School	.372	10.770
Some College	.488	13.209
College Degree	.784	22.478
Extra Certification	.019	.779
R^2	.22	

pleted both an apprenticeship and *Fachschule* (and most of those with *Fachschule* had only completed *Hauptschule or Realschule*) had the same expected earnings as did a respondent who had graduated from technical college or university (0.173+0.095+0.247= 0.515 vs. 0.548). The ready availability of economically valuable training credentials to workers who did not attend college implies narrower earnings differentials across levels of formal education than one finds in the United States, where extra certification outside of school had no obvious economic value. The second distinctive cross-national difference evident in table 10.1 concerns the earnings of Americans who did not complete high school. The earnings penalty for this group is considerably larger than for the comparable group in Germany.

Table 10.2 then elaborates table 10.1 by including the intervening variables mentioned above. These results support the claim that education and job placement are more tightly linked in Germany than in the U.S. and further suggest that the consequence of a looser linkage between education and job implies a stronger "direct" effect of education on earnings in the United States than in Germany. In the United States, the gap between the effects of college completion and high school shrank only slightly when

TABLE 10.2   Log Earnings, 1985 for the U.S. and Germany

	United States		Germany	
	Estimate	*T-Ratio*	*Estimate*	*T-Ratio*
Intercept	10.320	66.927	5.380	65.269
Age in 1985	0.061	7.438	0.048	11.161
Age^2	-0.001	-6.735	-0.001	-10.229
High School	0.228	7.041	—	—
Some College	0.322	8.978	—	—
College Degree	0.508	13.146	—	—
Other Cert.	0.018	0.786	—	—
Haupt/Real	—	—	0.036	2.252
Abitur	—	—	0.004	0.121
Uni/Fachhoch	—	—	0.191	5.398
Apprenticeship	—	—	0.070	5.038
Fachschule	—	—	0.144	5.667
Upper Prof/Mgr	0.621	13.505	0.550	21.994
Lower Prof/Mgr	0.421	12.671	0.227	10.625
Routine Nonman	0.180	4.384	0.157	5.493
Self-employed	-0.070	-1.299	0.394	11.278
Manual Superv	0.363	7.000	0.137	4.611
Skilled manual	0.250	8.072	0.062	3.727
Empl. Tenure	0.017	10.382	0.001	1.202
Union Member	0.181	6.876	0.034	2.930
Light Mfg	-0.200	-6.082	-0.054	-3.690
Comm/Tran/Util	0.005	-0.129	-0.110	-4.967
Whol/Ret Trade	-0.200	-5.497	-0.138	-5.277
Services	-0.236	-7.440	-0.173	-9.914
Term Contract	—	—	-0.111	-4.237
R^2	.35		.43	

intervening variables were included (from .412 to 0.28), while the gap between university and lower-intermediate schooling in Germany shrank more substantially (from .375 to 0.155). Similarly, the contraction is greater in Germany for the contrast between university completion and the lowest (omitted) educational category. One should note, however, that important direct effects of education and training remain for German males even after job attributes are taken into account. The existence of moderately strong direct effects of education and training suggest that job rewards differ in Germany even within the occupational and industrial categories specified in table 10.2, and that this within-category variation is directly linked to education. To phrase it differently, education and training credentials continue to affect earnings levels in Germany even after gross occupational and industry distinctions are taken into account.

The contrast between the strong effects of training on earnings in Germany and the absence of training effects in the United States is counterbalanced by the contrast between the virtual absence of employer tenure effects in Germany and their strong influence in the United States. In human capital models of American earnings, employer tenure is typically taken as an indicator of firm-specific training. From a human capital perspective, one might interpret the different pattern in the two countries as implying that the two systems for teaching job-related skills are functionally equivalent: American workers are rewarded for informal training, while German workers are rewarded for training credentials. However, this interpretation would be inadequate for two reasons. First, the absence of employer tenure effects on earnings in Germany remains even if training variables are removed from the model.[6] Second, the benefits of employer tenure in the U.S. are similar at all levels of educational attainment. In other words, the average American worker who lacks a college education does not offset this disadvantage via employer training (to state this more technically, there is no positive interaction between high school diploma and employer experience), while German workers who lack a college education can close the earnings gap between themselves and college educated workers by obtaining training certification.[7] Earnings returns to tenure are therefore a distinctive characteristic of American labor markets; they correspond to but are not equivalent to returns to training credentials in Germany. The employer tenure effect in the U.S. is undoubtedly an *average* effect that masks substantial variance at the individual level. But while an important component of such variation in Germany is manifestly measurable via training credentials, the variance in the U.S. is latent: it is an important aspect of American labor market structure, but it is not easily characterized.

Having established the connection between education and earnings in the two countries, we next focus on the relationship between education and earnings change. Table 10.3 examines the connection between earnings dynamics and education in the simplest possible way. Earnings change is represented as a dichotomous variable in which earnings gain (net of inflation) is distinguished from earnings decline.[8] The table shows a clear relationship between earnings gain and education in the United States, and a more ambiguous, weaker relationship in Germany. Overall, upward mobility was much more common during this period in Germany than it was in the United States, and the frequency with which it occurred appears to be largely independent of educational level. In the late 1980s, earnings mobility in Germany could accurately be described as a collective event that contrasts with the large variance in individual outcomes in the United States. Some of this variance in the United States is apparently attributable to education, since there is a noticeable pattern for college graduates to have higher probabilities of earnings gain than less educated workers. The pattern is strongest when comparing the extremes of the educational

TABLE 10.3   Earnings Mobility

Sample Limited to Those Employed at Start and End

	Germany			
	1985-1988		1988-1991	
	Upward	*Downward*	*Upward*	*Downward*
None/Other	83%	17%	77%	23%
Lower Intermediate				
No Apprenticeship	83%	17%	78%	22%
Appren/Vocational				
Training	82%	18%	74%	26%
Fachschule	83%	17%	78%	22%
Upper-Intermediate	88%	12%	71%	29%
University	83%	17%	71%	29%

	United States			
	1985-1988		1988-1991	
	Upward	*Downward*	*Upward*	*Downward*
Less than High School	58%	42%	43%	57%
High School Completion	60%	40%	51%	49%
Some College	60%	40%	48%	52%
College Completion	66%	34%	54%	46%

Sample Includes Those Not Working at Destination Time

	Germany			
	1985-1988		1988-1991	
	Upward	*Downward*	*Upward*	*Downward*
None/Other	72%	28%	71%	29%
Lower-Intermediate				
No Apprenticeship	73%	27%	71%	29%
Appren/Vocational				
Training	76%	24%	67%	33%
Fachschule	81%	19%	75%	25%
Upper-Intermediate	83%	17%	62%	38%
University	79%	21%	68%	32%

	United States			
	1985-1988		1988-1991	
	Upward	*Downward*	*Upward*	*Downward*
Less than High School	52%	48%	36%	64%
High School Completion	56%	44%	45%	55%
Some College	56%	44%	45%	55%
College Completion	63%	37%	50%	50%

distribution: the odds that a college graduate experienced a real earnings gain over three years were 30% higher than a high school graduate during 1985-88 and 40% higher than a worker who had not completed high school. The odds ratio for the contrast between college graduates and high school graduates narrowed somewhat during the second period, but the gap between college graduates and high school dropouts grew larger in the second period than the first.

The results described in table 10.3 are further confirmed in table 10.4, which shows the results of logistic regressions on the probability of earnings growth between 1985 and 1988 and between 1988 and 1991. When age and hours of work in the base year are controlled, American workers with college degrees were noticeably more likely to experience earnings gains than were workers with less education in both the first and in the second period. The German contrast between the top and bottom of the educational hierarchy is numerically as large as the contrast in the United States for the first period, though the standard errors are larger in Germany. Consistent with our predictions, the effects for the U.S. and Germany moved in different directions in response to the less favorable economic conditions in 1988-1991. The recession heightened the contrast between the earnings of American workers who had completed high school and those who had not. In Germany, full recession did not hit until 1992, but the period 1988-1991 was one of economic slowdown, exacerbated by the economic uncertainty which accompanied reunification. The slowdown actually reduced the effect of education or the direction of earnings change in Germany.

Table 10.4 is based only on the qualitative comparison of whether real earnings rose or fell over time. One might question whether the cross-national contrast would be as great if the analysis focused on changes in earnings rather than a dichotomous measure of earnings increase. We address this question by reporting regressions of the log of the ratio of earnings change in table 10.5.[9] The results without controls are presented in the left hand columns of each panel, while the results with controls for occupation, industry, employer tenure and other relevant variables are presented in the right hand panel for each set. Both sets of results suggest that cross-national comparisons based on the magnitude of earnings change differ from cross-national comparisons based on the direction of earnings change. In the first period (a period of prosperity), the total effects of education on earnings were actually greater in Germany than in the United States, which is not what our analysis of the direction of change showed. Education effects on the magnitude of change, however, disappeared in Germany during this period of economic slowdown, while they increased in the recessionary U.S. These results are consistent with the results we obtained using the direction of earnings change as the dependent variable. The increase in the size of the effects in the United States can largely be attributed

TABLE 10.4   Effect of Education on The Probability
of Upward Earnings Mobility

	United States					
	1985-1988			1988-1991		
	Estimate	Standard Error	Prob	Estimate	Standard Error	Prob
Intercept	8.082	1.0316	0.0001	5.5479	1.1265	.0001
Age	-.08	.0325	0.0142	-0.0781	.038	.0396
Age^2	.001	.0004	0.0788	0.0007	.0005	.1289
High School	.069	.1256	0.581	0.2599	.1378	.0594
Some College	.167	.1345	0.2155	0.2912	.1456	.0455
College Degree	.365	.1274	0.0041	0.4992	.1375	.0003
Extra Certification	-.024	.0882	0.7836	0.0214	.0934	.8188
Log hours/ month in base year	-1.142	.165	0.0001	-0.7656	.1622	.0001

	Germany					
Intercept	8.094	1.969	0.0001	3.511	2.19	0.1088
Age	-.044	.046	0.3361	-.047	.052	0.3638
Age^2	.0003	.0006	.5685	.00033	.00063	.6003
Lower/Intermediate	.17	.14	0.2234	-.074	.162	0.6473
Upper-Intermediate	.419	.366	0.2514	-.329	.328	0.3155
University	.342	.216	0.1126	-.134	.201	0.5053
Appren/Voc school	-.254	.135	0.0596	-.137	.14	0.3279
Fachschule	.049	.252	0.8452	.231	.239	0.3337
New Training	.372	.753	0.6215	.126	.656	0.8475

to the experience of those who lack a high school education, who did badly in the second period.[10]

The recession also changed the pattern of training effects in Germany. Vocational training had no discernible effect on earnings change in either period. The effect of gaining new training credentials during the three year period was important in the first period but not the second, while having a *Fachschule* certificate was important in the second period but not the first. The lack of stability in the German results may be due to the relatively small number of workers who gained new training credentials over a relatively short period of time. Overall, the results suggest that training, like education, has an impact in Germany on earnings trajectories apart from broad occupational and industrial categories, though the precise form of this relationship is somewhat ambiguous.

The results discussed so far are generally but not completely consistent with the hypotheses presented at the start of the paper. In general, the effects of education are more mediated in Germany than in the U.S. However, the cross-national contrast is not as crisp as it could be—educa-

TABLE 10.5   Effect of Education on the Log-Ratio of Earnings

United States

| | 1985-1988 | | | | 1988-1991 | | | |
| | Total Effects | | Partial Effects | | Total Effects | | Partial Effects | |
	Estimate	T-Ratio	Estimate	T-Ratio	Estimate	T-Ratio	Estimate	T-Ratio
Intercept	2.156	15.1	—	—	1.746	8.0	—	—
Age	-.017	-3.3	-.008	-1.5	.003	0.4	.004	0.5
Age²	.0002	2.4	.0001	1.0	-.0001	-1.2	-.0001	-1.4
High School	-.005	-0.3	.018	0.9	.056	2.0	.0644	2.3
Some College	.016	0.7	.03	1.3	.064	2.2	.062	2.0
College Degree	.031	1.5	.057	2.3	.092	3.3	.087	2.6
Extra Certification	-.01	-0.7	-.005	-0.4	.005	0.2	.004	0.2
Log hours/month in base year	-.33	-15.1	-.259	-10.6	-.342	-11.3	-.182	-5.2
R²	.09				.07			

Germany

| | 1985-1988 | | | | 1988-1991 | | | |
| | Total Effects | | Partial Effects | | Total Effects | | Partial Effects | |
	Estimate	T-Ratio	Estimate	T-Ratio	Estimate	T-Ratio	Estimate	T-Ratio
Intercept	.788	6.7	—	—	.518	3.1	—	—
Age	-.011	-3.9	-.004	-1.4	.001	0.2	.005	1.1
Age²	.00011	3.1	.00004	1.0	-.00004	-0.9	-.0006	-1.7
Low-Intermediate	.0083	0.9	.0045	0.4	-.004	-0.3	.01016	0.7
Upper-Intermediate	.035	1.8	.052	2.4	-.022	-0.9	-.003	-0.1
University	.062	4.9	.089	5.0	-.015	-1.0	.029	1.4
Appren/Voc school	-.001	-0.1	.008	0.9	-.001	-0.1	.006	0.5
Fachschule	-.001	0.1	.009	0.6	.04	2.2	.062	3.4
New Training	.1112	3.1	.0709	2.0	-.004	-0.1	.002	0.03
Log hours/month in base year	-.083	-4.0	-.042	-1.9	-.078	-2.7	.009	0.3
R²	.05				.03			

TABLE 10.6   Age-Education Interaction Effects on Log Earnings, 1985

Variable	United States	
	Estimate	T-Ratio
Intercept	10.397	57.546
Age	.06	6.854
Age^2	-.001	-6.797
High School	.213	3.259
Some College	.292	5.514
College Degree	.452	7.653
Extra Certification	.016	.712
HS * (Age-18)	.00008	.026
College * (Age-25)	.002	.476
College Degree * (Age-25)	.004	.999
	Germany	
Intercept	5.352	56.084
Age	.053	11.579
Age^2	-.001	-11.64
Lower-Intermediate	.026	.761
Upper-Intermediate	-.031	-.459
University	.051	1.039
Vocational Training	.067	4.911
Fachschule	.134	5.304
Lower-Inter * (Age-18)	.00032	.227
Upper-Inter * (Age-18)	.002	.558
University * (Age-25)	.009	3.292

In addition to the variables listed, these models include controls for all the variables found in Table 10.2, with the addition of interactions between (age-25) and upper prof/mgr, lower prof/mgr, routine nonmanual, and self-employed.

tion and training have important, significant direct effects on outcomes in Germany despite the tight linkage between educational and work institutions. To explore further the relationship between education and earnings change, we included interactions between age and education in the analysis of earnings *levels*.[11]   Table 10.6 shows significant interactions between education and age in both countries, even when interactions between occupation and age are included in the model. The interactions in both countries show the same form: higher education has a bigger effect on earnings for older than younger men. If this effect is a life-course effect, then it certainly contradicts the hypotheses of this paper, which predict that the direct effect of education in Germany should shrink quickly as the standardized credentials in Germany are converted into occupational positions. An alternative interpretation, however, is that the interactions between education and age reveal cohort effects, rather than life course effects. In this interpretation, the effect of higher levels of education were greater for older cohorts than they are for younger cohorts. Such an interpretation is consistent with a queuing interpretation of the value of credentials (Thurow 1975; Sakomoto and Powers 1994). In older cohorts, higher levels of education are less common (e.g., Mare 1980, Blossfeld 1987), and so the value of higher levels of education may be greater.

To improve our ability to distinguish cohort from life-course effects, we included interactions between age and education in our models for earnings change. These models which are reported in table 10.7, reveal a different story than do the models where earnings level is the dependent variable. In the American case, there is no significant effect of the interaction between education and age on earnings change. In Germany, the inclusion of the education-age interaction reveal significant educational effects on earnings change even in the second period, where the simpler models found no evidence of educational effects. In both German models, the interactions imply a *decreasing* effect of education on earnings through the life course. It is tempting to interpret this declining effect as evidence that job position is—like the theory predicts—increasingly masking the effects of education over the life course. However, this explanation appears to be inconsistent with the data, since the declining effect of education on earnings change at higher ages is found even in reduced form regressions that omit all measures of job. In fact, we are reluctant to interpret the greater effect of education on recent earnings change as a life-course phenomenon. Instead, we suspect that— as Blossfeld (1987) has argued—Germany's rigid labor market institutions segment the labor market by cohort more completely than do American labor markets, and the pattern found in the recent data are a reversal of the cohort effects found in the model for 1985 earnings. Additional research with data that cover a longer time period is necessary to evaluate this conjecture.

Tables 10.6 and 10.7 differ from table 10.2 in that they are regressions of earnings change rather than of earnings at a point in time. Because the dependent variable is change, we included controls for earnings level in 1985 on the change between 1985-88 and we included a control for the size and direction of the 1985-88 change on the 1988-1991 change. Any tendency for earnings change in one period to be offset by an opposing earnings change in the second period constitutes an earnings rebound. Table 10.8 shows that the earnings rebound was substantial in both countries, though somewhat larger in the United States. The possibility, indeed the fact of earnings rebound in both countries raises the question whether the incidence and extent of such rebound is influenced by education. To examine this question, we included an interaction between educational level and the size of the earnings rebound in the regression for 1988-1991 earnings

TABLE 10.7   Effect of Age-Education Interactions on Earnings Change

| | United States | | | |
	1985-1988		1988-1991	
Age	-.0088	-1.6	.0006	0.1
Age²	.0001	1.0	-.0001	-1.1
High School	-.037	-0.9	-.0033	-0.1
Some College	.0248	0.7	.0389	0.7
College Degree	.0578	1.5	.1076	1.9
Extra Certification	-.0057	-0.4	.004	0.2
High School * (Age-18)	.003	1.5	.0033	1.2
Some College * (Age-25)	-.0002	-0.1	.0015	0.5
College Degree * (Age-25)	-.0004	-0.2	-.0017	-0.5
	Germany			
Age	-.0041	-1.3	.00637	1.4
Age²	.00004	1.2	-.0001	-1.5
Lower-Intermediate	.0139	0.6	.067	1.8
Upper-Intermediate	.1443	3.2	.0858	1.3
University	.131	4.0	.1655	3.7
Lower-Inter * (Age-18)	-.0004	-0.5	- .0024	-1.7
Upper-Inter * (Age-18)	-.0048	-2.3	- .0039	-1.4
University * (Age-25)	-.003	-1.6	- .0082	-3.4
Vocational Training	.0075	0.9	.0051	0.4
Fachschule	.0115	0.7	.06	3.3
New certification	.0664	1.8	.0033	0.1

In addition to the variables listed, these models include controls for all the variables found in Table 10.2, with the addition of interactions between (age-25) and upper prof/mgr, lower prof/mgr, routine nonmanual, and self-employed.

change. Specifically, we included an interaction between the lowest educational category and educational level. If workers with higher levels of education who suffered earnings reversals in the first period were more likely to experience earnings gains in the second period, then this interaction term would be negative.

Table 10.8 shows that this term is instead insignificant in both Germany and the United States. While higher education has a positive effect on earnings and on earnings growth in both countries, it does not appear to provide significant advantages for those workers who do experience earnings decline. One possible explanation has to do with the reasons for earnings decline. Earnings decline can occur through several mechanisms: reduction in hours worked, reduction in wage or salary in the same job, or job changing. There is no particular reason why education would be associated with that part of earnings rebound that comes from reductions

TABLE 10.8 Earnings Change, 1985-1988, Including Effects
of Past Earnings Change

	United States		Germany	
Intercept	1.71	6.2	.829	4.2
Age	.004	0.5	.005	1.2
Age^2	-.0001	-1.4	-.0001	-1.8
High School	.073	2.5	—	—
Some College	.071	2.2	—	—
College Degree	.096	2.7	—	—
Extra Certification	.003	0.2	—	—
Lower-Intermediate	—	—	.008	0.6
Upper-Intermediate	—	—	-.002	-.1
University	—	—	.021	1.0
Vocational Training	—	—	.005	0.5
Fachschule	—	—	.049	2.7
New Training	—	—	.038	1.0
Upper Prof/Mgr	.107	2.8	.054	2.6
Lower Prof/Mgr	.057	2.0	-.007	-0.4
Routine Nonman	.039	1.1	.009	0.4
Self-employed	.117	2.6	.012	0.4
Manual Superv	.095	2.1	.022	1.0
Skilled manual	-.017	-0.6	-.007	-0.5
Empl. Tenure	.003	2.0	.001	0.9
Union Member	.027	1.2	-.007	-0.8
Term Contract	—	—	-.047	-1.5
Log Hours/month in base year	-.182	-5.2	.032	1.0
Light Mfg	-.036	-1.3	-.018	-1.6
Comm/Tran/Util	.014	0.4	-.047	-2.9
Whol/Ret Trade	.008	0.3	-.065	-3.1
Services	-.002	-0.1	-.024	-1.8
Log(Earn88/Earn85)	-.549	-10.7	-.316	-3.5
Log(Earn88/Earn85) (if +)	.481	6.4	.161	1.5
Log(Earn88/Earn85) * Low Education	.105	1.0	.051	0.7
Log Earnings in the 1985	-.075	-4.1	-.147	-7.7
R^2	0.13		0.10	

in hours or reductions in wages in the same job. One might argue, however, that education should be most useful to reverse earnings declines that are associated with job changes. To further explore the connection between education and earnings rebound, we included an interaction between education and earnings rebound for those respondents who changed employers during the period of earnings declined. We still found no evidence that the rebound in earnings depends upon educational level.[12]

Discussion

The results of this paper suggest that labor market structure shapes the nature of the connection between education and career outcomes, though not always in ways predicted by theory. Germany and the United States have quite different educational and training institutions, labor markets that differ in important ways, and very dissimilar linkages between educational and work institutions. Despite these differences, individual-level educational differences have rather similar impacts on earnings. Relatively more of the effects of education appear to be mediated through occupational position in Germany than in the United States which is in line with our theoretical predictions. However, significant direct effects remained even in the German case. The mediation of educational effects in Germany by job position was most apparent in the 1985 earnings regression. Such mediation was less visible in the earnings change models, particularly when interactions between age and education are included. On the other hand, the sharp differences in the effects of vocational training credentials, and the large difference in the role of employer tenure, were evident through the analyses presented here.

Cross-national contrasts are particularly strong during the 1988-1991 period. The fact that education played a greater role in the U.S. during the recession fits the interpretation of the American labor market as a place where individual resources are particularly important while positional resources are comparatively unimportant. It should be noted, however, that the most influential educational difference in the United States concerned the difference between having a high school diploma or not. There is no functional equivalent to this group in Germany, which is a principal reason why the German educational effects tend to be smaller than the American ones. Similarly, there is no functional equivalent in the United States to the training credentials of Germany, some of which continued to have an impact on earnings change even in the 1988-1991 period.

Finally, the analyses in this paper showed education's effects even in the individualistic American labor market to be less than pervasive. While education clearly affected both earnings levels and earnings change in the United States, education did not offer any special advantage to those American workers whose recent earnings trajectory was in decline. Workers who had lost ground in the recent past tended to make up a portion of their losses. The portion that they made up (around 55% in the United States, 40% in Germany) was the same on average regardless of the level of education. In other words, education offered attractive possibilities for earnings growth regardless of the recent history of a worker's earnings trajectory. But education did not improve a worker's chances of making up lost ground. It may be that more targeted training could serve this function, but such information was not available in the PSID, while the German results offer little support for this position.

In summary, the tightly structured labor markets of Germany differed substantially from the more loosely structured American markets in several ways – in the importance of training credentials, in the unimportance of employer tenure, and most obviously in the overall shape of the earnings trajectories, which moved in a relatively cohesive direction in Germany and diverged in the United States. Against this backdrop, the effects of individual-level resources have more prominent effects in the United States than in Germany. However, individual resources clearly matter even in tightly structured labor markets such as Germany's. These results caution against underestimating the heterogeneity of employment situations that exist in a complex economy, whatever the structure of its institutions.

Notes

This research has been supported partly by National Science Foundation Grant SES 92-09159, partly by a grant from Duke University's Arts and Science Council, and partly by a grant from the Trent Foundation. This research was made possible by a contract with the Deutsches Institut für Wirtschaftsforschung to use the English-language version of the German Socio-Economic Panel. Please direct any comments to the authors at the Department of Sociology, Duke University, Box 90088, Durham, NC 27708-0088.

1. The first wave of the GSOEP was collected in 1984.

2. This paper's use of recent panel data and its inclusion of foreign workers who reside in Germany (Ausländer) distinguish the sample used in this paper from the samples used in other analyses of earnings mobility in Germany (e.g., Carroll and Mayer 1986, Hannan, Schömann and Blossfeld 1990).

3. We would have preferred to use a measure of labor force experience rather than age, but it is difficult to construct an experience estimate comparable to the conventional age-education-6 measure used for American data.

4. We used age rather than labor market experience in these results because the differences in the education and training institutions of the United States and Germany make it difficult to construct comparable imputed measures of experience.

5. That portion of manufacturing/mining which fit Stinchcombe's (1979) definition of "large scale engineering" (this includes mining) was grouped into the omitted category.

6. The coefficients from this analysis are not included in the paper—they are available from the authors upon request.

7. The coefficients from this analysis are not included in the paper—they are available from the authors upon request.

8. It is of course possible for nominal earnings to stay level or rise while real earnings declines.

9. With this measure, the regression coefficients measure the percent change in the ratio of earnings at the two periods to a change of one unit in the covariate.

10. Relative to high school graduates, college graduates had 3% higher earnings growth in both the first and second period in the United States. The contrast between high school and college is significant at the .05 level in the first period, at the 0.1 level in the second period.

11. To be precise, we included interactions between high school completion and age-18, and between some college or college degree completion and age-25. In Germany, we included interactions between lower school completion or middle school completion and age-18, and between upper school completion and age-25. The constants are included for convenience of interpretation. The result of this approach is equivalent to the conventional method of incorporating labor force experience (measures of age - education - 6) under the assumption that years of schooling have no impact on earnings over and above the four dummy variables and the training variables included in our specification.

12. These results are available from the authors upon request.

References

Blossfeld, Hans-Peter. 1987. "Entry into the Labor Market and Occupational Career in the Federal Republic: A Comparison with American Studies." Pp. 86-118 in *Comparative Studies of Social Structure: Recent Research on France, the United States, and the Federal Republic of Germany*, edited by Wolfgang Teckenberg. Armonk, NY: M.E. Sharpe.

Blossfeld, Hans-Peter, Gianna Giannelli and Karl Ulrich Mayer. 1993. "Is There a New Service Proletariat? The Tertiary Sector and Social Inequality in Germany." Pp. 109-135 in *Changing Classes: Stratification and Mobility in Post-Industrial Societies*, edited by Gosta Esping-Andersen. Beverly Hills, CA: Sage.

DiPrete , Thomas A. and Patricia A. McManus. 1993. "Tenure, Mobility, and Incumbency: Comparing Observed Patterns of Earnings with Predictions from an Elaborated Theory of Occupational and Firm Labor Markets." *Research in Social Stratification and Mobility* 12:45-82.

DiPrete, Thomas A. and Patricia A. McManus. 1996. "Institutions, Technical Change, and Diverging Life Chances: Earnings Mobility in the U.S. and Germany." Forthcoming in *American Journal of Sociology*.

Ganzeboom, Harry B.G., Ruud Luijkx, and Donald J. Treiman. 1989. "Intergenerational Class Mobility in Comparative Perspective." *Research in Social Stratification and Mobility* 8:3-84.

Haller, Max. 1987. "Positional and Sectoral Differences in Income: The Federal Republic, France, and the United States." Pp. 172-190 in *Comparative Studies of Social Structure*, edited by Wolfgang Teckenberg. Armonk N.Y.: M.E. Sharpe.

Hannan, Michael T., Klaus Schömann and Hans-Peter Blossfeld. 1990. "Sex and Sector Differences in the Dynamics of Wage Growth in the Federal Republic of Germany." *American Sociological Review*. 55:694-713.

König, Wolfgang and Walter Müller. 1986. "Educational Systems and Labor Markets as Determinants of Worklife Mobility in France and West Germany: A Comparison of Men's Career Mobility, 1965-1970." *European Sociological Review*. 2 (2):73-96.

Mare, Robert D. 1980. "Social Background and School Continuation Decisions." *Journal of the American Statistical Association*. 75:295-305.

Mayer, Karl Ulrich, David L. Featherman, Kevin L. Selbee, and Tom Colbjornson. 1989. "Class Mobility during the Working Life: A Comparison of Germany and Norway." Pp. 218-239 in *Cross-National Research in Sociology*, edited by Melvin L. Kohn. Newbury Park, CA: Sage.

Rosenbaum, James E., Takehiko Kariya, Rich Settersten and Tony Maier. 1990. "Market and Network Theories of the Transition from High School to Work: Their Application to Industrialized Societies." *Annual Review of Sociology*. 16:263-299.

Sakomoto, Arthur, and Daniel A. Powers. 1994. "Education and the Dual Labor Market for Japanese Men." *American Sociological Review* (forthcoming).

Thurow, Lester C. 1975. *Generating Inequality: Mechanisms of Distribution in the U.S. Economy*. NY: Basic Books

11

Education and Credentialing Systems, Labor Market Structure and the Work of Allied Health Occupations

Robert Althauser
Indiana University
Toby Appel
Yale University

The influence of professional sovereignty on the division of labor in American medicine created fluid boundaries within the profession but . . . sharp boundaries between physicians and other occupations. . . . Moreover, the subordinate occupations, such as nursing and laboratory work, became more hierarchically stratified than did medicine. (Starr 1982: 225)

Introduction

We have long known that stratification within an organization or occupation can block mobility, by impeding access to jobs or occupations with more pay, responsibility and autonomy. As Starr suggests above, this is readily apparent in the careers of those working in 'subordinate' or 'allied health' (AH) occupations. Occupational stratification within AH occupations typically takes a dualistic form. For example, there are two tiers in the occupation of physical therapy: Physical Therapists (PTs) and Physical Therapy Assistants (PTAs). In this paper, we will treat forms of stratification within allied health occupations—their educational and credentialing institutions as well as their labor markets—as institutional obstacles to individuals' job mobility. We will evaluate existing explanations of blocked mobility within occupations and suggest more cogent alternatives.

In the social stratification literature, various proponents of functional, conflict and status competition perspectives generally try to explain restrictions on job mobility by analyzing in different ways the consequences of educational and other credentialing institutions (Bowles and Gintis, 1976; Collins, 1971,1979). In the conflict and status competition perspectives in particular, the most relevant aspect of these institutions is their internal stratification, starting with the fact that educational programs differ in content, length and difficulty. Similar stratification is apparent in credentialing or licensing exams and their prerequisites. Applied to AH fields, these perspectives view the relatively high degree of occupational stratification within AH occupations as a reflection of the degree of stratification within their educational and credentialing institutions. This should be especially apparent in the relative difficulty which those working in the lower tiers of each occupation have in accessing and completing educational and credentialing programs.

In the dual labor market literature, stratification within labor markets is the key source of blocked mobility. Most of the dual labor market (DLM) literature focuses on the dualistic character of national labor markets (Gordon 1972; Berger and Piore 1980). Labor market sociologists and economists have largely neglected the task of explaining how labor market dualism develops within specific occupations or organizations (with important exceptions—Peattie 1974; Finlay 1983; Osterman 1984, Parcel and Sickmeier 1988).

This paper develops answers to these key questions:

1. Is the blockage of mobility in the workplace the intended, even envisioned effect of this educational and credentialing stratification?

2. Is mobility blocked for the reasons adduced by stratification and labor market theories?

The answers we develop for these questions will finally lead us to a third question:

3. What alternative explanations have promise?

In our view, the internal stratification of such allied health occupations as respiratory, physical and occupational therapy represent at the very least a form of within-occupation labor market dualism. We first set out to establish the plausibility of this view. Then, turning to the first two questions above, we review the relevant portions of functional and status competition theories of stratification and of dual labor market theory, specifying how they would explain this sort of labor market dualism. We have drawn upon the explications of functional and status competition theory provided by Collins (1971, 1979). Baron and Hannan (1994: 1121) recently described his 1979 volume as "the most influential work in sociology on educational credentials in the labor market. . . ."[1]

Then, using the recent histories of several AH occupations as crucial data, we tackle the first two questions above. As envisioned in the creation and immediate justification of educational and credentialing programs, we find ample evidence that a clear division of labor between tiers in the (typically) hospital workplace was envisioned when the educational and credentialing systems of each occupation were initially created. This normative expectation of little or no overlap of responsibilities or duties between tiers of allied health occupations was expected to parallel the larger, normative separation of responsibilities between physicians and allied health workers. This strict division of labor (or 'task discontinuity', to paraphrase Offe (1976)) between tiers would result from and yet help reproduce the stratification within the education and credentialing system and also provide the mechanism by which that stratification would effect blocked mobility in the workplace.

However, our review of articles in the journals of these AH occupations as well as our own field work strongly suggests that such an explanation of blocked mobility and occupational dualism is inadequate. While upward mobility from lower to upper tiers remains blocked in formal and sometimes legal ways, we find permeable divisions of labor and far more 'task continuity', e.g., overlapping responsibilities in the workplace, than would have been expected by the usual stratification or dual labor market explanations. The stratification built into the educational and credentialing institutions of these occupations does not engender and maintain a clear division of labor, the theoretically expected mechanism for restricting mobility in the medical workplace. Pursuing alternative explanations for blocked mobility amidst this flexible division of labor, we examine relevant aspects of the histories of these occupations, isolating roles played by occupational associations, hospital administrations and by some key labor processes, such as 'routinization' and 'workplace assimilation'.

Theoretical Background

To develop our argument more fully, we first need some background from the literature on dual labor markets. In the initial writings on dual labor markets, what Berger and Piore later term a 'minimalist' (Berger and Piore 1980:17) version of dualism was presented—a primary and secondary market (Doeringer and Piore 1971; Gordon 1972; Edwards 1975). This reflected the intellectual origins of DLM theory, with its initial focus on urban unemployment and poverty. It sought to explain why productivity-related factors like years of schooling or vocational training failed to influence the employment of women or minority workers seemingly trapped in a sea of unstable, short-term jobs. The very name of this concept suggests (recalling Stinchcombe's insight about concepts as hypotheses) its core hypothesis (Gordon 1972: 49-51): that there is little mobility between dual markets during individual careers.

The Static Version of DLMs

As concepts, DLMs are commonly understood in very static terms. They are portrayed as wide divides between privileged jobs—'good', stable jobs with careers—and underprivileged jobs—'bad', unstable jobs without careers. The core DLM hypothesis reinforces the image of an impermeable barrier, unaltered by changing economic climates or changes in technology (such as advances in scientific and medical knowledge). By the middle of the decade, Piore (1975:126) and others (Edwards 1979, Gordon et al. 1982) found that distinctions within the primary market were as important as the distinction between the primary and secondary labor markets, adding the upper and lower tier primary labor markets to the original typology.

On this static view, the 'borderline' between markets is anything but theoretically problematic. DLM theory thus presented fails to pay any attention to the conditions under which a line of work, a job, or an occupation is found in one or another market.[2] Understood in this way, dual labor market theory seems almost inapplicable to the present case of internally stratified occupations.

Fortunately, what undermines this common static-model understanding are the arguments which appear (Doeringer and Piore 1971; Edwards 1975) as part of what Rosenberg (1989: 365-366) calls a 'richer version' of the original theory. Here, boundaries were not viewed as static. Doeringer and Piore (1971:169) downplayed the 'strict separation' of primary and secondary labor markets because they viewed the secondary market as a "mixture" of internal labor markets (ILMs) and non-ILM jobs. Craft work was also discussed as falling into its own labor market, a kind of anomaly on the face of the basic typology of labor markets (Piore 1975:133-4).

A Dynamic Version of DLMs

A more dynamic understanding of labor markets over time becomes apparent at this point, though much of the reasoning here has been neglected in subsequent empirical research. While not specifically sensitive to internal stratification within occupations, this dynamic understanding provides us with the theoretical opening needed to establish that the internal stratification of AH occupations is an example of labor market dualism within occupations.

There are two key starting points to this dynamic view. The first is that labor market segments have different types of mobility chains (Piore 1975: 129). The second is that jobs can move back and forth across boundary lines between the upper and lower primary or between the lower primary and secondary tiers. Doeringer and Piore (1971) and Piore (1975) discuss at length how jobs migrate between mobility chains, hence market segments (1975: 139-148): "... a particular job might lie on more than one type of mobility chain (Piore 1975:129)." These authors also describe this as a process of "adjustment" between employers' structuring of markets and the supply of workers with various behavioral traits (Piore 1975: 147 ; Doeringer and Piore 1971: 178f). From this reasoning we can see how physical therapy jobs, for example, could be located in more than one labor market segment.

The third key aspect of this alternative view of DLMs serves to correct the atheoretical character of the usual literal or concrete interpretation of dual markets. In his most extensive treatment of labor market dualism, Piore asserts (Berger and Piore 1980: 2, 26-7) that the 'significance of dualism' is not that markets are divided into two discontinuous segments, but that markets are lumpy segments.

> Whether or not there are two or more such lumps is not central to our conception, though the numbers of segments cannot be multiplied indefinitely . . .

This view is supported by the citation of findings from micro studies of labor markets of 'dualisms within dualisms', e.g., Lisa Peattie's finding (1974) of licensed and unlicensed street vendors in Bogota, previously thought to be a homogeneous secondary market. This notion of more microscopic dualisms embedded in more macroscopic dualism is consistent with our claims about the dualistic character of AH occupations' labor markets and of the more macroscopic labor market dualism dividing AH and physician occupations.

Hence, a simplistic classification of AH occupations into one or more of these dualistic or triple segments is not our intention here. Indeed, inconsistencies mark the many attempts [at least seven, according to Rosenberg (1989:369-371)] at placing occupations within the secondary market or the two tiers of the primary labor market.[3] Moreover, the occupants of the therapeutic occupations under study here are predominantly women; yet Piore admits that this typology of segmented labor markets was 'designed largely to explain male careers' (1975: 134).

Nor is our concern to establish the strictly dual character of segmentation within AH occupations. This would ignore the 'dualism within dualism' insights mentioned above and would be doubtful in any event in light of the occasional utilization of physical therapy aides, not to mention dental assistants (versus dental hygienists) or nurses aids working with LPNs and RNs.

The point is simply that in the more dynamic understanding of DLM theory apparent in a careful reading of the literature, market boundaries are treated as problematic and subject to movement. Ongoing adjustments continue at the boundary. The literature even offers a theoretical opening, rather than an impediment, to the treatment of within-occupational segmentation.

The fact that most of the previous work on DLMs, especially but not exclusively by economists, has treated occupations as homogeneous and entirely located within the borders of some market segment is a convenient but unnecessary oversight. Most of the early theoretical treatments of dual labor markets failed to consider the way in which occupations organize a great deal of work, or affect the character of whatever labor markets may operate in the workplace. The larger problem here is that for the most part, theorists have long glossed over workplace divisions of labor as a source of segmentation among occupations, much less within occupations.

There are four aspects of allied health (hereafter AH) work which strongly support the presence of a dualistic form of labor market segmentation *within specific AH occupations*. The first two are widely apparent to observers of these occupations and will not be further argued here: 1) strong wage differences between the two tiers of each occupation (Visit2, pg. 15[4]); and the blocked mobility between tiers.[5] The other two—inequalities in educational and credential prerequisites and the theoretical separation between the tasks and responsibilities assigned to each tier—are developed below.

We now turn to the task of specifying how dual labor market theory and functional and status competition schools of stratification theory can explain this dualism.

Occupational Dualism:
The Account of Dual Labor Market Theory

For the purposes of articulating a general account of dualism in ways applicable to occupational dualism, we draw primarily upon the most recent and useful work on dualism theory to date (Berger and Piore 1980). At points, this material extends the earlier writings in new ways; at other points, it restates arguments made earlier (Doeringer and Piore 1972, Gordon 1972, Piore 1975).

Berger and Piore (1980:57-80) argue that the labor market location of a job is a function of job structure, which essentially boils down to the number and complexity of tasks. Further, the structures of jobs reflect their location within a division of labor. A continuum of divisions of labor is imagined, with the extremes of Adam Smith's pin factory and craft labor.

The sort of division of labor utilized, the argument continues, is a function of the extent of the market (borrowing from Adam Smith), as well as the stability of demand and an ability to divide product demand into stable and unstable portions (57-70). Much of the evolution of the job structure of manufacturing work, particularly leading to increasingly specialized jobs that occurred during the rise of mass production, presumably reflects an expanding market. These jobs were primarily located in the lower tier of the primary market.

In Piore's earlier work, dual job strata are principally characterized by a contrast between 'general' and 'specific' behavioral traits required in their work (1975: 130-134), and by differences in the types of mobility chains found in each tier (128). In his 1980 essays (17-18), Piore argues further that

...the list of distinctive behavioral characteristics which define the strata are generated by a single, basic, underlying difference, that is, a difference in the way in which people learn, and subsequently understand, the work which they perform.

"Abstract learning" typifies upper tier jobs; "concrete," on-the-job learning is found in lower-tier jobs (20, 70-78). Abstract learning permits 'greater geographic and institutional mobility' and is typically acquired in educational settings. It is then reinforced when applied at work in upper-tier jobs, principally through progressions through upper-tier mobility chains (returning on this point to his 1975 (133) treatment). Concrete learning is developed on the job and is proportionate to the number of tasks carried out. What is learned is more specialized and less generalizable to other jobs or institutions. This difference in the 'way in which work is learned and understood' (1980: 21) establishes the differential linkage between educational attainment and labor market location.

We have now covered enough of Piore's argument to isolate the essential parts of a dualistic understanding of the kind of within-occupational strata we see in AH occupations and their work. The role of a growing market in stimulating a more specialized division of labor would suggest that

DLM hypothesis 1: a growing demand for services and the prospect of a large stable demand for services would be a prime condition for the emergence of lower tier AH strata.

While any simplistic association of 'abstract' learning with the upper tier and 'concrete learning' with the lower tier would face several obstacles, one would expect that

DLM hypothesis 2: the higher level of education and credentialing would include more theoretical or 'abstract' training for the upper than the lower tier.

Finally, the

DLM hypothesis 3: work of the upper tier occupants should require and utilize the more general skills and knowledge acquired in their educational program, while the work of lower tier occupants should utilize the more specialized knowledge acquired on the job.

In short, DLM theory offers three related grounds for effecting the blockage of mobility between tiers. While we will not attempt to directly test the hypotheses above, they do offer us a basis for projecting answers to our first two questions:

1. The blockage of mobility in the workplace should indeed be the intended, even envisioned effect of educational and credentialing stratifica-

tion with AH fields.

2. A blockage of mobility should be the result of several expected differences between the tiers: the lower tier should utilize specialized, on-the-job-based skills and knowledge rather than general and abstract knowledge, as part of a broader but fairly strict division of labor between tiers.

Occupational Dualism:
The Account of Two Stratification Theories

Functional Theory. Functional and status competition theories differently specify this linkage between education and work, as many have previously indicated (Collins 1971, Berg 1970). According to both accounts, the workplace is primarily a set of positions, often equated with distinct occupations. But in the functional account, these positions require technically determined and objective skills. These positions or occupations differ in level of skill, authority and control, and in 'rights and perquisites' (Davis and Moore 1945). People filling them differ in 'native and trained capacities and personality traits' (Featherman 1975:333)

Thus, functional theory sees a strong linkage between progress through educational institutions and both job placement and job attainment. It assumes that *there are corresponding differences in the content of the specific work done by those in these positions or occupations, e.g., a clear technical division of labor; those who complete educational and other credentials are placed in positions with distinctly different responsibilities.*

In functional theory, there is a structural isomorphism between occupational and organizational strata and stratified educational institutions. Access to work in different occupations and organizations is based on completing the requirements of variously stratified educational and credentialing institutions. Failure to complete the requisite level or degree of training and credentialing explains subsequent immobility between different positions. Thus, despite its individualistic orientation (Horan 1978), functional theory thus assumes the existence of stratified educational and credentialing institutions, the focus of our first question.

To sum up, blocked mobility is the unsurprising consequence of the underlying educational and credentialing stratification. AH positions exist within a clear, technical division of labor and have their respective educational and credentialing prerequisites. If individuals experience obstacles to mobility between lower and upper tiers, the (theoretical) reason must be that they have not progressed through all levels of the educational and credentialing institutions within their AH field.

Collins' Status Competition Theory. How, according to Collins' account, do credentials typically lead to positions with greater privilege and greater remuneration, a feature even of the upper tiers of AH fields? What is the process, the mechanism? Collins views positions as being a form of property, hence his concept of 'positional property'. A 'position' is "a collection of behavioral patterns . . . reserved for particular individuals under particular conditions of tenure". (1979:53-4).

How are credentials used to channel people? By conditioning access to the best jobs, especially at their entry levels (1979:50-51). According to this theory, there are three motives for restricting access: to control the training process (those with the highest level of credentials gain more control over their own reproduction); and to monopolize skill. Achieving these two serves the third motive — to legitimate forms of privilege, greater pay, etc.

Exploring the first two of these motives, Collins views professional monopolies as examples of Weberian 'status groups'. Their basis is "the practice of certain esoteric and easily monopolized skills and the use of procedures that by their very nature work most effectively through secrecy and idealization" (1979:134). Earlier (132), he explains that a strong profession 'requires a real technical skill that produces demonstrable results and can be taught. *Only thus can the [technical] skill be monopolized, by controlling who will be trained.*" (Our italics)

But how are privileges legitimized in the credentialist view? As part of his discussion of the historic evolution of 'education as status culture' and 'education as a mechanism of occupational placement', Collins (1971:1015) notes that: "With the attainment of a mass . . . higher education in modern America, the idea or image of technical skill becomes the 'legitimating culture' . . . [defining the] struggle for position [that] goes on." In other words, what legitimates inequality of privilege (in position and pay) is the appearance of greater skill and knowledge possessed and exercised in practice by those most highly credentialed. And this appearance is not just in the eyes of the public or the law, but in the beliefs of those in the workplace. This appearance is consistent only with a clear division of labor between different positions.

To sum up, in Collins' status competition theory, various work organizations and well-organized professions or occupations utilize credentials to achieve more privileged and better paid positions by restricting access to entry. They accomplish this by gaining and maintaining control over training and hence their own social reproduction, monopolizing their skills and thereby legitimating their level of privilege and pay. Their assumptions are embodied in public and legal jurisdictional settlements; both assume a clear division of labor.

Collins' concept of 'positional property' helps define the character of this clear social division of labor. In his discussion of ways to dismantle the 'credential society', Collins (1979:198-202) argues that the key step would be to break the 'current forms of positional property', ending the clear divisions of labor that keep those in the occupations of manager and secretary, or doctor or nurse, from sharing tasks and responsibilities and utilizing on-the-job learning of skills to the fullest extent. Such a breakdown is no more imaginable from a status competition than a functionalist perspective. But the flexible division of labor observed blurs the assumed line of demarcation in ways and to a degree which is not consistent with the tenets of conflict theory.

A convergence of functional and status competition theories? Despite their differences, we have shown that these theories share common assumptions about the centrality of positions and their location within a clear division of labor, even as they offer differing accounts of how positions in the workplace are linked to education. According to both views, positions differ in the skills they require. In status competition theory, these skill requirements of positions are more socially constructed and negotiated; in functionalist theory, positions require unequal amounts of technical skill and knowledge. In the first, the clear division of labor is socially defined; in the second, positions are embedded in a technical division of labor.

So for functionalists, the completion of required educational and credentialing 'entrance requirements' brings access to positions. For Collins (1971), status group membership certified by educational and other formal credentials lead to initial placement and later job mobility. How positions differ is variously described: in levels of skill, status honor, power and remuneration. Variations in these job characteristics reflect underlying and clear differences in the content of work performed, whether this division of labor is social or technical in character. For both theories, positions are clearly structurally differentiated, as are distinct occupations.

Applications to a History of AH Fields: An Overview. So understood, the shared logic of these theoretical perspectives can be applied to the labor market dualism apparent within AH occupations. Such dualism involves two sets of jobs with very limited mobility between each set. Market dualism may be based on the assumption of expert, cultural authority found in a professional model, or on the assumption of responsibilities for control and direction found in the management model. In either case, one finds dual labor market structures grounded on a division of more from less expert labor.

The view that such a division is appropriate has long guided the founding and continuation of educational and credentialing systems in general. In the case of AH fields, this anticipated division of labor within AH work is assumed in the very construction of a stratified educational system, with its separate educational tracks of unequal duration, non-cumulative curricula and limited transfer of credit hours from lower to upper tracks. In some instances, there are also two distinct levels of voluntary certification or state licensing exams. These typically presuppose and often require prior completion of educational prerequisites from accredited schools, providing a relatively tight linkage between educational preparation and the right to take the credentialing exam.

The application of this line of thinking to the boundary between medicine and allied health is already familiar. Physicians' educational and medical licensing systems share with allied health systems a common purpose—to gain control of specific tasks and hence defend themselves against potentially competing occupational groups, including (in the AH case) competition from lower tier workers. For various groups of physicians, increasing their own educational prerequisites and later their voluntary credentialing efforts (including the creation of the specialty certification) has enhanced such controls and achieved insulation from competing medical and allied health occupations as well (Stevens 1972: 198-200; Starr, 1982: 356-7; Abbott, 1988: 84). The basic dualism of physicians and allied health occupations results.

Ironically, as allied health occupations emerged, the model provided in this hierarchical differentiation between physicians and allied health occupations and their separate educational and licensing tracks was adopted by the leaders of allied health occupations, as they developed similarly stratified educational and certification tracks. As part of this deliberate imitation of these physician licensing and medical specialty boards, allied health occupations have developed their own dualistic structure as a means of formally identifying the elite members of their occupational group and controlling the activities of subordinate members (Gritzer and Arluke 1985: 166). The apparently more intense subordinate-level stratification Starr noted (1982:225) could be understood in part as a byproduct of an imperfect and more rigid replica of the basic physician—allied health division. This is reminiscent of DLM theory's portrayal of education's greater importance for upper tier primary market mobility chains, and its corresponding lesser importance for lower tier primary market jobs (Piore, 1975: 133).

Reviewing projected answers to key questions. This discussion of two stratification theories suggests a second set of projected answers to our first two questions:

1. Is The blockage of mobility in the workplace the intended, even envisioned effect of educational and credentialing stratification?

ANS: Though by different logics, according to both theories, the blockage of mobility in the workplace is the intended, even envisioned effect of educational and credentialing stratification within AH fields.

2. Is mobility blocked for the reasons adduced by stratification and labor market theories?

ANS: For both theories, an individual's potential for upward mobility is limited because they do not complete various levels of educational programs and credentialing exercises that are prerequisites for the upper or lower tier positions of AH occupational positions; and because individuals are placed according to their credentials in specific jobs with distinctly different responsibilities, within a strict division of labor between upper and lower tier work resembling similar divisions between physicians and AH occupations.

Before turning to our data to check these projected answers to these first two questions, we first need to provide some background on the emergence of the second tiers of specific allied health occupations.

Data

Our information is drawn from two types of sources. We have reviewed relevant articles across several decades of health occupation journals on the topics of education, certification, the application of new technology, and changes in the size and scopes of practice. Beginning in 1986, the first author conducted informal interviews and observations of respiratory, physical or occupational therapists in more than 20 hospitals located in seven states, one Canadian province and two Australian states. In addition, the staff or elected leadership was interviewed during visits to the national offices of all three associations.[6] Extensive interviews were conducted during one six-day 1986 annual convention of the American Association of Respiratory Care and two annual meetings of the Indiana chapter.

Occupational Dualism in Allied Health Occupations: Some Background

How did occupational dualism develop? Let us consider the lower tiers of three allied health occupations: certified occupational therapy technicians, physical therapy assistants and certified respiratory therapy technicians, and to a more limited extent, the case of licensed practical nurses.

Historically, the second tiers of physical, occupational and respiratory therapy formally developed in the late Fifties or during the Sixties: Certified Occupational Therapy Assistants (COTAs) began in 1958 (Cromwell 1974), Physical Therapy Assistants (PTAs) in 1967, and Certified Respiratory Therapy Technicians (CRTTs) in 1969 (only eight years after the appearance of the upper tier Registered Respiratory Therapists or RRTs). In all three fields, on-the-job trained 'nonprofessional' aides were used before and are still occasionally used now.

Certified Occupational Therapy Assistants (COTAs). In occupational and physical therapy, the lower tier or second level of therapy work was a creation of their respective occupational associations. By the 1950s, the entry level for occupational therapy (OT) was a bachelor's degree. Schools were accredited by the American Medical Association, but credentialing was under the control of the AOTA (OTs were not yet licensed). The AOTA maintained a registry open to those who had graduated from an

AMA-accredited program and passed an examination. There was a strong link between education and credentialing: graduation from an accredited program was necessary to become a member of AOTA; also, a high percentage of those who took the examination passed it. (Gritzer and Arluke 1985)

A proposal was first made to the American Occupational Therapy Association (AOTA) in 1949 to train OT assistants in psychiatric hospitals, but it took nine years of debate before the COTA was created. Recognition by the AOTA of a second level of workers in occupational therapy began in a limited way in 1958. A shortage of personnel and outside pressure to expand services were the immediate stimuli. The AOTA at first approved a plan to certify and train workers in psychiatric settings only. Two years later, AOTA permitted parallel training programs for general practice only. Finally, in 1963, programs trained assistants for all workplaces. These programs were originally set up in the work sites for those already employed as aides. In 1964, with the approval of AOTA, the training of COTAs began to shift to junior colleges. AOTA both certified aides and accredited educational programs to train them. Certification was initially available for those with work experience only; after educational standards were set, training became a prerequisite. No examination was required until 1977. COTAs were allowed to join AOTA, but for a long time they were not eligible for office nor allowed to vote (Hirama, 1986: 23-24; Cromwell, 1974)

OT assistants were originally to be used for ordering supplies, preparing equipment and maintenance, and 'diversion' (or therapy via crafts) (Adamson and Anderson, 1966). A 1968 "Guide for the Supervision of the Certified Occupational Therapy Assistant" stated that a COTA was to be supervised by an OTR, an experienced COTA, or an OTR designate.

Physical Therapy Assistants. Physical therapy (PT), like occupational therapy, had achieved a bachelor's degree entry-level to the occupation. As in OT, PT schools were accredited by the AMA. Membership in American Physical Therapy Association required graduation from an accredited school. By the 1950s, physical therapists were in the process of breaking down the domination of physicians through their support of new state licensing laws. Therapists in some states were already engaging in independent practice. State licensing eventually led to the closing of the physician-maintained Registry in 1971 (Gritzer and Arluke, 1985: 132).

The American Physical Therapy Association (APTA) resisted the movement to create a second level longer than did the AOTA. With the post-war increase in rehabilitation cases, a shortage of PTs was evident. Non-registered workers, or PT aides, were used in most work places (Blood, 1965). APTA's official policy was to encourage on-the-job training of aides in specific work settings, but to disapprove of separate courses for aides or assistants that had physical therapy in the title or that would award a certificate.

(Worthingham, 1965; Fowles and Young, 1965).

By 1964, when extended debate over establishing a second tier began, the worker shortage had become critical. With Medicare on the horizon, the demand for rehabilitation work with chronic care patients was expected to dramatically increase. It was generally agreed among PTs that not enough new bachelors-level PTs could be recruited to satisfy the growing demand (Worthingham 1965: 112-113). Federal reports were calling for more "manpower" in PT. Federal laws had been enacted to provide colleges and trade schools with funds to set up training programs for allied health workers. Junior and community colleges, constituting a strong lobby, were eager to obtain the federal funds to organize the training programs. Thus, there was considerable external pressure on PTs to extend services. The leaders felt that if they did not endorse a lower level of worker, some other group would undertake to train workers outside of the jurisdiction of PTs (Worthingham 1965: 115).

In 1967, after much spirited debate, the APTA authorized a second level credential (the PTA) to be based on education (White 1970). Programs were immediately set up in junior colleges. Unlike OT, there was no grandfather clause enabling those trained on the job to acquire the new credential. PTs, like RNs, worked to alter state licensing laws to provide for two levels with supervision of the lower by the upper. PTAs were made affiliate members of APTA to prevent them from establishing a competing organization, but given subordinate status and denied voting privileges.

Licensing laws for PTs were to specify that PTAs apply therapy procedures "only under the direction and supervision" of the registered PT (Rutan 1968: 1001). The responsibilities to be assigned to PTAs were clearly limited. As Fowles and Young (1965: 124 - 6) advocated:

> Using nonprofessionals in all of clerical, housekeeping, and messenger duties, limiting patient contact to the area of assisting the patient only when being supervised or directed by the physical therapist...By adhering to [this and other] simple principles,...the danger of less skilled workers carrying out the physical therapy techniques which are the PTs responsibility could be eliminated.

Of all the AH occupations, physical therapy has managed to keep its two tiers furthest apart, at least on a formal level.

Licensed Practical Nurses. For the sake of comparison we offer this rather brief synopsis of the development of LPNs (loosely drawn from Kalisch and Kalisch 1995: 358-362; Melosh 1984:482-496). As an early allied health occupation, nursing was the earliest group to develop a dualistic structure. RNs had been licensed since early in this century. In the late 1940s, most nursing education still took place in hospital diploma schools, but there were some collegiate programs awarding a bachelors' degree. The leaders of the American Nurses Association (ANA) hoped that the entry level of nursing practice would eventually become a bachelors degree. After the Second World War, however, nursing faced a critical shortage of workers. Although some trained practical nurses predated World War II, the great surge of schools for LPNs took place between 1948 and 1954. There was strong outside pressure, from surgeons, for example, for hospitals to train auxiliaries.

Previously, the nursing leadership had resisted trained auxiliaries as potential competitors to RNs. But after the war they conceded to the demand, endorsed the LPN, and sought to control standards and the division of labor between RNs and LPNs. The American Nurses Association (ANA) lobbied to rewrite state nursing laws to include LPNs, with the provision that they be supervised by RNs. LPNs were considered nonprofessional workers and not allowed membership in the ANA.

Question #1: Was Blocked Mobility the Intended Effect of Educational Stratification?

Even before we reach the rather different case of Respiratory Therapy, our review of the creation of a second tier within nursing and especially within occupational and physical therapy already suggests an affirmative answer to our first question.

OT, PT and LPNs: A Common Scenario; A Deliberate Linkage. When their dual systems of education and credentialing were first created, nursing, PT, and OT had several features in common:

1) membership in the occupational association was limited to those with recognized education and/or credentialing;

2) a severe shortage of workers was perceived which the occupation could not fill based on its current standards;

3) upper tier members dominating the associations strongly resisted the notion that lower tier occupants would receive any formal education or training, other than in-service hospital training (Fowles and Young, 1965: 125-6; Kirchman and Howard 1966, Gritzer, 1981: 275; Worthingham 1965; Reverby 1987: 163-6);

4) there were low level tasks that seemingly detracted from professional status that might be delegated to lower-tier workers, to the benefit of the upper tier (Perry 1964; Blood 1965);

5) although all fields had on-the-job trained auxiliaries, the association leaders wanted an institutionalized way to create more trained workers, fearing either that other occupations doing lower-tier work would emerge beyond the reach of the occupation's control or that administrators would substitute lower-tier workers (with their lower wage levels) for upper tier workers (Gritzer and Arluke 1985:52, 71,77,116).

Our review of the literature in PT and OT journals shows us that the founders of the COTA and PTA levels envisioned that a clear division of labor would prevail. Routine and *supervised* work would be confined to occupants of the new lower tiers; other tasks would be reserved for the upper tier. Some were reluctant to delegate any tasks. In 1980, a director of a PTA program reiterated that the 'roles and functions' of PT and PTA "are clearly separable," and that "the role of the PTA will not change in the next decade." (Canan 1980)

The occupational association, in each case, created or endorsed a second tier which the upper tier could control. The upper tier considered itself the "professional" level; the lower tier was labeled the "technical" or "assis-tant" level. (In OT especially, a continuing battle between COTAs and OTRs centered on the name to be given the second level). Certification or licensing was to remain under the control of the upper tier.

Staff members at the national headquarters in both the American Physi-cal Therapy Association and American Occupational Therapy Association reiterated this view. Assistant OTs (COTAs) are "not seen as junior level therapists"... "This profession believes there is a distinction between what the therapists do and assistants [do]." (Visit1, pg. 9). "....there is a real difference in the amount of responsibility, independent function, critical thinking and problem solving among PTs vs. PTAs." (Visit2, pg. 19)

Certified Respiratory Therapy Technicians (CRTT): Different Scenario; Same Result. Respiratory therapy (RT) was a second generation allied health field which emerged in the late 1940s. By comparison with the OT and PT fields, the creation of the CRTT in respiratory therapy took place in a somewhat different context. A combination of unusual conditions precipi-tated the creation of a technician level certification:

1) In the early 1960s, schools—which had just begun to be accredited by the AMA—were still in hospital settings. A separately incorporated registry board, with physicians holding the majority of votes, was established in 1960. Hence, the educational and, for the most part, the credentialing systems in RT were not under the control of the occupational association, known initially as the AAIT (American Association of Inhalation Thera-pists; and more recently as the AARC—American Association for Respira-tory Care).

2) Originally, the credential which the registry conferred, the Registered Respiratory (initially, Inhalation) Therapist or RRT, was exceedingly diffi-cult to obtain. Well over half of those who graduated from accredited schools could not pass the written and oral registry examinations, though the pass rates varied widely over time (Smith, 1989: 99,173,177.230)

3) Membership in the AAIT, unlike the APTA and the AOTA, was based in the 1960s on work experience and not on graduation from an accredited school.

4) The demand for respiratory therapy sharply increased in the late 60s, enhancing the perception of shortages of both RRTs and the more rapidly

growing segment of on-the-job trained technicians.

5) Thus the association was numerically dominated by those without any credential at all, most of them trained on the job (Smith, 1989; Burton and Barham, 1970). By 1969, when the CRTT was created, there were about 7000 members of the occupational association but only about 1600 RRTs (Smith 1989: 230).

6) Finally, the AAIT was repeatedly rebuffed in its efforts to persuade the registry, dominated by physicians and filled out by RRTs, to create a credentialing mechanism for technicians. (Smith 1989: 95-97).

So the AAIT boldly created their own "technician certification" mechanism, in part as a political act aimed at the physician-dominated registry board and in part as a means of producing more workers and providing a larger portion of existing workers and members of the AAIT with a usable credential. For a short time (1969 - 1972) the AAIT administered this precursor to the current CRTT examination. The exam was open at first to members of the AAIT with work experience only (Smith 1989:80,116); it was relatively easy to pass. But the AAIT came to see that it had a conflict of interest between expanding its membership and giving exams to its members. In 1974, faced with the competition from AAITs certificate, the registry elected to assume the responsibility for the technician level exam and also to reduce the physician dominance of the registry by reconstituting its board with equal physician and respiratory therapist representation (Smith, 1989: 79, 97, 139).

The minimum length of therapist education was eventually set at two years and the length of training for the technician at one year. Thus there is less of an educational difference between levels than in OT or PT. (Smith 1989: 71-73; Burton and Barham, 1970).

Even in this anomalous case, the AAIT while creating the CRTT wanted to preserve the higher, Registered Respiratory Therapy (RRT) credential. It tried to establish distinctions between the tasks for which the two levels were prepared (Julius, 1970). But of all the AH fields discussed here, respiratory therapy experienced the greatest difficulty in establishing a credential-based hierarchy in the workplace..

Immobility and Educational Stratification:
Summarizing Answers to Question #1

Let us sum up the answers these materials suggest to our first question, "is the blockage of mobility the intended effect of educational and credentialing stratification?" Occupational leaders expected that stratification within educational and credentialing institutions would shape workplace stratification and block mobility between tiers. This would be accomplished by restricting access to upper tier credentials in two ways. First, mobility from lower to upper tiers would be hampered because access to the exams that certify qualifications for jobs at either level was (and remains) limited to those who have completed accredited educational programs. For example, in respiratory therapy, the right to take credentialing exams has typically depended on completing educational prerequisites at accredited programs and in some instances, months to years of practical experience (Smith 1989: 97, 168, 178-9).

Second, academic credits gained in completing the lesser levels of training eventually established for lower tier degrees have rarely counted against the requirements for upper tier degrees. So experienced lower tier occupants who 'go back to school' while working part or full time find they must largely 'start over', a situation which is often lamented at all levels of these occupations (Kerr 1971).

As a result, respiratory therapy's two-track educational tiers, each tightly linked with two-track credentialing exams, combined to make career mobility difficult, even 'virtually nonexistent' in the early period of 1969-1973 (Smith 1989: 97, 165) and still difficult now. Indeed, PT educators have criticized high school counselors for misleading graduates into thinking that the associate degree program for PTAs is a stepping stone for entry into the "professional program." (White 1972).

In effect, those guiding the creation of assistant level programs with their very separate educational or certifying tracks viewed the work tasks central to each of the two levels as distinctly different, or 'discontinuous'. Their underlying model of working practice and appropriate training and education envisioned very little continuity across the whole range of tasks undertaken by upper and a lower tier AH workers. In their vision, functions sharply differ between the levels of this simple hierarchy—a prime example of what Claus Offe has defined as a "task-discontinuous status organization." (Offe 1976:25-27) This model also reminds us of the separation of control from execution, of thinking from doing, a key principle of 'scientific management'.

In short, *the restricted mobility* in this occupational context (which recalls that of a classic dual labor market) is the intended consequence of a considerable degree of educational and credentialing stratification, itself predicated on a vision of a clear division of labor and a task discontinuous organization of the statuses and appropriate work for each tier. What this explanation leads us to expect in practice is a clear division of labor, with highly skilled tasks reserved for upper and lesser skilled for lower tier workers. But is this the actual workplace arrangement which produces blocked mobility? Is the way in which mobility is actually blocked consistent with this explanation based on educational and credentialing stratification systems?

Question #2: Is Mobility Blocked for the Reasons Adduced by Stratification and Labor Market Theories?

If allied health fields were structured to imitate, however approximately, the medical profession's emphasis on credentials and education, one would expect a conformity or even an over-conformity to the practice norms accompanying this (greater) internal stratification. The work typically assigned to the upper tier should uniquely require their higher levels of education and certification; conversely, less demanding or responsible work would be consigned to lower tier incumbents. What is the point of having levels of medical occupations subordinated by certification and educational criteria if not to structure the strict separation of more routine, from less, discretion-filled from discretion-less tasks, on the basis of accepted qualifications?

But observations do not confirm this expectation. While the credentialing system may be an institutional extension of the educational systems, neither is at all consistent with the flexible division of labor found in actual occupational practice. How this comes about is relevant to our appraisal of the arguments drawn from dual labor market and stratification theories.

In actual practice, according to a great deal of our material from interviews, observation and articles in the occupation's journals, the scopes of practice of workers in the two tiers substantially overlap. We have found that in many though not all hospitals, lower tier occupants of the various dual labor markets encompassing several subordinate medical occupations are *not* uniformly exclusively assigned to less skill-demanding, discretion-exercising tasks. For example, in respiratory care units in hospitals, most of the hospital ICUs we observed or heard about could not staff ICUs around the clock with RRTs while confining CRTTs to general floor duties. In some hospital departments, PTAs and COTAs develop highly skilled areas of specialized care, becoming the care-givers of choice as well as consultants to their upper tier colleagues.

These observations are consistent with material we found in these occupations' journals. Task overlap among different levels of AH occupations has been amply documented (Goldstein and Horowitz: 1974: 21-38; Cromwell 1968; Adamson and Anderson 1966). "The overlap of skills and responsibilities must be recognized" in PTs work (Holmes 1970); Watts outlines factors which make "flexibility in delegation of responsibility highly desirous" (1971:32-3). "The skill levels of PTAs may far exceed" those for PTs "in the performance of certain tasks..." (White, 1970; see also Watts 1971: 33). One study documents that over one third of the working time of the earlier PT aides was spent doing lower skilled tasks (Blood 1965: 120). Another shows that aides were working outside of the areas they were originally expected to work in and much of the time were working without the expected supervision by PTs (Gray 1964). Another author warns against PT licensing laws that specify educational subject matter or duties and task allocations, because 'development in care techniques' may make any given division of labor and educational content obsolete (Rutan 1968). Over the histories of these fields it is apparent that AH fields in general and the upper tier workers in particular have similarly assimilated many aspects of treatment which was formerly the exclusive province of physicians. (Perry, 1964: 434; Melosh 1984:492).

What this and other evidence depicts, in short, is close to what Offe (1976) calls "task-continuous" status organization. As exemplified by the operations of a small craft workshop, functions, skills and knowledge overlap within the framework of a progressive development of skills, knowledge and responsibilities .[7] This is illustrated in the following excerpt from an interview with a physical therapy assistant (PTA):

> **Ques.: What are the differences in the work done by a PTA vs. a PT? What actually happens?** Ans: When an assistant goes to school, they concentrate on how modality is done, how to administer treatments. Therapists concentrate more on evaluating the problem and some therapists also carry out the treatment. The basic difference is: we don't evaluate how to take care of a patient. We can change treatments after discussion with the therapist. We can change or update the program if necessary. **Ques: Do you have to do that—discuss it with the therapist—first?** Ans: Kinda..., sorta. We use our own judgement: say if a patient is not getting relief, then we can try another modality. This is an assessment, based on our professional experience; we reassess what the patient needs. These have to be informal; at the initial evaluation, the PT puts a patient through the tests—I don't know the name of these tests, but these are part of the formal, initial evaluation. Assistants do informal reassessments instead. We can do muscle grades, test their strength, reassessments, similar to what was part of the initial tests.

While this passage shows expected differences in schooling and knowledge between PTs and PTAs, the PTA questioned combines a restatement of the normative assignment of initial assessments to PTs with the informal practice of PTAs doing reassessments.

These comments illustrate the overlapping scopes of practice of the two tiers in the workplace, an issue over which respiratory and occupational therapy have experienced considerable turmoil. A major role delineation study of respiratory care work in the mid-Seventies found that at 'beginning practice, [there was only] one level of practitioner . . . [whether therapist or technician, an individual performed]...the same set of tasks, irrespective of educational background..." (Smith 1989: 163). The result was an important political collision between the membership association and the credentialing body, resulting in a change (in 1983) in the content of the exams for the CRTT and RRT credentials and the designation of the CRTT as the only entry level exam.

In the field of OT, the same issue has drawn much attention. Before a decade of experience with COTAs has passed, Adamson and Anderson (1966, pg 78) reported that:

An assistant who is hired to take the place of an OTR is frequently on the same level in the organizational structure of the department as a staff therapist. Even the text of a "Guide for the Supervision of Certified Occupational Therapy Assistants" (1968:99) stated: "Inherent in the [supervision] relationship is the acceptance... of the fact that readiness for increased responsibility should when possible, be recognized by assignment to more demanding duties and rewarded by an appropriate adjustment in salary scale.

As an immediate past president of the AOTA, Ruth Brunyate fervently restates sentiments expressed at a recent (1968) workshop on the 'assistant movement' below; yet even these ideas reflect a common ambivalence about clear versus flexible divisions of labor. This passage of hers comes in an article authored and largely written by the then current AOTA president Florence Cromwell (Cromwell 1968: 379-380):

I submit that the goal of many voices here is to have as the profession's official stand, the fact that the COTA is an occupational therapist and not a subservient assistant to an occupational therapist; that within the profession there are varying avenues of educational preparation, qualifying criteria and levels of competence. I infer that we recognize that just as competence, capacity or judgement and exercise of responsibility vary with the level of preparation, so too do they exist with individual variation within either professional or technical level...there can and do exist COTAs whose competence for a given assigned responsibility exceeds that of a more elaborately educated but less endowed professional, just as there do exist COTAs and OTRs whose individual competence falls below our desired optimum for an assigned task." [OTRs must reassess their roles with assistants around] " . . . with the added manpower provided by the COTA the profession is now experiencing a reevaluation of what it does and does not, should and should not do. We now acknowledge that contained within many occupational therapy services are great pockets of activity programs under the guise of occupational therapy which did not shock or even disquiet the profession, until it saw that when the COTA functions with an appropriate pattern of supervision, he is highly skilled in performing parts of all facets and every stratum of the profession's practice.

Somewhat more restrained is the response of Florence Cromwell, the current AOTA president, as she completes this article. The unsettling adjustments which upper tier workers struggle to make in the wake of obviously overlapping scopes of practice are apparent as she writes:

We of the OTR group, having helped to create this needed level of function within our practice, also struggle with his role as his proficiency and potential increase, as demands on us change, as we attempt to identify our own rightful and most efficient function in today's practice.

In short, flexible divisions of labor are evident in practice. This is far from the vision of a clear division of labor upon which the educational and credentialing systems were grounded. In the face of blocked mobility between lower and upper tiers of these AH occupations and the inability of the educational and credentialing institutions to materially control workplace practice, what explanations of blocked mobility make sense, which also take into account these flexible divisions of tasks among upper and lower tiers?

Question #3: What Alternative Explanations Make Sense?

Future research in this area should focus on alternative explanations. We do not view any of these as likely to be established as the sole, best account. Allowing for the influence of unique features of each occupation and its work, a satisfactory explanation may well require some combination of all of these.

Actions of Occupational Associations. Occupational associations, like the ANA, AOTA, APTA or AARC, as well as respiratory therapy's independent registry and accreditation bodies, clearly have an interest in how labor is divided between lower and the controlling upper tiers. By dint of membership rules and patterns of historic dominance, graduates of upper tier schools, possessors of the top level credentials and occupants of upper tier positions have consistently dominated these associations (with the possible exception of some periods of the recent history of the respiratory therapy establishment). These associations can take actions which maintain market boundaries and block mobility between tiers. Among the types of actions that have been apparent, we briefly discuss three examples.

1. Creating, then Sabotaging an Alternative Career Ladder for COTAs. Occupational Therapy is an AH occupation which has probably devoted more effort and resources to creating a non-traditional avenue into its upper tier than any other. With some ongoing ambivalence, the American Occupational Therapy Association undertook a "career mobility program" in the Seventies. COTAs were permitted to take the exam leading to the registry on the basis of five or more years of experience, six months of 'professional field work' and a 'self-assessment', rather than having to fulfill the usual educational requirements (Visit1, pg. 1). The fact that such an end-run could be mounted reflects the realities of a workplace more flexible in its division of labor than formal dualism would be inclined to acknowledge.

Why did this 'mobility program' fail? A relevant but secondary factor in its demise was that the response to this program was light; fewer than 50 COTAs succeeded in becoming OTRs (Adams 1981). Doubts mounted with the ensuing costs in time and money. More essential were doubts that the OTR registration exam alone was sufficient to certify someone as an OTR, absent the usual educational prerequisites. (Visit1, pg. 8) But the fatal issue was not the technical quality of the exam. Faced with even modest prospects of success, the most important reason for its demise was finally articulated: no amount of experience however self-studied, supervised and documented by this program could by itself replace formal educational requirements. In effect, the experiment had clarified and strengthened the fundamental assumptions of educational dualism.

OTRs at the state level also exercised their veto through licensing laws: their states declined to recognize COTAs who became OTRs through the program, since they lacked the customary accredited educational credentials for becoming an OTR. (Hightower - Vandamm 1981; Ryan 1986: 27-30). The effective result was that a failed nine-year experiment had served to blunt the challenge to OTR domination from what some referred to as the "assistant movement" (Brunyate in Cromwell 1968). COTAs have since pressed for other forms of enhanced status within the AOTA, but no longer by the means of a job ladder linking COTAs and OTRs. The tension persists between the formal and informal patterns traced out above.

2. Raising minimum educational standards for upper tier recruits. While calls for increasing minimum educational requirements for nurses, OTs or PTs can be found in the histories of these fields, the projected impact on workplace practice of actually achieving these minimums is neither obvious nor as intended. Depending on the field, the intent was to eliminate or at least diminish the use of lower tier workers, or to enhance the occupation's standing in the medical community. Some leaders of respiratory therapy, however, have argued that the effect of already higher educational standards for upper tier workers in physical and occupational therapy has been to enhance the growth and use of lower tier workers and therefore have opposed proposals to move respiratory therapy toward a four-year minimum training period. However differently the leadership of a given occupation's upper tier foresees the consequences of raising educational standards, the division of labor between tiers is likely to be affected (Abbott 1988:84).

3. Delineating career ladders within the upper tier. During the last decade, the leadership of Australian nursing put through a restructuring of their conventional career ladder, which originally led from entry level registered nursing to various supervisory positions (Silver 1986b). An additional new track now permits nurses to remain heavily involved in clinical care, even at higher levels of expertise. Largely missing from the documentation of this development was the impact which this restructuring had on the skills that the Australian 'enrolled nurses' (ENs are roughly equivalent to LPNs in the U.S.) were allowed to develop and use on the job. While this redelineation of career lines was limited to RNs and did not directly reach down to ENs, the latter group experienced new pressure to confine themselves to the more routine, discretion-less duties of nursing, especially in the urban hospital settings. This is an interesting case of labor market boundaries being reconfirmed by a renewed reinforcement of a normative, clear division of labor, e.g., clamping down on well established tendencies for second tier nurses to assume the tasks and exercise the skills formally reserved to RNs (Jenkins 1989; Silver 1986a).

Hospital Administration. As in this latter instance, the other group of stakeholders with vested interests in how labor is divided are the hospitals. Given the opportunity for observation, no one can miss the remarkable degree of variation in the ways in which hospitals organize the work of allied health occupations. The strict division of labor found in some departments of hospitals resembles the vision of 'task-discontinuity' found earlier; in other departments, one sees the flexible division of labor even though mixed with heavily restricted chances for actual mobility. However national organizations approach jurisdictional issues, hospital and departmental administrators (and in some cases, medical directors) routinely create the kind of division of labor they want in their units. Some do this by creating clinical ladders for personnel. While generally not designed to bypass educational and credentialing institutions or to challenge the blockage of mobility still engendered by educational and credentialing institutions, these ladders do provide local status and financial recognition of growing skill and knowledge.

In short, occupational associations and individual hospital administrations act to directly shape the scopes of practice among upper and lower tiers of allied health occupations, quite apart from their nominal support of established institutions of education or credentialing.

Workplace Labor Processes: Routinization and "Assimilation". Abbott (1988:59-65;84) argues that 'control over tasks' is the 'central organizing reality of professional life'. Indeed, the issue of control over work is central to the sociology of work. The inability of credentialing or educational institutions of AH occupations to control the allocation of tasks in the health care workplace reminds us of the broad argument from students of the labor process literature: that social aspects of the labor process such as workers' struggle (Clawson 1980), worker's 'craft knowledge' (Kusterer 1978) or 'making out' (Burawoy 1979) and other workplace games have generally impeded attempts of external actors to control or influence various aspects of work—whether management or labor unions or here, educational and credentialing institutions, occupational associations and hospital institutions. Given the variable linkage between control over tasks and the possibility of job mobility evident above, what sort of labor processes may be helpful in explaining this strange combination of a flexible division of labor coupled with blocked mobility?

Abbott argues that control of tasks or jurisdictions is pursued in three arenas: the legal system, public opinion and the workplace itself. Settlement of these jurisdictional claims is subject to periodic renegotiation, but this is more frequently observed in the workplace than in the other arenas. In explaining why, his work identifies several related labor processes relevant to this alternative explanation.

As skill and knowledge develops and work practices evolve, a large proportion of treatments, tests, assessments, and diagnoses simply become routine. Abbott (1988: 126-7) who has already underscored the consequences of dividing professional work into its routine and nonroutine elements, describes as 'degradation' this shifting of increasing routine tasks to other professional or occupational groups. At the level of everyday practice, Abbott's concept of "workplace assimilation" specifically concretely captures the process of transferring knowledge and skill and recalls the spotlight on the important role of 'craft knowledge' (Kusterer 1978) in the labor process literature. Halpern (1990) has similarly described how the 'routinization of work' helps explain an intra professional jurisdictional adjustment between pediatricians and social workers, psychiatrists and pediatric nurse practitioners.

One interesting and relevant feature of the history of medical practice is the successive transfer of procedures initially reserved to medical specialists or ordinarily physicians into the daily responsibilities of various levels of allied health occupations. The passage of blood pressure measurements, venous blood sampling (Melosh 1984: 492) and more recently, arterial blood gas sampling represents some examples of this. What is more pertinent here is that the same downward distribution of skills and knowledge, supervised tasks and responsibilities occurs from upper to lower tier AH occupations. Hence this passage engenders part of the flexible division of labor we found above.

When groups of physicians delegate (or lose control over) routine procedures to allied health occupations, they presumably turn their attention to new, non-routine activities, enhance their academic research interests or otherwise hold exclusive jurisdiction over other tasks. Failing this, they risk extinction. There is ample evidence that the upper tiers of AH occupations envision moving themselves into new responsibilities when they similarly 'hand off' now routine tasks to lower tier members. The boundaries remain intact, however, whether between tiers of AH occupations or between physicians and AH occupations. In this way, the ongoing processes of routinization, workplace assimilation and degradation provide the steady social undercurrent driving the transfers of now routine tasks, consistent with the flexible division of labor we found above. In labor market terminology, boundaries between the tasks normatively assigned to physicians, upper and a lower tier AH workers are successively redrawn, providing for the continuation of blocked mobility.

Summary

We have argued that the upper and lower tiers of three allied health occupations represent an example of occupational dual labor markets. We have reviewed the way in which the assistant-level, lower-tiers of allied health occupations developed as a means of determining whether their establishment and operation have been consistent with dual labor market, functional and status competition theories of stratification.

Despite some differences in their accounts, these theories clearly anticipate a linkage between the educational and credentialing systems of allied health occupations, their placement of graduates of these systems into distinctive positions in the workplace and their subsequent job mobility or immobility. Even after their initial placement in entry-level positions, the mechanism facilitating the blockage of mobility between tiers is a clear division of labor between physicians and both tiers of allied health occupation. Envisioning such a division of labor, newly trained physicians, and upper and lower tier AH incumbents have been prepared for their respective tasks and responsibilities by their experiences in their distinctive educational and credentialing tracks.

Throughout much of the discussion found in the literatures of these therapeutic occupations, however, and from most of our observations and interviews in the workplace, the blockage of mobility is not accomplished by a consistent and strict division of labor. We finally considered several factors as possible explanations of both the substantial blockage of mobility between tiers and the absence of a strict division of labor among tiers. These included actions by these occupation's trade associations, their related accrediting and credentialing bodies, and workplace processes like routinization and downward assimilation of upper tier skills and knowledge.

Discussion

We anticipate three counter arguments to this paper and offer responses to each. First, some might argue that dualism within an occupation (or an industry) so far misrepresents the more aggregate form of dualism across occupations and industries as to comprise a trivial, not a strategic, test of extant theory. We might have sympathized with that view before starting this line of research. The trouble is, the occupational founders of the lower tier often write or talk as if they were schooled by a dual labor market or stratification theorist! We would argue that the divisions within the workplace which they envisioned in the details of their educational and credentialing institutions look very much like the broader forms of dualism. That the flexible division of labor we and they find instead is inconsistent with both extant theory and their own expectations is not a trivial failing.

Secondly, others may view the combination of task overlap and barriers to mobility as entirely consistent with a credentialist account which stresses the power inequalities manifested in the continued maintenance of mobility barriers, even in view of the kind of positional differentiation that all three theoretical perspectives assume and (we think) require. However, those having this view will have to specify other mechanisms by which those with credentials hold sway than they have previously specified. They cannot long evade the problem of how the legitimacy of credentials is maintained in workplaces with task overlap, while public understanding and legal codes seem oblivious to workplace realities. We doubt a credentialist account of unequal privileges in the workplace can explain the fair degree of task overlap between the unequally privileged positions.

We have suggested that in the view of status competition theory, the credentialed elite seek to legitimate their privilege and to restrict access into their ranks by claiming a connection between their superior credentials and their skills, knowledge and ability. Higher-level credentials are anchored in licensing law and in public belief that the credentialed do indeed have more skill or knowledge, as evident in the case of people who successfully masquerade for years as doctors. Proponents of this theory might argue that their theory does not require these skills to be real nor must the claim be factually correct. Their understanding of continued privilege and apparent power might even encompass a version of 'false consciousness' (see especially Bourdieu's account in 1977a:496). The indefinite lag which Abbott projected between initial changes in workplace jurisdictions (here represented by task overlap) and later public and legal resettlements of jurisdictions leave time for a variety of outcomes to develop, as suggested by Abbott's typology of jurisdictional settlements (Abbott 1988:69-79).

Can status group privileges be sustained on the basis of false belief in the face of an unclear division of labor between groups? From the vantage point of signaling theory, this is a case of 'Pareto-inferior' or 'inefficient signaling' 'equilibria' based on informational considerations' (drawing here on Baron and Hannan 1994:1122). How stable is this arrangement? According to Baron and Hannan, Spence (1974) views this type of equilibrium as fragile, especially in the face of competition and experimentation which may lead to recognition of a more 'superior' equilibrium. We believe a thorough treatment of the history of occupations and professions would turn up a variety of outcomes, including but not restricted to a) a decline in the power and numbers of upper tier workers (compare physiatry in relation to physical therapists, in the mid-1930s and late 1950s in Halpern 1992), b) a combination of upper tiers delegating routine work to lower tiers while moving themselves into new areas of undisputed expertise and exclusive responsibilities (note pediatricians' postwar shift into psychosocial pediatrics, relating actual care to non-physician groups in Halpern 1990:33-37), c) a contractual settlement designed to reestablish intra-occupational or intra-profession boundaries in the face of high levels of task overlap. The latter are apparent in Finlay's (1983) account of what happened when a group of steady but noncredentialed crane operators were sharing their high paying work with steadily working but credentialed operators. A new labor contract supported by both union and employer associations placed the noncredentialed but essentially equally skilled operators behind new barriers to mobility.

In our view, status competition theory cannot be restated to effectively ignore the legitimacy problem or to predict the inevitable victory of the initially more powerful, because more highly credentialed, tier of workers. A status competition theory dependent on public ignorance would have to predict that once the public decides that such beliefs are false, credentials will be delegitimized and the privileged status of the top tiers will end. The widespread abolition of licensure laws in the United States in the 1800-1860 period demonstrated just such a result: authority by license required an association of licensing and objective skill that the public and the law could not sustain (Starr 1982:58). Unless this theory can otherwise solve the problem of credentials' legitimacy, overlapping scopes of a practice pose continued risks to public belief in the objective skill and credentialed superiority of the upper tiers.

Notes

1. We do not draw upon the work of either Bourdieu or signaling theory (Spence 1974), two theories which could be linked to a status competition perspective. While Pierre Bourdieu is also considered a status competition theorist, we will not deal with this thought in this paper. His concept of 'habitus' or predispositions in many respects parallels Piore's argument (see below) about 'general' vs. specific behavior traits and the corresponding difference in the way people in the different tiers of a dual labor market learn from and understand their own work. However, we have not found a treatment of workplace stratification (1977a,1977b) along dimensions of status (as opposed to social class) in Bourdieu's work.

According to Rosenbaum's (1986) treatment of signaling theory, the general context of signaling theory is the difficulty employers have processing myriads of job applicants or candidates for promotion, as they attempt to infer ability from multiple pieces of information. While educational credentials would appear to be a central criterion for hiring or promotion, many other criteria are found important, according to Rosenbaum's review: job demands, as proxied by job status and earnings (149), differences in family social background and track placement in school (150), and the status of entry jobs (153) are others which come into play. The career pattern predicted by signaling theory, in Rosenbaum's view, is irregular: thus, he found 'no clear career structure' at the utility company he studied (152), no single selection criterion or no set of criteria could be linked to students' track placement, etc. In these many respects, signaling theory would appear wholly inapplicable to the AH case, without being fairly tested by the case

2. Many of the often cited explications of dual labor market theory by Edwards (1975,1979) and Gordon et al. (1982) reinforce this static understanding.

3. The empirical research (Osterman 1975) which first assigned occupations to the upper and lower tiers of the primary as well as to the secondary markets placed all of the incumbents of a given occupation into a single tier. For example, 'therapists and healers' was placed in the lower tier of the primary market. Setting aside the fact that his method of placement was entirely subjective, the criteria he used for placing occupations into markets were 'the degree of autonomy and personal participation' (for assignments to either tier of the primary market) and low wages and skill levels and unstable employment for assignment to the secondary market. More systematic is the use of measures of repetitiveness and Specific Vocational Preparation from the Dictionary of Occupational Titles by Spenner et al. (1982), which result in placing 'therapists' and 'therapist assistants' in the upper tier of the primary market.

4. All citations to "Visit1" refer to interview notes taken during a day-long visit on August 10, 1990 to the AOTA offices near Washington D.C.; those to "Visit2" to notes taken during a visit on August 15, 1990 to the offices of the APTA, also near Washington D.C.

5. To be sure, some aspects of AH work would also support locating AH jobs within ILM structures: the on - the - job acquisition of additional skill and knowledge in hospital settings, not to mention the persistent shortages of labor (Althauser and Kalleberg 1981; Althauser 1989). Yet very few ILM structures for AH occupations have emerged, despite some experiments to that end (Goldstein and Horowitz 1977).

6. These include the following groups: The American Occupational Therapy Association, The American Physical Therapy Association, The American Association of Respiratory Care, the Joint Review Committee for Respiratory Therapy Education and the National Board of Respiratory Care, Inc.

7. Offe (1976) further describes 'task-continuous status organization' as involving "A greater mastery of the [common, technical] rules and greater ability, knowledge and experience in production...." which differentiates those in the upper from lower strata. He continues: "...there is a wide area of technical rules to which equal obedience is required from all the occupants..." of the adjacent positions.

References

Abbott, Andrew. 1988. *The System of Professions*. Chicago: University of Chicago Press.

Adams, N.G. 1981. "Ladder to Professional Certification: The Career Mobility Program." *American Journal of Occupational Therapy* 35(5): 328-331.

Adamson, Margaret J. and Mary Alyce Anderson. 1966. "A Study of the Utilization of Occupational Therapy Assistants and Aides," *American Journal of Occupational Therapy* 20: 75-79.

Althauser, Robert and Arne Kalleberg. 1981. "Firms, Occupations and the Structure of Labor Markets: A Conceptual Analysis." Pg. 119-149 in *Sociological Perspectives on Labor Markets*, edited by I. Berg. New York: Academic Press.

Althauser, Robert. 1989. "Internal Labor Markets". *Annual Review of Sociology* 15:143-161.

Baron, James N. and Michael T. Hannan. 1994. "The Impact of Economics on Contemporary Sociology". *Journal of Economic Literature* 32:111-1146.

Berg, Ivar. 1970. *Education and Jobs: The Great Training Robbery*. New York: Praeger.

Berger, Suzanne and Michael Piore. 1980. *Dualism and Discontinuity in Industrial Societies*. Cambridge:Cambridge University Press.

Blood, Helen. 1965. "Their Use by the Profession". *Journal of the American Physical Therapy Association* 45: 118-124.

Bourdieu, Pierre. 1977a. "Cultural Reproduction and Social Reproduction". Pp 71-112 in Richard Brown, ed., *Knowledge, Education and Cultural Change*. London: Tavistock 1973. Reprinted in Jerome Karabel and A. H. Halsey. 1977. Power and Ideology in Education. New York: Oxford, pp. 487-511.

_____. 1977b. *Outline of a Theory of Practice*. Trans: Richard Nice. Cambridge and New York: Cambridge University Press.

Bowles, Sam and Herbert Gintis. 1976. *Schooling in Capitalist America*. New York: Basic Books.

Burawoy, Michael. 1979. *Manufacturing Consent*. Chicago: University of Chicago Press.

Burton, George C. [MD] and Virginia Z. Barham [RN, EdD] 1970. "Education and/ or Licensure in Inhalation Therapy," *Inhalation Therapy* 15: 143-149.

Canan, Betty. 1980. "What Changes are Predicted for the Physical Therapist Assistant in the 1980s?" *Physical Therapy* 60: 312.

Clawson, Dan. 1980. *Bureaucracy and the Labor Process*. New York: Monthly Review Press.

Collins, Randall. 1971. "Functional and Conflict Theories of Educational Stratification." *American Sociological Review* 36: 1002-1018.

_____. 1979. *The Credential Society*. New York: Academic Press.

Cromwell, Florence S. 1968. "Nationally Speaking: from the President." *American Journal of Occupational Therapy* 22: 377-379.

_____. 1974. "The Development of the Occupational Therapy Assistant: History and Status Report." *Journal of the American Speech and Hearing Association*. 16: 671-676.

Davis, Kinsley and Wilbert Moore. 1945. "Some Principles of Stratification". *American Sociological Review*. 10: 242-249.

Doeringer, Peter and Michael Piore. 1971. *Internal Labor Markets and Manpower Analysis*. Lexington, MA: DC Heath.

Edwards, Richard C. 1975. "The Social Relations of Production in the Firm and Labor Market Structure." Pg. 3-26 in Richard C. Edwards, Michael Reich and David M. Gordon (eds), *Labor Market Segmentation*.

———. 1979. *Contested Terrain*. New York: Basic Books.

Featherman, David L., Frank L. Jones and Robert M. Hauser. 1975. "Assumptions of Social Mobility Research in the U.S.: The Case of Occupational Status." *Social Science Research* 4:329-360.

Finlay, William. 1983. "One Occupation, Two Labor Markets: The Case of Long-shore Crane Operators." *American Sociological Review* 48: 306-315.

Fowles, Beth H. and Janet E. Young. 1965. "On-the-job Training." *Journal of the American Physical Therapy Association* 45: 124-126.

Goldstein, Harold M. and Morris A. Horowitz. 1977. *Entry-Level Health Occupations. Development and Future*. Baltimore: Johns Hopkins University Press.

Gordon, David. 1972. *Theories of Poverty and Underemployment*. Lexington, MA: DC Heath.

Gordon, David M., Richard Edwards and Michael Reich. 1982. *Segmented Work, Divided Workers*. Cambridge: Cambridge University Press.

Gossett, Robert. "What's the Answer? Queries and Replies of Concern to Therapists." *Physical Therapy* 52: 95-96.

Gray, Jim Mason. 1964. "Function of Nonprofesssional Physical Therapy Personnel." *Journal of the American Physical Therapy Association* 44: 103 - 109.

Gritzer, Glenn. 1981. "Occupational Specialization In Medicine: Knowledge and Market Explanations." *Research in the Sociology of Health Care*, 2 251-283.

Gritzer, Glenn and Arnold Arluke. 1985. *The Making of Rehabilitation*. 1985. Berkeley: Univ. of California Press.

"Guide for the Supervision of Certified Occupational Therapy Assistants." 1968. *American Journal of Occupational Therapy* 22: 99.

Halpern, Sydney A. 1990. "Medicalization as Professional Process: Postwar Trends in Pediatrics". *Journal of Health and Social Behavior*. 31:28-42.

———. 1992. "Dynamics of Professional Control: Internal Coalitions and Cross-Professional Boundaries." *American Journal of Sociology* 94 (4): 994-1021.

Hightower-Vandamm, M. 1981. "Soaring into the 80s New Directions." *American Journal of Occupational Therapy* 35: 767-774.

Hirama, Haru. 1986. "The COTA: A Chronological Review" in *The Occupational Therapy Assistant, Roles and Responsibilities: A Comprehensive Text for Practice and Education*, edited by Sally E. Ryan. Thorofare, NY: Slack.

Holmes, Thelma M. 1970. "Supportive Personnel and Supervisory Relationships." *Physical Therapy* 50: 1165 - 1171.

Horan, Patrick. 1978. "Is Status Attainment Research Atheoretical?" *American Sociological Review*. 43: 534-540.

Jenkins, Enid. 1989 "Nurses' Control over Nursing". Pgs. 193-208 in *Issues in Australian Nursing 2*, edited by Genevieve Gray and Rosalie Pratt. New York: Churchill Livingstone.

Julius, Louise H. 1970 "Depth of Knowledge of Technician and Therapist," *Inhalation Therapy* 15: 71-75.

Kalisch, Philip A. and Beatrice J. Kalisch. 1995. *The Advance of American Nursing*. Philadelphia: Lippincott)

Kerr, Elizabeth E. 1971. "Utilization and Preparation of Personnel to Deliver Health Care," *Respiratory Care* 16: 41-48.

Kirchman, Margaret M and Billie Howard. 1966. "The Role of the Certified Assistant in a General Hospital." *American Journal of Occupational Therapy* 10: 293 - 297.

Kusterer, Ken C. 1978. *Know-How on the Job: The ImportantWorking Knowledge of "Unskilled" Workers*. Boulder, CO: Westview Press.

Melosh, Barbara. 1984. "More than the 'Physician's Hand': Skill and Authority in Twentieth Century Nursing." Pg. 482-496 in *Women and Health Care in America*, edited by Judith Walzer Leavitt. Madison, WI: University of Wisconsin Press.

Offe, Claus. 1976. *Industry and Inequality*. London: Edward Arnold.

Osterman, Paul. 1975. "An Empirical Study of Labor Market Segmentation." *Industrial and Labor Relations Review* 28: 508-523.

_____. 1984. "White - Collar Internal Labor Markets." Pg. 163 - 190 in *Internal Labor Markets*, edited by Paul Osterman. Cambridge MA: MIT Press.

Parcel, Toby and M. B. Sickmeier. 1988. "One Firm, Two Labor Markets: The Case of McDonald's in the Fast Food Industry." *Sociological Quarterly*. 29: 29-46.

Peattie, Lisa. 1974. "The Other Sector: A Few Facts from Bogata, Some Comments and a List of Issues." Mimeo.

Perry, Jacqueline. 1964. "Professionalism in Physical Therapy." *Journal of the American Physical Therapy Association* 44: 429 - 434.

Piore, Michael. 1975. "Notes for a Theory of Labor Market Stratification." Pg. 125-150 in *Labor Market Segmentation*, edited by R. Edwards, M. Reich and David M. Gordon. Lexington, MA: DC Heath.

Reverby, Susan. 1987. *Ordered to Care:The Dilemma of American Nursing 1850 - 1930*. Cambridge: Cambridge University Press.

Rosenbaum, James E. 1986. "Institutional Career Structures and the Social Construction of Ability". Pp. 139 - 171 in John G. Robinson (ed), *Handbook of Theory and Research for the Sociology of Education*.

Rosenberg, Sam. 1989. "From Segmentation to Flexibility". *Labour and Society*. 14:363-407.

Rutan, Fred M. 1968. "Implications of Assistant-Training Programs for Physical Therapy: On Licensure." *Physical Therapy* 48: 999-1002.

Ryan, Sally E. 1986. *The Occupational Therapy Assistant, Roles and Responsibilities: A Comprehensive Text for Practice and Education*. Thorofare, NY: Slack.

Silver, Margaret. 1986a. "A Program for Career Structure. A Vision Becomes a Reality". *Australian Nurses Journal* 16:44-47.

_____. 1986b. "A Program for Career Structure. From Neophyte to Expert. *Australian Nurses Journal* 16:38-41.

Smith, Gary A. 1989. *Respiratory Care. Evolution of a Profession*. Lenexa, KS: Applied Measurement Professionals.

Spence, A. Michael. 1974. *Market Signaling: Informational Transfer in Hiring and Related Screening Procedures*. Cambridge. Harvard University Press.

Spenner, Kenneth, Luther B. Otto, and Vaughn R.A. Call. 1982. *Career Lines and Careers*. Lexington, MA: D.C. Heath and Company.

Starr, Paul. 1982. *The Social Transformation of American Medicine.* New York: Basic Books.

Stevens, Rosemary. 1972. *American Medicine and the Public Interest.* New Haven: Yale University Press.

Watts, Nancy T. 1971. "Task Analysis and Division of Responsibility in Physical Therapy." *Physical Therapy* 51: 23-35.

White, Barbara C. 1970. "Physical Therapy Assistants: Implications for the Future." *Physical Therapy* 50: 674-679.

_____. 1972. "What's the Answer? Queries and Replies of Concern to Therapists." *Physical Therapy* 52: 94-95.

Worthingham, Catherine A. 1965. "Nonprofessional Personnel in Physical Therapy." *Physical Therapy* 45:122-115.

12

Creating Capitalists: The Social Origins of Entrepreneurship in Post-Communist Poland

Barbara Heyns
New York University

A number of papers in this volume deal with career transitions in post-industrial labor markets in a comparative context. The institutional context, however, is invariably relatively stable and longstanding. Contrasting labor markets dominated by stable occupational structures with those organized by stable firms, for example, as Thomas DiPrete and Patricia McManus do, presumes that the institutions in question operate within similar markets for labor. Equally, if one aims to understand labor market segmentation as a function of union strength and prevailing policies toward employment and training, as Arne Kalleberg does, the presumption is that these are set within an established economic structure, albeit one that can expand or contract. Variability in education, occupational mobility, and earnings are understood as a function of the demand and supply for labor set by relatively fixed economic structures. The capacity of firms to adapt to changing economic conditions depends on managerial skills and business conditions; the potential of a work force depends on human capital, and on opportunities for training and mobility. The opportunity structure is presumed to provide the incentives for investing in human capital and for individual labor market behavior.

This paper deals with a different problem, and that is how labor markets form in the first place. In particular, I am interested in the growth and expansion of the new private sector and in the development of business values and entrepreneurial aspirations in post-communist countries. Insofar as market transitions entail a transformation of values, aspirations, and opportunity structures, the question becomes how values and aspirations are formed when the opportunity structure is undefined and fairly chaotic. Preliminary answers can, I think, be found by studying student attitudes and values in post-communist countries.

This chapter will present data from the first survey of business students in post-communist Poland. The approach is comparative, in that three different educational contexts will be compared, but the central questions concern first, the origins and relative importance of economic values in shaping career aspirations, and second, the degree to which pre-existing institutions, such as schooling or the family, influence these aspirations.

Education occupies a difficult and ambiguous position in post-communist countries. New skills, attitudes, and values are needed, along with increased investments in human capital; yet the guarantees of jobs and the security of employment promised under state socialism have been abruptly terminated. Students must be mobilized to achieve, yet setting career goals in the midst of chaotic economic change is extraordinarily difficult. The economic reforms have aimed to sever the traditional links between education and career. The contours of the emerging opportunity structure are obscure; the incentives for learning particular subject matter are still unclear. Knowledge about career possibilities is rather limited and quickly outdated. On the one hand, students have never had more freedom to define their own career goals; at the same time, calculating the value of credentials or the expected returns to education has never been as problematic. Although criticism of rigid "manpower planning" as practiced by the former regime is widespread, the connections between schooling and career rewards were at least clear. The economic transformation means fundamental increases in uncertainty at all levels, but particularly for students.

Uncertainties affect all fields, but they are endemic to business education, where the purposes of training can be somewhat obscure, even in the west (*The Economist*, June 4, 1994). One might ask whether it is rational to earn an unproven credential in business or economics rather than becoming an entrepreneur directly. One of the most phenomenal changes in post-communist countries has been the rapid development of new business schools, courses in economics, trade and commerce, as well as a host of other new training opportunities for budding entrepreneurs. Programs range from crash courses lasting a few days or several weeks, to year-long workshops and seminars, to fully accredited schools offering degrees in business administration. They attract students of all ages and backgrounds, from young school-leavers with grand ambitions to seasoned veterans of state enterprise; from opposition activists eager to dismantle the public sector, to senior managers and planning experts who hope to survive the transition. Classes in accounting and finance, trade, computer programming, management, marketing and other business skills have proliferated;

the most popular carry the added label "international," European, or simply "western." Language study, both formal and informal, is also experiencing a renaissance, with courses in "business English" leading the way. Reliable counts of the students involved are unavailable, but estimates of the number of courses offered in Warsaw alone are in the hundreds.[1] One state enterprise even offered the "old guard" of *nomenklatura* managers scholarships for executive training seminars as part of a their severance package.

While it is too early to hazard an evaluation of the schools or programs that have mushroomed since 1989, much less to assess their impact on economic reform, the growth of business education is as remarkable as the "cowboy capitalism" flourishing center stage (Grayson, 1993). Prior to 1990, business education did not exist in communist countries. One could study management, which meant the direction and administration of state enterprise, or one could study orthodox versions of socialist economics. In Poland, six specialized universities of economics and planning were in operation, while many 'ordinary' universities included a department of economics and management. With very few exceptions, however, it was all but impossible to learn about private, independent, or non-state economic activity.[2] Aleksander Müller, for example (1991: 175), concluded that "The economic higher schools have trained useless graduates for a non-existing economy."

Although schools of business are new, they are not entirely unprecedented. New educational programs are seldom constructed from whole cloth; they depend on existing philosophies, faculties and facilities as surely as they displace them. If one envisions establishing a new field of study, there are three possible strategies. First, one might affiliate with an existing university program, enlarging a department within an established institution. Second, one might capture or reform an existing specialized school. Finally, one might establish a new and altogether separate school.

Business education has blossomed in all three ways in Eastern Europe. Traditional management and economics programs within the university have expanded dramatically, renegotiating their mission and credentials, while retaining their connections to the university. Schools of economic planning have been reorganized, adding business and commerce as major new specializations. Finally, new schools of business administration have been established, typically with western capital. Throughout the region, the institutional lineages of new and reformed business schools can be traced to one of these sources.[3]

Despite profound shifts in philosophy and values, institutions tend to reproduce themselves. Despite new courses and revised curricula, schools tend to recruit and train students who share distinctive—and differing—attitudes toward business. Both the structure and organization are shaped by preexisting institutions; new programs recreate the ideological tensions found in the programs that went before. Even an entirely new school, with a radical new mission, perceives and responds to images lodged in the past. Contrasting programs with dissimilar origins can provide a broader understanding of the dynamics of educational reform. The next three sections briefly sketch the three schools studied, emphasizing the major differences and similarities.

Specialized Schools of Economics

In April of 1991, the Polish parliament restored the name *Szkoła Główna Handlowa (SGH)* to the largest and most renowned school of economics in Poland. For forty-two years, the school had been known as *Szkoła Główna Planowania i Statystyki* [Central School of Planning and Statistics], or *SGPiS*. With five different faculties or departments and several branch schools outside Warsaw, the school offered not only statistics and planning but management, foreign trade, and tourism. Economics was taught as an applied science in the Marxist-Leninist mode, although the faculty were familiar with capitalist theory and models. *SGPiS* was known for having strong political connections both to the party and to state government. Students at Warsaw University, not entirely in jest, described *SGPiS* as the school for "police and spies," rather than "planners and statisticians." Graduates aspired to become industrial *apparatchiks* or government officials, and the most successful eventually moved into high posts in the command economy. During the 1960s, the school achieved distinction and international recognition through the work of economists such as Michał Kalecki, becoming known as the "Polish Cambridge." Both Leszek Balcerowicz, the architect of the Polish transition, and the former Finance Minister, Jerzy Osiatyński, have worked and studied here.

SGH has made substantial changes in the last four years, despite the budgetary crises (Beksiak, Chmielecka, and Grzelońska, 1991). Deans and rectors retired or were voted out of office, and the curriculum has been extensively revised. The departmental structure has been completely revamped; students are now admitted to the school, rather than to a particular faculty; their course of study is reviewed by the full academic senate rather than by specialized units. Although the program is still highly structured, students have considerably more choice among courses than before these reforms. The first five semesters are standardized, although students are now allowed to choose their lecturers; thereafter, electives and tutorials replace compulsory courses. Enrollments at *SGH* are robust, and growing rapidly. In 1991-92, there were 877 day students; in addition, some 1,600 evening students paid nominal tuition fees. *SGH* recently added an MBA program, modelled after American programs. In 1992, for the first time ever, *SGH* published a course catalogue, listing the programmatic options that students can pursue (Chmielecka, 1992).

Management and Economics within the University

The faculty of Management and Economics at Warsaw University is smaller than *SGH*, but generally considered somewhat more prestigious. Although Management never achieved the stature accorded more academic disciplines, this program retained a fair amount of intellectual autonomy under communism because of its affiliation with the university. Course work tended to be much more theoretical and less applied than at the former *SGPiS*; the faculty were generally thought to be less "political" as well.

Like *SGH*, the Management and Economics program has launched curricular reforms and expanded admissions to meet increased student demand; in 1992, 210 students of management and 351 students of economics were enrolled in the undergraduate program, while advanced degree programs grew dramatically. Postgraduate courses and an MBA degree, in collaboration with the University of Illinois, are now offered at the International Management Centre and School. The programs in management and economics always enrolled a large number of part-time and evening students; since 1989, however, these courses have grown substantially, despite escalating fees.

Under the current Polish constitution, higher education is free. However, with the passage of the Higher Education Act in 1990, university programs are permitted to charge tuition for evening courses or for special extra-curricular programs. Fees can also be charged for "irregular" students, or those returning to school after a certain age. The Management School, particularly the programs affiliated with the postgraduate Centre, aspires to become an autonomous unit within the university, at least in fiscal terms. There have been recurring controversies over whether individual departments can keep the revenues generated by extra-curricular courses. Compared to *SGH*, dissension among faculty over educational reform and the restructuring of programs seems less prevalent than conflict between the School and the central university administration over fees and the disposition of grants from international donors. Thus, the Warsaw University program in Management and Economics represents a second site for business training in post-communist countries—an adjunct to, and a potential subsidy for, university programs.

Private Business Education

The third type of business school is the newest and, for socialist countries, the most radical. The first private business school in Poland, the *Prywatna Wyższa Szkoła Businessu i Administracji*, or the Private Higher School of Business and Administration, was founded in 1991.[4] This school is best described as the vision of one man, Dr. Tadeusz Kożluk, a Polish-American businessman from New Jersey and, most recently, Warsaw. Dr. Kożluk is justifiably proud of his efforts to establish this school, despite enormous red tape and prolonged delays from the Ministry of National Education. The school was finally approved in the spring of 1991, and the first three hundred students admitted the following fall. Like all new endeavors in Poland, the school has faced a number of problems in finding appropriate space, recruiting staff, and beginning operations; the fact that it has prospered, despite these obstacles, is a tribute to the persistence of Dr. Kożluk. At the time of the interview, Dr. Kożluk and the staff had begun reviewing applications for the second year; he expected the next entering class to be twice as large as that of the first year.

As the name suggests, *Prywatna* is thoroughly private. Tuition alone was two million złotys per month ($200) in 1992, close to the average monthly salary in the state sector; moreover, student scholarships or stipends are not available. In exchange for these steep fees, students are subjected to a rigorous and demanding regime, encompassing not only their course work but also personal habits, grooming, outside activities, and general behavior. Students are required to attend all classes, to be punctual, orderly, and well-dressed; unlike the rest of Warsaw, smoking is not allowed in either the building or the classrooms. These rules are formalized in a contract that each entering student must sign with the school, a contract that governs their conduct and defines the expectations of the school and staff.

The student contract and the plethora of rules and regulations convey an explicit message: Business requires discipline; discipline will be taught and strictly enforced. The objective is to equip students with the character and the diligence needed for business, as well as with new skills. The symbolic meaning is clear to students and staff alike. *Prywatna Wyższa Szkoła Businessu i Administracji* aims to undo the shoddy work habits and lackadaisical attitudes inculcated by socialism. Poland's economic problems are to be understood as cultural and psychological, rather than systemic; disciplined work habits—and the sense of responsibility and personal dignity that results—can provide a fresh start for individuals and for the economy.

Each of the three business schools is unique, although their students tend to be recruited from a common pool of applicants living in or near Warsaw. Each school offers a similar array of business and economics courses, and each hopes to establish and promote joint degrees and international exchange programs with business schools in other countries. Given the incentives for extra-curricular teaching, even their faculties overlap. Warsaw faculty moonlight extensively; teaching courses in the evening and part-time at other institutions is a popular way to augment income. The intellectual ambiance in every school was overwhelmingly pro-reform; students and faculty in each school endorsed economic reform and welcomed the arrival of a market economy with enthusiasm. Little if any nostalgia for the past could be discerned. The extent of actual curriculum change at the level of individual courses could, of course, be debated; at the same time, the training offered at *SGPiS* and at the University was considered high quality before 1989. Although the course work differs from conventional economics and management training in the West, faculty in each of the schools believes that their program offers high-quality instruction in business administration. Both faculty and students believe that education will be a decisive factor in creating a market economy. Business schools, even those that formerly trained socialist technocrats, have the unique mandate of cultivating managerial skills and a vigorous capitalist ethic.

Along with restructuring programs, business schools are actively constructing new, post-communist reputations. *Prywatna* takes pride in being the first private business school in post-communist Poland, while the two state schools are absorbed in creating new and reformed images. Considering the questions that might be raised about their past, it is surely in the best interests of the schools to do so. These schools are definitely not trying to protect their traditions or rest on their laurels; wisely, perhaps, each claims to offer a program that is very different than before.

The Research Problem

The sudden flowering of neo-liberalism in Poland and other post-communist countries, even in societies without a significant private sector, seems to be unprecedented (Kovacs, 1991; Szacki, 1990; Heyns and Jasinska-Kañia, 1993; Weil, 1993). The dominant pattern of governance in the region historically involved authoritarian regimes presiding over largely agrarian economies; the class structure was pre-industrial, with neither an established bourgeoisie nor a significant middle class. Commercial activity was dominated by Jews, Germans, or other ethnic minorities; landowners and the intelligentsia alike viewed business with disdain. Moreover, even under state socialism, the various opposition movements did not as a rule advocate free markets or liberal institutions. The church, for example, was certainly anti-communist, but it did not champion *laissez-faire* economic doctrines or individualism. In the political realm, democratic values seem to have antedated the collapse of communism (Weil, 1993), but the source and significance of neo-liberal economic philosophies are a puzzle.

There is, of course, longstanding sociological interest in questions linking values and economic behavior. Hypotheses for studying the values of post-communist students can be loosely derived from Max Weber's thesis on the Protestant ethic and related work (Weber, 1930; Collins, 1980; Brubaker, 1984). While there are precious few Calvinists in Poland, one would expect that students aspiring to be entrepreneurs would be more supportive of business, more hostile to governmental regulation and authority, and more individualistic; Weberian theory would also predict future entrepreneurs would be more self-reliant, more committed to hard work and the "acquisitive impulse," and perhaps more concerned about the ethics of commerce. Business students should be less inclined to favor collective strategies of all sorts, whether aimed at welfare and social security, at economic planning, or at international assistance.

The three business schools chosen seem likely to represent a range of values and aspirations sufficient to test these hypotheses. The students enrolling in *SGH*, the most applied school with the closest historic ties to state government, were expected to be the most oriented toward state policy and toward managing state-owned industry. Despite economic and political reform, *SGH* students were hypothesized to be the most collectivist and the least oriented toward *laissez-faire* economics; they were expected to gravitate to state employment, as either reformers or planners, rather than to the private sector, and to support state intervention and assistance more readily than students in the other two schools.

In contrast, students choosing to attend *Prywatna* would be the most individualistic and the most committed to developing the private sector. Enrolling in a new business school without an established reputation might be considered a costly, high-risk option, whatever the aspirations. Correspondingly, students at *Prywatna* were expected to express the strongest pro-business sentiments, to be the most individualistic, and the most likely to anticipate an entrepreneurial future. Management students were hypothesized to fall between these two extremes in both values and aspirations.

Value differences among students were assumed to depend on both socioeconomic background and the choice of school; more importantly, values were assumed to predict entrepreneurial aspirations among students, irrespective of their backgrounds. Ivan Szelenyi and his collaborators (1988) have argued that the origins of entrepreneurship under communism are predominantly cultural, and can be traced to family values, rather than to economic ones. Rural entrepreneurs in Hungary expressed values quite similar to those of a parent or grandparent working under market conditions before the Second World War. These values included "autonomy and risk taking, resistance to being subordinated to the bureaucratic order and to accepting ascribed ranks in a hierarchy, desire to be one's own boss, value attached to hard work, and willingness to delay consumption." (Szelenyi, et al., 1988: 65). The authors argue that despite the forty-year hiatus, pre-War entrepreneurial families had preserved a distinctive belief system, and had socialized their children to these values and behavior. Despite very limited possibilities for inheriting land or capital under communism, shared familial values explained entrepreneurship. Perhaps family relations foster neo-liberal philosophies in Poland as well.

These concepts linking economic reform and personal values structured the inquiry, but they provided sensitizing ideas as much as formal hypotheses. During the course of the research, a number of business students were interviewed informally, in an effort to understand their points of view. The majority ridiculed the notion of an economic ethos based on either ethical or religious ideals. In general, the students were skeptical that economic values had any bearing on economic reform or personal aspirations. Protest, they argued, and a decade of political opposition, had produced economic reform, not Protestantism. Although many students had been involved in the informal economy, they generally denied having relatives or family members with connections to a free market. By their accounts, entrepreneurship meant nothing more or less than freedom from state control. They even denied aspirations to get rich. The best way to make money in post-communist Poland was to work abroad or for a foreign firm based in Warsaw; entrepreneurial activity was excessively risky. Attitudes toward the government varied from cynical to supportive; but few students doubted that politics would dictate the course of economic reform, rather than individual values or entrepreneurial efforts.

The Data

The survey data to be presented are based on questionnaires distributed to full-time, first-year business students in each of the schools described above. Arrangements were made with the faculty teaching first-year classes to permit us to administer forms before class; student interviews were conducted during the last full week of school in May 1992. Hence, the sample is restricted to those students who were still active in the last weeks of the term and it probably overrepresents those who attended most regularly; in all, 423 questionnaires were collected, representing virtually all of the students present on that day.[5] The students are not, of course, a random sample of either Warsaw business students or the students in these schools; accurate enrollment lists were simply not available in any school at the end of the term. In each setting, the data were, however, collected in a similar manner. Students and faculty were cooperative and quite willing to be interviewed; only a handful of respondents returned incomplete questionnaires. In each school, a sizeable fraction of the full-time students in the first-year classes were interviewed, and the demographic profile in each school was generally consistent with other information. There is little reason to believe, therefore, that respondents are a biased sample of the target population. Although the findings should be treated with caution, the data appear to be representative of first-year students in these three business programs. Generalizations to all Polish students, much less to other post-communist countries, however, are not tenable.

The survey data are summarized in three sections. The next section contrasts students in each of the three schools and summarizes the construction of measures. Student values will be compared to those of all Poles, at the outset of the market transition. This section relies on an extensive battery of questions developed in Britain to measure liberal and authoritarian attitudes cross-culturally (Heath, 1991; Białecki and Mach, 1992). Then, I examine the determinants of student values in Poland, and compare the differences between schools. The objectives in this section are twofold; first, to understand recruitment patterns among schools, and second, to compare schools in terms of values and student background. The next section evaluates student career aspirations, and endeavors to predict who aspires to owning their own business in Poland. The final section compares male and female students in terms of values and aspirations.

The Students

Polish students entering business school in 1991-2 were truly pioneers. These students were the first class to be admitted to business and management since the beginning of the market transition and they will be among the first graduates of these newly-formed—or reformed—programs. Demographically, the business students resemble other first-year university students. The majority (54%) were male. Ninety percent of the respondents were between 18 and 20 years of age; two-thirds were exactly twenty. Less than ten percent had any previous work or business experience. Over half (51%) of the students had lived in Warsaw their entire lives. One in six (17%) had lived abroad for three or more months during the last three years; more than a third (38%) expected to travel abroad in the next three years. These data suggest that the business students are a fairly sophisticated and cosmopolitan group.

In terms of socioeconomic background, the students are clearly advantaged. Half of their mothers and sixty percent of their fathers had at least some university education. Their family incomes were by Polish standards quite high; over half (54%) reported that per capita family income was over 2 million złotys per month, or about $200. (In Poland as a whole, the average per capita family income in 1991 was 766,000 złotys per month, or less than eighty dollars.) Forty percent had at least one parent employed in the private sector. These figures imply that Warsaw business students are a relatively privileged group, even among university students.[6]

In several important respects the backgrounds of the students in the three schools differ, most noticeably between the private and state sectors of education. Students attending *Prywatna* live in families with substantially higher incomes than the students in either the Management program at Warsaw University or *Szkoła Główna Handlowa (SGH)*. In addition, private school students were much more likely to have self-employed parents working in the private sector. Considering the tuition, these differences are not terribly surprising. We will return to this issue when we discuss student recruitment and differences between schools; first, it is necessary to review the measures of economic and political values.

Political and Economic Values: Measuring Liberalism

Measuring political and economic values in post-socialist countries poses difficulties. The problem is twofold: research on political and economic values was not well-developed in communist countries, and few studies produced relevant measures that could be compared over time. Existing value scales with known properties include items that may be irrelevant to countries in transition; moreover, such measures may be problematic for cross-cultural comparison. One is, however, forced to choose between developing new and original measures with unknown properties, or adapting items that were initially developed and tested in other countries (Converse, 1964; Rokeach, 1979).

For this study, however, only one option made sense. A battery of eighteen items constructed to measure "core values" of liberalism in British electoral studies had been translated and administered to a random sample of Polish adults in 1991.[7] The English research conceptualized liberalism as an enduring set of values, characterized by three distinctive dimensions. Economic values are defined along a continuum representing the degree of support for *laissez-faire* economics opposed to socialist arrangements; political values are measured on a scale that varied from libertarian to authoritarian. The third dimension represents individualist versus collectivist attitudes. These items have substantial face validity, and they have been shown to yield stable and reliable measures of political and economic values in other national surveys. Moreover, the items were being used in parallel analyses based on several other subpopulations (Białecki and Mach, 1992). Hence, comparisons were possible among different groups of Polish respondents.

All items are measured on a four-point scale, from strongly agree to strongly disagree. A confirmatory factor analysis was performed on the items in each of the domains for the national and student samples separately. Each set of items yields a single underlying factor scale, with the principle components accounting for between .36 and .43 percent of their respective common variances. The factor loadings ranged from .46 to .74 across items; the relative contribution of each item to the composite scales was similar in both samples, although the business students scored higher than the national sample on virtually all of the individual items measuring *laissez-faire* or libertarian attitudes.[8] The reliabilities calculated for the student sample were, however, as high as those for the population, despite the implied ceiling effects. The alpha reliabilities calculated for the student sample and the items included are given below.

1) Laissez Faire - Socialist scale (7 Items, Alpha = .787).[9]

2) Libertarian - Authoritarian scale (6 Items, Alpha = .592)[10]

3) Collectivist - Individualist scale (5 Items, Alpha = .571).[11]

These reliabilities compare favorably with the British results; the similarities with the national sample suggest that these three composite measures capture consistent differences in values among the Polish respondents. The *laissez-faire*-socialist scale can be interpreted as either pro-business or as anti-socialist; libertarian-authoritarian values reflect respect for individual rights versus support for law, order, and traditional authority. The measure of individualism-collectivism seems to tap a sense of personal responsibility as well as punitive attitudes towards welfare and dependency. Although these items were not developed to assess values or value change for a population in transition, the three scales appear to discriminate between groups with different economic and political values at the outset of the economic transition.

How Liberal Are the Polish Business Students?

The three scales were constructed to measure "core" values, and hence relatively stable and enduring traits. Since their explanatory power, even as descriptive measures is not known, the first task is to locate the business students in terms of economic and political values on each of the three dimensions measured with reference to the national population survey. The business students are, obviously, an especially advantaged group. In terms of age, income, educational background, and urban residence, the student sample is quite select. Age, education, and urban residence have each been shown to influence values; it would be difficult to imagine that these and related factors are uncorrelated with attitudes and values.

In order to compare business students with the national population, each of the three value measures was regressed on the full range of background factors common to both surveys. The independent variables included age, sex, urban location, farm origins, the education of the household head and the spouse, the sector of employment and the total family income reported by the respondent. Since the majority of students lived at home, their parents education and family income were used rather than their own. Three dummy variables were also added, indicating whether or not the respondent had lived in Warsaw for most of their life, whether or not anyone in the household received a state pension, and whether anyone was unemployed.

The *laissez-faire*, libertarian, and individualism scales derived from the factor analysis were regressed on these background factors. In each equation, a dummy variable for student status was included to test the overall differences between the two samples; then three separate dummy variables, one for each school, were substituted, in order to test for differences between schools. I also examined interactions between school type and background status. Student status on both *laissez-faire* and libertarian values is highly significant, uniquely accounting for between 6-8 percent of the total variance. On the individualist-collectivist dimension, however, demographic and economic background factors are largely unrelated to the value scores, and the differences between students and the general population are not significant.

Table 12.1 presents the ordinary least squares regression of the values scales on social background for the merged national and student samples. As the regressions clearly indicate, the students differ dramatically from the average Polish citizen and, not surprisingly, especially on the dimension measuring economic values. Moreover, these differences persist irrespective of the full set of controls. *Laissez-faire* values tend to be the most linked to socioeconomic factors, while libertarian values tend to be a function of age and urban residence. With and without controls, the business students are nearly a full standard deviation more "*laissez-faire*" than the Polish population and approximately half a standard deviation more "libertarian." Even when the population sample is restricted to those with some higher education or to those who are under the age of 35, student status increases the variance explained in economic and political values by at least three percent. In contrast, with respect to individualist - collectivist values, the student scores are not significantly different from those of the national sample.

The regressions provide support for the proposition that these measures of liberalism yield value configurations for post-communist countries resembling those observed in the west. At the same time, the strength of their associations with traditional social factors, such as class or demographic background, tends to be lower than in Europe or the United States. There is evidence that economic background plays a role in economic values; having either parent owning a private business is second only to parental education as a factor predicting how strongly *laissez-faire* values

TABLE 12.1 Unstandardized Regression Coefficients of Laissez-faire, Libertarian, and Individualistic Values Regressed on Social and Demographic Background Factors, for the merged Polish sample, including the national random sample [N=915], and the business school students [N=423].

Independent Variables	Laissez-faire			Libertarian			Individualism		
	b	s.e.	t	b	s.e.	t	b	s.e.	t
Sex	-.013	.047	.70	-.035	.050	-.48	-.057	.056	-1.02
Age	-.002	.002	1.05	-.013	.002	-6.56	.003	.002	1.47
Education, Wife	.095	.016	5.79	.031	.017	1.86	-.032	.019	-1.67
Education, Husband	.055	.015	2.90	-.010	.015	-.49	.036	.016	2.05
Farm Background	.148	.092	1.61	-.068	.101	-.67	-.011	.334	-.78
Sector of Employment	.018	.034	.35	.011	.059	.85	-.001	.034	-.97
Private Owner	.233	.091	2.56	-.045	.100	-.65	.083	.113	.74
Family Income	.019	.010	1.98	-.016	.011	-1.16	.027	.012	2.13
Pension	.013	.073	.86	.092	.080	1.15	-.184	.088	-3.10
Unemployed	-.245	.183	-1.34	.039	.201	.20	-.151	.201	-.62
Size of Town	-.002	.000	-.56	.153	.017	3.48	-.081	1.651	-1.09
Warsaw Resident	.007	.318	.80	-.003	-.098	.97	.043	.971	.33
Student	.906	.083	10.96	.425	.051	4.78	-.107	1.06	-.29
Intercept	-1.064	.134	-7.89	.302	.148	2.04	.037	.167	.22
R²	.3607			.2126			.0306		
Student, SGH	.866	.083	9.94	.465	.097	4.81	-.177	.109	-1.62
Management	1.013	.097	9.32	.427	.119	3.59	-.113	.135	-.84
Prywatna	.950	.135	6.63	.315	.148	2.13	.194	.167	1.16
R²	.3651			.2214			.0395		

are expressed. Libertarianism, in contrast, is largely a function of age and urban residence, which do not discriminate among the students. As other analysts have found, socioeconomic status predicts political attitudes and values in post-communist countries rather weakly. This is typically inter-preted as indicating a disjuncture between social structure and values or as indicating that class interests have not yet crystallized (Adamski, 1993).

The final three rows given in Table 12.1 represent the net effects of each of the schools, with the full set of background and demographic factors controlled. These coefficients are the unstandardized values of the three dummy variables when school type is substituted for the single student status variable. The coefficients represent deviations from the omitted category, in this case the national population sample, on each scale. The differences between schools are not large; net of background variables they are significant only for the scale measuring individualism. The scores do, however, correspond to the hypothesized ordering between schools. The private business school is the most individualistic and the least libertarian; *SGH* is the least *laissez-faire*, the most libertarian and the most collectivist. On all three scales, the Management program at Warsaw University falls between the other two schools.

The next section explores the relationships between these "core" values and other characteristics within the business student sample. It must be emphasized, however, that in terms of economic and political values, the Warsaw business students are substantially more liberal than the average Polish citizen, even when compared to those with similar demographic characteristics and comparable economic and cultural resources. The evidence that the three business schools have a distinctive pattern of values is much more tentative. Although the differences between schools are in the predicted direction, their magnitude is not large. When demographic factors and socioeconomic background of students are controlled, value differences between schools are insignificant.

Values and Student Recruitment

Despite the enormous demand for business education that now exists, to some extent these three business schools compete for clientele. Each of the schools tends to recruit students from the same catchment area, which includes Warsaw and the surrounding region. Moreover, the schools differ in cost, in expectations for students, and in their assigned positions under the previous regime. Although only the private school is or expects to remain completely dependent on tuition, attracting students is increasingly important throughout Polish education.

In spite of reform, the two established state schools were expected to recruit a student body that resembled their historic constituencies. The new private school, in contrast, must secure a niche in the marketplace, largely by competing for the clientele of state schools. We expected *Prywatna* to attract students with a strong commitment to the new private sector, who would be willing and able to pay high tuition in a somewhat risky setting. State schools, however, despite lower tuition and numerous reforms, no longer have secure and well-defined channels for either recruitment or placement. Hence, the characteristics of students at each school can be thought of as indicators of both continuity and change between schools.

The observed value differences between schools support those hypothesized in terms of the relative magnitude of effects, even if the differences in absolute size are not significant. The first question that must be asked, however, is whether these distinctive value configurations should be considered an intrinsic aspect of each school, or a consequence of differential recruitment patterns. Although there is little variance between schools in age, parental education, or sex composition, as we have seen, the schools do differ in the socioeconomic status of their students in consistent ways. In this section, we will pursue the question of whether socioeconomic differences between schools account for expressed value differences.

Two distinct hypotheses guided this work. First, we expected differences between the private and public sector in business education; second, we expected differences within the public sector would reflect whether students were recruited from Warsaw or from outside. Parental employment should be reflected in school choice, because private sector parents may prefer private education, and because private schools are considerably more expensive than their public sector counterparts; students enrolling in *Prywatna*, as we have seen, are from families with substantially more income than in either of the other two schools. Moreover, in this first year of operation, *Prywatna* admitted students quite late in the year, after exams had been completed by the other two faculties. We were interested in comparing students who chose to attend private business school over the state alternatives, in terms of their values and objectives.

Historically, the most significant difference between the two state schools is a consequence of specialization and the degree of emphasis on practical as opposed to theoretical economics. Both the training and the credentials offered by *SGPiS* were substantially more vocationally-oriented than those of the University program. The applicant pool was also significantly more diverse, and included students from small towns and rural areas in Poland. Students growing up outside Warsaw tend to be more provincial than those who attended secondary schools in the city. Within the public sector, we expected business students to hold different values depending on whether or not they grew up in Warsaw. If value differences between schools can be explained fully by these three characteristics, family income, sector of employment, and family residence, it strongly suggests that value differ-

TABLE 12.2 Logistic Regression Equations Predicting School Choice by Student Background, Polish Business Students, 1992.

Independent Variables	Dependent Variables					
	Private vs. State School			SGH vs. Management		
	Coefficient	(s.e.)	Sig.	Coefficient	(s.e.)	Sig.
Applied elsewhere	3.95	.57	.000	-1.48	.80	.065
Passed Exams	-1.85	.59	.002	.12	.86	.893
Family income	.17	.07	.014	-.17	.05	.003
Self-Employed	1.49	.41	.000	.13	.35	.713
Warsaw Resident	-.07	.38	.851	-.51	.26	.051
Values						
Laissez-Faire	-.04	.27	.875	-.17	.18	.325
Libertarian	-.04	.23	.847	.11	.15	.463
Individualistic	.37	.20	.069	-.09	.13	.494
Constant	-3.99	.53	.000	1.93	.32	.000
-2 Log Likelihood	201.19			370.00		
Model Chi-Square	111.79***			35.82**		
Degrees of freedom	8			8		
Number of cases	423			362		
Goodness of Fit	427.18, (p=.016)			328.41, (p=.251)		

ences between schools should be attributed to recruitment, rather than socialization. Although a particular business school may reinforce values, differences that are due to such background factors imply that prior family influences, rather than business school experience, are critical for the emergence of new economic and political values.

Table 12.2 presents two logistic regressions designed to test these hypotheses. The dependent variables in each case are the log odds of enrolling in a particular school.

The first equation predicts private sector enrollment compared to the two state schools, while the second compares only the two schools in the public sector, SGH and the University of Warsaw Management program. In each equation, Warsaw residence, family income and sector of employment are entered, with each of the three dimensions of liberalism previously discussed. Two additional dummy variables assessing recruitment are included: whether or not the student had applied to another business school and, if so, whether the student had passed the exams for that school. Only a minority of students (20%) had applied to a second school, and two-thirds of these stated that they had either passed the exams or that none were required. However, these variables account for a large part of the difference between the private and public sectors in business education.

The coefficients estimated in the first equation address the question of differences between sectors, or in this case differences between *Prywatna* and the two state-supported schools. The results imply that both sector of parental employment and family income are strongly and positively related to the probability of enrolling in the private school, while Warsaw residence is not. Students choosing *Prywatna* were the most likely to have applied to at least one other business school (65% had done so), and the least likely to have passed exams. *Prywatna* was approved quite late in the spring of 1991, and, since applicants could not know in advance whether the school would be approved, most prospective students had already applied for admission to other schools. But to some extent, *Prywatna* seems to have served as a back-up option for students who might be denied admission; at the same time, nearly half (47%) of those attending *Prywatna* who had sought admission elsewhere said that they had passed the exams; presumably, these students had chosen *Prywatna* over the established state schools. An important function of private sector business schools, however, seems to be allowing relatively advantaged students access to training and credentials, despite being denied admission to public sector schools. The major factor determining enrolling in a private school, however, which holds equally among those who did and did not apply to another school, is family income.

When socioeconomic factors are controlled, differences in values are uniformly insignificant between the private and the public sector. Individualism is the only value dimension that approaches significance, and even this difference is small when background differences are controlled. The coefficients in Table 12.2 include the three value measures, although they are correlated; entering them separately, however, does not significantly improve their explanatory power. The interactions between background and values, although somewhat larger than the main effects, are also insignificant. These results imply that virtually all of the observed value differences between the public and the private sector in these data can be explained by distinctive recruitment patterns between sectors.

The second equation compares recruitment between the two public schools, omitting the *Prywatna* students. Socioeconomic status is less important in predicting enrollment within the public sector than it is in distinguishing public from private sector enrollments. Family income and Warsaw residence are both significantly higher for Management students, however. Once these two factors are controlled, the differences in the liberalism scales between *SGH* and the Management School are small and insignificant. Although *SGH* students tend to be both more collectivist and anti-authoritarian than students at the Management School, these differences appear to depend on family background. *SGH* students, as noted previously, are the most likely to be recruited from outside Warsaw; correspondingly, family incomes are lower. Once income and place of residence are controlled, however, value differences between the two state schools are insignificant. The two state sector schools still recruit and enroll students that resemble their former constituencies to a striking degree. The second equation was also estimated by entering each value dimension separately; these coefficients were slightly higher, of course, but still insignificant in every case. Additional background variables, including those introduced in Table 12.1, do not alter these conclusions.

To summarize, economic and political values among the Warsaw business students are related, in the expected direction, to both family income and to having a self-employed parent in the private sector. Value differences among the schools, although consistent with predictions, are small and largely insignificant. Differences between schools appear to be a consequence of the demographic and socioeconomic factors that determine selective recruitment and enrollment. Variation in liberal values appears to be largely a consequence of residence, private sector experience of parents, and family income. Parent's education, which is uniformly high in all three schools, does not predict liberal values independently of parent's economic status. The residual differences in the liberal values measured here, do not justify assuming a strong causal role for business education in shaping values. Perhaps one year of business schooling is too short a time to influence economic and political values. Or perhaps students acquire *laissez-faire*, libertarian and individualistic values from their families directly, prior to entry. In any event, once socioeconomic background is controlled, liberal values are not significantly different between schools, irrespective of private or public sector control or the institutional legacy. For the two state schools, demographic patterns appear to be consistent with those that prevailed before the transition began, suggesting that these two schools continue to recruit from the same applicant pools, despite educational reform. *Prywatna*, in contrast, seems to be carving out a specialized niche, as a consequence of the high demand for business schooling and growth in the number of families who can afford private education.

Student Aspirations

Warsaw business school students, even more than their parents, aspire to work in the fledgling private sector. The most popular career destination is a private firm in Poland (39%), followed closely by owning one's own business (38%), or working for a foreign firm, (35%). In every school, more students aspired to own their own business than to work for a foreign firm or a joint venture in Poland. Moreover, employment in state firms was overwhelmingly rejected, despite the fact that this had been the dominant career track under communism. Less than ten percent (9.4%) of the students aspire to work in a state firm in Poland, although close to one-third concede that reforming state enterprises would be challenging. When asked what they considered the "greatest challenge" confronting Polish business, 40.5 percent of the students said starting a new firm, 30.4 percent said "restructuring state enterprise," and 9.6 percent said "privatization." One out of five students aspires to work abroad, while research in a university or scientific institute (4%) was the least popular career choice. The major reason students chose to attend business school, by a considerable margin, was that it provided "a chance to make money," with 58 percent mentioning this goal. The second most important reason was somewhat more patriotic; 29 percent started this course of study because the "Polish economy needs educated businessmen."[12]

The career aspirations of students differ more than their economic and political values, although only *Prywatna* students differ once gender and family background are controlled. In every school, aspiring entrepreneurs are more likely to be male, and to have fathers or mothers who are self-employed and earning more income than average. Future entrepreneurs differ in terms of values as well. Those who aspire to start their own businesses score significantly higher on *laissez-faire* attitudes as well.

By way of summary, Table 12.3 presents the logistic regression of hoping to start one's own business on selected background variables and economic values. The background variables included in the equation are gender and having at least one self-employed parent; family income is largely redundant when private sector employment and the school attended is included. Two additional measures of student motivation are included: the number of occupations chosen by the respondent and two dummy variables, one indicating that the primary reason the student chose business school was to make money and the other indicating that starting one's own business was the greatest challenge for Polish business. Although these variables are quite highly related to the dependent variable, they improve the fit of the logistic model without reducing the size or significance of the independent variables of interest. The school attended was included as a categoric variable with two degrees of freedom, and coded as deviations from the overall mean. Finally, scores on *laissez-faire* values and on a variable measuring the extent to which the respondent believed that the economy should be completely unregulated were included. Tests were conducted for first- and second-order interaction terms, as well as a number of other variables; these were uniformly insignificant and are excluded from the final model.

The final column of Table 12.3 presents the antilogs of the logistic coefficients, allowing one to see their relative strength as additive effects. The values imply, for example, that males were more than twice as likely to aspire to owning their own businesses, since $e^{.72} = 2.05$. This effect, with

TABLE 12.3   Logistic Regression of Ownership Aspirations on
Student Background and Economic Values, 1992

Independent Variables	Coefficient	(s.e.)	p	Exp(B)
Sex	.720	(.231)	.0019	2.05
Self-Employed	.589	(.264)	.0255	1.80
Business School				
Management	-.669	(.188)	.0004	.51
SGH	-.137	(.160)	.3914	1.15
Laissez-Faire	.296	(.154)	.0542	1.35
Challenge - Own	.663	(.224)	.0031	1.94
Money	.406	(.226)	.0728	1.50
Number of Careers	.839	(.247)	.0007	2.31
No Regulation	.197	(.089)	.0280	.82
Constant	-1.616	(.438)		

-2 Log Likelihood	490.190, with 414 degrees of freedom
Model Chi-Square	15.958 p = .0003
Goodness of Fit	372.789 (p = .4063)

other variables controlled, is the largest substantive difference in the model, since to some extent, the number of careers chosen necessarily increases the log odds of wanting to own one's own business. We will return to this point. The school attended exerts a smaller influence, but as the coefficients indicate, *Prywatna* students are the most likely to aspire to ownership. Private business schools, although still very small, seem both to enroll and train a disproportionate share of the private sector.

The final model correctly predicts 70 percent of the student's choices between business ownership and all other careers. The two background measures, sector of parental employment and gender, explain most of the differences between *Prywatna* and the Management program; *SGH* students, however, remain the least likely to aspire to own their own businesses. The values predicted to explain proprietorship aspirations are also significant; aspiring owners are among the most *laissez-faire* and the most likely to think the economy requires no regulation at all. Values contribute to the explanation of ownership aspirations independently of background or other attitudes; potential owners are also the most likely to regard starting a business as the biggest challenge, and the most likely to have entered business school in order to make money. Although these results are not too surprising, they support the conclusion that economic values distinguish different career tracks among these future Polish businessmen, even when student backgrounds, aspirations, and choice of school are controlled. Moreover, they suggest that one of the primary functions served by the private sector in business education is to provide training and credentials for private sector entrepreneurs. Although aspirations differ by social background and by choice of school, Warsaw business students aspire to private sector jobs and entrepreneurship in large numbers. The single factor that seems to reduce the desire to own one's own business is gender. And to that we now turn.

Gender, Values, and Proprietorship

Throughout East Central Europe, one of the most disconcerting trends has been the increase of gender-based inequalities (Einhorn, 1993; Mogdaham, 1993; Muller and Funk, 1992; Hauser, Heyns, and Mansbridge, 1992; Rueschemeyer, 1994). Women tend to be overrepresented among the unemployed and underrepresented in the new political leadership. Although mining and heavy industry were generally regarded as the most problematic economic sectors, the first firms to be closed were in the industries dominated by women, such as textiles or small electrical appliances. Even in those sectors of the economy in great demand, such as the services, women have tended to remain in the impoverished state sector, while males "privatize" their medical practices, law offices, and business services of all sorts. Child care, maternal leave, and reproductive rights of all sorts are defined as forms of socialist paternalism, too costly to be retained, while unemployment benefits and retraining for men are considered urgent priorities. Informally, there is enormous pressure on women to return to the home, to accept the "choice" of full-time motherhood that was denied them under state socialism, while men are encouraged to become entrepreneurs and businessmen. The market transition in Eastern Europe seems to have redefined the concept of private along gender lines: for women, "private" means the home and a return to domesticity, while for men it means entrepreneurship and economic activity without any state interference.

Gendered labor markets are not new, of course. Sex segregation and wage inequalities have been well-documented in Poland as well as in other countries of the region (Einhorn, 1993; Reszke, 1989). Despite the rhetoric, it is easy to show that labor force participation did not "emancipate" women under state socialism, if by this term one means economic equality between men and women. State socialism did, however, create a unique configuration of "feminized" labor markets. Professions requiring higher education, for example, particularly those in the human services, tended to be feminized, if not absolutely, at least dramatically more so than their counterparts in the west. Medical and dental care, law, economics, and a host of positions in middle-level management were dominated by women. Women held many jobs in economics and planning, and in accounting and administration within state enterprises. To be sure, these positions rarely entailed the responsibility, status, or the salary of equivalent job titles in western companies; under centralized planning, such positions were typically fairly routine and even clerical. Moreover, relative to skilled industrial jobs, the service sector as a whole was starved for funds (Heyns and Białecki, 1993; Białecki and Heyns, 1993).

The transition to a market economy in Eastern Europe will involve dramatic changes in both labor markets and stratification more generally. Whether one attributes change to the collapse of state socialism or to the dawn of a market economy, the emerging patterns of employment offer a rare opportunity to observe the sources and consequences of gender inequality in the labor market. Educational institutions of all sorts are under considerable pressure to reform the curriculum, and to educate a new, market-oriented elite. Yet as we have seen, educational programs, including those in business and economics, tend to recruit students from the same social groups as before. Currently, women are as well-represented in higher education and in economics as they were in the past. Despite dramatic increases in the proportion of students studying business and economics, the percentage of women is still high, if western patterns are taken as the norm. Ironically, many recruiters have been nonplussed by the sex composition of many jobs and professional training programs.[13]

Each of the business schools studied enrolls roughly equal numbers of women and men, and these programs are not atypical for Poland as a whole. As we have seen, however, the values and aspirations of women students differ from those of the men, particularly with respect to starting their own business. The question becomes whether we can account for gender-specific aspirations among students by differences in background and values. Ultimately, of course, occupational mobility depends on factors not anticipated by students and not measured in this research. But we can begin to unravel the sources of gender difference in attitudes and values that predict entrepreneurial aspirations.

Table 12.4 presents the complete list of occupational destinations separately by gender for the Polish business students. As this table makes clear, both men and women business students aspire to diverse occupational roles. The women are at least as likely to favor private firms as the men, and both men and women overwhelmingly reject state enterprise. Moreover, female students do not seem indecisive about their goals or career plans; they are at least as likely as the men to have formed specific ambitions during their initial year, and these ambitions resemble those of men students in most respects. The single item that significantly distinguishes men and women students is their propensity to aspire to owning and running their own businesses. Almost half of the men, compared to less than one woman in three hopes to be the proprietor of their own firm.

TABLE 12.4   Career Aspirations and Challenges by Gender,
Polish Business Students, 1992

PERSONAL ASPIRATIONS[1]	Males	Females	Total
Own one's own business	45.4	29.9	38.3*
Private Firm	38.0	40.2	39.0
State Firm	11.8	6.7	9.5
Foreign Firm or			
Joint Venture	31.4	40.2	35.5
In Poland	12.7	16.0	14.2
Abroad	21.8	17.5	19.9
Research, Continue			
Education	7.0	6.2	6.6
Don't know, No Answer	11.4	9.3	10.4
The greatest challenge for business in post-communist Poland is			
Organizing and running a new business	41.1	36.6	39.0
Restructuring, reforming state enterprise	29.4	29.3	29.3
Other, Don't Know	29.5	34.1	31.7
The primary reason for attending business school is to make money	63.8	50.0	57.5

[1]Students were allowed to choose multiple answers to the question of occupational destinations, hence the percentages do not equal 100%.
* This is the only sex difference that is significant, ($p < .01$).

Polish business schools offer a unique laboratory for comparing gender differences in aspirations and values. Historically, business and economics attracted more women than men; hence, women were available as both role models and peers to a much greater extent than is true in the west. Neither minority status nor tokenism within business and management would be expected to depress Polish women's aspirations and achievement, as seems to occur in western firms (Kantor, 1977).

There are several alternative explanations for the relationship between gender and ownership, and some evidence in favor of each. One might argue that women are more realistic about their career plans than men, and less likely to aim for distant, unreachable goals. Perhaps women's aspirations are more dependent on their family of origin than those of men. Finally, sex-specific economic values could also influence the differences. Paula England (1993) and other feminists have argued that neo-classical economics assumes a value structure that is inimical to women's special contributions, by focussing on self-interest and on rational, profit-maximizing behavior that ignores concerns for the collectivity. The women in this sample consistently scored lower than male business students on *laissez-faire* values, although there were no significant gender differences in the national sample. The question becomes can the differences in proprietorship be explained by a gender-specific configuration of values, aspirations, or status.

A very large literature on gender differences in achievement has aimed to distinguish between aspirations, values, and parental status. (Marini, 1978; Hout and Morgan, 1976). Explanations tend to emphasize differences in socialization and aspirations as the key variables. However, there are persistent differences in attainment between men and women that are relatively independent of either background or aspirations. While the Polish business students are a relatively select group, family resources, values, and aspirations predict ownership aspirations. However, family income and sector of employment explain differences in values at least as well for men students as for women students. Moreover, both men and women students grew up and were socialized in a society that did not endorse liberal economic values or business aspirations; hence, there seems no reason *a priori* to expect that the relationship between values and aspirations would differ by sex.

The modelling strategy adopted was based on extending the logistic equation presented in Table 12.3. However, each of the independent variables was redefined as a gender interaction. Predicting the log odds of aspiring to own one's own business was assumed to be a function of social background, private school enrollment, the perceived challenge of proprietorship, the desire to make money, and the measures of *laissez-faire* and collectivist values. To some extent, each of these factors is different for men and for women. Male students are more influenced by having a self-employed parent or by enrolling in the private school, although the direction of effects are similar. Women students are somewhat less likely to perceive owning a business as the greatest challenge, and considerably less likely to admit making money was the primary reason they enrolled. However, these variables influence proprietorship for both sexes, and their effects are largely additive. Measures of values, however, influence aspirations very differently for men and for women. Women are .2 of a standard deviation less *laissez-faire* than men, and there is little relationship between scores on this variable and any measure of aspirations. In fact, women who want to make money score significantly lower on *laissez-faire* values than women who do not. Individualism, in contrast, does not distinguish men from women; however, collectivist values operate to inhibit aspirations only among women. The combination of these two factors, operating in tandem, is sufficient to reduce the effect of gender to insignificance. A fully specified gender model, with all effects defined as interactions, is not

TABLE 12.5 Logistic Regression of Ownership Aspirations on Student Background and Values, Polish Business Students, 1992.

Independent Variables	Coefficient	(S.E.)	p	Exp(B)
Self-employed	.581	(.260)	.025	1.787
Private school	.591	(.316)	.061	1.806
No. Destinations	.390	(.107)	.000	1.477
Challenge-Own	.740	(.222)	.001	2.096
Money	.401	(.223)	.072	1.493
Laissez-faire-Men	.236	(.194)	.225	1.266
Individualism-Women	-.370	(.179)	.039	.691
Sex	.354	(.284)	.212	1.425
Constant	-2.208	(.307)	.000	
-2 Log Likelihood	504.130,	with 414 degrees of freedom.		
Model Chi-Square	58.886			
Goodness of Fit	421.859	(p=.3842)		

significantly better than the model with only values allowed to interact with
gender. This model, given in Table 12.5, implies that background, careers
chosen, challenges perceived, desires to make money, and private school
enrollment significantly influence ownership aspirations for both men and
women. Sex-specific values, including the positive effect of *laissez-faire* on
men and the negative influence of individualism, account for gender
differences. Among these Polish business students, values supporting
collectivism diminish economic aspirations, but do so only for women.
Despite the fact that for both men and women, the correlation between
individualism and *laissez-faire* attitudes is positive, and for both men and
women, background is equally predictive of values, their effects are quite
specific by gender.

Conclusions

Most of this paper has been relatively descriptive, with little attention to
the larger issues of the economic transition in East Central Europe. Perhaps
concluding on a more speculative note is, therefore, justified. One might
well ask whether the institutions studied have much to do with the labor
markets and training institutions in stable post-industrial societies, that are
not "in transition." One question, in particular, recurs: Are business schools
"rational," as a means for creating or joining a market economy? For most
of this paper, the intentions of the schools and students have been taken at
face value. The analysis focussed on the consistency of liberalism, and on
the determinants of career decisions.

From an economic point of view, post-communist business schools seem rather paradoxical. The economic failures of socialism are seen in the lack of market rationality linking supply and demand. Whether one sees planning as too complex or the state as too powerful, the failure of socialism is the same. Markets, in turn, rest on individual effort and competition, without, if possible, state intervention. Entrepreneurship and innovation, two systemic deficiencies of socialism, involve skills and risk-taking that cannot be taught. To create a market economy, one needs private property and a relatively stable polity to protect individual rights; incentives for self-interested, profit-maximization are assumed to be innate. Credentials, in contrast, create possibilities for monopoly, closure, and exclusivity. Establishing schools for training entrepreneurs and business leaders would seem to be icing the cake before it is baked.

At the outset, I argued that "market transition" really means a period of time or a place of social change, involving the supposition that markets should replace state control in every sphere; as such, they provide a perspective on how societies and ideologies are organized and how they change. On the one hand, there is the universal assumption that market processes will rationalize labor markets and make them more competitive and efficient. On the other, when the process is as extreme as in East Central Europe, established institutional processes have all but collapsed and new incentives and mechanisms for job placement have yet to emerge. Education, in particular, has been divested of a major motivational incentive, the power to determine the economic fate of their students. Although individuals are now "free" to save or spend their resources, and to plan their futures without state interference, the information that would make such calculations possible is not yet available. Ironically, however, education, and particularly business education, is expanding throughout the region.

From an institutional point of view, post-communist business and economics education is a growth industry. The new or reformed schools claim to have the expertise needed for a new era; moreover, the demand for their services has never been greater. Their traditional mission, however, their faculty, and virtually all of their assets are inherited from the past. The basis of their power and status has, however, undoubtedly shifted. The schools have lost a privileged relationship to state planning as well as their monopoly of selection and placement. What they retain, and which apparently is their most critical resource, is the claim to possess and transmit specialized expertise in economics. The schools claim to be sure, that they have reformed to meet the new challenge, yet their resource base is the same as before. They reform not by hiring new faculty or discharging the old, building new facilities or developing new curricula; this would be costly. Instead, they "liberate" their resources from the state, "marketize" their products, and transform their administrative structures. The most visible aspects of reform consist of rhetorical debates and untested claims of business perspicacity and competence.

From the point of view of students, the system works in much the same way as before, but with a very different rhetoric. There are, to be sure, new and diverse options and opportunities for training, although these are uniformly quite expensive. It would be understandable if students were rather dubious about the claims or the mission of economics education. Prolonged training requires commitment, and in this case, it is not clear where it will lead. The credibility of economics could be challenged, as well as the authoritative claims of their instructors, especially when the returns to schooling are still unclear. The incentive to invest in human capital presumes that one can calculate an expected return, discounting the lost opportunities of "early" market entry. The primary motivation of the business students, as we have seen, is to make money. Yet instead of actually starting a business or seeking employment in the expanding private sector, they choose to study the subject, spending scarce resources in the hope of acquiring knowledge and credentials that will, at least in the long run, "pay-off."

The rationality of either providing or investing in business education rests on the conviction that with knowledge and expertise, especially if authoritative and accredited, one can understand, manipulate, and control market forces. The idea that education and informed planning can outwit the market was common in virtually all socialist countries, particularly those that ceased to rely on terror or overt coercion. Moreover, education was assumed to be the best strategy for reforming the system, and for creating new values and "new socialist citizens." Post-communist business schools have not changed this conception of their role; the content of the message has changed, but the assumptions about purpose and mission are much the same as before. Why does this idea persist, when so many other aspects of socialist ideology have been forcefully discredited?

The answer, I believe, is central to understanding the market transition. Faith in the magical power of schooling to create new personalities and a new social order is not unique to post-communist countries; education is heralded as the panacea for every kind of reform, especially in times of national crisis. What is unique is the enormous economic uncertainty prevailing in East Central Europe and the claim that specialized business expertise is the most appropriate cure.[14]

For both business students and business schools, conceptions of expertise serve to reduce uncertainty. There is, to be sure, the added incentive of possibly being the vanguard of a new, still dimly envisioned, social order. For the faculty, few alternatives but reform are possible. For the students, however, choosing to attend business school involves a calculated gamble. Education no longer offers a clearly planned career trajectory; the established links between the skills learned and the jobs assigned have been terminated. But there is the possibility, however slight, of vast riches just around the bend. While the schools no longer offer certainty about career prospects and rewards, they can and do furnish examples of successful entrepreneurs, and they circulate advertisements for positions with unbelievably high salaries. However remote these possibilities may be in actuality, and however irrational and chaotic the current marketplace in fact is, business schools reduce the risk of unemployment at least in the short run, and they offer the possibility of immense wealth in the future. Business education is not "rational," if by this we mean the expected returns are greater than the costs that are likely to be incurred, either socially or individually. These societies risk creating far more disillusioned graduates than successful entrepreneurs. At the same time, their primary function may be to reduce the uncertainties inherent in market processes, rather than preparing entrepreneurs.

Notes

Funding for this research was provided by the National Council on Soviet and East European Research. A preliminary report of this research was presented at the Midterm conference of the Sociology of Education section in Amsterdam, July 1992.

1. Between 1990 and 1992, the number of schools of higher economics education increased from five to fourteen, and enrollments from 24 to 40 thousand in Poland. By 1993, 14.6 percent of all post-secondary students in Poland were studying Economics, compared to 10.6 percent in 1990-91. *Szkoły Wyższe w Roku Szkolnym 1992/93*, (Warsaw: *Glowny Urzad Statystyczny*, 1993).

2. In recent decades, the dearth of training may have been a practical response to labor market planning, as much or more than ideological distaste. Socialist countries did provide specialized training in business and economics when needed. Agricultural universities, for example, offered courses in economics and marketing, because farming in Poland remained overwhelmingly private. Departments of foreign trade provided instruction in western banking, trade regulations, and international finance sufficient to handle imports and exports.

3. A fourth site for business training might be the Polytechnic University. In Warsaw, the *Wydzial Mechaniczno-technologiczny* trained mechanical engineers; this school recently announced their intention to admit and train managers for heavy industry.

4. *Prywatna* was the second private school in Poland, the first being the Catholic University in Lublin, which had survived the entire communist era. In 1992-93, the Private Higher School of Banking and Insurance was approved, as well as a second private business school in Warsaw. By 1994, thirty-three private post-secondary programs were in operation.

5. Permission to interview students was granted rather late in the academic year, and it was not possible to sample classrooms or to follow-up absent students. Questionnaires were distributed and collected in large introductory classes at the

Management School and *SGH*. In the case of the private business school, students were approached during required computer workshops. The coding of questionnaires was done by the *Centrum Marketingu i Analiz Spolecznych*, under the direction of Joanna Konieczna. Questionnaires were administered to 122 students at the Warsaw University Management Department, out of a total enrollment of 190 first-year students. At *SGH* two hundred and forty students out of 720 first-year students completed questionnaires, and 61 out of 220 first-year students at *Prywatna*.

6. As a rough comparison, a national sample of university students in 1991 [N=2,428] reported that 41 percent had fathers with some higher education, and 20 percent worked in the private sector (Wnuk-Lipinska, 1992). Warsaw students are not, of course, representative of the country as a whole, and private sector employment has grown dramatically since 1991.

7. The items were selected from the "short" scales developed by researchers at Nuffield College, Oxford, for the British Elections Project. The scales were constructed to measure "fundamental" dimensions of political values, or stable "core beliefs." See A. F. Heath (1991) for a description of the items and an assessment of their reliability and validity in Britain.

8. Several exploratory factor analyses with LISREL-7 were performed on the complete set of items. The first two factors for both the national sample and the business students have similar structures, but they are not identical. Formally, testing the equivalence of factors requires five independent tests: 1) Equality of covariance matrices, 2) The measurement model or factor pattern is common to both groups, 3) Assuming common factors, equivalence of correlations, 4) Assuming equal correlations, common error matrices, and 5) Assuming all of the above, the equivalence of Phi, the variance-covariance matrix for exogenous factors (Bollen, 1989). For the *laissez-faire* scale, the first hypothesis is rejected, the second and third are accepted, while the final two tests must be rejected. Hence, one concludes that although the scales are highly correlated, the two samples have different variance-covariance matrices and different error structures. Since identical scales were needed in order to compare the determinants of values between samples, the items were pooled, and a single factor extracted for each of the three dimensions. For both samples, the pooled factor scores correlated with the principal components very highly, and never less than .935. The means and variances for each scale, however, are specific to the pooled sample, and hence the student scores are greater than 0 and the variance less than 1.

9. The items for the Laissez faire-Socialist scale were 1) "Ordinary working people do not get a fair share;" 2) "There is one law for the rich and one for the poor;" 3) "Management-labor cooperation is impossible;" 4) "Big business benefits owners;" 5) "Government should equalize incomes;" 6) "Management exploits labor;" and 7) "People are poor because of social injustice."

10. The items included in the Libertarian-Authoritarian Scale were 1) "Schools should teach obedience;" 2) "The punishment for breaking the law should be more severe;" 3) "Young people today lack respect;" 4) "For some crimes, the death penalty is appropriate;" 5) "The law must be obeyed;" and 6) "Censorship is necessary to uphold moral standards."

11. The items measuring Collectivism-Individualism were 1) "Welfare benefits are too generous;" 2) "Poverty is usually a person's own fault;" 3) "Many people

who get social benefits do not really deserve them;" 4) "When someone is unemployed, it is usually their own fault;" and 5) "Government gives too many handouts."

12. Other responses to this item were that they had been interested in business for some time (8%), that this particular program had been discussed (8%), or that it had been recommended to them (7%), that their parents (2%) or employer (1%) had suggested it. Twelve percent of the students chose "another reason."

13. As part of this project, a number of western business executives and representatives of international foundations were interviewed. Many expressed concern at the large number of women in economics and management programs; "affirmative action" for men might be necessary, we were told. The pattern was interpreted by our informants as indicative of the low status of business and commerce under communism; enhancing the status of these training programs might require discriminating in favor of men.

14. The faith in education was widespread, but perhaps not as pervasive as the faith in free markets. At least one faculty member commented that educational reform was utopian, and hearkened back to enduring tenets of socialism. His comment was that Poland needed capital, not capitalists.

References

Adamski, Władysław W., Ed. 1993. *Societal Conflict and Systemic Change*, Warsaw: Polish Academy of Science, Institute of Philosophy and Sociology.

Beksiak, Janusz, Ewa Chmielecka, and Urszula Grzelonska. 1991. *Kierunki zmian w wyższym szkolnictwie ekonomicznym*, [Direction of Changes in Higher Economics Schooling], Warsaw: Materiały Fundacji im Stefan Batorego.

Białecki, Ireneusz and Bogdan Mach. 1992. "Social and Economic Orientations of Polish Legislators Against a Background of the Views of Polish Society," *The Polish Sociological Bulletin* 2: 167-186.

Bollen, Kenneth A. 1989. *Structural Equations with Latent Variables*. New York: Wiley.

Brubaker, Rogers. 1984. *The Limits of Rationality: An Essay on the Social and Moral Thought of Max Weber*. London: George Allen and Unwin.

Chmielecka, Ewa. 1993. *"Katalog Szkoły Głównej Handlowej,"* [The SGH Catalogue] *Nauka i Szkolnictwo Wyższe* 1. Warsaw: Centrum Badań Polityki Naukowej i Szkolnictwa Wyzszego.

_____. 1993. "Market Economy and the Reform of Education in the Warsaw School of Economics," Paper presented at the Conference, *Change in the Systems of Higher Education in Central European Countries*, Madralin, Poland, October.

Collins, Randall. 1980. "Weber's Last Theory of Capitalism: A Systematization," *American Journal of Sociology* 45 (December): 925-942.

Converse, Philip E. 1964. "The Nature of Belief Systems in Mass Publics," Pp. 206-261 In *Ideology and Discontent*, edited by David E. Apter. New York: Free Press.

Einhorn, Barbara. 1993. *Cinderella Goes to Market: Citizenship, Gender, and Women's Movements in East Central Europe*. New York and London: Verso Press.

England, Paula. 1989. "A Feminist Critique of Rational-Choice Theories: Implications for Sociology," *American Sociologist* 20: 14-28.

England, Paula. 1993. "The Separative Self: Androcentric Bias in Neoclassical Assumptions," In *Beyond Economic Man: Feminist Theory and Economics*, edited by Marianne A. Ferber and Julie A. Nelson. Chicago, University of Chicago Press.

Editors. 1994. "The Flawed Education of the European Businessman," *The Economist* 331, 7866 (June 4): 61-62.

Grayson, Leslie E. 1993. *Paving the Road to Prosperity: Management Education in the Czech Republic, Slovakia, Hungary, and Poland*, Laxenburg, Austria: International Institute for Applied Systems Analysis, August.

Hauser, Ewa, Barbara Heyns, and Jane Mansbridge. 1993. "Feminism in the Interstices of Politics and Culture: Poland in Transition," In *Gender Politics and Post-Communism*, edited by Nanette Funk and Magda Mueller. New York: Rutledge Press.

Heath, Anthony F. 1991. "The Measurement of Core Beliefs and Values," Working Paper #2, Nuffield College, Oxford (August).

Heyns, Barbara and Aleksandra Jasińska-Kania. 1993. "Values, Politics, and the Ideologies of Reform: Poland in Transition," Pp. 169-194 in *Democratization in Eastern and Western Europe: A Research Annual*, Vol 1, edited by Frederick D. Weil, (Greenwich, Connecticut: JAI Press.

Heyns, Barbara and Jan Szczucki. 1992. "Educating Entrepreneurs: Values, Educational Reform, and the New Polish Business Schools." Paper presented to the International Sociological Association, Research Committee on the Sociology of Education, Midyear Conference, July, Amsterdam, Netherlands.

Hout, Michael and W. R. Morgan. 1976. "Race and Sex Variations in the Causes of the Expected Attainments of High Schools Seniors," *American Journal of Sociology* 81: 364-94.

Inglehart, Ronald. 1988. "The Renaissance of Political Culture: Basic Values, Political Economy and Stable Democracy." *American Political Science Review* (December).

Kantor, Rosabeth. *Men and Women of the Corporation*. New York: Basic Books, 1977.

Kovacs, Janos M., Ed. 1991. *Rediscovery of Liberalism in Eastern Europe*, Special Issue of *East European Politics and Societies* 5, 1.

Marini, Margaret M. 1978. "Sex Differences in the Determinants of Adolescent Aspirations: A Review of Research," *Sex Roles* 4: 723-53.

Müller, Aleksander. 1991. "Changes in the System of Higher Economic Education in Poland: The Case Study of *Szkoła Główna Handlowa*," in *Transformation of Science in Poland*, edited by Antoni Kukliński, (Warsaw: State Committee for Scientific Research, 1991).

Paul, Ellen Frankel, Fred D. Miller, Jr., and Jeffrey Paul, Eds. 1993 *Liberalism and the Economic Order*. New York: Cambridge University Press.

Reszke, Irena. 1989. "Sex Inequalities in the Labour Market in Poland," *Sisyphus* 6: 83-102.

Rokeach, Milton. 1979. *Understanding Human Values*. New York: The Free Press.

Rueschemeyer, Marilyn, Ed. 1994 *Women in the Politics of Postcommunist Eastern Europe*. Armonk, New York: M. E. Sharpe, 1994.

Szacki, Jerzy. 1990. "A Revival of Liberalism in Poland?" *Social Research* 57, 2 (Summer):463-491.

Szelenyi, Ivan in collaboration with Robert Manchin, Pál Juhász, Bálint Magyar, and Bill Martin. 1988. *Socialist Entrepreneurs: Embourgeoisement in Rural Hungary.* Madison, Wisconsin: University of Madison Press.

Weber, Max. [1904-1905] 1930. *The Protestant Ethic and the Spirit of Capitalism* [Translated by Talcott Parsons]. New York: Scribner's.

Weil, Frederick. 1993. "The Development of Democratic Attitudes in Eastern and Western Germany in a Comparative Perspective," Pp. 195-225 in *Democratization in Eastern and Western Europe: A Research Annual*, Vol 1, edited by Frederick D. Weil, Greenwich, Connecticut: JAI Press.

Wnuk-Lipińska, Elzbieta. 1992. "University Student Survey," *Bulletin of the Centre for Science Policy and Higher Education*, University of Warsaw.

PART FOUR

Social System Contexts

There is no sharp distinction between the papers in Part IV and at least two of those in Part III. Both DiPrete and McManus and Heyns situate their analyses and interpretations in the nature of societal systems. However, the papers in Part IV have a somewhat broader concern with the relevance for mobility patterns of the varied and changing nature of the societal systems within which stratification processes occur.

In the first paper in Part IV, Michael Hout points to inter-societal variations in social mobility and suggests ways in which actions by the state can affect the degree and kind of mobility observed. He suggests one particular way in which actions of the state can indirectly alter mobility patterns, namely, through the level of support of post-secondary education. He describes the different responses of three nations (Ireland, Italy and Russia) to the post-World War II increased demand for university education and how the three approaches affected the degree of access different social classes had to higher education. He argues that past actions of the U.S. state and national governments have increased equal access and facilitated intergenerational mobility. But he sees current policy as threatening to reduce access for potential students in the lower classes. National higher education policy is thus seen as a very significant factor in determining the degree of "openness" of a society's mobility pattern.

Seymour Spilerman and Hiroshi Ishida use their study of a large Japanese financial firm to point up several ways in which a society's cultural norms affect the career patterns of the firm's workers. There are sharp contrasts between this Japanese firm and comparable American firms in the role of gender in occupational placement, the firm's recruitment methods, the firm's commitment to workers, the degree of specialization, and the structure of rewards. Given these differences, Spilerman and Ishida's primary concern is to understand promotion patterns within the Japanese firm's managerial work force. They find a very gradual sifting process rather than a tournament or cumulative advantage patterning of careers. Strong Japanese cultural norms of social harmony, respect for elders, and putting collective goals before personal ones help explain both the structural features of the firm, and the career experiences of workers.

Also making comparisons between societies, Arne Kalleberg's paper suggests ways in which current and recent shifts in the world economy can affect the way firms operate in different societies. He argues that firm "flexibility" is increasingly necessary for successful world competition. Using various societal contrasts, he shows how a society's institutional and political-economic characteristics affect the ease with which various kinds of flexibility can be introduced. Assuming a growing need for flexibility, Kalleberg develops two sets of possibilities for the future: an "optimistic scenario" foresees an overall up-grading of the skill level of the labor force, but a "pessimistic scenario" foresees increased polarization of the labor force into a small high skill flexible core and a large residualized periphery. He speculates about the conditions that might lead to one or the other.

The papers in Part IV identify societal and inter-societal characteristics that affect the distribution of the population into stratified levels. Spilerman and Ishida show how a society's cultural norms and definitions provide a matrix of forces that help to define possible and "appropriate" moves in the labor force. Hout demonstrates how national political decisions can enlarge or limit students' access to high level educational credentials. And, finally, Kalleberg discusses ways in which inter-societal economic relationships can feed back on intra-societal institutional arrangements and the labor force experiences of a society's workers. All of these papers show how societies shape the flow of individuals into their stratification systems.

13

The Politics of Mobility

Michael Hout
University of California, Berkeley

Social mobility gauges the openness or closure of a society. An open society will exhibit a high level of social mobility due to a low persistence of privilege from one generation to the next; a closed society will exhibit a low level of social mobility due to persistence of social position across generations. As citizens and social scientists we endorse equality of opportunity, even when we disagree about the appropriate absolute level of inequality, so openness is a widely shared goal. We might even say that although we study mobility for many reasons, none is more important than to study social mobility in order to change it for the better. That said, we might go on to ask how the accumulation of research on social mobility over the past decade guides that interest in making society better.

Research over the past decade has contradicted several widely cited conclusions from earlier research and speculation. Among the key new findings:

>Social mobility varies significantly among societies.

>Social mobility has changed over time in most societies—although change over time is less than differences among societies.

>Variability in social mobility—once thought to be due more to so-called structural mobility—in fact reflects differences in openness.

>Variability in openness—once thought to reflect certain law-like properties of industrialization—in fact reflects political choices.

>Two kinds of political choices can influence the degree of openness in society. Capitalist social welfare policies can promote openness by providing a wide range of social service jobs while mitigating the effects of losing out in the jobs competition by redistributing incomes. Free market employment and investment policies typically increase income inequality but they

can nonetheless foster openness if the state pursues aggressive investment in higher education (which in turn directly fosters openness).

I point only to the lessons of the past decade's research for political sociology in this chapter, so my reading of the research literature is restricted. Breiger (1995) provides a more comprehensive review.

Structural mobility is the outcome of factors that affect all origin classes proportionally. For the most part, structural mobility occurs because some classes grow while others shrink over time, e.g., the historically significant decline of agriculture and the growth of professional managerial employment has increased the opportunity for upper white collar employment for all workers regardless of their origin class.

Definitions

Social mobility occurs between social classes. Much of the research over the last decade has addressed the issue of defining classes (Wright 1985; Erikson and Goldthorpe 1992a). However, if we step back from this (admittedly important) detail we can draw conclusions that apply to the work of political sociologists so long as any reasonable class scheme is employed. By "reasonable" I mean that the scheme contains sufficient information about the hierarchy of positions in society to be useful while at the same time making concessions to the amount and kind of data available and other exigencies of research practice. Of course, it is possible to have serious disagreements on these matters (e.g., Wright 1987; Hout and Hauser 1992; Erikson and Goldthorpe 1992b). I will do my best to focus instead on the points that the major neo-Marxist and neo-Weberian approaches have in common.[1]

Mobility studies commonly feature the concepts of structural and exchange mobility. Structural mobility arises because the marginal distributions of origins and destinations typically differ, making it impossible for all persons to have a destination in the class of their origin.[2] Typically, structural mobility refers to all those factors that are independent of origins but that also account for all differences between the distributions of origins and destinations (Featherman and Hauser 1978; Sobel, Hout, and Duncan 1985). By convention, exchange mobility is that part of the mobility process that produces equal flows between origin-destination pairs (Sobel et al. 1985). Structural mobility plus exchange mobility does not necessarily equal total mobility. Some asymmetry in the association between origins and destinations can produce additional mobility.[3] The Sobel et al. framework for studying structural and exchange mobility departs from prior approaches in three beneficial ways: (1) it avoids the tendency to view either structural or exchange mobility as the residual left over when the other is accounted for, (2) it provides a one-to-one correspondence between concepts and measures, and (3) it reorients thinking about structural mobility by replacing a society-wide concept with one that applies to each occupational category. Recent work has tended to drop the strict SHD formulation of the problem and to adopt the definition of structural mobility that stresses that it is the sum of only the factors responsible for dissimilarity between the marginal distributions of origins and destinations that are independent of origins.

Exchange mobility is the symmetrical part of the association between origins and destinations (Sobel et al. 1985; Hauser and Grusky 1988; Hout and Hauser 1992). The *ij* terms capture all of that association, but do so relatively inefficiently. A wealth of models offer many more efficient ways of expressing the association between origins and destinations (e.g., Goodman 1972, 1979, 1984, 1991; Hauser 1979; Clogg 1982; Logan 1983; Hout 1983, 1984; Hout and Hauser 1992; Yamaguchi 1987; Xie 1992; Breen 1993). The goal in modeling is to: (1) make statistical results more useful for theory and practice by giving mathematical expression to a theory about mobility, (2) improving statistical efficiency and parsimony, and (3) facilitating comparisons by reducing the number of coefficients that must be compared.

Since the 1960s, immobility has received special attention (Goodman 1965). Nearly all data evince immobility in excess of that expected on the basis of association in the off-diagonal cells. Yamaguchi (1983) refers to this distinction between immobility and off-diagonal association as the "specific" and "general" effects of origin on destination. In this paper I modify his terminology slightly and refer to "diagonal" and "general" effects.

Variation in Structural Mobility

A commonplace of the 1970s was that structural mobility accounts for most of the mobility differences among countries and over time (e.g., Hauser, Dickinson, Travis, and Koffel 1975a, 1975b; Featherman, Jones, and Hauser 1975). Recent research calls that conclusion into doubt (Wong 1990, 1992; Hout and Hauser 1992). Cross-national studies that rely on parameter estimates—usually drawing on the SHD formulation—instead of decompositions of chi-square show that class differences in the force of structural mobility are very large but national differences are small. Figure 13.1 (from Hout and Hauser 1992) illustrates the point. For the seven Western European and two Eastern European nations that comprise the core of the CASMIN project, there is surprisingly little cross-national variation in structural mobility. Figure 13.1 shows the results for the nine European nations in the CASMIN project (Hout and Hauser 1992). In every nation, the professional classes (and to a lesser extent routine white collar workers, technicians, and foremen) grew at the expense of the agricultural classes.[4]

FIGURE 13.1 Structural Mobility Coefficients for Nine European Nations (CASMIN project) by Class, c. 1972

source: Hout and Hauser 1992.

FIGURE 13.2 Structural Mobility Coefficients for Six Countries by Occupational Category, c. 1972

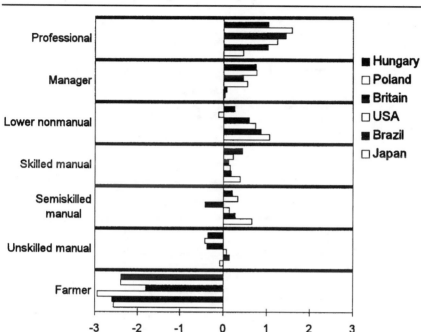

source: Wong 1992.

Scotland and Britain have less structural mobility than the rest of the countries and Hungary has more, but the overall impression is of more variation from class-to-class than from nation-to-nation. Adding the United States, Japan, and Brazil to the analysis (Figure 13.2) introduces more nation-to-nation variation (Wong 1992). The US profile resembles that of the CASMIN countries, but the level (Wong uses the 1973 US data) is slightly higher than that in Western Europe.[5] Japan has a substantially different structural mobility profile than the other nations have (also Ishida 1993). The professionals grew little; the managers grew almost not at all. On the other hand, routine white collar and skilled blue collar jobs grew more relative to their growth (or stagnation) elsewhere. Brazil conforms to the CASMIN profile surprisingly well. Brazil lags behind the CASMIN countries in the creation of management positions, and it is still in the phase of blue collar growth appropriate to its level of economic development.

Women's structural mobility substantially exceeds men's in most countries that have been studied (Roos 1986; Hout 1988; Jonsson and Mills 1993; Wong and Hauser 1992). Figure 13.3 (from Hout 1988) shows the results

FIGURE 13.3   Structural Mobility Coefficients for Men and Women in the
United States by Occupational Category and Year, 1972-75 and 1982-85

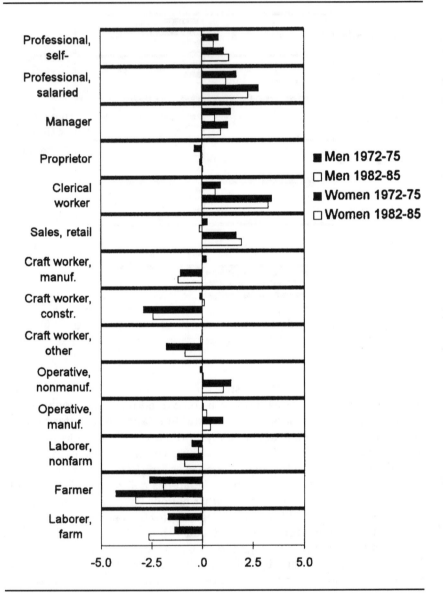

source: Hout 1988.

from the United States at two time points by way of example. Because women are underrepresented in farming and crafts, there is substantial structural mobility out of these classes for women. The huge structural mobility of women into routine white collar jobs offsets the manual and farming deficit. Structural mobility has declined in the U.S..

This evidence makes clear that gender and class differences in structural mobility far outweigh the cross-national and temporal differences. Although the differences among countries and within the USA over time are statistically significant, only Japan has a distinct pattern among the ten countries I consider here - a group of countries that includes two socialist countries and one developing nation.

Cross-National and Temporal Differences in Association

The Lipset-Zetterberg hypothesis of no cross-national variation in mobility (Lipset and Bendix 1959) was supplanted in the 1970s by the FJH hypothesis of no cross-national variation in the association between origins and destinations (Featherman, Jones, and Hauser 1975; Grusky and Hauser 1984; Hauser and Grusky 1988). Early returns comparing Britain with France (Erikson, Goldthorpe, and Portacarero 1979) and the United States (Kerckhoff, Campbell, and Laird 1985; Erikson and Goldthorpe 1985) supported FJH. Sweden and other social democratic countries stood out, though, as having a more open mobility pattern than other regions (Erikson et al. 1979; Grusky and Hauser 1984; Pontinen 1984; Erikson and Goldthorpe 1987). The Netherlands resembles Sweden in openness (Ganzeboom 1984; Ganzeboom et al. 1989). The CASMIN project (Erikson and Goldthorpe 1992b) has made cross-national differences in association abundantly clear. Germany, Ireland, Hungary, and Poland each has a distinct national variant on the "core" pattern (see Sorensen 1992). Japan and Brazil differ from the other cases as well (Wong 1990, 1992). Furthermore, changes over time in the United States (Hout 1988), Hungary (Wong and Hauser 1992), and the Netherlands (Ganzeboom and de Graaf 1984; Ganzeboom et al. 1989) refute the FJH hypothesis as it pertains to change within countries.

Thus, not only are mobility differences due to structural mobility smaller than expected, but mobility differences due to association are also larger than expected.

Both diagonal and general effects differ among nations and over time. Figure 13.4 shows the results for cross-national variation in general association from the Western European nations in the CASMIN project (from Hout and Hauser 1992). Germany, France, and Scotland have the strongest general association; Sweden and Northern Ireland have the weakest. Only Northern Ireland is a surprise in this group. That is where cross-national differences in diagonal association become important. Diagonal association

FIGURE 13.4 Logits for Lower Professional versus Unskilled Manual Destination by Origin SES, as expected under a Linear (shown by lines) and Composite (shown by dots) Model of Origin Effects, Country Differences in Intercepts Removed, Seven Western European Nations (CASMIN project), c. 1972

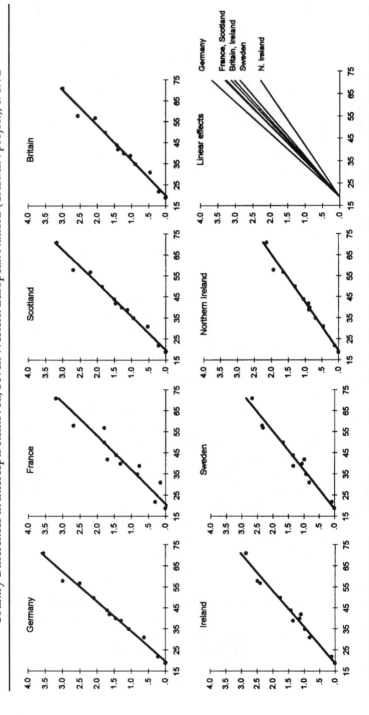

source: Hout and Hauser, 1992

FIGURE 13.5 Measures of General Association and Diagonal Association
for Seven Western European Countries (CASMIN project)
normed to Zero Mean and Unit Variance

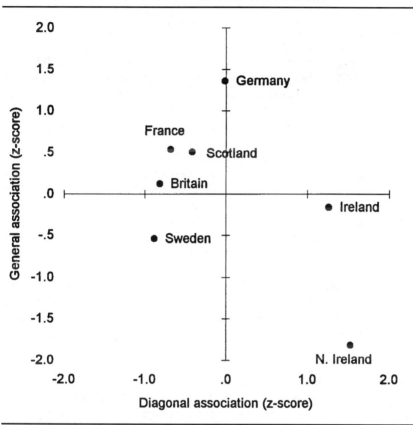

source: Hout and Hauser, 1992.

in Northern Ireland is significantly stronger than in any other nation in the
CASMIN set, although the Republic of Ireland is close. Figure 13.5 shows
cross-national differences in general and diagonal association in two dimensions. The two Irish nations stand out for having a combination of low
general and high diagonal association. Sweden is the only nation in the
CASMIN set with low general and low diagonal association. Notably, none
of the CASMIN nations has high general and high diagonal association.
Results for other data sets indicate that Japan conforms to the low general-high
diagonal pattern (Goodman and Hout 1993).

Over time, general association has changed more than diagonal association in the United States (Hout 1988) and the Netherlands (Ganzeboom and

de Graaf 1984). In both countries the general association has declined by more than 30 percent since the mid-1960s while diagonal association has changed little if any.

Explanations for Cross-National and Temporal Differences

The leading alternative to the Lipset-Zetterberg hypothesis of no cross-national differences in mobility was the thesis of industrialization (Treiman 1970). The main proposition of the thesis of industrialization concerns the rationalizing effects of bureaucratic management. As firms compete for talent in a legal environment defined by the rights of citizen job-seekers, they will be forced to assess workers on observable criteria: "This does not mean that family background no longer influences careers. What it does mean is that superior status cannot any more be directly inherited but must be legitimized by actual achievements that are socially acknowledged" (Blau and Duncan 1967, p. 430). Blau and Duncan call this process "expanding universalism." The thesis of industrialism posits that expanding universalism will immutably erode the class barriers represented by the association between origins and destinations.[6] From this point of view, social progress can be measured in the rate of decrease in the association between origins and destinations (Kerr 1959).

This emphasis on law-like, exogenous change, has given way in the 1990s to a focus on political determinants of mobility in general (Nee 1991, for state socialist societies; Esping-Anderson 1992, for market economies) and the association between origins and destinations in particular (Grusky and Hauser 1984; Erikson and Goldthorpe 1987, 1992a; Ganzeboom et al. 1989). The diffuse pressures brought on by rationalizing forces were insufficient, in and of themselves, to foster equality of opportunity. On the other hand, intercepting market forces through the power of the welfare state or state socialism can be very effective in leveling social distinctions, including distinctions based on origins. The politics of redistribution in Sweden and Hungary have made very clear how the state has the potential to affect equality of opportunity by affecting social mobility. The differences among Hungary, Poland, and Czechoslovakia caution against making too much of a reified "state socialist" regimen (Erikson and Goldthorpe 1992a, p. 373). Anchoring the other end of the political spectrum, Ireland and France (and, in its way, Japan) defend small, family-based enterprise in ways that reinforce diagonal association. The German emphasis on industrial employment and a stratification by skill in the working class reinforce the level of association there (Erikson and Goldthorpe 1987; Esping-Anderson 1992).

The American combination of rapidly changing oppportunity in a context of little or no state activity is difficult to reconcile with the emerging political theory. The federal state does virtually no redistribution from class-to-class, yet the general effects decline (Hout 1988). The federal initiative to advance the civil rights of African Americans actually increased class differentiation within the black population (Wilson 1978; Hout 1984b; 1986). Of course the federal government is not the only source of public services, and, as I argue in the next section, the educational policies of individual states, especially their support for their state universities, fostered mobility.

Public Higher Education

Public policy can affect the association between origins and destinations either directly or indirectly. The most pervasive reform of the twentieth century has been the worldwide expansion of secondary and higher education (Meyer et al. 1982). Among its many consequences is the effect it has had on mobility and life chances. As government action, it is the exemplar of the indirect policy instrument.

Everywhere women have been educated in large numbers, closing the gap between the amount of education sons and daughters receive at the very time when sons' education was rising rapidly (Blossfeld and Shavit 1993). Even when the reforms have little or no effect on the specific transitions from school-to-school that make up the educational system, the association tends to decline because origins are more important for the early transitions than for the later ones (Mare 1980; Smith and Cheung 1986; Raftery and Hout 1985; Shavit and Blossfeld 1993). In many countries the improved access to education leads to improved employment prospects as well, reducing the association between socioeconomic origins and destinations in many countries (Ganzeboom et al. 1989).

The United States shows the potential for a successful approach that operates indirectly through education (and without much coordination among disparate policy-making jurisdictions). In part the American case is instructive precisely because educational expansion is the only attempt to use public action as a means of fostering equality of opportunity. If several policies were in place, it would not be so clear that educational expansion was the effective policy. It is also clear that expansion was the operative factor; little effort was expended to affect the other parameters of educational stratification. Contemporary debates stress cost as a factor because the costs of higher education are rising so rapidly and so visibly. They miss the importance of access. When the cost of staying in school is the main impediment to educational advancement, reducing costs through public subsidy is a highly effective policy device for increasing equality of educational opportunity and equality of educational outcome. However, experience has shown that cost is not always the main impediment to educational advancement.

Britain's famous reform of 1944 greatly reduced the cost of education to students and their families without reducing the differences among classes in their rates of educational advancement. In post-war Britain, the pre-reform system of private academic education could not meet the needs of the growing middle class who wanted academic educations for their children but could not afford them. Once the cost was reduced, the middle classes immediately took advantage them. The working classes did not respond as quickly. The net result was that each class's participation in academic education after 1944 was in proportion to its participation prior to the reforms (Halsey, Heath, and Ridge 1980; Jonsson and Mills 1993; Kerckhoff and Trott 1993). Among the factors blunting working class participation are the "cultural" bases of selection embedded in the testing instruments (Bourdieu 1977; Ogbu 1987; Clancy 1986; Lynch 1990) and the signals (subtle and otherwise) from teachers that poor and working class students are not fit for academic work (Willis 1979; MacLeod 1987). Potentially more relevant than these indirect factors for understanding why reducing cost had so little effect on class differentials (but unresearched as far as we know) is the perceived rate of return to academic education (Becker 1975). Children of the "affluent workers" of the late 1950s and 1960s (Goldthorpe et al. 1969) may have inferred a low rate of return to academic education from their fathers' combination of low education and comfortable income - a perception likely to lead to "underinvestment" in academic education (Becker 1975).

Costs are more directly linked to income per se than to social class.[7] The work linking costs to class barriers implicitly assumes that social classes defined by occupation have different levels of income. If every class has the same economic standing (income and wealth) on average, then changing the cost of education may affect some individuals at the low end of their class's distribution of economic standing, but will not be likely to affect class differences in educational participation rates. Few societies are at risk of income inequalities disappearing. However, this factor complicates analyses of trends in educational opportunity in societies where the income distribution has changed. Most notably, the decrease in income inequality in Sweden in the twentieth century introduced ambiguities into the interpretation of the changes observed by Jonsson (1993; also Jonsson and Mills (1993).

Educational policy makers control the size of the public educational system as well as the cost of attending. Within broad bounds they can directly affect educational outcomes as effectively by manipulating the number of students admitted as by changing the tuition. The expansion of publicly funded academic education, especially secondary education, contributed at least as much as lower tuition to equality of educational opportunity in the twentieth century in many countries (Mare 1980; Smith and Cheung 1986; Hout 1989; Shavit and Blossfeld 1993; Raftery and Hout 1993).

FIGURE 13.6   Enrollments in Higher Education as a Percentage
of 18-22 Year Olds by Type of Institution, United States, 1948-1992

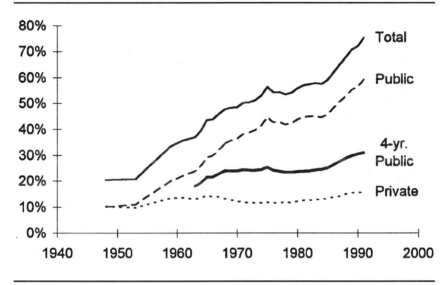

Expansion creates opportunity by eliminating most forms of selection, including class-based selection, at the lower levels of the educational system. Equality of educational *outcomes* does not necessarily follow, as the expansion spreads not only through secondary schools but also through universities and graduate schools. Expansion works to reduce the association between class and educational outcomes because, in most societies, the degree of class-based selection is greater at the lower than at the higher rungs of the educational ladder (see Shavit and Blossfeld 1993 for a review of the evidence). With the rungs that figure most in class-based selection no longer a point of departure from the system, the overall association between class and outcome is typically reduced.[8]

The sheer size of the expansion of American public higher education is important to bear in mind first because greater size means higher cost and second because the expansion was undertaken under extremely high demographic pressure. The federal government provides funds to US schools, but it administers only the military academies. State and local governments administer the public schools; there are also many private schools and universities (Coleman et al. 1982; Hout et al. 1993). Between 1945 and 1992, post-secondary enrollments as a proportion of American youth 18-22 years old rose from 20 percent to 77 percent even as the size of cohorts increased (see Figure 13.6).[9] Nearly all of that growth was in the

FIGURE 13.7 Three Measures of the Share of Public Higher Education as a
Portion of all Higher Education – the ratio of enrollments in 4-year public
colleges and universities to total enrollments, the ratio of enrollments in
4-year public colleges and universities to enrollments in all public institutions,
and enrollments in private colleges and universities to enrollments in
4-year public colleges and universities, United States, 1963-1992

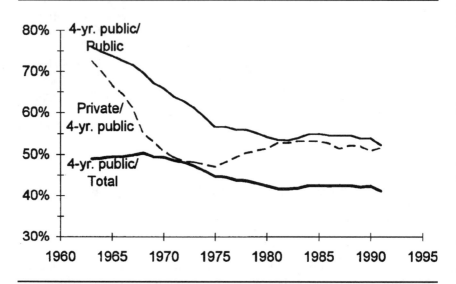

public sector; private college and university enrollments have grown only
slightly faster than the eligible population (from 12 percent in 1965 of the
cohort to 15 percent in 1992). Meanwhile enrollments in public four-year
colleges and universities as a fraction of the college-age population doubled
(from 17 percent to 34 percent) between 1962 and 1992. Enrollment in
community colleges and other two-year programs accounts for a huge share
of the overall growth as total public enrollment raced ahead of enrollment
in public colleges and universities with four-year degree programs. In 1963,
three-fourths of students in public post-secondary institutions were in
four-year colleges and universities; by 1975, four-year institutions' share
had fallen to just over half of the public enrollment (Figure 13.7).

The period of expansion for public colleges and universities was 1952 to
1969. In addition to accommodating a rising fraction of each cohort, public
colleges and universities' share of total enrollment grew until the 1960s
when half of all students in higher education attended public colleges and
universities. During the first half of the 1970s, public colleges and universities continued to grow, but they could barely keep up with cohort growth
as baby-boomers put pressure on their facilities. Then in the mid-1970s they

began to lag behind both community colleges and private universities. Enrollment ratios have gone up again since 1984 through a combination of slightly higher admissions, more fifth-year seniors, and smaller cohorts.

Private colleges and universities have begun to catch up with the public ones. Their enrollment ratios have grown faster since the early 1980s than at any point between 1960 and 1980. Prior to 1955, private colleges and universities enrolled more students than the public sector did. By 1975, the ratio of private-to-public (four-year) enrollments had fallen below 50 percent (dashed line in Figure 13.7); it rebounded to 55 percent by the early 1980s and remains there. All of which means that, despite growth, public colleges and universities play a smaller role in US higher education in the 1990s than they did in the 1960s and 1970s. They may also be "socially smaller" in the sense that rapidly rising in-state tuition for state universities in New York, Massachusetts, Michigan, and California remove some of the distinction between public and private universities.

Impending demographic changes will absorb any growth that may be attempted in the next five years and for the first ten years of the next century. The number of 18 to 23 year olds will increase from 15 million in 1991 to 21 million in 2001 - a 40 percent increase in a decade (U.S. Bureau of the Census 1994). That kind of growth led to a flowering of the public colleges and universities between 1966 and 1975. But in most states, especially the largest ones, there is neither the financial nor political support for a second wave of growth. For example, cuts in state support have led California to cut faculty instead of increasing it while postponing plans for a new UC campus that was slated to absorb the increase. Educational needs will have to compete with mandated prison expenditures in the next decade - compounding the pressures on colleges and universities in California. If the public institutions cannot grow, then the enrollment rates will have to fall. How American higher education responds will affect the future of opportunity just as its expansion prior to 1975 did.

The consequences of not meeting the needs of bigger cohorts will reach beyond the public colleges and universities themselves. Openness in education is important for the politics of mobility because higher education— and by inference *public* higher education—promoted equality of occupational opportunity in the United States between 1962 and 1985. Contraction may portend the end of that era. In documenting the 1962-85 improvements, I showed that expanding higher education—not "expanding universalism" —was critical (Hout 1988). I speculated that the growth of public colleges and universities was an especially important component of educational expansion, at least as it related to the association between social origins and destinations. If I was right, then inequality of occupational opportunity ought to remain at the level it reached by the mid-1980s and may even increase in the next decade.

Several European countries have experienced enrollment bottlenecks similar to the one about to jam American universities. Ireland, Italy, and Russia all experienced very rapid growth in their populations eligible to enroll in public universities due to a combination of population growth and an expansion of academic secondary education. In Ireland the costs of higher education are borne by the state. With no tuition money, expansion must be met out of general revenues (Clancy 1982). The Irish Ministry of Education could not build new facilities or hire new faculty fast enough to accommodate a rising pool of eligibles that came of age between 1970 and 1984. Irish policy makers responded by allowing enrollments to increase only very slowly—significantly slower than the size of the eligible pool was growing. Consequently, enrollment rates as a proportion of academic secondary school leavers fell from 1970 to 1984 (Clancy 1986; Raftery and Hout 1985, 1993). The available positions were allocated on the basis of test scores, and the historical pattern of no association between class origins and entry to university was maintained (Raftery and Hout 1993; Breen and Whelan 1992).

In Italy the enrollment crisis was met by a laissez-faire approach. Admission to university in Italy is by formula. The formula was not changed as the pool of eligibles grew, so a constant fraction of that rising pool was admitted to university (Barbagli 1982). The money to construct new facilities or to hire sufficient faculty was not allocated. Consequently, students admitted to university found that they could not be admitted to courses they needed. Dropout rates—called "abandonment" in Italy—increased sharply. The time to degree increased among those who did not drop out (Schizzerotto 1988), and an association between class origins and the probability of graduating from university emerged (Cobalti and Schizzerotto 1993; Shavit and Blossfeld 1993).

In Russia, too, a combination of larger cohorts and a higher rate of qualifying for university admission by graduating from an academic secondary school put pressure on the universities to admit more students. The student fees were trivial, so the universities had to win appropriations for their growth from the central government. However, the government's priority was universal academic secondary education (after 1966; see Connor 1991; Gerber and Hout 1995), leaving little money for new higher educational facilities. Unlike Ireland, Russia had a history of sharp class differences in university attendance. When the bottleneck developed at the point of entry to university, enrollment rates fell for all classes, but faster for classes that traditionally had low enrollment rates than for the sons and daughters of the "intellegencia" (Gerber and Hout 1995). The net result was a significant increase in the class differentials in access to the universities among cohorts born after 1960.

Thus, we have three countries responding differently to enrollment bottlenecks similar to the one American universities (especially public ones) are about to face. They each responded differently. Ireland restricted admissions but kept class differences from appearing. Italy deflected the crisis from the university to the individual lecture and kept class differences from appearing at the point of entry while imposing stratification on graduation prospects. Russia rationed admissions but because there were significant class differences to begin with, rationing increased inequality of opportunity. Because tuitions and other costs are rising at public and private universities in the United States, it seems unlikely that the Irish model will emerge in the USA. The choice between the Italian and Russian models is neither pleasant nor unfamiliar. At many of the campuses of the California State University system, frustration due to overcrowding and increased time from matriculation to degree has been building. Rationing admission and financing growth by raising tuition has led to sharp increases in the family incomes of freshmen at UC-Berkeley, UCLA, and the University of Michigan (Fishlow 1993).

Direct Policy Approaches

Sweden has pursued the direct approach to fostering equality (Erikson 1983). The Swedish program of full employment (much of it in the public sector), high quality jobs, and progressive income redistribution has fostered equality of both educational and occupational opportunity (Erikson and Goldthorpe 1992; Jonsson and Mills 1993; Jonsson 1993). Full employment in the Swedish case means not only low unemployment but also high overall employment—almost 80 percent of Swedish adults participate in the labor force (Esping-Anderson 1992). The state provides some "public works" employment, but most state jobs are in health, education, and welfare services. As such, they offer high wages, steady employment, and career opportunities to state employees (Esping-Anderson 1992). Because the state recruits persons from disadvantaged backgrounds to fill these positions, the net result is a lower association between origins and destinations than might otherwise be the case, and certainly lower than other countries have achieved (Wong 1993).

The Netherlands undertook massive educational reform in the 1960s. It reduced the association between social origins and educational attainment both by increasing the access to academic education for all Dutch youth and by lowering the effect of social class on the probability of entering academic secondary school (DeGraaf and Ganzeboom 1993). In the process, it may well have equalized the pattern of occupational mobility as educational expansion did in the United States. However, the key change in the Netherlands was the establishment of a welfare state that rivals the Swedish one in comprehensiveness. The combination dramatically reduced the association between occupational origins and destinations in the Netherlands between the mid-1960s and the mid-1980s.

State socialism was expected to foster the same kinds of equalization of opportunity as the Swedes and Dutch have achieved. European state socialist states have not done so. Quotas for secondary and university admissions in Hungary increased working class enrollments, but did little to redress the differences in chances between privileged and underprivileged students (Szelenyi and Aschaffenberg 1993). The evidence even suggests an upturn in inequality in the most recent cohorts. In Poland, the places opened by educational expansion were filled by young women, not the sons (or daughters) of the working class (Heyns and Bialecki 1993). In Czechoslovakia, class was a weaker factor in school progress than elsewhere (except the Netherlands and Sweden) both before and during the state socialist era. As we have seen, the enrollment crisis in Russia—brought on by egalitarian secondary school expansion—led to *rising* class barriers to university enrollment (Gerber and Hout 1994).

Conclusion

The main point of this review has been to show the accumulation of knowledge about social stratification that has accrued from mobility research since the early 1970s. Very little of that research has had a policy focus, yet the implications of our work for social policy are very important. The clearest point is the last: supporting higher education promotes openness in society. The indirect effect of expanding public support for higher education on equality of opportunity in the United States has been a great success story. The effect of class origins on class destinations has fallen by between 30 and 50 percent since the early 1960s. Much of that change is attributable to the expansion of public support for higher education. That support has not continued to grow. In important states like New York, Michigan, Texas, and, most recently, California, it has begun to shrink in real terms. Building is deferred. Fees are hiked far faster than the modest rate of inflation.

The jokes during the 1992 U.S. Presidential campaign about the choice between making potato chips and computer chips is a real one. To say that societies *choose* the distribution of jobs overstates Esping-Anderson's (1992) argument somewhat, but the public choice of educational, employment, and welfare policies directly affects the mix of "good" and "bad" jobs in the economy. Investment in human capital through public investment in secondary and higher education is paramount.

Notes

The UC-Berkeley Survey Research Center and Committeee on Research provided funding. Thanks to Richard Arum and Gustavo Resendiz for research assistance and to the conference participants for helpful comments.

1. The one controversial criterion that I will impose on materials I review here is that they contain sufficient evidence of hierarchy in the data. By this I mean that to be considered by me, a class scheme must admit to substantial variation in income, prestige, and credentials (see Hout and Hauser 1992 for more discussion).

2. Origin need only be a class that is occupied at some time in the past; destination refers to current class. In this paper, I restrict my attention to intergenerational mobility so origins refer to the class in which a person grew up. Significant research on intragenerational mobility will feature in other presentations.

3. The product of structural mobility and exchange mobility (along with parameters that set the size of the sample and the relative sizes of the origin classes) imply the model of quasi-symmetry according to the formula: $F_{ij} = \alpha_j \beta_i \beta_j \delta_{ij}$ where F_{ij} is the number of persons expected in cell (i, j), α_j is the structural mobility multiplier for class j, $\beta_i \beta_j$ sets the sample size and the relative sizes of the origin classes, $\delta_{ij} = \delta_{ji}$ are the exchange mobility parameters for combinations (i, j). See Sobel et al. (1985) for statistical details such as identification restrictions and estimation techniques. This parameterization is referred to as the SHD formulation or the SHD model.

4. Since the Polish and Hungarian studies did not inquire whether self-employed persons had employees the values for the two employer categories are missing not zero in these two nations.

5. The US level reduced in the late 1970s and early 1980s (Hout 1988), so using data from 1982-85 would conform to the CASMIN pattern quite closely.

6. The original Blau-Duncan formulation simply posited that more of the association would become indirect via education (Blau and Duncan 1967, p. 430).

7. An individual's or family's social class derives from the source(s) of his/her/its income not from the amount of income itself (Jencks 1991; Erikson and Goldthorpe 1992; Hout, Brooks, and Manza 1993).

8. Explanations for why class affects early selection more than later selection differ. Mare (1993) reviews the literature on this subject and presents a model for testing some of the competing theories using data on siblings (assuming that siblings share the same class background). His results indicate that most if not all of the familiar pattern of class effects being stronger at lower levels of education than at higher levels is due to the noncausal correlation between class and factors actually being selected and not to a causal connection between class and survival.

9. These figures are not strict cohort measures because the requisite data are not recorded. We have simply divided enrollments by the size of the population in an appropriate age group. The numerator includes all students, regardless of age. The denominator is the typical age range of post-secondary enrollment. Even this ratio could not be calculated without some manipulation of the data at hand. Counts of persons by single year of age are not available for most years, so we took the number of 20-24 year olds two years later as our estimate of the number of 18-22 year olds in a given year. Because the numerator covers just one year while the denominator covers five, the percents in figure 13.6 are 500 times the ratio of enrollments to

persons 18-22 years old.

10. Changes in the association between origins and destinations will lag 10 to 15 years behind changes in higher educational policies because (a) the students have to finish their degrees and establish themselves in careers while (b) the older, less educated cohorts pass out of the labor force.

11. In California fees at the UC and CSU campuses have gone up 144 percent in three years while the consumer price index has gone up 6.5 percent.

References

Barbagli, Marzio. 1982. *Educating for Unemployment*. New York: Columbia University Press.

Becker, Gary. 1975. *Human Capital*. Chicago: University of Chicago Press.

Blau, Peter M. and Otis Dudley Duncan. 1967. *The American Occupational Structure.*. New York: Wiley.

Bourdieu, Pierre. 1977. *Reproduction in Education, Society and Culture*. Beverly Hills: Sage.

Breen, Richard and Christopher T. Whelan. 1992. "Explaining the Irish Pattern of Social Fluidity: The Role of the Political," Pp. 129-151 in *The Development of Industrial Society in Ireland*, edited by J.H.Goldthorpe and C.T. Whelan. Oxford: Oxford University Press.

_____. 1993. "From Ascription to Achievement? Origins, Education and Entry to the Labour Force in the Republic of Ireland During the Twentieth Century." *Acta Sociologica* 36:3-17.

Breiger, Ronald. (forthcoming). "Socioeconomic Achievement and Social Structure." *Annual Review of Sociology* 21

Clancy, Patrick. 1982. *Participation in Higher Education*. Dublin: Higher Education Authority.

Clancy, Patrick. 1986. "Socialisation, Selection, and Reproduction in Education." Pp. 116-136 in *Ireland: A Sociological Profile*, edited by Patrick Clancy, Sheelagh Drudy, Kathleen Lynch, and Liam O'Dowd. Dublin: Institute of Public Administration.

Clogg, Clifford C. 1982. "The Analysis of Association: Models for Social Data." *Journal of the American Statistical Association* 71: 803-815.

Cobalti, Antonio and Antonio Schizzerotto. 1993. "Inequality of Educational Opportunity in Italy." Pp. 155-176 in *Persistent Inequality: Changes in Educational Opportunities in Thirteen Countries*, edited by Yossi Shavit and Hans-Peter Blossfeld. Boulder, Co.: Westview Press.

Coleman, James S., Thomas Hoffer and Sally Kilgore. 1982. *High School Achievement: Public, Catholic and Private Schools Compared*. New York: Basic Books.

Connor, Walter D. 1991. *The Accidental Proletariat: Workers, Politics, and Crisis in Gorbachev's Russia*. Princeton: Princeton University Press.

De Graaf, Paul M., and Harry B. G. Ganzeboom. 1993. "Family Background and Educational Attainment in the Netherlands for the 1891-1960 Birth Cohorts." Pp. 76-100 in *Persistent Inequality: Changing Educational Attainment in Thirteen Countries*, edited by Yossi Shavit and Hans-Peter Blossfeld. Boulder, CO: Westview Press.

Erikson, Robert, John H. Goldthorpe, and Lucianne Portocarero. 1979. "Intergenerational Class Mobility in Three Western European Societies: England, France, and Sweden." *British Journal of Sociology* 30:415-430.

Erikson, Robert. 1983. "Changes in Social Mobility in Industrial Nations: The Case of Sweden." *Research in Social Stratification and Mobility* 2: 165-195.

Erikson, Robert, and John H. Goldthorpe. 1985. "Are American Rates of Social Mobility Exceptionally High?" *European Sociological Review* 1:1-22.

_____. 1987. "Commonality and Variation in Social Fluidity in Industrial Nations I." *European Sociological Review* 3:54-77.

_____. 1992a. *The Constant Flux: Comparative Analysis of Social Mobility in Industrial Nations*. Oxford: Oxford University Press.

_____. 1992b. "The CASMIN Project and the American Dream." *European Sociological Review* 8:283-306. 1992.

Esping-Anderson, Gosta. 1992. "Changing Classes: Mobility Regimes in Post-Industrial Economies." European University Institute. Unpublished manuscript.

Featherman, David, F. Lancaster Jones, and Robert M. Hauser. 1975. "Assumptions of Mobility Research in the United States: The Case of Occupational Status." *Social Science Research* 4:329-360.

Featherman, David and Robert M. Hauser. 1978. *Opportunity and Change*. New York: Academic Press.

Fishlow, Harriet. 1993. *Statistical Profile of Berkeley Freshmen*. Oakland, CA: Office of the UC President.

Ganzeboom, Harry B. G., and P.M. De Graaf. 1984. "Intergenerational Mobility in the Netherlands in 1954 and 1977," in *Social Stratification and Mobility in the Netherlands.*, edited by B. Bakker, J. Dronkers and H.B.G. Ganzeboom. Amsterdam: SISWO.

Ganzeboom, Harry B. G., Donald J. Treiman, and Ruud Luijkx. 1989. "Intergenerational Class Mobility in Comparative Perspective." *Research in Social Stratification and Mobility* 8: 3-84.

Gerber, Theodore P., and Michael Hout. 1995. "Educational Stratification in Russia During the Soviet Period." *American Journal of Sociology* 101: forthcoming.

Goldthorpe, John H., David Lockwood, Frank Bechhofer, and Jennifer Platt. 1969. *The Affluent Worker in the Class Structure*. Cambridge: Cambridge University Press.

Goodman, Leo A. 1965. "On the Multivariate Analysis of Three Dichotomous Variables." *American Journal of Sociology* 71:290-301.

_____. 1970. "The Multivariate Analysis of Qualitative Data: Interactions Among Multiple Classifications." *Journal of the American Statistical Association* 65:226-256.

_____. 1972. "Some Multiplicative Models for the Analysis of Cross-Classified Data." Pp. 649-696 in *Sixth Berkeley Symposium on Mathematical Statistics*, edited by Luciene Le Cam. Berkeley: University of California Press.

_____. 1979. "Simple Models for the Analysis of Association in Cross-Classifications Having Ordered Categories." *Journal of the American Statistical Association* 74:537-552.

_____. 1984. *The Analysis of Cross-Classified Data Having Ordered Categories*. Cambridge, MA: Harvard University Press.

_____. 1991. "Measures, Models, and Graphical Displays in the Analysis of Cross-Classified Data." *Journal of the American Statistical Association* 86:1085-1138.

Goodman, Leo A., and Michael Hout. 1995. "Statistical Methods and Graphical Displays for the Analysis of Association as it Varies Between Countries, Among Subgroups, and Over Time." Paper presented at the annual meeting of the American Sociological Association, Washington, D.C., 18 August 1995.

Grusky, David, and Robert M. Hauser. 1984. "Comparative Social Mobility Revisited." *American Sociological Review* 49:19-38.

Halsey, A.H., A. Heath, and J.M. Ridge. 1980. *Origins and Destinations*. Oxford: Clarendon Press.

Hauser, Robert M., Peter J. Dickinson, Harry P. Travis, and James M. Koffel. 1975a. "Temporal Changes in Occupational Mobility among Men in the U.S." *American Sociological Review* 40:279-297.

Hauser, Robert M., Peter J. Dickinson, Harry P. Travis, and James M. Koffel. 1975b. "Structural Changes in Occupational Mobility among Men in the U.S." *American Sociological Review* 40:585-598.

Hauser, Robert M. 1979. "Some Exploratory Methods for Analyzing Mobility Tables and Other Cross-Classified Data." *Sociological Methodology* 11:141-158.

Hauser, Robert M., and David Grusky. 1988. "Occupational Composition, Structural Mobility, and Cross-National Variation in Mobility." *American Sociological Review* 53:723-741.

Heyns, Barbara, and Ireneusz Bialecki. 1993. "Educational Inequalities in Postwar Poland." Pp. 303-336 in *Persistent Inequality: Changing Educational Attainment in Thirteen Countries*, edited by Yossi Shavit and Hans-Peter Blossfeld. Boulder, CO: Westview Press.

Hout, Michael. 1983. *Mobility Tables*. Beverly Hills, CA: Sage.

_____. 1984. "Status, Autonomy, and Training in Occupational Mobility." *American Journal of Sociology* 89:1379-1409.

_____. 1984b. "Occupational Mobility of Black Men." *American Sociological Review* 49:308-322.

_____. 1986. "Opportunity and the Minority Middle Class: A Comparison of Blacks in the United States with Catholics in Northern Ireland." *American Sociological Review* 51:214-223.

_____. 1988. "More Universalism, Less Structural Mobility: The American Occupational Structure in the 1980s." *American Journal of Sociology* 93:1358-1400.

_____. 1989. *Following in Father's Footsteps: Social Mobility in Ireland*. Cambridge, MA: Harvard University Press.

Hout, Michael, and Robert M. Hauser. 1992. "Symmetry and Hierarchy in Social Mobility." *European Sociological Review* 8:239-265.

Hout, Michael, Adrian E. Raftery, and Eleanor O. Bell. 1993. "Making the Grade: Educational Stratification in the United States, 1925-1989." Pp. 25-50 in *Persistent Inequality: Changing Educational Attainment in Thirteen Countries*, edited by Yossi Shavit and Hans-Peter Blossfeld. Boulder, CO: Westview Press.

Hout, Michael, Clem Brooks, and Jeff Manza. 1993. "The Persistence of Classes in Post-Industrial Societies." *International Sociology* 3:259-277.

Ishida, Hiroshi. 1993. *Social Mobility in Contemporary Japan*. Stanford, CA: Stanford University Press.

Jencks, Christopher. 1991. "Is the Urban Underclass Increasing?" Chapter 2 in *Urban Underclass*, edited by Christopher Jencks and Paul E. Peterson. Washington, D.C.: Brookings Institution.

Jonsson, Jon O. 1993. "Persisting Inequalities in Sweden." Pp. 101-132 in *Persistent Inequality: Changing Educational Attainment in Thirteen Countries*, edited by Yossi Shavit and Hans-Peter Blossfeld. Boulder, CO: Westview Press.

Jonsson, J.O. and C. Mills. 1993. "Social Class and Educational Attainment in Historical Perspective: A Swedish-English Comparison, Parts I and II." *British Journal of Sociology* 44:2-3.

Kerckhoff, Alan C., Richard T. Campbell, and Idee Winfield-Laird. 1985. "Social Mobility in Great Britain and the United States." *American Journal of Sociology* 91:281-308.

Kerckhoff, Alan C., and Jerry M. Trott. 1993. "Educational Attainment in a Changing Educational System: The Case of England and Wales." Pp. 133-154 in *Persistent Inequality: Changing Educational Attainment in Thirteen Countries*, edited by Yossi Shavit and Hans-Peter Blossfeld. Boulder, CO: Westview Press.

Kerr, Clark, J.T. Dunlop, F.H. Harbison, and C.A. Myers. 1960. *Industrialism and Industrial Man*. Cambridge: Harvard University Press.

Lipset, Seymour Martin, and Reinhard Bendix (eds). 1959. *Social Mobility in Industrial Society*. Berkeley, CA: University of California Press.

Logan, John A. 1983. "A Multivariate Model for the Mobility Table." *American Journal of Sociology* 89 (September): 324-349.

Lynch, Kathleen. 1990. "Reproduction: The Role of Cultural Factors and Educational Mediators." *British Journal of Sociology of Education* 11:3-20

MacLeod, Jay. 1987. *Ain't No Makin' It*. (First edition). Boulder: Westview Press.

Mare, Robert D. 1980. "Social Background and Educational Continuation Decisions." *Journal of the American Statistical Association* 75: 295-305.

_____. 1993. "Educational Stratification on Observed and Unobserved Components of Family Background." Pp. 351-376 in *Persistent Inequality: Changing Educational Attainment in Thirteen Countries*, edited by Yossi Shavit and Hans-Peter Blossfeld. Boulder, CO: Westview Press.

Meyer, John W., and W. Richard Scott. 1983. *Organizational Environments: Ritual and Rationality*. Beverly Hills, CA: Sage.

Nee, Victor. 1991. "Between Redistribution and Markets in China." *American Sociological Review* 56:267-282.

Ogbu, John U. 1987. "Variability in Minority School Performance: A Problem in Search of an Explanation." *Anthropology & Education Quarterly* 4:312-334.

Pontinen, Seppo. 1984. *A Comparison of Mobility in Scandinavian Countries*. Helsinki Sociological Institute.

Raftery, Adrian E., and Michael Hout. 1985. "Does Irish Education Approach the Meritocratic Ideal?" *The Economic and Social Review* 16 (January): 115-140.

_____. 1993. "Maximally Maintained Inequality: Expansion, Reform, and Opportunity in Irish Education, 1921-1975." *Sociology of Education* 66:41-62.

Roos, Patricia. 1986. *Gender and Work: A Comparative Analysis of Industrial Societies*. New York: State University of New York Press.

Schizzerotto, A. 1988. "Il ruolo dell'istruzione nei processi di mobilitá." *Polis* 1:83-123.

Shavit, Yossi, and Hans-Peter Blossfeld, (eds.) 1993. *Persistent Inequality: Changing Educational Attainment in Thirteen Countries.* Boulder, CO: Westview Press.

Sobel, Michael E., Michael Hout, and Otis Dudley Duncan. 1985. "Exchange, Structure, and Symmetry in Occupational Mobility." *American Journal of Sociology* 91:359-372.

Sorensen, Jesper B. 1992. "Locating Class Cleavages in Inter-generational Mobility: Cross-National Commonalities and Variations in Mobility Patterns." *European Sociological Review* 8:267-279.

Smith, Herbert L. and P.P. L. Cheung. 1986. "Trends in the Effects of Family Background on Educational Attainment in the Philippines." *American Journal of Sociology* 91:1387-1408.

Szelenyi, Szonja, and Karen Aschaffenberg. 1993. "Inequalities in Educational Opportunity in Hungary." Pp. 273-302 in *Persistent Inequality: Changing Educational Attainment in Thirteen Countries,* edited by Yossi Shavit and Hans-Peter Blossfeld. Boulder, CO: Westview Press.

Treiman, Donald J. 1970. "Industrialization and Social Stratification." Pp. 207-234 in *Social Stratification: Research and Theory for the 1970s,* edited by Edward O. Laumann. Indianapolis: Bobbs-Merrill.

Willis, Paul. 1979. *Learning to Labour.* London: Saxon House.

Wilson, William Julius. 1978. *The Declining Significance of Race.* Chicago: University of Chicago Press.

Wong, Raymond Sin-Kwok. 1990. "Understanding Cross-National Variation in Occupational Mobility." *American Sociological Review* 55:560-73.

———. 1992 "Vertical and Nonvertical Effects in Class Mobility: Cross-National Variations." *American Sociological Review* 57:396-410.

———. 1993. "Postwar Mobility Trends in Advanced Industrial Societies." *Research in Social Stratification and Mobility* 12:121-144.

Wong, Raymond Sin-Kwok, and Robert M. Hauser. 1992. "Trends in Occupational Mobility in Hungary Under Socialism." *Social Science Research* 21:419-444.

Wright, Erik Olin. 1985. *Classes.* London: Verso.

———. 1987. "Rethinking, Once Again, The Concept of Class Structure." Pp. 269-348 in *The Debate on Classes,* edited by Erik Olin Wright, Uwe Becker, Johanna Brenner, Michael Burawoy, Val Burris, Guglielmo Carchedi, Gordon Marshall, Peter F. Meiksins, David Rose, Arthur Stinchcombe, and Philippe Van Parijs. London: Verso.

Xie, Yu. 1992. "The Log-Multiplicative Layer Effect Model For Comparing Mobility Tables." *American Sociological Review* 57:380-395.

Yamaguchi, Kazuo. 1983. "The Structure of Intergenerational Occupational Mobility: Generality and Specificity in Resources, Channels, and Barriers." *American Journal of Sociology* 88:718-745.

———. 1987. Models for Mobility Tables: Toward Parsimony and Substance." *American Sociological Review* 52:482-494.

14

Stratification and Attainment in a Large Japanese Firm

Seymour Spilerman
Columbia University
Hiroshi Ishida
University of Tokyo

Introduction

Japanese management policy has been a source of keen fascination to social scientists in the United States. Many issues relating to the organization of efficient, high quality production and delivery of services have been resolved in a manner that is believed to be quite different from U.S. formulations. Japanese industry, for example, has instituted practices such as quality control circles, just-in-time delivery, affiliated satellite firms, and contracting out arrangements—administrative structures that have few precedents in the United States.

The human resource systems of large companies in Japan are also characterized by practices quite different from those in U.S. firms, both in the assumed employment relation and in the approach taken to career development. Notions of life-time employment, hiring "permanent" workers directly from school, the rarity of lateral entry, the seniority reward system (nenko), and salary compression are some of the features that are distinctive to personnel management in Japan (Cole 1979; Koike 1988). This is not to suggest that these practices are entirely absent from U.S. firms, but it is rare for several to appear in the same company, though IBM in past decades may have been an exception (Foy 1975). In large Japanese companies[1] these features tend to be components of an integrated personnel system, possibly reinforced by cultural norms that stress social harmony, primacy of corporate goals over individual aspirations, and deference to elders (Dore 1973, pp. 51-52, 297-298; Koike 1988, pp. 4-7; Roland 1988, pp.

72-75; but also see Lincoln and Kalleberg 1990).

When examining the human resource system of a Japanese firm one can readily observe how some of the component features are knit together and work in tandem, as well as identify strains in an otherwise coherent set of personnel practices. Contracting-out arrangements, for example, facilitate a policy of lifetime employment by permitting fluctuations in product demand to be passed on to an affiliated satellite firm (Dore 1973, p. 39). An early mandatory retirement age—55 to 60 is the common range—often followed by rehiring the superannuated worker (at a lower wage) provides additional flexibility to a firm in adjusting to the economic cycle, since the rehired worker is no longer protected by the "lifetime" commitment.

A decision to offer lifetime employment carries several implications. First, personnel selection must be done with great care since a strategy of disposing of workers who later reveal themselves to be poor performers is not available to management. Second, where lifetime employment is coupled with a linkage of salary to seniority, worker motivation and wage cost containment can become problems since management is denied the use of some potent behavioral reinforcers. Third, although lateral entry is not formally foreclosed by a policy of lifetime employment, when many firms follow this practice few mid-level job changers are likely to be available for recruitment. These considerations heighten the importance of training and socialization. The skills that will be required by a company have to be developed internally; moreover, future corporate leaders must be selected and groomed from the young recruits (Peck and Tamura 1976; OECD 1973; Cole 1979, pp. 40-42). This circumstance helps explain the long-term relationships with particular schools that are often sought by employers, since the educational institutions can evaluate students on the basis of several years of observation (Rosenbaum and Kariya 1989).

Tensions arise because some personnel practices do not mesh well with others. For example, the socialization of managerial recruits is intended to instill commitment to the firm and reinforce cohort bonding (Dore 1973, pp. 46-54). Identification with the firm, rather than with a subunit, is promoted by a policy of rotating employees among occupational tasks and organizational units; in practice, encouraging a "generalist" orientation (Hirono 1969, pp. 260-61). According to Ballon (1969a, p. 26), job rotation is essential for advancement to senior management. Yet, large firms must also develop specialists, and economic rationality suggests that such individuals be encouraged to work within the domain of their expertise. We know little about how specialization is motivated or rewarded in a work context that is largely geared to promoting a generalist orientation, though see Koike (1991) and Pucik (1964a) for some insights into the career implications of specialization.[2]

Similarly, the selection of employees for advancement to senior positions entails a process of differentiation among cohort members—a problematic activity in a context in which cohesion is prized. There is some consensus to the effect that these conflicting objectives are managed by segregating them in time. Solidarity is emphasized during the first decade or so of employment, facilitated by a policy of automatic promotion through the junior ranks. Only afterwards does differentiation begin in earnest, with some employees earmarked for high administrative ranks (Clark 1979, p. 112-119; Yoshino and Lifson 1986, pp. 146-147).

How this process unfolds is not clearly understood. Following Rosenbaum (1984), Pucik (1985, p.77) contends that after the first decade of employment attainment can be described by a "tournament model," in which employees who have advanced rapidly from one rank have sharply higher prospects for swift promotion in the subsequent rank (see Hanada 1987 for a similar assessment). In Rosenbaum's formulation (1984, pp. 61-62), early winners —measured by rapid promotion in the initial ranks—have an opportunity to compete for high statuses, while losers can compete only for lesser jobs. A derivative feature of the tournament model of careers is its weakness in accommodating "errors of exclusion." It lacks a mechanism for bringing early losers back into the competition for senior positions (Rosenbaum 1984, p. 288).

Ballon has suggested a very different decision calculus, one in which productivity in the early ranks is not a dominating consideration in later promotion decisions. The question for Ballon is what is meant by productivity? "[I]n Japan economic performance is not so much a matter of individual employees as [it is] of an entire organization" (Ballon 1969a, p.26). Promotion, in turn, is less tied to the details of work performance than to "proper organizational values." These are expected to mature with age and tend to reveal themselves only in late career stages. Assuming, then, that rapid advancement in the early ranks reflects *individual* productivity, one prediction from Ballon's thesis is that slow initial mobility may not be a handicap in later promotion decisions.[3]

There is also the related issue of the *consequence of advancement* and how the effects of loss in the career competition are managed. This is a serious issue in a context of "lifetime employment" because a worker who has been passed over for promotion must still be motivated to perform effectively in lower ranked positions. The fact that the seniority component of salary is often large in Japanese firms (Cole 1979, p.41; Okochi, et. al. 1974, pp. 499-500) operates to mitigate the problem, since this arrangement limits the material effects of loss in the promotion competition. Clark (1979, p. 122) also describes a set of titles accorded to employees on the basis of seniority —"honorable consolation prizes"—but which lack the authority that derives from high rank in the principal status hierarchy of the firm.

In this paper we examine the related themes of status advancement and compensation level in a large Japanese company in the mid-1990's. We organize the analysis around the following specific issues: (a) What are the determinants of promotion and how do they vary by rank in the firm? (b) What is the consequence of status attainment (relative to the effect of seniority) for remuneration level? (c) What kind of conceptual imagery—e.g., Rosenbaum's tournament model; Ballon's formulation—best describes the way that opportunity and advancement are structured for employees?

The information for this study comes from the employee data base of one of the ten largest financial service companies in Japan. Our data set is unusually rich in that we have complete work histories of employees current as of 1993, which permits personnel issues to be addressed in some detail using the methods of survival analysis. Moreover, while we have emphasized career features that are fairly distinctive to Japan, there have been suggestions of change and a trend toward adoption of practices common in western countries—in both salary determination and promotion policy (Marsh and Mannari 1976, p. 120; Yoshino and Lifson 1986, pp. 152-155; Wolferen and Murphy 1994, p. IV-13). Because the firm we have studied is considered by its officers to be fairly typical of large companies (in the financial service sector) in its human resource practices, by examining the extent to which our findings deviate from earlier accounts of Japanese work systems we can assess the evidence for change and convergence to western arrangements.

The Stratification System for Managerial Employees

Before turning to the analysis of rank advancement and salary determination, it is useful to outline the main features of the stratification system of the Japanese firm. Also, for a reference standard, we compare the Japanese company with a large financial service organization in the U.S., which has been studied in some detail (Spilerman and Lunde 1992; Petersen and Spilerman 1990).

Analogous to the U.S. firm, the Japanese company is divided into clerical and managerial specialties. However, (1) all clerical workers are women and almost all managerial employees are men.[4] In the U.S. firm, by comparison, women constitute 91% of clerical workers and 46% of administrative employees. (2) In the Japanese company there is no mobility across the clerical/managerial divide; recruits to the managerial ranks come directly from college. In the U.S. firm, in contrast, there are extensive "posting and bidding" provisions to facilitate job transfers, and these have resulted in approximately half of managerial entrants coming from the clerical ranks of the company.

Regarding entrants from the external labor market into the managerial ranks, in the U.S. firm some 55% have had prior work experience,[5] a background that is rare in the Japanese company. In the U.S., new managerial hires exhibit differences in level of educational attainment, which is not the case in Japan where all entrants have a college degree. (3) In Japan, there is a distinction between "non-permanent" and "permanent" workers, which is virtually coterminous with the clerical/managerial dichotomy. Only permanent employees are promised lifetime employment.

To summarize, in the Japanese firm managerial employees are male; they have been recruited directly from college; they comprise an entering cohort that is homogeneous in age and in education; and most expect to spend their full working lives within the company. Clerical employees, in comparison, are female, usually without a college degree. They are not recruited into the managerial ranks and their tenure with the firm normally ends with marriage or childbirth. The significance of this distinction in the personnel categories is conveyed by the fact that the employee data base of the Japanese company contains work histories of only managerial employees. Hence, our investigation is restricted to managerial employees and to men.

It should also be emphasized that the sort of analysis a student of careers can do with the Japanese materials is less rich than what is commonly undertaken with U.S. data. In the study of the U.S. financial service company, for example, much of the research effort was devoted to examining the effects on attainment of gender, years of schooling, entry age, and entry portal (promotion from the clerical grades versus entry by a new hire directly into the managerial ranks). In the Japanese company, however, there is little variation on any of these variables. Indeed, this tendency to homogeneity of an entry cohort—a frustration to the researcher—combined with the practice of encouraging a "generalist orientation," facilitates the common corporate policy of rewarding employees principally on the basis of seniority. *If there is little differentiation on other human capital variables, the significance of seniority as a determinant of productivity and performance is heightened.*

The structure of rewards

In large work places in the U.S. the reward structure is commonly based on the principles of modern compensation design (e.g., Wallace and Fay 1983; Sibson 1981). The essential features of such human resource systems are a set of ranked salary grades (there are 20 in the U.S. company), the slotting of job titles into the grade levels on the basis of a job evaluation procedure, and a definition of promotion as an upward movement in the salary grade structure, rather than in terms of a change in job title. As remarked elsewhere (Spilerman and Petersen 1994), the attractiveness of this arrangement is that it frees management from the tyranny of a technologically determined occupational distribution that constrains promotion allocations to the presence of "vacancies." In the salary grade formulation management can more easily award promotions on the basis of merit. Lacking a vacancy, a job title can either be reclassified into a higher grade or the number of grades associated with the position can be increased.

In comparison, the reward structure in the Japanese company has three distinct dimensions. First, there is a system of *status ranks* (often referred to as "standard ranks" [e.g., Clark 1979, p. 104]), a hierarchy which lacks a counterpart in U.S. industry. The standard ranks—titles such as department head, section head, sub-section head—adhere to the individual and are not necessarily descriptive of the job he does. The standard ranks are fairly universal in Japan; as a result the titles convey meaning throughout the society about an individual's status and provide a basis for social comparisons among employees of different firms. In the U.S. the closest parallel is status in the military, in which rank conveys authority and patterns deference relationships but is not indicative of an officer's job assignment.

The second dimension relates to *functional responsibility* in the company—one's managerial authority. While there is a correspondence between this dimension and standard rank, they are not formally identical. Clark (1979, pp. 111-115), for example, describes an organizational setting in which senior level supervisory positions are sometimes left unfilled, in order to permit capable junior employees to take on duties normally associated with high standard rank, which they lack the tenure to acquire. As Dore (1973, p. 68) notes, "[t]he advantage of this flexible system is that it allows faithful service by men of mediocre ability to be rewarded by an increase in rank without the disadvantage of dysfunctionally promoting them to positions of greater authority."

The third dimension concerns *salary grade*. The U.S. financial service company utilizes a set of 20 grades, essentially a system of overlapping salary ranges. In the Japanese company which we examined there are 34 grades, each of which specifies a base salary rate that is adjusted for seniority. More consequential is the different significance of the salary grade hierarchy in the two countries. As noted earlier, in the U.S. company salary grade constitutes a unified reward dimension. There are no "personal" status ranks; also, the job titles—which convey functional responsibilities—are mapped onto the salary grades. Promotion, in turn, is defined as movement in this grade hierarchy.

In contrast, in the tripartite division of the Japanese company, standard rank constitutes the central factor in the allocation of status, authority, and career rewards (Rohlen 1974; p. 25). Also, promotion is defined in terms of movement within this hierarchy. While salary grade is correlated with standard rank, the former is often tied to seniority, especially at the beginning of the career (Dore 1973, p. 68; Rohlen 1974, p.156). Indeed, this emphasis on seniority in the setting of salary—rather than job assignment—

is rational in an environment in which job rotation is encouraged and employment is long-term. While a worker's wages might not reflect his specific job duties at a given time point, the compensation model—as well as notions of equity and employee expectations—is formulated in terms of *lifetime career rewards*, not statically (Yoshino and Lifson 1986, p. 152; Koike 1988, p. 134).

Since the system of standard ranks is the principal dimension of stratification in the Japanese firm, we have focused our investigation on mobility within this status hierarchy. Because of the complex relation between compensation and status rank—high remuneration is both a reward for attainment and, possibly, a consolation prize as well for passed-over employees—we also examine the consequence of rank attainment for compensation level.

The Attainment Process in the Firm

In Table 14.1 we present cross-sectional information on the distribution of personnel in management ranks in 1993 (column 1). From the duration figures (column 3) it is evident that a long period is spent in the "non-management" or "trainee"[6] status and that there is little variation in duration in this rank (column 4, row 1). This finding is consistent with the reports of other investigators (e.g., Yoshino and Lifson 1986, 146; Pucik 1985, p. 74), who have noted that the trainee period lasts from 10-15 years and that promotion is automatic after a fixed interval in this status. (We shall, however, have more to say about this assessment.) The figures in column (5) provide rough evidence for the stability of the organization in size and in status distribution, indicating that turnover in ranks 20 to 40 has been fairly constant at about 110 persons/year. In ranks 20 and 30 this turnover consists largely of promotions; however, many of the exits from rank 40 are retirements and hence the decline in turnover in the highest positions.

Which variables predict to promotion? This issue is addressed in Table 14.2 using Cox's proportional hazard model (Blossfeld, Hamerle and Mayer 1989, chap. 3) with career history data from the 1961-82 entry cohorts. The Cox model specifies that

$$h(t \mid \underline{X}) = h_0(t) \exp(\underline{X}'\underline{B}) \qquad (1)$$

where $\underline{X}'$ is a vector of covariates, $\underline{B}$ is the vector of respective regression coefficients, t is the waiting time to promotion, and $h_0(t)$ is an unspecified base rate that is the same for all individuals. To permit the possibility that the determinants vary with level in the organization, we examined promotions from ranks 20, 30, and 40 separately. Thus, the regressions in each

TABLE 14.1 Distribution of Personnel by Status Rank in the
Japanese Financial Service Company, 1993[a]

Status Rank[b]	Name	(1) N	(2) Mean Age of Entry into Rank (years)	(3) Mean Duration in Rank[c] (years)	(4) C.V.[d] of Duration	(5) N/ Mean Duration
20	Trainee/Non-Management	1,106	23.05	11.03	.067	100
30	Sub-Section Chief	542	34.04	4.65	.260	117
40	Section Chief	921	38.89	8.46	.225	109
50	Sub-Dept.Head	110	47.71	2.8	.421	39
60	Depart. Head	146	49.61	1.75[e]	—[f]	—[f]
70	Director	5	—	—	—	—
N		2,830				

[a]Omitted from the study are female employees, lateral transfers from other companies, and employees without a college education. Exclusions for these reasons amount to less than 5% of the firm's labor force.

[b]Some minor ranks (in 20's) and ranks with small N's (45, 80, 90) have been grouped with an appropriate major rank.

[c]Based on completed durations.

[d]Coefficient of variation = s.d. of duration/mean duration.

[e]Mean duration in rank 60 is based on current incumbants, not completed spells.

[f]Value is not comparable to others in the column. See note e.

panel are based on spells in the particular rank. An employee can contribute only one spell to a panel; however, if he has progressed through several ranks he can contribute a spell to more than one panel. In each model, the regressors predict to the rate of promotion from the noted rank; incomplete spells as of July 1993—the data collection date—are treated as censored observations.

For reasons outlined earlier—the homogeneity of managerial recruits in terms of educational attainment, gender, and (absence of) prior work experience – the available regressors are few. Nonetheless, some distinctive patterns emerge. With respect to advancement from the "non-management" status (Panel A), neither age at hire (on which there is a range of some 3 years) nor college major predicts to promotion. However, the models in columns (3) and (4) indicate a negative association between size of an entry cohort and the promotion rate, which would suggest a corporate policy of insulating the higher ranks from annual variations in magnitude of the intake. This finding would seem at variance with the contention that promotion from rank 20 is "automatic;" however, we will shortly make clear that even at this early career point the company has begun to make distinctions among employees as well as to fine-tune the advancement regime.

In the analysis of promotion from rank 30 (Panel B), we introduce a regressor for duration in the prior rank. This term is intended to assess whether individuals who have previously advanced rapidly are advantaged with respect to current promotion prospects. The significant negative coefficient that we find—long prior duration reduces the promotion rate – supports this possibility (column 1). One explanation for the finding would emphasize the sorting of workers on the basis of either tournament success or ability (unmeasured in our data set); however, these initial results are also consistent with a tracking or gate-keeping explanation.

Further insight into the mechanics of the attainment process can be obtained from an analysis of promotion in rank 40 (Panel C). These results provide support for a "tracking" type of explanation. In particular, while we continue to find a significant negative coefficient for time in rank 20, there is no effect of duration in rank 30, the prior status level (column 1).[7] This result is not consistent with an "ability sorting" thesis or with a "tournament" model; both would suggest that recent job performance—indexed here by duration in prior rank—should have greater impact on promotion chances than less proximate performance measures. Instead, our results suggest a process in which a critical evaluation is made early in an employee's career and it is this decision, rather than later job performance, which determines the worker's subsequent promotion prospects.

Finally, we note from columns (3) and (4) of the several panels that entry cohort size has no impact on the promotion rate after the trainee years (rank

TABLE 14.2 Promotion Regressions, by Status Rank in the Company[a]

PANEL A. Promotion from Rank 20				
Variable[b]	(1)	(2)	(3)[e]	(4)
Age[c] (years)	.0114	.0020	.0726	.0130
College Major:[d]				
Business/Law		-.0126		
Science		.1353		
Cohort Size			-.0012*	-.0061**
-2LL =	19296.60	19278.37	19827.53	19287.47
N =	1486	1485	1486	1486
Percent censored =	0.5%	0.5%	0.5%	0.5%

PANEL B. Promotion from Rank 30				
Variable[b]	(1)	(2)	(3)[e]	(4)
Age[c] (years)	.0013	.0233	.0046	.0001
Duration in Rank 20 (years)	-.1679*	-.1925**	-.1667*	-.1681*
College Major:[d]				
Business/Law		.3697*		
Science		.1405		
Cohort Size			.0005	.0010
-2LL =	12397.41	12373.84	12415.88	12397.18
N =	1119	1118	1119	1119
Percent censored =	11%	11%	11%	11%

PANEL C. Promotion from Rank 40				
Variable[b]	(1)	(2)	(3)[e]	(4)
Age[c] (years)	.1605	.1959	.1392	.1632
Duration in Rank 20 (years)	-.4770**	-.5114**	-.4981**	-.4890**
Duration in Rank 30 (years)	-.0567	-.0552	-.0344	-.0610
College Major:[f]				
Business/Law		.6714*		
Cohort Size			-.0006	-.0081
-2LL =	1830.74	1812.10	1834.75	1830.23
N =	300	299	300	300
Percent censored =	37%	37%	37%	37%

*p<.05, **p<.01

[a]Regressions are Cox proportional hazard models. Clock for the models is duration in rank. Data are from 1961-82 entry cohorts for rank 20 employees, 1961-78 cohorts for rank 30 workers, and for 1961-70 cohorts for rank 40 employees.

[b]Dummy terms for entry year are included in each equation.

[c]Age at entry into the rank.

[d]Humanities major is the omitted category.

[e]Entry year dummies omitted from this model.

[f]Humanities and Science major is the omitted category.

investigators in several key respects:
dominant role in compensation deterr
two decades of employment (Pucik 1⁹
differentials become important for sa
(Yoshino an Lifson 1986, p. 154); and (c
sion, in comparison with western com
272; 1974b, p. 92). In particular, the mos
data set received 2.3 times the salary o
the U.S. financial service company th
mately 5.0.

The salary practices we have observ
descriptions published several decade
1971, chap. 3), despite suggestions of a
mode of compensation (e.g., Clark 197⁹
152-155).[11] This stability is not surpri
strategy of a firm cannot be isolated
practices. Rather, it is a key element in
a low variance in human capital variab
orientation during the training peri
lifetime employment. Seniority-base
cally rational in the early years of a
employee differentiation; it is also a re
years, after differentiation has taken
"failure." In a context of lifetime e
consideration since commitment and
the less successful employee.

Formulations of R

What sort of conceptual imagery b
the Japanese company? Should it be
a process of cumulative advantage, (c
(d) a gatekeeping operation, or (e) a
which the criteria for promotion to a
from judgments about performanc
sufficiently rich to distinguish defin
nations, though we are in a position
conceptual imageries may appear
descriptions, once the explanation
from several of the formulations ten
and (b) are difficult to disentangle;
In its simplest form, the tourna
contests in which only winners adv

20). In contrast, college major, which has little effect during the trainee years —possibly because new recruits follow a generalist career path—attains significance at higher organizational levels, where specialization is more common (Suzuki 1981), with a business/law major predicting to early advancement. Thus, what can be said from these data is that trainee assessments—as indexed by duration in rank 20—have a profound effect on advancement prospects over the career course and that, in the higher corporate ranks, college major also predicts to promotion. As to the individual-level variables which discriminate among employees during the trainee period—surely an interesting question—we have no information. Because of the homogeneity of new recruits on most observable human capital measures and the absence of a work history at the trainee stage, we lack variables that might differentiate among employees in this early career period.

Compensation level

The second dimension in our description of the stratification process concerns the determinants of monthly salary. There is some consensus that, at least in past decades, seniority has constituted the principal consideration in the calculation of salary level in large Japanese firms (Marsh and Mannari 1976, pp. 154-156; Yoshino and Lifson 1986, pp. 152-153). Moreover, we have argued that such an arrangement meshes well with several distinctive features of industrial organization in Japan: little differentiation among workers on human capital measures; a practice of rotating employees among jobs; and a need to mitigate the consequence of failure in the promotion competition. A policy that pegs compensation to seniority would appear consistent with these organizational practices. At the same time, other researchers (e.g., Cole 1971, pp. 81-84; Clark 1979, pp. 154-155) have suggested that Japanese firms have been moving away from a largely seniority based reward structure to job specific payments and performance wages.

In a large Japanese firm an employee's compensation level is the sum of several components: base salary, rank supplements, family and commuting allowances, and a bonus payment. In the following analysis, we limit our consideration to the base salary component (which includes additions for seniority) and the rank supplements.[8] OLS regressions of monthly compensation (in July 1993) are reported in Table 14.3.

The coefficients in column (1) show the effects of seniority and status rank on log monthly salary. In this semi-log specification, exponentials of the rank coefficients can be interpreted as multiplier terms. Thus, holding seniority constant, the cumulative salary returns to rank—relative to the base category (rank 30)—are: an 8.5% increase in rank 40 (i.e., a 1.085 multiplier), a 15.8% increase in rank 50, and a 23.6% increment in rank 60.

TABLE 14.3   Determinant:

Variable	
Constant	2.
Current Rank[b]:	
40	.
50	.
60	.
Seniority (years)	.
(Seniority)^2	-.
Duration in Current Rank x10^{-2} (years)	
Rank 40 x Duration (x10^{-2})	
Rank 50 x Duration (x10^{-2})	
Rank 60 x Duration (x10^{-2})	
R^2 =	
N =	

*p<.05, **p<.01
[a]Dependent variable is log o
(yen) = 587,200.
[b]Excluded category is Rank

In comparison, holding rar
tenure at the 10, 20, and 30 y
145%, and 168% over entry
Columns (2) and (3) repo
nation process. In column (
and for interactions betwee
of the high correlation betwe
tion of this variable is used.
Because the rank effects
compare the returns to seni
assess the latter at different
to seniority is a 170% increas
different: a 182% increment.
ranges for instance from z
relative to the omitted categ
entrants to 9.6% at the five y
and in rank 60 it is 22.1% to
hardly inconsequential, the
to tenure, especially over th
To summarize, our res

Rosenbaum (1984, p. 243): "This leads to a system in which selections are continually occurring [to decide who will be promoted and who will be] eliminated from the tournament and moved into the category of loser, from which there is limited opportunity to advance." In Rosenbaum's *tournament model of careers*, "winners" are operationalized by time in rank—they are the employees who have been promoted early. Also, in place of strict elimination, the careers model posits a slower rate of promotion for "losers" and consequentially a lower peak rank at retirement. There are three implications of the model which can be examined with our data: (a) careers are structured in terms of a sequence of selections, (b) individuals with a short time-duration at one level are likely to be promoted rapidly from the next rank, and (c) there is little opportunity for "losers" to recover. Support for the tournament imagery in a large Japanese firm has been reported by Pucik (1985).

Unfortunately, many of the implications of the tournament model also follow from a process of *cumulative advantage*, such as would occur from the sorting of employees in each corporate rank on the basis of ability or performance. Even without a notion of structured competition and the elimination of "losers," some workers will advance rapidly while others fall behind. In both formulations we should find that senior level employees progressively pulled ahead of their peers, having spent shorter durations in a rank and consequently having arrived at each successive status with less seniority. Rosenbaum (1984, pp. 265-267) attempted to disentangle the two models by associating the tournament formulation with a "labeling" process—rapid prior mobility *signals* an employee's high potential, in contrast with reliance by management upon contemporaneous evaluations of performance—but this embellishment does not help to distinguish between the formulations with the personnel data available to us.

A *sponsorship* model (Turner 1960; also see Rosenbaum 1984, p. 17), entails an early selection decision and the assignment of employees to two or more tracks. The selection determines an individual's prospects of eventually achieving a senior administrative rank. Contingent on the track assignment, an employee's subsequent performance—and his rate of promotion from mid-level ranks—is relatively unimportant. What counts is the early sorting decision, which may be followed by special job assignments and "grooming" for elite status. A *gatekeeping operation* suggests an analogous filtering process early in the career course. A subtle distinction between the models is that "sponsorship" is usually associated with elite selection whereas "gatekeeping" suggests an objective of insuring minimum competence. Both models, however, involve a tracking decision at an initial career point.

Turner (1960) also introduced the notion of *contest mobility*, in which decisions about elite status are delayed well into the career course, permitting employees an opportunity to overcome poor early evaluations or otherwise "grow with experience." Ballon's (1969a, pp. 25-26) description of career dynamics in a large Japanese firm echoes this formulation, with his emphasis on time-in-rank prerequisites for advancement and his stress on the nuances of socialization ("proper organizational values"), in place of narrow work performance. The conclusion by Spilerman and Lunde (1991), from data on the U.S. firm, to the effect that different talents become relevant to promotion decisions as one rises in the corporate hierarchy also supports this formulation.

The above alternative models, or competing imageries, provide a framework for assessing the structure of the attainment process in the Japanese firm. In Table 14.4 we examine the effects of duration spells in prior ranks on the promotion rate. Column (1), a repeat of Table 14.2, Panel B, column (1), is presented for continuity with the earlier analysis and reports a significant negative effect of duration in rank 20 (the trainee status) on the promotion rate in rank 30. Because the linear specification of the duration variable might be masking non-linear returns to different interval lengths, which would be revealing of the consequence of "early" and "late" promotions, we divided the duration variable into four categorical terms: early promotion, on-time promotion, late promotion, and very late promotion.[12] "On-time," which is defined as the modal category, is the reference term. The results are reported in column (2).

Relative to "on-time" promotion, the tournament model would predict rapid advancement from rank 30 for employees who were promoted early from the prior rank ("winners"), and slow promotion for laggards. Our results make clear that laggards do, indeed, have poor advancement prospects, but they fail to show an advantage for early movers. It is also worth noting that the two laggard categories sum to only 15% of personnel (see note 12); in short, rather than a process of gleaning the very best employees and preparing them for elite positions, the selection mechanism appears to be oriented to eliminating the chaff—the small proportion of "recruitment errors."

Columns (3) to (5) refer to promotion from rank 40. From column (3) we observe the effect of duration in rank 30—the prior status—to have no impact on the promotion rate. In column (4) we introduce a term for duration in rank 20, a repetition of the model in column (1), Panel C of Table 14.2. As explained in regard to that table, the present formulation is identical to a model containing variables for seniority and duration in the prior rank, though for reasons that have been noted the present representation is preferred. Even in the presence of this control we find no effect of duration in rank 30. This model does indicate, however, a continued negative effect of duration in the trainee status. In column (5) a model is reported in which the duration terms have been divided into categorical

TABLE 14.4   Promotion Regressions: Effects of Duration in Prior Ranks[a]

Variable[b]	Promotion from Rank 30			Promotion from Rank 40	
	(1)	(2)	(3)	(4)	(5)
Age[c] (years)	.0013	.0171	-.0467	.1605	.1074
Duration in Rank 20:					
Continuous (years)	-.1679**			-.4770**	
Early Promotion[d]		-.1872			-.1472
Late Promotion		-.2245*			-.6813**
Very Late Promotion		-.6098**			. . .[e]
Duration in Rank 30:					
Continuous (years)			.1742	-.0567	
Early Promotion[d]					-.1540
Late Promotion					-.0961
Very Late Promotion					-.0049
-2LL =	12397.41	12391.86	1840.31	1830.74	1826.05
N =	1119	1119	300	300	300
Percent censored =	11%	11%	37%	37%	37%

*p<.05, **p<.01

[a]Regressions are Cox proportional hazard models. Clock for the models is duration in rank. Data cover 1961-82 entry cohorts.

[b]Dummy variables for entry year are present in each equation.

[c]Age at entry into current rank (30 or 40).

[d]Set of four dummy variables for duration in rank. Deleted term in regressions is "On-Time Promotion," which is defined as the mode waiting time (11 years for duration in rank 20; 4 years for duration in rank 30).

[e]Because of small N, "Very Late Promotion" is combined with "Late Promotion" in the the rank 40 regressions.

variables to ascertain whether the linear specifications have masked distinctive non-linear returns to particular duration intervals.[13] Again, we fail to find an effect of duration in the prior grade.

Taken together, these results do not support a tournament formulation or a cumulative advantage model as a description of the attainment process in the Japanese company. There is no evidence of sequential selections among "winners," as Rosenbaum (1984, p. 243) requires for the tournament model, nor an accumulation of rapid promotions by the presumably more able employees. Moreover, we fail to find any indication of a return to "winners," in that rapid mobility in the prior rank provides no discernable advantage over the modal rate of advancement.

If our results do not support a tournament model, they are consistent with a selection process in which an early tracking decision, based on evaluations during the trainee period, influences an employee's attainment

TABLE 14.5 Distribution of Spell Durations in Rank 30 by Seniority at Entrance into Rank 30[a]

		Duration in Rank 30 (years)[b]									
		1	2	3	4	5	6	7	8	9 or more	N
	10				9	14	3	1			27
	11			80	298	294	89	23	9	5	798
Seniority at Entrance to Rank 30 (years)[c]	12		5	27	38	43	18	10	6	2	149
	13	1	4	3	6	3		2		1	20
	14	1	3			1					5
	15	3				1					4
	N	5	12	110	351	356	110	36	15	8	1003

[a]Data are for completed spells that ended in a promotion.
[b]Mean duration in rank 30 = 4.6 years, median = 5.0 years.
[c]Seniority at entrance into rank 30 (= mean duration in rank 20) = 11.2 years, median = 11.0 years.

prospects over the career course. Yet this selection mechanism does not appear to be one of anointing the most promising employees, rather it operates as a gatekeeping process that weeds out the least capable trainees. Contingent on this tracking decision, the promotion rate in the middle ranks does not appear consequential as a determinant of an employee's eventual peak status in the firm.

The negative coefficients of *early* promotion in the prior status, which we observe in the dummy variable formulations of both the rank 30 and rank 40 regressions, do not reach significance (columns 2 and 5). Nonetheless, if the data are organized somewhat differently we can observe that these are not chance effects, but arise from the very specification of promotion criteria in the company.

In Table 14.5 we present a cross-tabulation of duration in rank 30 by duration in rank 20 (seniority at entrance into rank 30). Note first the diagonal in the upper left corner. It makes clear that there is a minimum requirement of 14 years seniority (duration in ranks 20 plus 30) before one can be considered for advancement to rank 40. As a consequence, employees promoted early from rank 20 (10 years duration) must wait four years before advancement, whereas slow movers from rank 20 can be promoted again within a year. It is this seniority requirement which produces the

TABLE 14.6   Distribution of Spell Durations in Rank 40 by Seniority at Entrance into Rank 40[a]

		Duration in Rank 40 (Years)[b]									
		4	5	6	7	8	9	10	11	12 or more	N
	14					3	3	1	2	2	11
	15				1	12	11	6	2	4	36
Seniority at Entrance to Rank 40 (years)[c]	16			3	15	22	12	9	5	8	74
	17	1		6	13	6	5		1	32	
	18				2	2	2	1	1		1	9
	19		1	1	1	1		2			5
	20	1									1
	N	2	1	12	32	45	32	19	9	16	168

[a]Data are for completed spells that ended in a promotion.
[b]Mean duration in rank 40 = 8.4 years, median = 8.0 years.
[c]Mean seniority at entrance to rank 40 = 16.1 years, median = 16.0 years.

negative effect of early promotion in the prior grade, noted in columns (2) and (5) of Table 14.4, and which undermines the possibility of a tournament/cumulative advantage process describing attainment in the firm.

The rows and columns in Table 14.5 can be interpreted as deviations from their respective medians. In particular, the entries in the first four columns represent early promotions from grade 30. Thus, among employees who served 10 years in rank 20 (row 1), 33% (9/27) were promoted early from rank 30. Among employees with 11 years duration in rank 20, 47% were promoted early from grade 30. For 12 years service the early promotion rate is also 47%; and for 13 or more years in rank 20 it is 72%. To emphasize that these results are not idiosyncratic of the particular rank, we report in Table 14.6 an analogous cross-tabulation between seniority at entrance into rank 40 and duration in rank 40. The effects are almost identical to those reported in Table 14.5.[14]

To summarize, these findings run counter to a contention that rapid advancement from one rank increases an employee's prospects of early promotion in the next rank—an imagery that underlies both the tournament model and the cumulative advantage process. Instead, as a consequence of the firm's promotion rules, we find a tendency for short durations to be coupled with long stays in the succeeding rank. Pucik (1985) concluded that a tournament model adequately fits career evolution in the Japanese company he studied, however we do not find support for this imagery. Moreover, the specification of a seniority minimum for rank entrance (sometimes, an age minimum) has been reported by other investigators of Japanese industrial practices (e.g., Yoshino and Lifson 1986, p.147; Marsh and Mannari 1976, chap. 7; also see Koike 1988, pp. 210-215 for a comparison between Japan and European countries). Thus, even though our assessment is based on data from a single firm, it is unlikely that a tournament/cumulative advantage model is widely applicable in the Japanese industrial context.

Advancement to senior ranks

What more can be said about the attainment process? In particular, what can be ascertained about the selection of senior personnel—the rank 60 managers? Table 14.7 speaks to this question, as well as providing summary information about career dynamics. These data examine current (1993) status for employees hired during the time interval 1962-67—the entry cohorts that are approaching retirement age. Since we do not have data on personnel who have left employment, this sample provides our best insight into the achievement of high level positions. Table 14.7 describes current status, contingent on seniority at entrance into lower ranks.

With respect to seniority at entrance into rank 30 (duration in rank 20), there is a clear division in terms of prospects for reaching status 60 (Panel A). On-time entrants (specified by median seniority) and early entrants are twice as likely as late arrivals to achieve this level. However, there is no advantage to rapid prior advancement—"winners" in Rosenbaum's formulation—nor is there a special disadvantage to employees in the very slowest category. In this specification of the seniority categories, some 65% of employees are in the two groups that show superior prospects for reaching rank 60.[15]

Panel B reports the likelihood of reaching the different 1993 ranks, contingent on seniority at entrance into status 40. Focusing on status 60, we again see evidence of a step function effect: little apparent difference in the attainment prospects of "early," "on-time," or "moderately tardy" employees, as measured by prior rate of movement, but a clear disadvantage to very slow movers (15% of the sample), who exhibit an advancement rate into status 60 that is less than half that of the other categories.

Thus, in ranks 30 and 40, the advancement regime appears to operate as a gatekeeping process which does not differentiate between rapid and average movers, nor (in rank 40) between these groups and modestly tardy employees, with respect to prospects for achieving elite status. A minority of employees are penalized, namely those with very slow rates of prior

TABLE 14.7   Status Rank in 1993 by Seniority at Entry into Prior Ranks,
1962-67 Entry Cohort

PANEL A. Rank in 1993, by Seniority at Entry into Rank 30[a]

			Rank in 1993			
Seniority (mos.)	60	50	40	30		(N)
<132	.64	.18	.18	.00	1.00	(11)
132	.61	.27	.11	.01	1.00	(148)
133-144	.32	.26	.38	.04	1.00	(77)
>144	.30	.20	.40	.10	1.00	(10)
All	.51	.26	.21	.02	1.00	(246)

PANEL B. Rank in 1993, by Seniority at Entry into Rank 40[a]

			Rank in 1993		
Seniority (mos.)	60	50	40		(N)
<192	.58	.31	.12	1.01	(52)
192-203	.60	.27	.12	0.99	(81)
204-215	.50	.17	.33	1.00	(48)
>215	.21	.24	.55	1.00	(33)
All	.51	.25	.23	0.99	(214)

PANEL C. Rank in 1993, by Seniority at Entry into Rank 50[a]

		Rank in 1993		
Seniority (mos.)	60	50		(N)
<277	.96	.04	1.00	(26)
277-288	.82	.18	1.00	(39)
289-300	.70	.30	1.00	(30)
301-312	.47	.53	1.00	(19)
>312	.19	.81	1.00	(26)
All	.66	.34	1.00	(140)

[a]Entries are percentages of the seniority group.

mobility, yet, even here, there is substantial opportunity for recovery, which is not a feature of the tournament imagery (Rosenbaum 1984, p.42). Some 20 - 30 percent of the "laggard" category do succeed in reaching the highest status.

Promotion from status 50 exhibits a different pattern. Whereas, in lower ranks, the advancement regime appears to operate by curtailing the attainments of a minority of employees (a gatekeeping operation), we now see evidence of *progressive* differentiation in terms of prior service (or age[16]). In particular, employees who have advanced the most rapidly to rank 50 have

TABLE 14.8   Status Rank in 1993 by Seniority at Entry into Prior Ranks, 1962-67
Entry Cohort, Employees with 132 or Fewer Months in Grade 20 Only

PANEL A. Rank in 1993, by Seniority at Entry into Rank 30[a]

| | *Rank in 1993* | | | |
Seniority (mos.)	60	50 or lower		(N)
<132	.64	.36	1.00	(11)
132	.61	.39	1.00	(148)
All	.61	.39	1.00	(159)

PANEL B. Rank in 1993, by Seniority at Entry into Rank 40[a]

| | *Rank in 1993* | | | |
Seniority (mos.)	60	50 or lower		(N)
<192	.62	.38	1.00	(39)
192-203	.67	.33	1.00	(66)
204-215	.58	.42	1.00	(24)
>215	.38	.62	1.00	(8)
All	.62	.38	1.00	(137)

PANEL C. Rank in 1993, by Seniority at Entry into Rank 50[a]

| | *Rank in 1993* | | |
Seniority (mos.)	60	50		(N)
<277	.96	.04	1.00	(23)
277-288	.81	.19	1.00	(31)
289-300	.65	.35	1.00	(23)
301-312	.54	.46	1.00	(13)
>312	.17	.83	1.00	(12)
All	.70	.30	1.00	(102)

[a]Entries are percentages of the seniority group.

the best prospects of reaching rank 60; the slower the prior progression, the poorer an individual's chances.

A more refined assessment of the attainment process can be obtained from Table 14.8, in which the calculations of Table 14.7 have been repeated but with the "laggards" in Panel A removed (employees in the last two rows). We now observe a virtual absence of a tenure effect at entrance into rank 40 on one's prospects of achieving high status in the organization (Panel B); in short, little differentiation takes place at this career stage. The fall off with tenure, noted in Panel B of Table 14.7, was largely an artifact of the inclusion in that table of employees who failed the gate-keeping cut. (The fall-off with tenure that remains in Panel B refers to 5% of employees and the N is too small to establish statistically that the rate is below the category average.) With respect to the impact of seniority at entrance into rank 50, our results are very different from the lower grades and exhibit a strong tenure effect (Panel C).

In regard to conceptual imagery, these findings add up to what can be considered a *two-step process*. First, a screening or gate-keeping decision is made in the lowest grades to weed out poor performers, as indexed by very slow rates of prior mobility. The remaining employees—perhaps 70% of an entry cohort—are not differentiated with respect to prospects for attaining elite status as they move through the middle ranks of the organization. Possibly, this is intended to maintain morale by avoiding an early labeling of employees as "winners" and "losers"—an understandable strategy in a firm in which demoralized workers cannot be dismissed. Possibly, as Ballon (1969a, pp. 25-26) has contended, elite selection is delayed because the ability to perform senior tasks effectively is revealed late in the career course. At any rate, it is only at the second stage, promotion from rank 50, where there is clear evidence of a graduated return to prior mobility and where length of service is an effective indicator of prospects for attaining the highest status.

Conclusions

In contrast with Pucik's (1984b; 1985) assessment of the attainment process, we find little evidence to support the imagery of a tournament model of careers in the Japanese financial service company. As we have noted, in a context of lifetime employment it makes sense for a firm to delay revealing (and perhaps deciding) who will be permitted to reach the highest ranks. Other elements of the reward structure—such as seniority based compensation, with only small additions to salary for achieved rank—also contribute to cohesion and to the morale of the workforce.

There have been suggestions of impending change in the structure of careers and rewards in Japanese industry, such as hiring experienced workers and increasing salary payments for achieved rank (e.g., Cole 1971, chaps. 3,4; Marsh and Mannari 1976, pp. 307-314). However, in the firm we have studied there is little evidence to suggest much movement away from the kind of reward structure that was described some 25 years ago (e.g., Ballon 1969b). Moreover, because of the tight interrelation of the component features of the reward structure, we suspect that when change does come it will not be gradual or piecemeal.

Finally, what can be said about who achieves elite status? Actually very little. There is markedly little differentiation among employees through rank 40, in part because the entry cohorts are homogeneous with respect to education, age, gender, and (lack of) prior experience. In the later career stages, where differentiation does take place, it appears to reflect subtle considerations of "suitability" and values (Ballon 1969a, chapter 1) in addition to job performance—measures that are not usually present in the personnel records made available to researchers. Interestingly, there is also evidence from the U.S. financial service company (Spilerman and Lunde 1991) that the role of education in promotion decisions is weaker in high corporate ranks than in the middle levels. There, too, it was argued that the criteria for effective performance are quite different for elite managers than for mid-level employees, that considerations of social style and personality play a greater role in the senior ranks than do assessments of cognitive ability.

Notes

This research was supported by a grant from the U.S.-Israel Binational Foundation (to Spilerman) and by an Abe Fellowship from the Social Science Research Council (to Ishida). We would like to thank Kuo-Hsien Su for assistance with the computations.

1. In Japan, size of firm is a key differentiating variable in the stratification system. Both the status characteristics of workers (educational attainment, household wealth) and the rewards of employment (occupational prestige, income) are more favorable for employees of large companies (Ishida 1993, pp. 208-226).

2. Koike (1991), in one of the few studies which addressed the issue of specialization and skill formation in Japanese companies, documents the practice of specialization among white-collar workers but also shows that employees tend to experience a broad range of jobs within a specialty.

3. We note that there is a counterpart literature with respect to attainment in western firms which argues that the personality demands of jobs at different organizational levels can be quite distinct. Moreover, the character type and coping style of an employee that is effective in low organizational ranks may be dysfunctional in higher grades (Silver and Spilerman 1991).

4. Since enactment of the Equal Employment Opportunity Law in 1986 women have moved into the managerial ranks in Japan, although they are still very few in number. Only one percent of career-track employees in the financial service company are women.

5. We lack data on employment history prior to entry into the U.S. firm. This estimate is based on the proportion of hires who are age 25 and older.

6. The Japanese company uses the term "non-management employees" and these workers are placed in the lifetime queue from the time of employment. We prefer the term "trainees" because this is the better fitting description in the American context. These workers are not promoted from lesser positions based on performance but are hired directly into this fixed-duration status from which most progress to management positions.

7. It is more common to introduce "seniority" and "duration in prior rank" as the temporal variables. In a model with exactly two prior ranks, as in the Panel C regressions, this specification can be obtained by a simple transformation of the reported covariates, since "seniority" = "duration in rank 20" + "duration in rank 30". In particular, the model equivalent to column (1) has coefficients for seniority and duration in rank 30 equal to -.0397** and .0350**, respectively . The negative effect of seniority on the promotion rate makes sense in terms of the reports of other researchers (e.g., Rosenbaum 1984, pp. 169-170); the positive effect of duration in the prior grade is less comprehensible until one observes that, with seniority held constant, a positive duration in rank 30 is equivalent to a negative duration in rank 20—which is the effect we report. Our presentation of the two duration terms as covariates, in place of seniority and duration in prior rank, permits a more direct interpretation of the findings.

8. Entertainment allowances are omitted from this investigation. Since the allowances increase with rank, our results somewhat underestimate the true rank effects on monthly salary.

9. Despite the small increase in R^2 in moving from equation (2) to equation (3), the set of added terms is highly significant based on a conventional F-test.

10. This value is calculated from the monthly salary data and is somewhat smaller than the regression-based multipliers reported in the preceding paragraph. Note, also, that while Pucik (1984a, 1984b) applies the term "salary compression" to the small salary dispersion found when seniority is held constant, our comparison refers to unadjusted salary figures.

11. Part of the reason for the stability in compensation practices derives from the fact that the Japanese company is in the financial service sector. The seniority component of compensation has been traditionally high in this industry (Higuchi 1991).

12. The duration in rank 20 terms are defined as follows: "early promotion" (10 years in rank) contains 18% of observations, "on-time promotion" (11 years) contains 66% of observations, "late promotion" (12 years) contains 12% of observations, and "very late promotion" (13 or more years in rank) contains 3% of observations. There were no promotions before 10 years in rank.

13. The duration in rank 30 categories are defined as follows: "early promotion" (1-3 years in rank) contains 14% of observations, "on-time promotion" (4 years) contains 36% of observations, "late promotion" (5 years) contains 35% of observations, and "very late promotion" (6 or more years in rank) contains 16% of observations. "On-time" promotion, which is defined as the modal category, is the reference term in the regressions.

14. How material is the exclusion of incomplete spells from Tables 14.5 and 14.6? This has no consequence with respect to the diagonal pattern in the upper left corner of the tables because the diagonals derive from short durations in the adjacent grades. The exclusion of long spells is potentially more serious in the calculation of early promotion rates, but an examination of incomplete spells (durations in current state) reveals no major disparities from the results we have presented.

15. There is much lumpiness in the data, which permits little flexibility in the assignment to seniority categories. In particular, 148 employees were promoted exactly 11 years after entrance into the company. Similarly, about 95% of employees

in the next category were promoted at exactly the 144 month point. Thus, there is no possibility for exploring the sensitivity of the reported findings to the seniority category boundaries. Note, also, that no employee was promoted to rank 30 with less than 10 years service.

16. Because of the small age variance in each entry cohort, the argument of this section, which stresses seniority, can be formulated equivalently in terms of employee age.

References

Ballon, Robert J. 1969a. "The Japanese Dimensions of Industrial Enterprise." Pp. 3-40 in Robert J. Ballon (ed.), *The Japanese Employee*. Tokyo: Sophia University.

_____. 1969b. "Lifelong Remuneration System." Pp. 123-166 in Robert J. Ballon (ed.), *The Japanese Employee*. Tokyo: Sophia University.

Blossfeld, Hans-Peter, Hamerle, Alfred, and Karl U. Mayer. 1989. *Event History Analysis*. Hillsdale: Erlbaum Associates.

Clark, Rodney. 1979. *The Japanese Company*. New Haven: Yale University Press.

Cole, Robert. E. 1971. *Japanese Blue Collar: The Changing Tradition*. Berkeley: University of California Press.

_____. 1979. *Work, Mobility and Participation*. Berkeley: University of California Press.

Dore, Ronald. 1973. *British Factory-Japanese Factory*. Berkeley: University of California Press.

Funahashi, Naomichi. 1973. "The Industrial Reward System: Wages and Benefits." Chap. 10 in *Workers and Employers in Japan*, K. Okochi, B. Karsh, and S.B. Levine (eds.). Princeton: University of Princeton Press.

Foy, Nancy. 1975. *The Sun Never Sets on IBM*. New York: William Morrow.

Hirono, Ryokichi. 1969. "Personnel Management in Foreign Corporations." Pp. 251-272 in *The Japanese Employee*, Robert J. Ballon (ed.). Tokyo: Sophia University.

Ishida, Hiroshi. 1993. *Social Mobility in Contemporary Japan*. Stanford: Stanford University Press.

Koike, Kazuo. 1988. *Understanding Industrial Relations in Modern Japan*. London: MacMillan Press.

Marsh, Robert M. and Hiroshi Mannari. 1976. *Modernization and the Japanese Factory*. Princeton: Princeton University Press.

OECD (Organization for Economic Cooperation and Development). 1973. *Manpower Policy in Japan*. Paris: Organization for Economic Cooperation and Development.

Okochi, Kazuo; Karsh, Bernard; and Solomon B. Levine. 1974. "The Japanese Industrial Relations System: A Summary." Pp. 485-517 in *Workers and Employers in Japan*, K. Okochi, B. Karsh, and S.B. Levine (eds.). Princeton: University of Princeton Press.

Peck, Merton and Shuji Tamura. 1976. "Technology." In *Asia's New Giant*, Hugh Patrick and Henry Rosovsky (eds.). Washington, D.C.: Brookings Institution.

Petersen, Trond and Seymour Spilerman. 1990. "Job Quits from an Internal Labor Market." Pp. 69-95 in *Event History Analysis in Life Course Research*, Karl U. Mayer and Nancy B. Tuma (eds.). Madison: University of Wisconsin Press.

342

Pucik, Vladimir. 1984a. "White-Collar Human Resource Management in Large Japanese Manufacturing Firms." *Human Resource Management* 23 (3), pp. 257-276.

_____. 1984b. "White Collar Human Resource Management: A Comparison of the U.S. and Japanese Automobile Industries." *Columbia Journal of World Business* 19 (3), pp. 87-94.

_____. 1985. "Promotion Patterns in a Japanese Company." *Columbia Journal of World Business* 20 (3), pp. 73-79.

Rohlen, Thomas. 1974. *For Harmony and Strength*. Berkeley: University of California Press.

Roland, Alan. 1988. *In Search of Self in India and Japan*. Princeton: Princeton University Press.

Rosenbaum, James E. 1984. *Career Mobility in a Corporate Hierarchy*. New York: Academic Press.

Rosenbaum, James and Takehiko Kariya. 1989. "From High School to Work: Market and Institutional Mechanisms in Japan." *American Journal of Sociology* 94 (6), pp. 1334-1365.

Sibson, Robert E. 1981. *Compensation*. New York: AMACOM.

Silver, Catherine and Seymour Spilerman. 1991. "Psychoanalytic Perspectives on Occupational Choice and Attainment." *Research in Social Stratification and Mobility* 9, pp. 181-214.

Spilerman, Seymour and Tormod Lunde. 1991. "Features of Educational Attainment and Job Promotion Prospects." *American Journal of Sociology* 97 (3), pp. 689-720.

_____ and Trond Petersen. 1994. "Occupational Structure, Determinants of Promotion, and Gender Differences in Attainment." Submitted for publication.

Suzuki, N. 1981. *Management and the Industrial Structure in Japan*. New York: Pergamon Press.

Turner, Ralph. 1960. "Modes of Social Ascent Through Education: Sponsored and Contest Mobility." *American Sociological Review* 25, pp. 855-867.

Wallace, Marc J. and Charles H. Fay 1983. *Compensaton Theory and Practice*. Belmont, Calif.: Kent Publishing Co.

Yoshino, M.Y. and Thomas B. Lifson. 1986. *The Invisible Link*. Cambridge, Mass.: MIT Press.

Wolferen, Karl van and R. Taggart Murphy. 1994. "Tough Love for Japan." *New York Times*. February 20, 1994, p. IV-13.

15

Changing Contexts of Careers: Trends in Labor Market Structures and Some Implications for Labor Force Outcomes

Arne L. Kalleberg
University of North Carolina at Chapel Hill

Labor market structures are major institutional contexts which help to define the structures and processes that generate earnings, employment contracts, patterns of job changing and unemployment, and other aspects of careers. In the past quarter century, considerable progress has been made in understanding both the structure of labor markets and their impacts on these important labor force outcomes. Conceptions of labor markets have not been static; the view dominating at a particular time reflects in part theoretical developments in sociology and economics, as well as political, social, and economic events that heighten concerns with particular issues and problems and render other questions moot. The dominant conception of labor markets at a particular time, in turn, affects the kinds of labor force issues and aspects of careers that are deemed important to study.

This paper discusses some of the main conceptions of labor market structures in the past quarter century, and how they have influenced research and thinking about careers. The first section summarizes three approaches to labor markets: dualism; segmentation; and flexibility. I then speculate on some implications of current changes for future labor market structures and various career-related outcomes.

Approaches to Labor Markets

Dualism

The resurgence of interest in labor markets in the late 1960s was prompted by concerns among radical economists to account for why the black urban poor in the United States remained poor despite efforts to alleviate their poverty (see the summary in Gordon, 1972). The answer was because the poor participated in the secondary labor market, the segment of the economy characterized by low wages, job instability, and generally bad jobs. The situation in the secondary labor markets was radically different from that in the primary market, which consisted of stable, well paid, and generally desirable employment. Though the imagery of two distinct labor market segments was important, the existence of *two* labor markets was less important than the idea that there was a radical discontinuity in labor market processes between them (see Berger and Piore, 1980).

Dual labor market theorists argued that the origins of primary and secondary markets were rooted in workers' characteristics (such as their behavioral preferences for stable vs. unstable work), as well as in technology and skill (for a review, see Kalleberg and Sørensen, 1979). Some of these mechanisms (such as technology) are consistent with neoclassical economic theory; others (such as the assumption that peoples' preferences and attitudes aren't exogenous to the labor market) are not. The dual labor market theory was fairly static in its focus on the existence of unequal structures of pay and stability, despite its assumptions about the polarization of jobs accompanying the evolution of capitalism.

The idea of labor market dualism soon expanded beyond ghetto labor markets to include the analysis of national labor markets in advanced industrial societies, and the micro-level dual labor market theory was linked to the macro-level dual economy theory (e.g., Averitt, 1968; Bluestone, 1970). The latter focused on the duality between core and periphery industries and firms, and provided both economists and sociologists with a useful way of conceptualizing qualitative divisions resulting from the evolution of the organization of capitalist production. Taken together, these dual theories posited a correspondence between primary labor market segment jobs and core sector industries and firms, and between secondary labor market segment jobs and periphery sector firms and industries.

Dualism and Research on Careers. The first generation of dualist research was mainly concerned with demonstrating that there were radically different processes of earnings determination in the two segments. It also sought to assess the extent of inter-segment mobility; the absence of mobility between segments was an assumption integral to the view that there was social closure within markets. Studies supported the view that there were few mobility channels that people might use to exit from the secondary market. This focused attention on the constraints faced by poor workers who sought to experience upward mobility by investing in education and other forms of human capital. Training and skills were not particularly valued in secondary labor market jobs, nor useful as resources for upward mobility.

Dual labor market researchers also examined how and why certain categories of workers—usually white males in the United States—were integrated into the core of the socioeconomic system (whether viewed in terms of core sectors or primary labor markets), while others—women, blacks, and other minorities—were assigned to the periphery of this system by lack of human capital, discrimination, or inappropriate behavioral dispositions. These studies helped to explain why these minorities found themselves in a permanent precarious socioeconomic position (see Kalleberg and Sørensen, 1979, for a review of this research).

Segmentation

Interest in labor markets accelerated rapidly in the 1970s. Sociologists who sought to explain patterns of social stratification saw labor markets as a way of incorporating institutional and structural variables in the model of the socioeconomic achievement process that originated in Blau and Duncan (1967), and in explanations of mobility and income inequality more generally. Radical economists and Marxists found the notion of labor markets attractive for explaining changes in the organization of work and the labor process that were associated with capitalist development. This second generation of labor market researchers recognized that dual labor market theory oversimplified the complex mechanisms that create and maintain labor market structures in industrial societies. They thus focused more on the diversity and forms of labor market segmentation.[1]

There were two main thrusts of research on labor market segmentation in the 1970s and early 1980s. The first, *aggregated* approach sought to describe the structure of labor markets in a society as a whole by, for example, deriving clusters of relatively homogenous occupation-industry categories (e.g., Freedman, 1976; see also Spilerman, 1977). Other researchers used time series data to analyze changes in inequalities between core-periphery industry groups and/or between primary-secondary occupation groups. Reich (1984), for example, argued that the post-World War II United States was marked by a segmentation phase characterized by growing distinctions among both occupations and industries.

A second, *disaggregated* approach to segmentation research focused on specific occupations and organizations. This approach centered on the concept of the internal labor market (ILM), which was originally discussed by institutional economists in the 1950s. ILMs are job ladders characterized by entry at the bottom and upward movement associated with a progressive development of skill and knowledge; they are found in both occupations (OILMs) and firms (FILMs) (see Althauser and Kalleberg, 1981).

Both aggregated and disaggregated approaches sought to account for the processes by which internalization occurred within firm and occupational labor markets. The hierarchical—as opposed to market—governance of employment relations was argued to result from the operation of social forces (such as employer control, unionization, licensing, educational credentials) as well as from technical factors (such as skill specificity and the imperatives of on-the-job training).

Some writers recognized explicitly that labor market segmentation does not proceed in a steady, linear fashion, but rather reflects broader economic conditions. Organizations seek to adapt to boom and bust business cycles by increasing or decreasing their employment. Sengenberger (1981), for example, showed that German firms decreased their number of primary-type jobs during the mid-1970s recession, thereby creating a smaller core workforce and increasing the number of short-term contracts and employee leasing arrangements. This strategy represented a retrenchment from employers' emphasis on internal labor markets to bind scarce labor to the firm in the previous decade, when unemployment was very low. This tendency is consistent with a common response of employers to crises, which is to marginalize or externalize part of their workforces (see below).

Segmentation and Research on Careers. The notion of internal labor markets helped researchers explain how labor market structures shaped individuals' careers. The concept of FILMs proved particularly useful for studying differences in career patterns and promotion opportunities within organizations, and job ladders provided a way to account for patterns of mobility within firms (e.g., Baron et al., 1986; Cohen and Pfeffer, 1986; Pfeffer and Cohen, 1984; Spilerman and Ishida, this volume; see the review in Althauser, 1989). FILMs were also central to descriptions of bureaucratic control systems within large firms in the post-World War II period. Thus, FILMs enabled managers to control workers by promising them opportunities for future advancement in return for their commitment and loyalty to the organization (Edwards, 1979).

Flexibility

Research on labor market segmentation during the 1960s and 1970s—especially in the United States, but also in many other industrialized nations—was conducted within a context of relative stability and growth. During periods of relative prosperity, issues such as career advancement and earnings differences among full-time workers become important to study. Accordingly, questions of labor market uncertainty and structural change were given relatively minor roles (see Rosenberg, 1989). By contrast, the 1980s were marked by diminished growth and high unemployment rates in many industrialized nations. Product markets became increasingly complex, uncertain, variable, and marked by rapid change (Piore and Sabel, 1984). These altered economic conditions prompted a shift in labor market research away from topics of segmentation, and toward a focus on dynamic changes in labor market structures and how they could be restructured to increase flexibility (Rosenberg, 1989).

The issue of labor market flexibility stimulated considerable debate on both sides of the Atlantic. It was generally agreed that employers need the flexibility to reorganize employment relations in response to rapid developments in technology, growing international competition in product markets, and changes in labor markets such as the increased labor force participation of women.

The flexibility debate focused on the firm, and attention centered on three main types of flexibility (Atkinson, 1987; Boyer, 1987; Lane, 1989; Meulders and Wilkin, 1987; Piore, 1986; Rosenberg, 1989): (1) *functional flexibility*, the extent to which employers are able to move their existing (relatively permanent, full-time) employees from one task or department to another, and/or to reorganize the content of jobs to adjust to changing technologies and economic conditions; (2) *numerical or employment flexibility*, the employers' freedom to alter workers' hours (numerical) or to adjust the sizes of their workforces (employment) to respond to changing conditions; and (3) *wage flexibility*, the ability of employers to adjust wages downward when economic conditions warranted.

Maximizing all three types of flexibility simultaneously is difficult: strategies designed to achieve functional flexibility may undermine the ability of employers to obtain numerical and/or wage flexibility, since the conditions that promote the former (e.g., commitment to the firm) are incompatible with policies that emphasize layoffs and wage reductions. One way that an organization might balance its needs for various types of flexibility is suggested by the notion of the **flexible firm** (see Atkinson, 1987, Pollert, 1988; also called the "core-periphery" model—Osterman, 1988; or the "shamrock" organization—Handy, 1989) (see Figure 15.1). This idea applies dualist notions of core-periphery to the firm level. It suggests that there are divergent processes of labor market segmentation within the firm that are based on a combination of market and hierarchical governance systems. Optimal cost effectiveness is achieved by dividing the labor force into fixed and variable components. The fixed component consists of a core of highly committed, functionally flexible workers who are integrated into the firm via long-term employment contracts, are trained to perform multiple skills, and are often empowered to participate in decision-making. This is similar to the "salaried" internal labor market model that combines relatively flexible administrative procedures with high employment secu-

FIGURE 15.1   The "Flexible Firm"

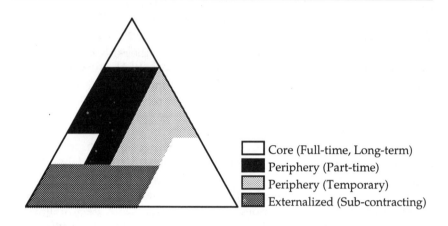

☐ Core (Full-time, Long-term)
■ Periphery (Part-time)
▨ Periphery (Temporary)
▩ Externalized (Sub-contracting)

rity (thus achieving high functional flexibility at the expense of low employment flexibility).[2] Two additional, variable components provide organizations with wage and numerical/employment flexibility: (1) a periphery group of temporary and part-time workers who are only weakly attached to the organization; and (2) an externalized set of activities (subcontracting) that are performed by people who are not permanent organizational members (see Atkinson, 1987; Handy, 1989; Atchison, 1991).[3]

A country's institutional, political-economic environment will affect the extent to which employers are able to segment their workforces in ways suggested by the model of the flexible firm. In the United States, the relative weakness of unions and "employment at will" enable employers to achieve relatively high wage and numerical/employment flexibility.[4] By contrast, in Germany, the combination of unions' strength, dominance of occupational markets and strong systems of vocational training has constrained the development of peripheral labor forces within firms. This has motivated German companies to place greater emphasis on fostering functional flexibility in order to adapt to changes in business conditions and technology (Lane, 1989; see also the studies in Boyer, 1988; Sengenberger and Kohler, 1987). The Japanese form of human resources management is often cited as the exemplar of the "flexible firm." It appears to achieve both functional *and* numerical/employment flexibility by: (1) segmenting the organization's labor force into a "core" set of permanent jobs/employees (*honko*) and a "periphery" group of temporary, contingent jobs/employees (Koike, 1978); and (2) a well-developed system of subcontracting.[5]

The ability and willingness of organizations in particular nations to segment their labor forces also depend on their size. Large firms in the United States tend to rely more heavily on temporary workers than do small and medium-sized firms, because larger organizations have a harder time firing people and adjusting their hiring practices to changing conditions (Mangum et al., 1985). In Japan, on the other hand, the ratio of regular (core or long-term) workers to temporary and day laborers decreases as the size of the firm increases: temporary workers are more commonly found in small companies. Larger Japanese organizations rely more on various kinds of subcontracting relationships, as opposed to hiring large numbers of temporary workers.

Industrial differences will also affect the degree of labor market segmentation within firms. The use of temporaries in the U.S. is more common in industries exposed to fluctuating product demand (Mangum et al., 1985). In Japan, the nature of subcontracting varies among industries: in industries such as steel, shipbuilding or chemicals, there is widespread use of *shagaiko* or employees of other companies who are leased to the parent firm on a temporary basis; in the automobile, electrical machinery and construction industries, activities are subcontracted out to smaller firms whose employees do not actually work in the parent firm (Tokunaga, 1984). In Norway, highly unionized banks have relatively large core and small peripheral labor forces; while the opposite is true in the relatively weakly unionized retail industry.

Flexibility and Research on Careers. Concerns about flexibility gave added significance and impetus to research on unemployment and patterns of labor force attachment. Unemployment rates were found to have increased less in the late 1970s and early 1980s in countries where wage flexibility was high (U.S., Japan) than in European nations that had less wage flexibility (Boyer, 1987). This is consistent with the assumption of economists' market models that wage and employment flexibility are trade-offs: increasing wages reduces employment; and vice versa (see Piore, 1986).

Research on temporary, part-time, and subcontracting employment relations also became more prevalent and pressing in the 1980s, as long-term employment contracts became less common. The term "contingent employment" was coined in the mid-1980s to describe the growing trend toward these types of "non-traditional" employment relations that have emerged from the concerns for workplace and employment flexibility. Studies found that the growth of contingent employment in the United States was due in part to the growing labor force participation of women (who increasingly seek flexible work schedules) as well as to organizations' greater needs for flexibility (see Pfeffer and Baron, 1988).

Future Trends in Labor Market Structures

Some of the key trends that are likely to have a major impact on future labor market structures in many industrial nations are already clear. These changes in labor markets reflect both managerial/organizational imperatives and the changing nature of the labor force, and are occurring at both organizational and societal levels. To a considerable extent, labor market structures will vary among countries, depending on a nation's employment and training policies, employer strategies, unionization and structure of industrial relations, economic conditions, position in the world economy, welfare state structures, and so on.

Continued Need for Functional Flexibility

Functional flexibility will continue to be important to the modern corporation, since firms must have a trained and adaptable workforce to be able to adjust to rapid changes in technology and business conditions. In the United States and in most industrial nations, then, there is likely to be a continued emphasis on practices that facilitate a multi-skilled workforce (such as employee involvement, "total quality management," job rotation, and retraining). There should thus be considerable pressures on organizations to adopt a "salaried" model of internal labor markets in both blue-collar and white-collar occupations, with a corresponding decline in the "industrial" model of internal labor markets (see Osterman, 1988).

Technological advances and the continued need for functional flexibility are likely to increase the importance of education, a view that is consistent with mainstream theories of post-industrialism (e.g., Bell, 1976). Education will become perhaps the most important determinant of job placement and life chances, and the gap separating high and low educated people will grow. This will increasingly divide labor force insiders from outsiders, and insiders among themselves. The emphasis on training (and re-training) also underscores the necessity to study other sources of skills in addition to formal education, such as company training, vocational apprenticeship systems, and so on.

Continued Need for Numerical/Employment Flexibility

Organizations' needs for numerical/employment flexibility are also likely to continue into the future. Recessionary business conditions and the challenges introduced by global competition have led many employers to downsize their workforces in order to stay in business and/or to maintain profits. Bunning (1990), for example, reports that 35% of 1200 personnel managers in the United States in a 1988 survey worked for companies that had downsized during the past twelve months. This downsizing largely represents "delayering," or a flattening of the corporate pyramid due to a reduction in middle-management positions (Cheek and Cameron, 1990). As a result of downsizing and patterns of job creation, employment in the United States is continuing to shift toward middle- and small-sized firms (see Granovetter, 1984). These trends are also observed in Europe, though there employers generally have less wage and employment flexibility due to constraints imposed by collective bargaining agreements and other laws governing industrial and labor relations (but see Note 4).

Growth of Inflexible Labor

At the same time that employers are increasingly likely to need a more flexible workforce, labor force trends in the United States are tending to produce a more inflexible labor force. For example, the average age of the American labor force is likely to increase, as the baby boom cohort ages and a smaller number of young persons from the baby bust cohort enters the workforce (Johnston and Packer, 1987). The labor force thus will be made up more of older men and women who are less mobile because they have considerable experience with firms and occupations, and who are less willing and able to be retrained for new jobs. In addition, women workers may more often seek permanent employment in the future, making them less available for part-time and temporary work (see Osterman, 1988).

These labor force trends will constrain employers' ability to achieve functional as well as numerical/employment flexibility. These trends also point to the need for research on the changing labor force. For example, the combination of an aging workforce and decline in long-term employment raises important questions regarding patterns of retirement and portability of pensions. (See the discussion on life course changes by O'Rand, this volume.)

Future Labor Market Structures: Two Scenarios

While these three trends are likely to help shape the labor market structures of the future, their exact contours cannot be predicted with a high degree of confidence. There are both optimistic (upgrading) and pessimistic (polarization) scenarios that might describe these future labor market structures.

Upgrading of Jobs and Skills. Organizations' needs for functional flexibility—coupled with an increased emphasis on education—may result in massive upgrading of the skill levels of organizations and occupations. This is reminiscent of Bell's (1976) description of the post-industrial knowledge society. Piore and Sabel (1984:279) describe this scenario as resembling the "artisans' republic envisioned by Rousseau and Proudhon." In this scenario, employees will have fairly high levels of job security, and there will be a decline in secondary labor market jobs.

One way by which this scenario might be implemented is through the development of "network organizations." The network organization is characterized by reciprocal patterns of communication and exchange and is an alternative governance structure to markets and hierarchies (see Powell, 1990). Network organizations represent clusters of downsized, focused business units coordinated by market mechanisms rather than by layers of middle-management planners and schedulers (Snow et al., 1991). These networks take various forms, including consortiums (e.g., the Japanese *Keiretsu*), joint ventures, and contractual partnering of different kinds designed to extend an organization's capabilities. These patterns are already common in many industries in the United States, including: construction, book publishing, film and recording, banking, autos, telecommunications and computers. They are also represented by the Emilian model in Italy and the Japanese textile industry (Powell, 1990).

The network organization is one possible solution to the organization's needs for both functional and numerical/employment flexibility. Network organizations tend to be relatively small and thus have the capacity to achieve higher levels of functional flexibility than is feasible in larger organizations. Firms that participate in such networks will have a small permanent core, and increasingly use subcontractors such as consulting firms to provide non-permanent employees. IBM, for example, has been vendoring lower-level services (such as internal cafeterias and mail rooms) for some years, and has also spun off higher-level functions, such as many activities associated with employment, that are carried out by an affiliated company. These non-permanent employees (from the point of view of IBM's commitment to them) might themselves be relatively permanent members of their consultant firms. Over fifteen percent of work organizations in the United States in 1991 sub-contracted one or more occupational activities (see Kalleberg and Schmidt, 1996).

Achieving this optimistic scenario is likely to require some state intervention. A national employment policy appears to be necessary in order to provide adequate training, which is a precondition for upgrading in many kinds of occupations. Public policies are also needed to facilitate employment security, which is a key component of the "salaried" model of internal labor markets. European countries such as Germany and Sweden have had quite effective employment policies in this regard; by contrast, the United States traditionally has lacked such an employment policy (see Osterman, 1988). These points have not been lost on the Clinton Administration, which has emphasized the importance of retraining and of employment security, rather than job security.

The emergence of network organizations suggests the need to study careers as they unfold between organizations, not just within them. Job search and information networks become more salient if workers and managers need to change organizations more often. Flows of human capital among organizations also need to be investigated. For example, we know very little about sources of training other than formal education or on-the-job training. Moreover, patterns of sub-contracting and other forms of contingent employment among networks of organizations remain largely unexplored.

Polarization between Core and Periphery. On the other hand, organizations' efforts to achieve greater functional and numerical/employment flexibility might result in a polarization of the labor force into a small group of full-time, functionally flexible permanent core workers (who have autonomy, a great deal of human capital, and often high trust relations with their employers) and a large group of peripheral workers (who may be relatively unskilled and/or outsiders to the labor market). These peripheral workers represent a modern, post-industrial version of Marx's reserve army of the unemployed: they are "stand by" or "disposable" workers who are available when needed and discarded when they are not (see also Braverman, 1974; Michon, 1981). Harrison (1994) refers to these peripheral workers as the "dark side" of flexible production. Piore and Sabel (1984:279) describe this regime as resembling "... the old Bourbon kingdom of Naples, where an island of craftsmen, producing luxury goods for the court, was surrounded by a subproletarian sea of misery."

There are at least two versions of this pessimistic scenario (see, e.g., Esping-Andersen, 1993). Within a nation, there can be a polarization between a small core of highly upgraded core insiders, and either: (1) a large service proletariat consisting of lots of bad jobs; or (2) a relatively few bad jobs and a large population of labor force outsiders. The type of polarization that occurs depends on factors specific to a country, including: the role of the welfare state (such as the opportunities provided by the welfare state for extra-labor market support); barriers to entering the labor market; and the system of industrial relations. In the United States, for example, the growth of a low wage labor force in the weakly unionized service sector would be likely, if it were not for the constraints on such development imposed by the lack of persons who are willing to accept relatively low paying, unstable, and otherwise inferior jobs (Osterman, 1987). (On the other hand, the study by Alexander and Entwisle, this volume, suggests that there may be more such low skilled and educated persons than we might have assumed.)

This scenario suggests greater urgency for certain kinds of studies of careers. For example, research is needed on the correlates of unemployment. As in the early research on dual labor markets, it would also be important to study the conditions underlying and perpetuating secondary labor market work and the barriers that hinder secondary workers from entering the primary labor markets. Again, studies of the sources of education and training, and the transitions from the sites where skills are taught to the workplaces where they are utilized, are likely to take on added importance.

It is too early to tell whether the optimistic or pessimistic scenario will more accurately describe future labor market structures in the various industrial nations. Nevertheless, there are several reasons to suspect that the former, more optimistic scenario might be more appropriate in many industrial countries. A number of factors constrain the expansion of a low wage labor force in industrial societies; these range from the considerable power of unions in many European countries, to national employment policies in countries such as Germany and Sweden, to the unavailability of persons willing to work in secondary market jobs. Increased international competition may also encourage firms to remain small and highly functionally flexible. Evidence from the U.S., U.K., Canada, Germany, Norway and Sweden indicates that "...everywhere, the trend favors the higher-grade occupations such that the shape of the post-industrial occupational hierarchy is biased toward the top and the middle, rather than the bottom" (Esping-Andersen et al., 1993: 53).

These two scenarios are of course oversimplified, and these ideal types need further development and refinement. One complication is introduced by the trend toward internationalization of production. What is good for one country may not be so good for another. The outsourcing of semi-skilled jobs from the U.S. to other countries, for example, is optimistic from the point of view of the country gaining jobs, but pessimistic from the standpoint of communities in the United States that may lose jobs.

In any event, what is clear is that changes in labor market structures pose new empirical questions that constitute an agenda for future research. Studies of these issues require comparative, cross-national data on work organizations and their employees that are based on representative samples drawn from diverse populations. These studies need to be complemented by investigations of specific industries, organizations and occupations. Research also needs to focus on networks of organizations, to explain how employers interact with other organizations to obtain and train new workers. Such studies are necessary to understand better the linkages between work organizations and broader labor market contexts.

Notes

1. "Segmentation" describes a general approach to studying labor markets that goes beyond the dual framework. Labor market segmentation theory posits the existence of distinct labor markets that differ in their processes of earnings determination and other outcomes. In this view, dual labor market theory is a specific example of labor market segmentation theories.

2. By contrast, the traditional "industrial" internal labor market model organizes work into a series of narrowly defined jobs that are tied to clear duties and responsibilities (thereby obtaining high numerical/employment flexibility but low functional flexibility) (see Osterman, 1987; 1988).

3. Such externalization of employment represents a retreat from internalized bureaucratic employment relations to a set of ongoing transactions with the open labor market (Pfeffer and Baron, 1988). This harkens back to an earlier era in economic organization when factory labor was not continuously employed but rather subcontracted from the outside (Williamson, 1985).

4. The United States legal context is generally perceived as being more flexible than many European nations in its policies regarding layoffs. However, the greater flexibility of U.S. employers in this regard is often exaggerated: the U.S. courts have been increasingly restrictive in their interpretations of the employment-at-will doctrine, and this has made U.S. employers very cautious about exercising it. In 1986 in California, for example, plaintiffs won 78% of wrongful-discharge cases with an average total award of $424,527 (Fulmer and Casey, 1990). As a consequence, it has been argued that the degree of employment and wage flexibility in the U.S. is not qualitatively different from that found in Europe (Piore, 1986).

5. It is the temporary workers—more than the regular workers—who provide what little formal definition there is to the boundaries of the permanent employment system in Japan, since it is the temporaries—not the regulars—who are issued employment contracts clearly delineating the fixed-term nature of their attachment to the firm. The dependence on an immense quantity of peripheral labor is a prior condition for why the Japanese are able economically to implement many of the organization structures that promote commitment (Tokunaga, 1984). (Some of these peripheral workers were formerly regular, "permanent" employees, who were hired back as temporaries at lower wages after their "retirement.") However, the negative features of the "dual" structure of Japanese industry are often overstated: subcontractors in Japan are relatively independent from the larger, parent firms—at least in industries such as machine tools—and employees of subcontracting firms are often highly skilled and relatively well paid (see Friedman, 1988; Chalmers, 1989).

References

Althauser, Robert P. 1989. "Internal Labor Markets." *Annual Review of Sociology* 15:143-161.

Althauser, Robert P. and Arne L. Kalleberg. 1981. "Firms, Occupations and the Structure of Labor Markets: A Conceptual Analysis" Pp. 119-149 in Ivar Berg (ed.), *Sociological Perspectives on Labor Markets* (New York: Academic Press).

Atchison, Thomas J. 1991. "The Employment Relationship: Un-tied or Re-tied." *Academy of Management Executive* 5:52-62.

Atkinson, John. 1987. "Flexibility or Fragmentation? The United Kingdom Labour Market in the Eighties." *Labour and Society* 12:88-105.

Averitt, Robert T. 1968. *The Dual Economy: The Dynamics of American Industry Structure.* New York: Norton.

Baron, James N., Alison Davis-Blake, and William T. Bielby. 1986. "The Structure of Opportunity: How Promotion Ladders Vary Within and Among Organizations." *Administrative Science Quarterly* 31:248-273.

Bell, Daniel. 1976. *The Coming of Post-Industrial Society.* New York: Basic Books.

Berger, Suzanne and Michael J. Piore. 1980. *Dualism and Discontinuity in Industrial Societies.* Cambridge: Cambridge University Press.

Blau, Peter M. and Otis Dudley Duncan. 1967. *The American Occupational Structure.* New York: Wiley.

Bluestone, Barry. 1970. "The Tripartite Economy: Labor Markets and the Working Poor." *Poverty and Human Resources Abstracts* 5:15-35.

Boyer, Robert. 1987. "Labour Flexibilities: Many Forms, Uncertain Effects." *Labour and Society* 12: 107-129.

Boyer, Robert (ed.) 1988. *The Search for Labour Market Flexibility: The European Economies in Transition.* Oxford: Clarendon Press.

Braverman, Harry. 1974. *Labor and Monopoly Capitalism.* New York: Monthly Review Press.

Bunning, Richard L. 1990. "The Dynamics of Downsizing." *Personnel Journal* 69: 68-75.

Chalmers, Norma J. 1989. *Industrial Relations in Japan: The Peripheral Workforce.* London: Routledge.

Cheek, Gerald D. and Walter Cameron. 1990. "Corporate Downsizing: An American Trainer's Affliction." *Industrial and Commercial Training* 22:26-31.

Cohen, Yinon and Jeffrey Pfeffer. 1986. "Organizational Hiring Standards." *Administrative Science Quarterly* 31:1-24.

Edwards, Richard. 1979. *Contested Terrain.* New York: Basic Books.

Esping-Andersen, Gøsta. 1993. "Post-Industrial Class Structures: An Analytic Framework." Pp. 7-31 in Gøsta Esping-Andersen (ed.), *Changing Classes: Stratification and Mobility in Post-Industrial Societies.* London: Sage.

Esping-Andersen, Gøsta, Zina Assimakopoulou and Kees van Kersbergen. 1993. "Trends in Contemporary Class Structuration: A Six-nation Comparison." Pp. 32-57 in Gøsta Esping-Andersen (ed.), *Changing Classes: Stratification and Mobility in Post-Industrial Societies.* London: Sage.

Freedman, Marcia K. 1976. *Labor Markets: Segments and Shelters.* Montclair, New Jersey: Allanheld, Osmun.

Friedman, David. 1988. *The Misunderstood Miracle: Industrial Development and Political Change in Japan.* Ithaca, New York: Cornell University Press.

Fulmer, William E. and Ann Wallace Casey. 1990. "Employment at Will: Options for Managers." *The Academy of Management Executive.* 4:102-107.

Gordon, David M. 1972. *Theories of Poverty and Underemployment.* Lexington, Massachusetts.: D.C. Heath.

Granovetter, Mark. 1984. "Small is Bountiful: Labor Markets and Establishment Size." *American Sociological Review* 49:323-334.

Handy, Charles. 1989. *The Age of Unreason.* Boston: Harvard Business School Press.

Harrison, Bennett. 1994. *Lean and Mean: The Changing Landscape of Corporate Power in the Age of Flexibility.* New York: Basic Books.

Johnston, William B. and Arnold H. Packer. 1987. *Workforce 2000: Work and Workers for the 21st Century.* Indianapolis: Hudson Institute.

Kalleberg, Arne L. and Kathryn Schmidt. 1996. "Contingency Workers and Contingent Work: Part-Time, Temporary, and Subcontracting Employment Relations in U.S. Organizations." In Arne L. Kalleberg, David Knoke, Peter V. Marsden, and Joe L. Spaeth, *Organizations in America: A Portrait of their Structures and Human Resource Practices.* Newbury Park: Sage.

Kalleberg, Arne L. and Aage B. Sørensen. 1979. "The Sociology of Labor Markets." *Annual Review of Sociology* 5:351-379.

Koike, Kazuo. 1978. "Japan's Industrial Relations: Characteristics and Problems." *Japanese Economic Studies* 7:42-90.

Lane, Christel. 1989. *Management and Labour in Europe: The Industrial Enterprise in Germany, Britain and France.* Brookfield, VT: Gower.

Mangum, Garth, Donald Mayall, and Kristin Nelson. 1985. "The Temporary Help Industry: A Response to the Dual Internal Labor Market." *Industrial and Labor Relations Review* 38:599-611.

Meulders, Daniele and Luc Wilkin. 1987. "Labour Market Flexibility: Critical Introduction to the Analysis of a Concept." *Labour and Society* 12:3-17.

Michon, Francois. 1981. "Dualism and the French Labour Market: Business Strategy, Non-standard Job Forms and Secondary Jobs." Pp. 81-97 in Frank Wilkinson (ed.) *The Dynamics of Labour Market Segmentation.* New York: Academic Press.

Osterman, Paul. 1987. "Turnover, Employment Security, and the Performance of the Firm." Pp. 275-317 in M.M. Kleiner, R.N. Block, M. Roomkin, S. Salsburg (eds.), *Human Resources and the Performance of the Firm.* Madison, Wisconsin: Industrial Relations Research Association.

Osterman, Paul. 1988. *Employment Futures: Reorganization, Dislocation, and Public Policy.* New York: Oxford University Press.

Pfeffer, Jeffrey and James N. Baron. 1988. "Taking the Workers Back Out: Recent Trends in the Structuring of Employment." Pp. 257-303 in Barry M. Staw and Larry L. Cummings (eds.), *Research in Organizational Behavior, Vol. 10.* Greenwich, CT: JAI Press.

Pfeffer, Jeffrey and Yinon Cohen. 1984. "Determinants of Internal Labor Markets in Organizations." *Administrative Science Quarterly* 29:550-572.

Piore, Michael J. 1986. "Perspectives on Labor Market Flexibility." *Industrial Relations* 25:146-166.

Piore, Michael J. and Charles F. Sabel. 1984. *The Second Industrial Divide: Possibilities for Prosperity*. New York: Basic Books.

Pollert, Anna. 1988. "The 'Flexible Firm': Fixation or Fact?" *Work, Employment and Society* 2:281-316.

Powell, Walter W. 1990. "Neither Market Nor Hierarchy: Network Forms of Organization." *Research in Organizational Behavior* 12:295-336.

Reich, Michael. 1984. "Segmented Labour: Time Series Hypothesis and Evidence." *Cambridge Journal of Economics* 8:63-81.

Rosenberg, Sam. 1989. "From Segmentation to Flexibility." *Labour and Society* 14:363-407.

Sengenberger, Werner. 1981. "Labour Market Segmentation and the Business Cycle." Pp. 243-259 in Frank Wilkinson (ed.), *The Dynamics of Labour Market Segmentation*. London: Academic Press.

Sengenberger, Werner and Ch. Kohler. 1987. "Policies of Workforce Reduction and Labour Market Structures in the American and German Automobile Industry. Pp. 245-269 in Roger Tarling (ed.), *Flexibility in Labour Markets*. Orlando: Academic Press.

Snow, Charles C., Raymond E. Miles and Henry J. Coleman, Jr. 1991. "Managing 21st Century Organizations." *Organizational Dynamics* 20,4:5-20.

Spilerman, Seymour. 1977. "Careers, Labor Market Structure, and Socioeconomic Achievement." *American Journal of Sociology* 83:551-593.

Tokunaga, Shigeyoshi. 1984. "The Structure of the Japanese Labor Market." Pp. 25-55 in Shigeyoshi Tokunaga and Joachim Bergmann (eds.), *Industrial Relations in Transition: The Cases of Japan and the Federal Republic of Germany*. Tokyo: University of Tokyo Press.

Williamson, Oliver E. 1985. *The Economic Institutions of Capitalism*. New York: Free Press.

About the Book and Editor

In this book some of the leading stratification scholars in the United States present empirical and theoretical essays about the institutional contexts that shape careers. Building on recent advances in theory, data, and analytic technique, the essays in this volume work toward the goal of identifying and assessing the processes by which a birth cohort is distributed in the stratification system, given its position of origin in that system. Alan Kerckhoff's introduction situates the studies in this volume within the context of previous stratification research over several generations, making the book an invaluable resource for scholars and graduate students.

Alan C. Kerckhoff, professor of sociology at Duke University, is the author of many important books and journal articles on careers, education, and social stratification.